The Bitter Waters
of Medicine Creek

The Bitter Waters
of Medicine Creek

*A Tragic Clash Between White
and Native America*

RICHARD KLUGER

MAR 1 5 2011

Montante Family Library
D'Youville College

THIS IS A BORZOI BOOK
PUBLISHED BY ALFRED A. KNOPF

Library of Congress Cataloging-in-Publication Data
Kluger, Richard.
The bitter waters of Medicine Creek : a tragic clash between
white and native America / Richard Kluger.—1st ed.
p.   cm.
Includes index.
ISBN 978-0-307-26889-1
1. Nisqually Indians—History—19th century.   2. Nisqually
Indians—Government relations.   3. Leschi, Nisqually chief, d. 1858.
4. Leschi, Nisqually chief, d. 1858—Trials, litigation, etc.
5. Stevens, Isaac Ingalls, 1818–1862.   6. Puget Sound (Wash.)—
History—19th century.   I. Title.
F99.N74K55 2011
979.7004'979435—dc22   2010034249

Jacket images: (background) *Puget Sound and Olympic Mountains,*
Washington, U.S. © UpperCut Images / Alamy; (insets, top to bottom)
Brigadier General I. Ingalls Stevens by Joseph E. Baker, J. H. Bufford's
Lith., Boston, MA, 1861 (detail), Washington State Historical Society;
Chief Leschi, Nisqually by Raphael Coombs, 1894 (detail),
Washington State Historical Society
Jacket design by Chip Kidd
Maps by Darin Jensen

Manufactured in the United States of America
First Edition

For Adrianne and Mike—
warm, wise, witty,
and ever venturesome

LISTEN

Once people could see beyond space
And watch the eagle fly toward the sun.
Power is coming back to you.
You've been looking down,
Now it's time to look up.
The spirit warms the blood
And electrifies the heart.
Like spring coming out of winter;
Like a boy learning to ride,
Or a young hawk wavering
Across the sky.
Songs will be heard by those who listen.
People are chanting;
Something bigger is coming,
Of dreams promised long ago.
A new song is heard.
People will find unity,
For the Lord nourishes all.
He speaks to all people.

—Jack Iyall

CONTENTS

PREFACE

A Fresh Reckoning

A FEW YEARS BACK, I was casting about for an appealing subject on which to base a historical novel, a genre in which I had published three earlier works. In both my fictional writing and my books on American social history, I had dwelled frequently on the law and its majesty along with its debasement by malpractice and misapplication. And so it occurred to me that a stirring narrative could be crafted dealing with the adventures of a fictional circuit-riding judge during the frontier days of the Old West, when life brimmed with peril and where the line between virtue and villainy at times grew indistinguishable.

Hoping to blend literary license with historical authenticity, I needed to discover at the outset whether legal documents have survived from that earlier time—in particular from the territorial era before states were carved from vast expanses of wilderness, where the law was largely an abstract premise, heeded fitfully and enforced haphazardly if at all. Research on an earlier book had taught me that Washington, before it was granted statehood in 1889, had been a U.S. territory for thirty-six years—long enough to have generated a considerable record of rough-and-ready jurisprudence, assuming the authorities had taken the trouble to preserve it. I phoned the state law library at the Temple of Justice, as Washingtonians, with admirable reverence, have named their Supreme Court building in Olympia, the state capital, and spoke with a pleasant and cooperative librarian.

"Oh, yes," she said, "we have all the opinions of the court from the territorial period—and they're all available online." And she gave me the Web link.

I thanked her with anticipatory glee.

"You might," my librarian friend added a bit tentatively, "want to have a look at case number three in the first volume of the territorial reports."

"Because . . . ?" I asked.

"It was the first capital case in the history of Washington Territory to be appealed to the Supreme Court—that was the direct predecessor of our present State Supreme Court." The year, she said, was 1857.

"I see," I said, not quite catching her drift. "And was there something special about the case that I ought to . . . ?"

"It dealt with a notorious murder conviction," said the librarian. "And the decision was reviewed two years ago."

"You mean—that would be, what—one hundred forty-seven years later?"

"Yes," she said and explained that a special tribunal had assembled, presided over by the current chief justice of the Supreme Court of the state of Washington, to reconsider the matter.

Recalling the law's hoary precept that justice delayed is justice denied, I ventured, "Wasn't that a little late in the game?"

She gave a pleasant laugh and urged me to check into the circumstances. And so I have.

What follows is not a historical novel but rather the story surrounding that case, *Washington Territory v. Leschi, an Indian,* an all but forgotten episode from our nation's past, which occurred in a then remote but breathtakingly beautiful setting in the farthest northwest corner of the country. The very obscurity of these circumstances, I feel, invites cool reflection on the issue at its core instead of aversion from it as a too familiar and depressing eyesore on our shared cultural landscape. Call it a fresh reckoning.

I logged on to the site and read the court's 1857 ruling. Its first few sentences betrayed a transparently racist tone suggesting that something less than a disinterested quality of justice was about to be rendered. Events over the three years preceding the court's decision, my subsequent investigation led me to conclude, were shaped by a similarly phobic disposition among Washington Territory's citizenry at large. Why this should have been so is a question, I believe, worthy of consideration even at this seemingly late date. For we are still a young nation, and despite all our feats, our united prospects are likely to turn on our ability to learn from how we have erred as well as succeeded.

White Americans cannot deny their long history of abusive transactions with people of color. These offenses, it should be noted out of fairness, can be explained in part by the fact that no other sizable national state has ever been formed from the confluence of so many diverse ethnic streams. All our heterogeneous ferment no doubt made contentiousness inevitable. In retrospect, it is hardly surprising that whites would assert privileges of entitlement flowing from their fortunate economic status and social rank (also known as the accident of birth) and assign nonwhite minorities the status of a permanent servile class. And in accord with the precepts of Social Darwinism, this uncivil subjugation was facilely intellectualized as neither commendable nor reprehensible; it was merely human nature in the raw. Everywhere and always, the strong have dominated the weak, as with every species in the jungle and individuals within every social subset. No one said what emerged from the melting pot had to look, smell, or taste very good.

A moral problem, however, intruded on this ready excuse for our racial perversion. The American colonies and the nation heir to them were conceived as a white enterprise, even if not certified as exclusively so. Yet on declaring its independence and designing its mechanics of governance, the United States proclaimed the equality of all mankind and sought to deploy political power in ways intended to check the tyranny of the mighty over the needy—a noble aspiration at sharp divergence from the habits of every previous society. Sadly, high-minded rhetoric was overmatched by self-interest and the sustained impulse to mastery by the ruling whites.

Lately, many—perhaps even most—white Americans, mindful of this thick catalogue of incivility, have been afflicted by an epidemic of something closely resembling a national guilty conscience over their past mistreatment of people of color. A cynic might dismiss this belated acknowledgment as timely in view of the swiftly rising proportion of nonwhites among the U.S. population and the corresponding surge in their social and economic power. The 2008 election of the country's first African American president—an attainment unthinkable to the many who could remember when Jim Crow still stalked the land—is of course the most dramatic evidence of this swelling tide of racial tolerance, but it is by no means an isolated incident. Blacks have been advancing as never before in many pursuits, though not yet nearly in ratio to their numbers, and multitudes remain unredeemed.

President Obama's first appointment to the U.S. Supreme Court, a Hispanic woman, suggests that the nation has similarly started to recognize and make amends for its long denigration of Latinos, now the largest ethnic minority in the United States. True, the presence of millions of impoverished or struggling illegal migrants from Mexico has aroused resentment across America. And yet there has been no general outcry to round up and deport these aliens. Instead, there is a growing, though far from universal, appreciation that most of these border violators, like most before them who risked fleeing their homelands for haven here, have come to live free and to earn a decent livelihood—and thus deserve to be dealt with humanely. Asian Americans, too, have been tipping the scales of social empowerment away from the formerly overwhelming white preponderance. Their numbers, like the soaring Hispanic presence, have been multiplied by refugees seeking asylum from political persecution and economic hardship in the teeming places of their birth. This burgeoning Asian community has demonstrated a remarkable degree of self-discipline and incentive to achieve wide material success. And its social and cultural distance from the American mainstream has begun to narrow in the younger generation as academic institutions and industry are welcoming, as never before, the highest achievers among them.

Far less visible amid the nation's surge of multiracial validation, and rarely granted more than lip-service acknowledgment of their victimization throughout the peopling of the continent by settlers of European ancestry, has been the oldest and now the smallest racial minority in the United States—those of native blood, a classification finally accorded the dignity of full citizenship in 1924, who are the remnant of a so-called red race that migrated to this hemisphere from Asia and Oceania starting some 10,000 years ago. Their antiquity has hardly served to ensure their survival or enhance their status in the American social hierarchy.

For nearly 400 years the confrontation between the natives of North America and the arrivals from the Old World was marked by the newcomers' conviction that they were entitled, by virtue of their cultural superiority, moral standards, and God's grace, to displace the Stone Age inhabitants of the broad, bountiful continent and make it their own. Shoved to the fringes of the landscape, Native Americans were permitted to choose between slow extinction on bleak reservations or self-exile from Indian Country to uncongenial urban surroundings, where acculturation often proved traumatic. By the beginning of this century, more of the estimated 2.75 million people (roughly 1 percent of the national total) electing to identify themselves as Native Americans—which generally required possessing at least one-quarter Indian blood—lived in cities and towns, not on or close to reservations.

The drastic decline of the natives as a distinctive ethnic classification has become a sad, irksome chapter in our national narrative. Those remaining as members of the roughly 500 federally recognized tribes, communities, and bands have for several generations now been more pitied than scorned. The methodical removal of their once vast holdings, the rest of us lament—when pestered about it—was the regrettable price that had to be paid if human evolution was to progress on this continent. At least we no longer deride tribal people as savages or make movies depicting them as good for little more than target practice by the U.S. cavalry. But far from viewing them as a national treasure with a culture worth preserving, Americans by and large tend to think of Indians as an exotic *memento mori,* anomalous curios, broken and unfixable. Only a recent and controversial exercise of massive affirmative action by the U.S. government, in the form of laws licensing gaming casinos in Indian Country, has begun to bring about promising change to parts of Native America.

Why, then, in owning up of late to the grievances of its other wronged racial minorities, has the nation registered such minimal awareness of its tribal people, such scant concern over their condition, and so little sorrow for their past degradation?

One reason for this dismissive attitude, I believe, is the failure by non-tribal people to appreciate the nature of the natives' grievance and how to address it. The Indians do not clamor for the nation's ear, demanding economic parity and the profits of free enterprise, because they are not animated by the American Dream of maximum personal self-aggrandizement. They are not worshippers at the shrine of rugged individualism. They are, through cultural conditioning that has endured for millennia, a communal and interdependent people; they need one another. And they are, for the most part, a more spiritual people than most who dwell in America, however godly the rest of us may profess ourselves, and they are, for the most part, less materialistic and mercenary. Liberty and prosperity for all, in their case, mean freedom from harassment by outsiders and a shared commonwealth of well-being, not greater opportunity for the most aggressive among them to thrive while the rest are left to founder. The tribes are collectives, whose pursuit of happiness is a shared venture—a practice decidedly against the American grain.

In recent years, under the spell of an insistent, presumably soothing political correctness, we have shied from using the word "Indian"— a misnomer from the beginning—and taken to calling tribal people "Native Americans." But "American" is, of course, a European-derived word and concept; the natives here were not Americans but *pre-Americans*. Their ancestors preceded the white settlers by thousands of years, and they do not ask for or need to be granted social certification by races who have avidly muscled them out of the way.

What the natives want, I believe, and what they have wanted from their first encounters with white intruders, is to abide, to be left to themselves, to remain on their home ground—or a goodly portion thereof—and to live (with a few bows to modernity such as electricity and sanitary waste disposal) much as they were accustomed to, in harmony with their natural surroundings and ancient beliefs. But the rest of us have ordained otherwise, telling Indians they don't know what's best for them and nudging them ever deeper into the shadows between their own values and pressing alien ones.

The Bitter Waters of Medicine Creek does not attempt an encyclopedic survey of the interaction between the red and white races on these shores—so calamitous to the former, so ignoble of the latter. It is meant to be not a compendium but an illustration. In focusing on the experience of a single small tribe, the book aspires to make a monumental tragedy more accessible and comprehensible; the smaller the scale, the keener our perception may become of an unfolding human drama.

To attempt a coherent narrative of this sort and bring the contending participants to life without heavy reliance on legend and hearsay is a challenge for the modern narrator, given the understandable reluctance of whites to record their transgressions with candor and the complete absence of written testimony on the natives' side. With help from many others, I was able to assemble a sizable body of documentary sources. These include administrative, military, and court records of the federal government, official and private correspondence, family memoirs, Washington State archival materials, old newspaper files, books (many of them rare), oral recollections, and the collective Nisqually tribal memory. While even the most conscientious present-day investigator of occurrences long ago in Indian Country—and I do not claim to be such—cannot escape indulging in a good deal of speculation and surmise, I hope the result here is a substantially faithful recounting of what occurred. If so, perhaps it will encourage the reader to rethink the place we have assigned the natives in our minds as well as on the land we took from them for our own sake. The cost of contemplating history is often an uneasy conscience.

—R.K.

PART I

The Governor
and the Chief

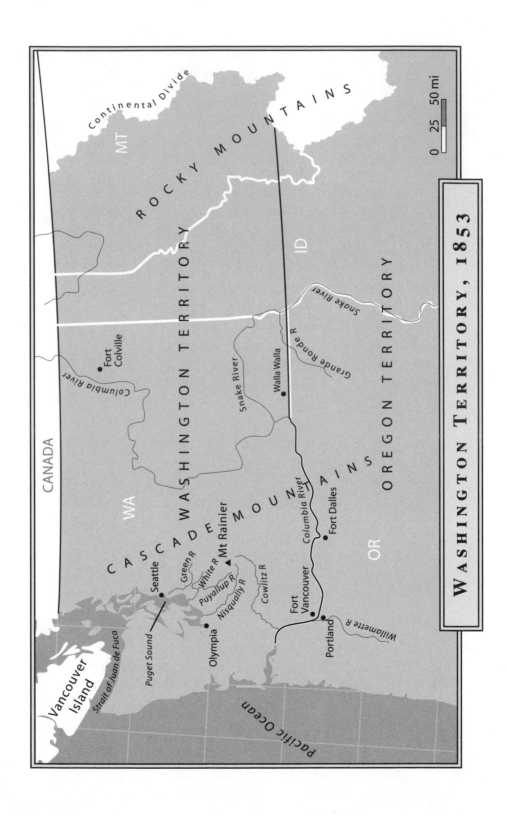

WASHINGTON TERRITORY, 1853

CANADA

Vancouver Island

Strait of Juan de Fuca

Pacific Ocean

Puget Sound

Seattle

Olympia

Nisqually R

Cowlitz R

Puyallup R

White R

Green R

Mt Rainier

Fort Vancouver

Portland

Willamette R

Fort Dalles

Columbia River

CASCADE MOUNTAINS

WA

OR

ID

MT

WASHINGTON TERRITORY

OREGON TERRITORY

ROCKY MOUNTAINS

Continental Divide

Fort Colville

Columbia River

Snake River

Snake River

Walla Walla

Grande Ronde R

0   25   50 mi

I

"I Know What I Am About"

THE ENTIRETY of Isaac I. Stevens's incandescent but recklessly sacrificed life may best be understood as a classic case of overcompensation.

One symptom of this tendency was his aptitude as a tireless communicator. In person he could be talkative, at times insufferably so, and inclined to dominate the conversation until he got his point across. On paper Stevens was likewise prolific and prolix, a compulsive letter writer and drafter of memoranda, some of them compelling reading but at times long-winded. Much that he wrote survives in official archives since he was employed by the American government for his entire adult life. His own writings, the responses to them, and the testimony of many contemporaries who knew and dealt with him form the documentary basis for two substantial biographies of Stevens. The first, published in 1901, is a worshipful two-volume compendium by his son, Hazard, a Congressional Medal of Honor winner but not a gifted litterateur. The second, a far more balanced and stylistically graceful account, is by a scholar and regional historian, Kent Richards, who subtitled his 1979 work *Young Man in a Hurry*. Stevens's passionate striving for personal advancement, along with his patriotism, courage, and intelligence, may be readily gleaned from this mass of material. Ironically, though, Isaac Stevens is remembered today, if at all, not for his daring or any luminous achievement but for his vendetta aimed at destroying the last chief of an obscure Native American tribe—a man who was, so far as modern scrutiny can tell, a patriot no less devoted to his little nation, equally brave, and just as smart by his own culture's determinants.

In the biography by Professor Richards, the reader is offered a word portrait of Second Lieutenant Isaac I. Stevens at age twenty-one, in dress uniform fresh out of the U.S. Military Academy at West Point, where he ranked first in his class academically. We are told of a handsome gallant with "expressive, attentive, large dark-hazel eyes . . . thick black hair which curled over his ears and collar, a small goatee carefully trimmed, straight nose, and firmly set lips and chin." His good looks, a bit more seasoned but no less dashing, were also evident in a stylized lithograph of the Union army's Brigadier General Stevens twenty-two years later, proudly wearing a buttoned-over, high-collar military tunic with epaulets and wielding a spyglass in his right hand, presumably for surveying the nearest battlefield. Not disclosed by either the verbal or graphic portrait was the elegant worthy's stature. Stevens was born with short, stumpy legs—a malformation likely traceable to a faulty pituitary gland—and a large head that appeared out of scale with the rest of his body. Some who would later have to deal with his driving energy, stand before his commanding presence, and confront those burning eyes fixed on whatever prize he was pursuing at the moment were convinced that Stevens was ruled by a casebook Napoleonic complex. It may well be a coarse simplification to suggest that his whole life played out as a compensatory reflex for his shortness—he probably stood only two or three inches above five feet, though no medical records survive—but of his dynamic nature there is no doubt.

He was an eighth-generation member of an American family that was among the first to settle the town of Andover, twenty miles above Boston in the Massachusetts Bay Colony. John Stevens, an Anglican convert to the Puritan sect, reached the New World in 1638 at the age of thirty-three and with his brood of eight children headed for Andover, on the Merrimack River. The town, later to become the site of the nation's oldest— and among its most elite—private college preparatory academies, would remain the Stevens clan's home for several centuries while its members coped, with varying degrees of success, as farmers, millers, soldiers, and civic leaders of their community. Isaac I. Stevens's grandfather Jonathan fought with the American revolutionaries at Bunker Hill, expanded the family farm, opened a tannery, and built a lakeside mansion to house his fourteen children.

Jonathan's seventh son, Isaac (father of Isaac I.), began grown-up life as a teenage adventurer, sailing to China, but was not enchanted by the nautical life. He returned to Andover to run a hay farm, a malt mill, and a general store with an adjacent inn that served as a crackerbarrel meeting place for local gentry and a hotbed of political palaver. Isaac married Hannah Ingalls, a local woman of similar background, though more affectionate and religious by nature. Hannah had good sense, ran her home efficiently, and bore seven children, five daughters and two sons, during a thirteen-year marriage that ended tragically.

Her husband, frugal, hardworking, and high-minded, had one unfortunate vice—he drove his horse and wagon like a fury. One day, with his wife seated beside him, he took a turn too fast and overturned the wagon, causing Hannah to hit her head sharply on the ground. She lingered for two years, never recovering from the accident. The family's collective grief was compounded when Isaac married his sullen housekeeper, who lavished little love on her stepchildren, and vice versa. None of the Stevens children was more emotionally scarred by the loss of their mother than her third-born, and first son, Isaac Ingalls Stevens, who was nine when she passed.

Isaac was so small and frail at his birth on March 25, 1818, that his survival was in doubt for a time. Family legend had it that Hannah, as tender-hearted a mother as ever walked the planet, was nevertheless so wearied from keeping house and minding her two older children that she let the undersized baby boy languish in his crib until his grandmother liberated him when he was three. If the story was true, little Isaac appears to have hit the ground running and remained in motion pretty much the rest of his days.

Whatever the lad lacked in physique, he soon gave evidence that his outsized head held a large and agile brain. His powers of memory and a precocious talent for numbers were demonstrated early on, and there was no lack of mental stimulus around the home. Isaac's father, while the very model of Yankee thrift, industry, and canniness, was also a well-read man of ardent convictions, a devout Unitarian of decidedly liberal views about religion and the evils of slavery, and a regular subscriber to the moralizing precepts espoused in the weekly edition of Horace Greeley's *New York Tribune* and William Lloyd Garrison's crusading *Liberator*. He generously shared his newspapers and books with his neighbors as well as his outspoken views, among them devotion to the tenets of populist Jacksonian democracy—disfavored in mercantile New England—and antipathy for liquor and tobacco as diabolic enticements to ruin.

These persuasions made the elder Isaac a demanding taskmaster where his bright boy's school lessons and study habits were concerned. Sent to school before he was five, the lad was preternaturally attentive, recited without flaw and beyond requirement, and was so accomplished in arithmetic that after a time his teacher no longer instructed him in the subject because she said his knowledge of it had outstripped hers. While striving to satisfy his intimidating father, young Isaac gravitated toward his more compassionate mother and frequented her bedside during the two years she survived her husband's reckless wagon-driving. The happiness went out of his childhood thereafter, dimmed by a father who was unsympathetic to the boy's sensitive nature. Isaac poured himself still more zealously into his schoolwork when, at age ten, the year after his mother died, he was sent to a private academy his grandfather had started, where the boy excelled from the first. He was not so devoted a bookworm, though, that he avoided the usual boyish exertions, like scaling the splendid elm trees that bordered the Stevens property, wrestling with his school chums, and working in the family's fields and orchards, sometimes to the point of exhaustion and once suffering from near-fatal sunstroke. It was as if he had to demonstrate to everyone around him that his pint size was no limitation to his physical prowess. One day, at the age of twelve, he pushed himself too hard pitching hay and suffered a serious groin rupture, which never fully healed, required him to wear a truss the rest of his life, and agonizingly recurred at several most inconvenient moments in his adult career.

To take a breather from his studies, at which he had overtasked himself (with his stern father's complicity), and to escape a less than embracing home life, Isaac apprenticed himself for a year at his uncle's nearby woolen mill, where once more he proved a quick learner (but was required to surrender all his wages to his pinchpenny father). Resuming his education, Isaac was sent for his final sixteen months of secondary schooling to nearby Phillips Academy for boys, where he did chores to pay for his room and board. Again he displayed formidable talent at mathematics, completing college-level studies and solving problems that puzzled his instructors. The law and the ministry were considered respectable career choices, if not exactly attuned to the youngster's gifts, but higher education was a cost his father was not eager to bear. The intervention of Isaac's uncle saved the day. He appealed to the local congressman, an acquaintance of his, to select his nephew for all-expenses-paid appointment to the U.S. Military Academy at West Point; the lawmaker agreed that Isaac's sterling school record merited reward.

· · ·

WEST POINT, under challenge in that era as a bastion for overprivi-
leged youth, was hardly known for its intellectual rigor. But neither was it
heralded for the way it taught military theory and tactics or for turning
out skilled officers. What it did well was train army engineers, and young
Isaac Stevens, already familiar with the rudiments of surveying—an
invaluable skill in territorially expansive America during the early nineteenth century—had come well prepared for induction into that branch of
the army.

The aura of the Point, its traditions and patriotic fervor, the ramrod
bearing of its officers—all of it enthralled the impressionable plebe
Stevens. On the other hand, as the product of a deeply moralistic, teeto-
taling, antitobacco home life, he was shocked by the cussing, boozing,
and smoking common among his peers. Isaac made no secret that, like
his father, he found such habits repellent—an earnestness that, combined
with his shortness, made him a ripe target for bullying, of which he suffered more than his share. But the scrappy, speedy young Stevens was
bent on winning his fellow cadets' respect; he did so by fighting back—
and winning a goodly number of demerits for misconduct—and by proving himself the smartest member of his class. He got up ahead of
everyone else each morning and vigorously hiked the Point grounds
before breakfast. He overcame his aversion to public speaking by joining
the Dialectic Society, one of the academy's few extracurricular activities.
He learned some social graces, including how to dance, though he
remained shy with girls other than his five sisters. And, of course, he pursued the vocational skills he thought might best advance his career, such
as how to build forts and bridges, the strategic emplacement of field
artillery—Napoleon's specialty—and first-rate horsemanship while
maintaining soldierly bearing. He sought as well to broaden his horizons
and mental acuity by delving into the liberal arts as his time and curricu-
lum allowed, reading the classics and British literary masters, keeping
himself abreast of politics and public events as his father did, and
improving his writing and drawing skills. A latent streak of rebellious-
ness led to his helping launch an underground student newspaper poking
fun at the army in general and at particular faculty members; it also featured vaguely subversive essays like one of his own titled "Has Man a
Conscience?"

As he neared the end of his cadet years, Isaac wrote his father, "I have
endeavored to make it my rule never to relinquish any undertaking, but
always to *try* till success crowned my efforts. I have thus got along pretty

well"—sweet words to a sire who, despite their clashing temperaments, had done much to imbue that dogged spirit in his son. So gifted had young Isaac shown himself to be at mathematics that he served as a temporary assistant professor in the subject during the last part of his time at the Point, and it was no great surprise when his grit and wits earned him the role of Class of 1839 valedictorian.

In a nation at peace with foreign powers since Andrew Jackson had thoroughly routed the British at the Battle of New Orleans a quarter-century earlier, service in the small standing U.S. Army did not require much in the way of derring-do. Jackson's victory and the pronouncement of the Monroe Doctrine had combined to tell the Old World that the young American republic had staked a claim on the New World as its sphere of influence—and woe be to any nation with dreams of newly colonizing the Western Hemisphere. U.S. soldiers stood vigil over the country's shores and boundaries, safeguarded settlers pushing west against attacks by resentful Indian tribes, or—if, like Isaac Stevens, they had been admitted to the select Army Corps of Engineers—were assigned to oversee federal construction projects, usually fortifications, roads, and canals and other waterways in need of dredging as the nation sprouted.

Stevens's first tour of duty was to superintend the final phase of a twenty-year construction program at Fort Adams in Newport, Rhode Island, the largest defensive citadel in the nation. The exacting nature of the job—he had to be all over the place dealing with personnel of a wide occupational variety—brought him to the attention of the outgoing supervisor of the massive project, Joseph Totten, a stickler for detail who had just been named chief engineer of the U.S. Army, a post Stevens hoped to hold himself someday.

A pleasing fringe benefit of the assignment was its locale. Newport was well established as a commercial and recreational nexus and the home of families of wealth and social position, where neatly groomed young military officers like Stevens were always in demand for cotillions and holiday parties. Isaac soon met local belle Margaret Hazard, whom he called Meg, a year his senior and the issue of two ranking families of Newport gentry. Her father, Benjamin, was rated among the ablest lawyers in Rhode Island and had represented Newport in the state legislature for three decades. A proper courtship followed, with long walks on the beach, high-speed horseback rides, and readings aloud of tender poetry. Before long the restless young army officer was beginning to find more drudgery than challenge in his labors as foreman at the fort and to reflect that a legal career might be more stimulating and rewarding, especially in the firm of Meg's father, who could open many a door for a bright-eyed son-in-law. But a virulent case of tuberculosis struck down Benjamin Hazard not long before Isaac and Meg were married in a subdued wedding celebration. The law no longer beckoned to the calculating second lieutenant.

By twenty-four, he was the father of a son, Hazard, but his career was not keeping pace with his family responsibilities. His transfer from Newport to take charge of repairs to the old fort at the whaling town of New Bedford, Massachusetts—a low-priority project—seemed a dead end. Nor did Stevens's initiative at his new workplace sit well at first. "The people in New Bedford are disposed to criticize my plans," Isaac wrote his father, "but they will find out that I know what I am about, and that they had better save their sneers for some other object."

Such combativeness and self-certitude would surface with increasing frequency and become the least appealing elements of his indefatigable work ethic. Before long, Stevens's nervy competence won him simultaneous command of construction at five installations in northern New England, including a new forty-gun bastion to be called Fort Knox along the Maine coast at the narrows of the Penobscot River opposite the town of Bucksport. Keeping close tabs on so many job sites required him to act as engineer, architect, personnel director, labor negotiator, purchasing agent, and paymaster—a crash course in management for any young aspirant to high rank and authority.

Stevens's youthful appearance belied the skill with which he performed his multiple tasks. An old Down East farmer who owned the land on which Fort Knox was to be built was so disdainful of the twenty-five-year-old lieutenant's callow looks that he refused at first to sit down across the bargaining table to arrange the terms of purchase. Advised that Stevens had been entrusted by the army not only to buy the real estate for the new fort but to manage its entire construction, the old-timer relented—and found, as many others would over time, that Isaac Stevens was one tough bargainer. Meanwhile, he was earning points with Chief Engineer Totten down in Washington.

FOR ALL Stevens's dutiful handling of his growing responsibilities, advancement in the peacetime army was excruciatingly slow. He thus welcomed the Mexican War as a chance to display courage and prowess in combat, the surest means of military promotion. To be sure, he believed the war was just and necessary, blaming it not on U.S. territorial ambitions but on Mexico's stubborn refusal to acknowledge the successful rebellion of Texas and its recent annexation by Congress. In this view, Stevens parted company with his father, who believed—not without cause—that the war had been cooked up by President James Polk, himself a slaveowner, in cahoots with southern politicians who wanted to extend the reach of the slavocracy all across the southern tier of the nation to the Pacific shore.

As the first blood was shed along the Rio Grande, Stevens put in for transfer to a combat zone. His request was not granted until the climactic final campaign of the war in 1847, when he was assigned as adjutant to the field commander of the Corps of Engineers accompanying General Winfield Scott, the highest-ranking officer in the U.S. Army, on his drive from Mexico's largest seaport, Veracruz, on the Gulf of Mexico, to Mexico City to force an unconditional surrender. Stevens's function would be to provide reconnaissance and logistical advice on troop movements through the steep and tangled highlands that dominated the 200-mile route to the Mexican capital. "I go," Isaac wrote to Meg, "without a single foreboding. . . . I trust I shall have full strength to do my full duty. I know this will accord with all the wishes of your own heart." Did ever a young patriot profess greater fervor on the brink of mortal peril?

Stevens was quickly baptized in the brutal realities of warfare. He watched in sorrow as the big guns on the U.S. Navy ships bringing Scott's task force to Veracruz pounded the port city for four days without opposition after its defenders refused to surrender. As the fighting raged up into the steamy mountain jungles, Isaac's letters disclosed a similar measure of sympathy for the bravery and suffering of the poorly trained, supplied, and led Mexican soldiers. Yet he actively took part in destroying the poor wretches who stood in the way of his nation's destiny. The action often took Stevens behind enemy lines or into the perilous gap between the opposing armies in order to find and map the least hazardous path of advance. In doing so, he won high marks from his commanders for cool, courageous, and resourceful conduct.

On one particularly harrowing assignment, leading a scouting party of fifty men through rough terrain in quest of the safest river crossing they could find for the U.S. attack force, Stevens exerted himself so strenuously that his old groin rupture reopened and left him in stunning pain. Ingloriously confined to a field hospital bed, he rallied and despite warnings not to overdo it was soon back in the field alongside fellow West

Point engineer Robert E. Lee and other colleagues in the elite cadre gathering essential intelligence for the final push on Mexico City.

As U.S. troops approached the outskirts of the capital, its defenders fell back to the satellite towns and rallied to put up stiff resistance at Contreras. There Isaac scaled a nearby church steeple—questionable therapy for a convalescent hernia—to obtain a panoramic view with his spyglass of the movements of the backpedaling Mexican troops. Seeing that the enemy was in full, disorderly retreat, he sent word to General Scott, who promptly ordered swift pursuit, with Stevens assigned to accompany the attackers. Their headlong surge brought the Americans to the town of Churubusco, where a strongly fortified convent slowed the pursuers. Stevens recommended the placement of artillery and infantry units close to the enemy guns for maximum firepower and quick assault. The advice, though accepted, was given without his awareness of the intervening, heavily manned enemy breastworks that were obscured from his view by a field of tall corn. The daring maneuver exposed the U.S. soldiers to a severe pounding and caused many casualties. In the end only a fixed-bayonet charge dislodged the diehard Mexicans in one of the deadliest encounters of the war. The sight and smell of so many mangled corpses on both sides left Stevens dazed and remorseful, but neither General Scott nor his top aides—knowing wars were won by bold strokes, not excessive caution about the price to be paid in blood—faulted the zealous engineer.

During the mop-up stage of the fighting, though, Stevens suffered a serious foot injury from an enemy rifle ball that shattered small bones and severed tendons. His usual grit was sorely tried by pain and a two-week fever brought on by blood poisoning, but he pulled through and wound up the war roundly commended for his manly, unstinting efforts. If he was not a medal-bedecked hero, he returned home with his future as an ascendant officer seemingly ensured.

THE DEMOBILIZED U.S. ARMY had more hands than work to busy them, so Isaac Stevens, promoted to brevet major for his wartime exploits, was nevertheless returned by the Corps of Engineers to his old assignment of keeping the coastal forts of northern New England in good repair. With his days of patriotic gore and glory on the battlefield still a fresh memory, he felt marooned, wondering if he ought to remain in the military.

For the first time he became active in politics, supporting the 1848 presidential aspirations of Senator Lewis Cass, Democrat of Michigan, who lost to Mexican War hero Zachary Taylor of the fading but still breathing Whig Party. His involvement now oriented Stevens's thinking toward the nation's capital, where his exemplary record won him a plum assignment in 1849—assistant to the director of the U.S. Coastal Survey. The nation's victory over Mexico had given it vastly expanded boundaries. The United States now claimed legal title to all the territory between the Rockies and the Pacific Ocean from the forty-ninth parallel on the north to the Rio Grande and bottom of California on the south as a result of successful diplomatic encounters with Spain (in 1819) and Britain (in 1846) and the recent military rout of Mexico. The task of mapping this expanse would be performed by some of the seventy-seven Corps of Engineers surveying parties then in the field. Charting every inch of America's new 1,200-mile-long Pacific coastline would soon follow. It did not take a visionary to perceive, along with Major Stevens, that the sooner Americans settled that immense domain, the safer it would become and the more certain the nation's emergence as a bicoastal colossus.

This vital geographical enterprise was coordinated by a seventy-man office in Washington, D.C., and because its director was almost always away troubleshooting at the survey sites, his assistant served as the acting, and highly active, boss of the operation. Stevens saw the job, which planted him in the midst of the federal government apparatus of a relentlessly expansionist nation, as a stepping-stone to a yet more responsible and challenging post.

The rigidity and passivity that too often define the bureaucratic mindset were not tolerated by Stevens, whose direct and sometimes confrontational ways of getting things done ruffled the feathers of older hands in the Coastal Survey office. Perceived by a number of his underlings as a martinet, he treated the intraoffice combat as a personal challenge. As he wrote to Meg, living at their Rhode Island home with their children—Hazard now had three sisters—while Isaac roomed at a boardinghouse on the limited pay of a brevet officer:

> I am bringing to bear upon the men my personal weight, and you know I rarely fail whenever I am brought into direct personal contact. . . . They know I am firm and steadfast, but I am as true to them as I am to the work itself. Every man will know that he can have entire confidence in my justice, and in my judgment of his merits.

Stevens, given his ambitions, did not limit his ambit to strictly parochial matters involving the coastline of the United States. His after-hours fraternizing, mostly with fellow younger officers, provided the occasion for him to voice his ideas about the need for a stronger, more professional standing army, better trained and paid, to protect the enlarged nation. In particular, he favored much strengthened artillery units and new fortified posts to safeguard the steadily heavier flow of wagon trains from what he called the "murderous Indian tribes in the West." His moral compass seemed not to allow for the possibility that the natives may have been acting in self-defense.

The restless major now began to mingle with civilian politicians, particularly younger ones on the rise, such as Stephen Douglas of Illinois, a newcomer to the U.S. Senate, only five years Isaac's senior and a Democrat like himself. Douglas would shortly emerge as a major figure in Washington and a conciliator in the intensifying regional divide over slavery. Stevens agreed with the Illinois lawmaker that while slavery was an abomination, for Congress to abolish it, as his father and growing anti-slavery multitudes favored, would very likely tear the Union apart. What made more sense to him was so-called popular sovereignty (a/k/a "squatters' rights"), allowing the citizens of new territories to determine for themselves whether, upon attaining statehood, they would permit or outlaw slavery.

In the course of his social rounds, Stevens wandered far from his upbringing and its strictures against indulging in alcohol. After arriving at West Point, he began to have an occasional nip to be one of the gang. He almost certainly drank during the Mexican War to dull the pain of his recurring rupture, the ache in his wounded foot, and the horrors of witnessing mass death from hot lead and rampant disease. As a Washington bureaucrat on the make and beyond the scrutiny of his genteel wife, he found pleasure in "whiskey punches for which Stevens achieved something of a reputation," according to his biographer Kent Richards.

To spread his name and ideas—and likely to curry favor with the gifted but insufferably vain Major General Winfield Scott, still the highest-ranking officer in the U.S. Army—Stevens took umbrage at an 1849 account of the Mexican War that he felt undervalued Scott's leadership and gave undue credit to politically appointed generals. Stevens greatly admired Scott's handling of the army in Mexico, and the admiration seemed mutual, since the general introduced him around Washington, according to Hazard Stevens's biography of his father, as "my young friend, Major Stevens, to whose courage and ability I owe much of my success in Mexico." Accordingly, Stevens turned out a barbed critique of the 1849 account of the war, setting the record straight by his lights, and submitted it to one of the leading literary periodicals of the day, the *North American Review*. The magazine rejected his offering as too contentious and personally demeaning to some of Scott's rivals. Stevens took the criticisms to heart and recast his essay after sharing it with his wartime colleague Robert E. Lee, who urged him to publish it in order to alert the public to the need for a much better army than the thrown-together, improperly prepared force President Polk had sent to Mexico. The 108-page, author-subsidized treatise was issued in a limited edition in 1851, and Stevens sent a copy to Scott, who he naturally expected would appreciate the writer's kind words. The words were apparently not kind enough, for Scott returned the book unopened and without explanation. Hazard Stevens's biography speculated that, for all its fulsome praise, his father's book erred by daring to second-guess several of Scott's decisions.

The snubbed author gained a measure of satisfaction the following year after Scott won the Whig nomination for President. Stevens bolstered the candidacy of Democratic standard-bearer Franklin Pierce of New Hampshire, who had come under scurrilous attack in the press for his role as a general in the Mexican War. Offended by charges that Pierce had been spineless on the battlefield, Stevens wrote a series of letters to leading papers in Boston and Washington in praise of the wartime service of his fellow New Englander and Democrat. Stevens's letters pointed out that Pierce had been esteemed in Scott's own written reports on military operations and had "done his whole duty as a son of the Republic . . . and that it has added a laurel to his beautiful civic wreath; as a citizen he has been ready to make sacrifices for his country; as a soldier and commander, he has shown gallantry before the enemy." Since Scott enjoyed the political support of most of Washington's military brass, Pierce was particularly appreciative—and needful—of the brevet major's efforts in his behalf.

Stevens's partisanship, encouraging military men to side with Pierce, stirred resentment in the War Department of President Millard Fillmore, a Whig, who had succeeded Zachary Taylor after he died in office. Soon Stevens received a letter of rebuke from Secretary of War Charles Conrad for butting into political affairs in a manner unbecoming a military careerist. Adopting a courteous but forceful style in his response, Stevens wrote he had not supposed that by his service as an army officer he had forfeited his rights as a citizen to advocate public measures he thought best for his country and to champion those he judged most suited to carry them out. Indeed, General Scott himself, in seeking the presidency, exemplified just such participation in politics that Stevens supported. Stevens never heard back from the Secretary of War—and Pierce won a decisive victory in the electoral college.

But Stevens was now in a pickle, professionally. He had won esteem for the diligence, efficiency, quality of workmanship, and high morale in the Coastal Survey office and, as a result, had been named to the board in charge of the nation's lighthouses and appointed to a commission responsible for improving navigation on the James, Appomattox, and Cape Fear rivers. Yet he was not advanced in rank from brevet major, had no keen sponsors among the upper echelons of the military, and had undoubtedly gained an enemy in Scott, still the army's first officer.

Increasingly irked that his talents were going unappreciated by his superiors, Stevens now actively cultivated friendships with key men in Congress, made a point of trying to meet other leading figures who visited the capital, and on occasion dropped by the lobby of leading Washington hotels like the Willard, sometimes with Hazard in hand, to chat up friends and would-be friends who might hold the key to his advancement. With Pierce due to arrive in the White House in March 1853, Stevens nurtured hopes of a political appointment as his way out of an atrophying army career. Like many other younger men approaching their prime—he was now thirty-five and the father of four—he cast his eyes westward, where the problems and challenges of the immense frontier opened by the victory over Mexico and the Gold Rush seemed to offer expansive opportunities. In his case, the object of pursuit was not wealth but power and position to use it.

In his last days in office, President Fillmore signed a bill that captured Stevens's interest because it seemed to offer a ready-made vehicle for his restless drive. The bill created the Washington Territory, an area larger than New York State and all of New England combined. Here was a huge virgin domain in the northwest corner of the nation, far less populated than roiling California or suddenly sprouting Oregon, and thus a *tabula rasa* on which Stevens could project his destiny and demonstrate his skills. He lost no time in asking Pierce to recommend him to Congress for appointment as the first governor of Washington Territory.

It was a canny choice of an arena for performing a star turn. Not many politicians were eager to win assignment to a frontier posting, with rough living conditions and few cultural amenities. Not long before, relatively unknown Abraham Lincoln, defeated in his reelection bid after one term in the House of Representatives due to his opposition to the Mexican War, had turned down the chance to be the first governor of Oregon Territory. The governorship of Washington Territory was likewise perceived as a tart political plum, so not only did Stevens face limited competition for the post but his credentials seemed ideal for the position: fourteen years in the military with combat experience; proven administrative skills; training and practice as an engineer, geographer, and surveyor; plus the energy of youth and driving ambition. The appointment, too, was an easy way for the new president to pay back the major who had flouted military propriety to advance Pierce's candidacy. Request granted, and Congress obliged.

2

Paradise for Free

IN TRADING THE HONOR, duty, and hierarchal rigidity of military
life, with its prospects of occasional high drama and the certainty of
long stretches of tedium for the vagaries of a political career, Isaac
Stevens resolved to make the most of his opportunity on the far side of
the nation. He had been to war and performed well, but he was—for all
his fiery competitiveness—a rock-ribbed New Englander, an officer, and
a gentleman, not a freewheeling adventurer familiar with the wilds of the
frontier and the everyday perils lurking there. His first task was to learn
all he could about the fiefdom on the nation's fringe that he had been
handed to transform from wilderness to a governable political subdivi-
sion. The trouble was that nobody back east knew very much about the
Washington Territory.

Of the prize Stevens had been awarded, this much was known: it covered, according to the best estimates of surveyors and cartographers,
about 110,000 square miles, possessed one of the most varied and spectacular landscapes on earth, and was populated by a few thousand white
people and probably six or seven times that many natives. Disarming the
local tribes and separating them from the lands of their forefathers would
be the first order of business for the novice governor of the new territory.

Ever since the first British settlement was planted on the opposite side
of the continent in tidewater Virginia 250 years earlier, the natives of the
far northwest had been spared the ravaging impact of white intruders,
largely because of their sheltering geography. To reach the heart of their
sanctuary overland from the east, settlers of European descent would
have had to traverse dense forests, myriad rushing rivers and swirling
streams, steep hills, deep valleys, narrow ravines, prairies without end,

parched badlands, sheer canyons, the rugged Rockies, and, at the end of their travail, the forbidding, snowcapped Cascade range. It would have been a far less taxing ordeal and taken a shorter time to get there traveling mostly by water from the nearby Pacific—if mariners had learned the route sooner. But neither French explorers who had navigated the full length of the Mississippi River, Spanish adventurers who had plundered the warmer climes of the New World, nor Russian fur traders plying the Pacific coastal waters to the north had ever ventured upon what the United States now called the Washington Territory.

No British seaborne voyagers had approached the region until the last years of the eighteenth century, and no American party came anywhere near it until Lewis and Clark's epochal 1805–6 expedition of discovery passed swiftly by some 100 miles to the south. Even after a chain of Spanish missions was strung along the California coast starting in 1769, maritime probes farther north were rare except for the frenetic international hunt for the sea otter and its luxuriously soft fur in the frigid waters along the northwest Pacific shoreline of modern Alaska. Monterey, 100 miles below San Francisco Bay and Mexican territory until 1848, was the only significant seaport along the Pacific coast from California north. While the Gold Rush turned San Francisco's slumbering little waterfront into a clamorous harbor, 1,000 miles of sea still separated it from ready access to most of the tribes in the new Washington Territory.

In addition to their remoteness, the natives there were insulated from outside contacts by the natural riches of the region, allowing them to stay close to home for their sustenance. The warming waters of the Japanese Current, the Pacific Ocean's equivalent to the Atlantic's Gulf Stream, brushed the northwest U.S. coastline, sending mild, moisture-laden air inland on prevailing west-to-east winds. These grow cool passing over the mountaintops of the nearby Olympic Range and form plump clouds that remain trapped for a time in the basin cupped on the east by the Cascades; the result is abundant annual rainfall throughout what was then the local Indian Country. The region was also well watered by spring-fed lakes and rivers rising in the Cascades—five from the ice packs on the slopes of 14,410-foot Mount Rainier, the snow-coned volcanic giant that stirred awe and dread among the Indians, who called it Tahoma ("white mountain")—that nourished lush valleys and fecund bottomland. Before white settlement began to take its heavy toll on the primeval forests, immense cedars, firs, and hemlocks, some soaring 200 feet or higher, formed thick woodlands that ascended upland hillsides and mountain slopes. This sea of trees and interspersed prairies of rippling grassland made a mantle of velvety green, draped across a gracefully sculpted countryside.

The wet, temperate climate nurtured a long growing season, and pristine waterways teemed with edible marine life—especially five varieties of delectable salmon and many kinds of shellfish, including clams larger than anywhere on the planet. The woods, too, made the survival of the aborigines far more secure and comfortable than that of most other hunter-gatherer societies. Their forests abounded in deer, elk, and bear, whose flesh, bones, and skin met many of the Indians' daily needs. The sky was alive with game birds and waterfowl. The plains, flattened by prehistoric glaciers, sprouted with nutritious wild bulbs, roots, and greens that supplemented the natives' protein-rich diets. The moist coastal soil rimming the prairies was bursting with berries of infinite variety, picked on summer excursions by tribal women and eaten right off the stem, dried for winter consumption and seasoning meats, or swirled into fruit drinks, a favorite Indian beverage in the innocent times before the white man brought liquor to the region.

Of nature's inedible gifts to the natives, none was of greater utility than the giant western red cedar. Its wood, savored for its sweet, musky aroma, was lightweight but strong, impervious to moisture so it did not decay in that often dank ecosystem, easy to split—a wedge made of elkhorn was the most common tool for that purpose—and highly malleable. These properties allowed tribesmen, strangers to metal tools, to fashion planks and beams with relative ease and assemble them into tall, remarkably sturdy residential lodges, some as long as 100 feet and as wide as 30, that stood for centuries. Cross sections of a single tree trunk five feet in diameter were hewn into ornamented canoes. And cedar bark, finely cut and shredded, was pounded into coarse thread for making women's skirts as soft as fabric, rain-repellent ponchos, intricately woven watertight baskets, floor mats, storage boxes, hats, sanitary pads, and baby diapers.

The Indians whom Isaac Stevens would soon encounter were truly blessed children of nature. It was their misfortune that history was about to catch up with paradise.

THE NATIVES' serene, secluded, and gloriously nurturing habitat was not intruded upon by white men until the last quarter of the eighteenth century, and no day-to-day contact began for another fifty years.

On his around-the-world exploratory voyage launched in 1778,

British captain James Cook sailed along the northwest coast of North America and later reported the existence of a channel just north of the forty-ninth parallel opening eastward from the Pacific between what would later be called Vancouver Island and the Olympic Peninsula in Washington State. Cook's travels did not allow him time to investigate the channel, but among sailors and empire-builders, the question arose whether this opening in the coastline might be the final stretch of the long-sought Northwest Passage, a hypothetical shortcut between the Atlantic and Pacific that would save months of ocean-going travel around Cape Horn at the southern tip of South America and open up commerce with vast new Asian markets. Another English captain, Charles Barkley, ventured partway into the channel in 1787, but only far enough to determine that it was a waterway of considerable length. Thereafter the mysterious channel was named the Juan de Fuca Strait after a Spanish explorer who, his nation belatedly claimed, had discovered the passage two centuries earlier. Five years after Barkley, another British sea captain, George Vancouver, who had been a midshipman on Cook's voyage fourteen years before, was assigned by the Admiralty in London to determine just how far east Juan de Fuca Strait extended.

As skipper of the sloop-of-war H.M.S. *Discovery,* the thirty-four-year-old Vancouver had been given the task of charting the northwest coast and its inlets in detail. After several days of due-east travel covering 100 miles from the open sea through the fifteen-mile-wide Juan de Fuca Strait, the *Discovery* encountered a wider north-south sea lane bordered on the east by an unbroken mainland shore. Vancouver veered to starboard, where he hoped the southerly route might eventually turn east again and lead all the way to the Atlantic. He was greeted instead after a few hours' sail by a vista of breathtaking beauty—a verdant, undulating landscape of immense trees stretching from the shore as far as the eye could see, framed at either end by a whitecapped mountain range of a scale rivaled in Europe only by the Alps. Sixty miles to the southeast rose the highest peak, which Vancouver dutifully named Mount Rainier after a British rear admiral of modest distinction.

Threading his way through the inlet with its jigsawed shoreline, Vancouver dropped anchor a little below modern Seattle out of fear the inlet might soon become too narrow and shallow for his large craft to maneuver in, even though the water at that point registered a depth of 210 feet—remarkable for that distance from the ocean. To continue the exploration, he ordered young second lieutenant Peter Puget to take a twenty-foot rowboat with ten oarsmen to see how far inland this crooked arm of the Pacific might reach. What they found on their meandering, two-week trip was a small inland sea 100 miles long, with many islands, large and small, and long, jabbing peninsulas that created a lacework of channels and bays. There was no link to a passage east. Of particular note, however, was the great depth of the water throughout the sound that would soon bear Puget's name—a phenomenon of nature that, along with its many potential harbor sites, identified the region as an ideal setting for a great future seaport, or series of ports, close to the ocean but protected from its often tempest-tossed waters at that latitude.

Puget, twenty-eight at the time, and his armed crew made wary contact with the equally wary but nonetheless welcoming natives. The Indians shared their delicious salmon, clams, and oysters with the white intruders, who found their hosts to be, in Puget's words, "a farce of savageness." Despite their suspicious looks, virtual nakedness, long filthy black hair, and limited communication skills, they seemed an unthreatening lot. Puget's party marveled at their handsomely carved canoes and finely wrought cedar baskets. The amity ended, though, when several of Puget's men went fishing in the Sound without license from the natives—a clear violation of what they believed to be their ancient territorial prerogatives, as their disapproving expressions and brandished spears made clear. Puget hurriedly rowed off into the sunset.

It proved an informative expedition, but the finding that Puget Sound did not turn into an interocean northwest passage was a deep disappointment to the Admiralty and the crown, always hopeful of widening British commercial dominion. As a consolation, Vancouver was honored by having the 12,000-square-mile island that formed the northern shore of Juan de Fuca Strait named for him. It is the largest island off the western coast of both American continents.

In spring of the same year as Vancouver's probe—1792—American navigator and fur trader Robert Gray, captaining his ship, *Columbia,* also entered Juan de Fuca Strait but turned back well short of Puget Sound. Instead Gray returned to the coast and continued south for another 200 miles before coming upon the estuary of a great river that Cook and no doubt others had failed to glimpse because of the fog and misty weather that often cloaked it from passing vessels. The estuary with its many sandbars was a perilous trial for any helmsman, but after passing through it Gray discovered a wide, stunningly beautiful river, the longest one emptying into the entire eastern coastline of the Pacific Ocean. He named it for his ship. White men had found the gateway, albeit over water, into the temperate, thickly timbered northwest corner of sub-Arctic North America. The natives' days of unchallenged occupancy were numbered.

After Lewis and Clark came upon the Columbia River from the land side thirteen years later and tracked it to the sea for the final westward leg of their legendary journey, they planted the American flag at a winter camp they built close to the Pacific shore, claiming U.S. hegemony over the entire Columbia basin. This expansive gesture of labeling so huge a wilderness American territory well before any permanent settlement there won swift disapproval from the British, who a few years later, in the War of 1812, sent a gunboat to seize a U.S. trading post and its protective garrison near the old Lewis and Clark campsite on the coast and raise the Union Jack over what the royal sailors renamed Fort George after their king. The two nations were on a collision course over ownership of the region that was soon being called the Oregon Country.

A *modus vivendi* to avoid bloodshed over that visually astounding land, as yet uninhabited by whites, was reached by a pair of treaties that U.S. Secretary of State John Quincy Adams crafted in 1818 with Britain and the following year with Spain. The Spaniards, on the brink of losing most of their New World empire to rebel colonists and politically aroused natives, agreed to drop all territorial claims north of the forty-second parallel, which serves as the northern boundary of both modern California and contiguous Nevada. The concession meant that the Oregon Country, directly to the north, was up for grabs.

Instead of a military confrontation so far away from their respective homelands, the United States and Britain reached an accord, open-ended in duration, covering half a million square miles. The area ran from the Continental Divide along the ridge line of the Rocky Mountains, where American territory acquired by the Louisiana Purchase ended, west to the Pacific and from the forty-second parallel border with Spanish territory north to just above the fifty-fourth parallel, where Russian America, to be renamed Alaska half a century later, began. This terrain was declared open to both American citizens and British subjects under the common jurisdiction of both nations but with neither serving as the governing authority or providing law enforcement. It was the truly wild Northwest, a limboland where only a few white hunters and mountain men had ventured.

Time and geography were on the Americans' side. For the next quarter-century, though, British commercial interests acted quickly to make good on the opportunity they saw at the western end of the continent before the United States could gain traction. The British presence was exercised almost exclusively by the Hudson's Bay Company (often called "the Company" or just "the Bay" by contemporaries, and ever since), the Montreal-based, government-backed trading house. In 1824 the Bay closed down the small post it had been operating near the mouth of the Columbia and transferred its operations ninety miles upriver to a site on the north bank close to where the Willamette River, a major tributary, flowed into the larger waterway from the south. It was a perfect spot from which to control trade throughout the Columbia basin, and the Bay's new post, Fort Vancouver, was scaled to handle the job. Described as "a cedar castle" by one observer at the time, Fort Vancouver (though not located on that island) soon grew into a stockaded, self-contained community with a store, workshops, a sawmill, a shipyard, grain storage and milling, and enough employees to allow the place to serve as the central supply depot, emporium, and bank for the whole Oregon Country— and its de facto capital. For all its solidity, the Bay's prospering quarters on the Columbia became neither a rooted community nor the springboard for systematic British colonization in the region; Fort Vancouver was essentially a company town, with more than its share of transients, many of them French Canadians, Scotsmen, and, in time, imported Hawaiians.

To further solidify future British claim to territorial dominion north of the Columbia, the Bay opened an auxiliary trading post in 1833 in the midst of Indian lands at the head—the southern end, actually—of Puget Sound. The new unit, perched on a hillside above the north shore of the Nisqually River delta, took its name from that river, which flowed from the slopes of Mount Rainier to the Sound. Fort Nisqually was a risky venture, not least of all because the nearest white settlement was more than 100 miles and a three-day journey away.

The natives, to judge from accounts left by Bay personnel, viewed with apprehension the arrival in the south Sound of the whites they called "King George men." The Bay set up shop with scarcely a by-your-leave bow to the Indians and threatened their command of the region by declaring monopolistic new trading rules and introducing diseases that would shortly prove lethal to tribal people. But the Bay was eager to receive all the beaver, fox, and mink pelts and deer and bear skins that Indian hunters wished to trade for the whites' manufactured items like clothing, blankets, guns, knives, and tools. Word was quickly passed throughout Indian Country around Puget Sound that the King George men treated the natives with respect, did not cheat them detectably, and did not dismiss their spirit faith as pagan sacrilege, their illiteracy as stupidity, or their warm-weather nudity as savagery.

The Bay's local operations were eventually headed by affable, hardworking chief factor William Fraser Tolmie, who by virtue of his position and nature was easily the most influential white man in the northern sector of the Oregon Territory. Tolmie, a slender, fair-haired, twenty-one-year-old Scottish physician fresh from the University of Glasgow, was first sent as a company employee to Fort Nisqually in 1834 and asked to lend a hand however he could while the Bay's facilities were being hammered together. At first he had been so uneasy about the natives' potential intolerance for the white incursion that he would go to sleep with five pistols on his bedstand. A gifted communicator and anything but aloof, Tolmie soon learned the local Indians' Salish dialect and spoke it regularly to the natives trading or working at the fort. He inquired into their customs and beliefs, ate their food, and immersed himself as time allowed in their milieu. He relished hiking, led by Indian guides, deep into the wilds to study and catalogue the flora and fauna. On at least one occasion that he recorded, Tolmie donned Indian garb for a winter trek into the Cascades, becoming the first white man to explore the heavily timbered lower slopes of Mount Rainier. In his journal he described the sleeping volcano's pyramidal shape and triple-peaked crown, reported how his guides shared their venison and body heat with him inside their blanket bundles against the wickedly chilling elements, and referred to them as "my Indians" and "my companions . . . Cannot call them my attendants."

Tolmie was soon assigned elsewhere in the region while the Bay's venture at Fort Vancouver and its chief northern satellite operation at Fort Nisqually firmly established British commercial dominance in the Oregon Country. When the European demand began to slacken for the furs gathered by native and French Canadian trappers in the overhunted forests north of the Columbia, British and Bay officials altered their strategy for mastery of the Oregon Country. In 1838 the Bay was granted permission by London to expand its activities at Fort Nisqually by chartering a subsidiary, the Puget Sound Agricultural Company (PSAC), intended mainly to raise crops and livestock to supply British and Russian posts along the Pacific coast. The new farming and ranching enterprise, it was hoped, would materially strengthen British claims to the northern two-thirds of the Oregon Country when the moment arrived to divide the region with the U.S. government. By the time Tolmie returned to take charge of Fort Nisqually and its agricultural subsidiary in 1843, the thriving PSAC extended over a dozen "stations" or farms, where wheat, peas, and potatoes were the main crops, and luxuriant grasslands covering more than 160,000 acres for thousands of grazing cattle and sheep and hundreds of horses.

The tribes of the region did not object to or harass the extensive British farming and ranching presence, set down on their appropriated ancestral prairie without compensation, in part because of the King George men's respectful conduct, as exemplified by Dr. Tolmie. The Bay overseers, moreover, were providing jobs and teaching skills to the natives, who were glad to be paid for working the fields and tending the flocks and herds side by side with white and mixed-blood laborers. Tolmie insisted that the indigenous people be treated with dignity and encouraged intermarriage by way of expanding the company-run community as men from the fort and the farming stations eventually went off the Bay's payroll to set up homesteads for themselves nearby.

Tolmie, whom the natives fondly called "the *tyee* [meaning, roughly, 'honorable'] doctor," was in command of every detail of his benevolent barony's operations. He made himself accessible to the Indians no less than to the rest of the frontier community. As a physician, too, he did his best, with limited medical supplies, to stem the white men's ravaging diseases that inevitably spread to the Indians throughout Puget Sound. Tolmie introduced vaccination to willing natives and promoted the use of their own herbal remedies that he found effective in combating malaria. His occasional small acts of generosity added to his popularity among the Indians. Once he donated several yards of good cotton to wrap the remains of a murdered tribesman for burial rites, and he helped others buy their way out of slavery or obtain a wife. While studiously fair-minded, Tolmie was hardly lax where crime was concerned. Indeed, he was zealous about its detection and punishment and known to pay informers generously, especially in cases of theft from the PSAC's herds.

American settlers who began to arrive in the south Sound in the mid-1840s were also glad for the helping hand Tolmie and his company offered new arrivals during their arduous early years of homesteading. One of their lot, Ezra Meeker, who later wrote a memoir celebrating those pioneer days, commended Tolmie as "a noble man, with noble impulses, honorable in his dealings, courteous in his intercourse." No man, native or white, was more highly regarded west of the Cascades than the indefatigable Scotsman. Under his genial and astute direction, the trading post at Fort Nisqually thrived as a vibrant marketplace, the busy crossroads for interracial and intertribal exchanges. As such, the British enterprise and its majordomo would become prime targets for Isaac Stevens almost immediately upon his arrival in the vicinity.

AN AMERICAN presence in the primeval surroundings of south Puget Sound was first detectable a dozen years after the Hudson's Bay Company had secured a beachhead at Fort Nisqually. The catalyst for the American incursion was a six-ship task force launched by the U.S. Navy in 1838 under Lieutenant Charles Wilkes, who, as an astronomer and mathematician as well as an able mariner, was one of the few certified scientists in the armed services. Wilkes's mission was to explore the Pacific in search of opportunities to expand U.S. commerce and to identify the best harbor sites on North America's West Coast.

By far the two most promising locations for a seaport there, Wilkes reported to Congress after his three-year voyage, were San Francisco Bay, then in loosely held Mexican territory, and the more isolated deep-water Puget Sound, far inside Oregon Country. Wilkes and his sailors carefully refined the charts of the Sound's shoreline, a complex puzzle of islands, inlets, bays, and channels, which had been hastily sketched half a century earlier during Peter Puget's rowboat survey. Wilkes roamed about inland as well, ranging far enough to become entranced by the grandeur of the landscape, with its dreamy forests, fertile valleys, swaying grasslands, and crystal rivers rising in the Cascades and allowing easy access to the Sound and the world beyond. "We entertain the belief that the whole of this magnificent country," he wrote, "so rich in the bounties of nature, is destined to become part of the American Republic. . . . The time will come when these hills and valleys . . . will contain cities and farms and manufacturing establishments"—not precisely the Indian vision of a happy hunting ground.

Word seeped out about this alluring paradise, and several parties of settlers who headed for the Oregon Country chose not to stake a claim in the Willamette Valley below the Columbia River, where much of the best land had been taken by the mid-1840s, but to veer north instead and head for the virgin country around Puget Sound. Congress and others in the U.S. government duly noted what Wilkes's discerning eye had fallen upon and the commercial development he predicted for the area. When

American and British diplomats sat down soon thereafter to thrash out how the Oregon Country should be apportioned, thus fixing the northern boundary of the United States, State Department officials proposed that the border line should simply be extended from its existing western terminus, where the Continental Divide atop the Rockies met the forty-ninth parallel, straight to the Pacific. Such a demarcation would have pushed the border 200 miles north of the Columbia River and enclose all of Puget Sound and its surroundings, where the merest handful of Americans had lately arrived but where the Bay's extensive installations and operations thoroughly dominated commerce in the region. The crown's presence there was amply evidenced by the many British place-names, such as Mount Hood (after a Lord of the Admiralty), Mount St. Helens (after the royal minister to Spain), and, of course, the Fraser River, Vancouver Island, and Puget Sound itself, all named for their British discoverers. American settlers might be heading west, but they would not get there overnight. Besides, the British-owned sector of North America, too, had a great western frontier, even if only a fraction as many northern pioneers were undertaking the brutal trudge across the western plains and over the mountains.

The royal ministry in London, serving vital British mercantile interests, had no intention of yielding any of the Pacific coastline and the choice harbor sites on Puget Sound to the feckless claims of land-greedy American settlers and Yankee cargo-carriers. They could jolly well accept the Columbia River as the international boundary west from where the forty-ninth parallel intersected with it, thus keeping 200 miles of Oregon coast, the best stands of fir and cedar, and gemlike Puget Sound firmly in British hands.

When Prime Minister Robert Peel refused the cheeky U.S. demand, American jingoists raised their battlecry of "Fifty-four forty or fight!" and threatened war to seize the whole Oregon Country, no matter that American discoveries and settlements were confined to the southern portion comprising at most one-third of the jointly held territory. The exasperated British held fast for a time, but U.S. President James Polk, a nervy little man with a very large appetite to expand his nation to the far edge of the continent, calculated that Peel was facing severe political pressure at home from the demands for relief by the increasingly impoverished British masses and could not undertake the financial burden of going to war over a chunk of wilderness 10,000 sea miles and six months' journey from England. In the ensuing stare-down, Peel was the first to blink. Under the 1846 agreement between the two governments drawing the border along the forty-ninth parallel as the Americans had brazenly first asked, the United States gained some 60 percent of the Oregon Country, including the precious prize of Puget Sound. The treaty provided that the Bay's lucrative trading posts at Fort Vancouver and Fort Nisqually could continue to operate until the U.S. government made an acceptable offer to the company for its property.

For the next few years almost all the 5,000 or so settlers in the 285,000-square-mile Oregon Territory, as the American portion of the newly divided Oregon Country was now officially designated by Congress, continued to reside in the Willamette Valley, with some small settlements farther east in the Columbia basin and the Walla Walla River Valley. Once the new U.S. territory formally became American turf so far as the white race was concerned, the number of homesteaders struggling by wagon train up the Oregon Trail surged. The newcomers squatted on the finest farmland they could find, confident that their nation would grant them legal title to it as soon as a governmental presence could be established.

No one bothered to ask permission of the native people before hunkering down in their midst. In fact, U.S. law prevented the settlers from doing so formally. The Northwest Ordinance as adopted in 1789 by Congress promised that no Indian land would be taken without tribal consent and decreed that only the federal government could acquire title to the natives' territory. To clarify how land ownership should be bindingly transferred from the natives to American settlers, federal lawmakers enacted a series of statutes between 1790 and 1834 explicitly interposing the U.S. government between the tribes who occupied the land and the whites who wanted to buy it, usually for a pittance, or just to take it, at gunpoint if necessary. These so-called Trade and Intercourse Acts stated that no private transactions like trading goods with or acquiring land from the natives could be conducted except under the surveillance of U.S. officials acting as go-betweens. No federal oversight apparatus was installed, however, in the years right after the 1846 Oregon Treaty with Britain. Pioneers who helped themselves to the land had to risk the consequences of Indian displeasure over the rising tide of "Bostons," as the natives called all American settlers.

Tribal hostility was fed by three forms of incitement. First was the whites' seizure, fencing off, and plowing up of much of the best land in Indian Country without offering any compensation. Second was the disparagement of native culture and religion as backward, savage, and in need of immediate replacement by the white man's ways and creeds— a program tirelessly propagated by the evangelizing church missions that served as the underpinning of the new Oregon settlements. Third were the diseases the white traders and settlers introduced with such deadly, if unintended, effect into native territory, especially venereal disease, tuberculosis, and malaria. In 1836–37 influenza as well was ravaging tribes in southern Puget Sound, and 10,000 deaths were reported among the Chinook-speaking people nearer the Pacific.

Indian resistance at first was sporadic and ineffectual. Terror tactics targeting wagon trains and isolated farms took lives here and there but hardly put a brake on the invasion, any more than the efforts by tribal patrols to collect tribute money for passage across Indian homelands or to charge the white travelers for shooting game and gathering wild plants for food—demands that the wayfarers mistook for impertinence or beggary. In November 1847, the Cayuse tribe in eastern Oregon struck a blood-curdling blow felt by every white farm family in the territory. The principal target of the natives' wrath was Marcus Whitman, a New York–trained physician who had become a Congregationalist missionary and led one of the first wagon trains to reach Oregon. Setting up his mission in 1836 a few miles west of the present-day city of Walla Walla, Dr. Whitman established a school, built a gristmill, and taught the natives crop rotation and other aspects of agronomy in addition to trying to convert the Cayuse tribe, the primary purpose of his community. The simmering resentment among the Cayuse toward the entrenched white settlement and its insistent do-gooding came to a boil in 1847 when a measles epidemic, accompanied by cholera, dysentery, and pneumonia, took the lives of half the tribe despite Whitman's best medical efforts. In keeping with the Indian belief that shamans, no matter their race, who did not save their patients might be put to death themselves, the Cayuses murdered Whitman, his wife, and twelve others, took fifty-four women and children hostage, and destroyed most of the buildings at the mission. Never before had such wholesale interracial violence occurred in the Northwest.

The Whitman Massacre sent an unmistakable message to oncoming American settlers and government officials that native people would not yield their homelands without extracting a steep price from the intruders, however well-intended their preachments. The pretense that white civilization was dedicated to the betterment of tribal culture rather than its extinction had been rudely shaken by the Cayuses' brutal response. Stunned settlers, still relatively few in number, slowly organized for righteous reprisal. What followed was eight years of sporadic warfare during which white posses reinforced by U.S. Army regulars chased down almost any natives they could find and eventually exacted a toll well in excess of those slain at the Whitman mission.

In upper Oregon Territory, Patkamin, the wily and combative chief of the Snoqualmies on the northeastern shore of Puget Sound, was strongly affected by news of the Whitman Massacre, the catastrophic epidemic that had triggered it, and an awareness that sympathetic Britons like William Tolmie and his whole Hudson's Bay Company apparatus would soon be leaving because the white nations had agreed that the region was now officially and exclusively U.S. territory. Doom awaited their race, Patkamin and his followers believed, if they let the Americans settle in multitudes around the Sound as they were now doing farther south. The first organized Indian act of armed confrontation with the whites in northern Oregon occurred in May 1849 when Patkamin, allegedly in pursuit of rival tribesmen who had insulted his people and taken refuge at Fort Nisqually, stormed the trading post, where Americans now formed a rapidly growing part of the clientele. Poorly organized, the incursion turned into a desultory skirmish causing minimal damage and resulting in only one fatality, an American.

The fallout from the attack, though, was considerable. Appeals for protection from further Indian violence led to the construction the following year of the first U.S. Army post on Puget Sound, located at its southeastern end. Garrisoned by only a few dozen soldiers at first, Fort Steilacoom, named for an Indian who had helped build it, was a barebones compound that consisted of a barracks, a mess, a small jail, and a few storage buildings edging a parade ground. Lacking a stockade, which nearby British-owned Fort Nisqually offered as a protective enclosure, the American military base seemed a feeble fortress. But its very existence cheered the little colony of settlers and encouraged more to come.

FURTHER ACTION by the U.S. government in 1850 signaled an imminent change in the white presence around Puget Sound and its impact on the natives. When gold was discovered in the river valleys above San Francisco just weeks after the peace treaty with Mexico had been signed, adding the entire West between the Rio Grande and the Pacific to the

United States, the flood of fortune-seekers was so swift and immense that Congress quickly granted statehood to California, slave-free under the Compromise of 1850. But fewer than 10,000 Americans were living in the adjacent Oregon Territory at the time, a smallish number to secure the U.S. grip on the 400-mile-long stretch of Pacific coastline between California and British America. To speed settlement there Congress passed the Oregon Donation Land Act, granting any white man over eighteen who had farmed a claim in the territory for four years title to a homestead of 320 acres without cost, and twice that amount—or one square mile—if he was accompanied by his wife. The offer proved an attractive lure to those hesitant to join the treasure-hungry swarm headed—perhaps already too late—to California to strike gold, a chancy hope at best. Earning a living the old-fashioned way, by farming, was no doubt less adventurous, but the free land in Oregon was a sure thing, and, if reports were to be credited, it was some of the best soil on the planet.

However well intended, the Donation Land Act was a mischievously careless piece of legislation. In promising settlers an opportunity to put down roots that would yield a bountiful future, Congress failed to specify that title to the land could not be certified until it was first formally vacated by the natives who lived on or regularly made use of it. The legal basis of this requirement was long established, even if it had been more honored in its breach than in its fulfillment. But Congress had put the cart before the horse—or perhaps alongside the horse—in the Oregon Territory by passing, in addition to the Donation Land Act, a law authorizing the federal government to make pacts for the purchase of tribal lands in the Pacific Northwest. Under this legislation the signatory Indian nations had to pledge nonbelligerency against both whites and other tribes and accept removal from their homelands to much smaller areas reserved for them, generally in places where they would avoid contact and conflict with white settlers.

On the ground in Oregon, the twin statutes framed by a distant Congress did not function in tandem as intended. Settlers were not waiting for treaties to be agreed to and ratified before filing their Donation Land Act claims with territorial officials and moving in. The federally appointed governor and his aides pushed hard for a series of Indian treaties in the Willamette Valley and the southern region of the territory in the 1851–53 period, but none of them was ratified by the U.S. Senate, in part because federal officials thought the terms too generous to the natives. Meanwhile, incidents of violence continued on both sides as infuriated natives, feeling betrayed by the Great White Father beyond the mountains after they had resigned themselves to the treaty terms in the hope they would provide Indian sanctuaries inviolable by American intrusion, struck randomly at white settlements, and territorial militias and vigilantes replied in kind.

Farther north, above the Columbia River, the upswing in white newcomers, especially around Puget Sound, had yet to create much racial friction. For one thing, an 1853 tally of the region revealed there were no more than 2,000 whites living there, compared with an estimated six times as many Indians. A considerable number of the latter, moreover, were being employed as a result of the prosperity the white Oregonians were enjoying as a by-product of the Gold Rush and boom in the settlement of northern California. Demand for Oregon's lumber, livestock, and flour rocketed, and almost any able-bodied white man could earn a nice livelihood by chopping away at the thronged stands of sky-high fir and cedar, milling the felled timber or scythed wheat, or raising cattle, sheep, fruits, and vegetables for shipment to the frenetic wharves of San Francisco. On any given day fifty or more cargo vessels would be anchored or moored in Puget Sound, eagerly waiting to haul away a shipload of trimmed lumber—masts, boards, beams, pilings, shingles, anything you could put a saw or hammer to—to California ports or as far away as South America and China.

Scruffy villages now sprang to life around the Sound. The biggest and busiest of them, Olympia, was at the southernmost reach of the Sound and a dozen or so miles below the mouth of the Nisqually River. Steilacoom, built close to the army fort of the same name, was a similar distance north of the Nisqually estuary and at once became Olympia's principal rival in both commerce and political activity. Fifty miles farther north along the eastern shore of the Sound, the little settlement of Seattle was established immediately adjacent to the Duwamish tribe under its sad-eyed old chief, Sealth. So heavy was the demand for lumber from the region that San Francisco financiers were backing start-up logging and milling operations at many places on or near the Sound's shoreline. And so hectic was the activity and so short the supply of labor that a skilled mill hand at Steilacoom could earn $20 a day, a fabulous wage for that time. Natives were willingly pressed into service to do the heavy lifting and hauling and, once persuaded the act did not gravely offend the Great Spirit, to help cut down the forests.

In the early phase of the first sizable wave of white settlement around the Sound, the natives remained calm, curious, and wary. The arriving

Bostons were evidently not inclined to do them harm, so long as the Indians did not interfere as the newcomers built their log cabins, fenced off farms, tended crops, domesticated animals, and made money by felling trees—private pursuits not perceived at first as directly threatening native culture or well-being. As the white man's hirelings and customers for his manufactured wares, the tribes of the south Sound won certain comforts and conveniences, but they came at a price: growing exposure to the settlers' fatal diseases, submission to their stupefying alcohol, and, not quite so obviously, erosion of their own ancestral skills like archery and crafts like weaving baskets and blankets. Nevertheless, there seemed to be plenty of room for the whites so long as they did not attempt to stop the natives from fishing, hunting, and gathering roots and berries in their accustomed places. And why should they? Mother Earth was there for all humankind to enjoy, revere, and thrive upon. Why worry about commingling with hardworking Bostons peaceably squatting by the Sound and along the river bottoms?

This unresisting response served only to embolden the oncoming Americans. As they kept filing claims for the free farms promised by Congress, no talk was heard yet about the need for treaties in the northern sector of the Oregon Territory; the silence pleased both races. Whites kept settling in the most fertile areas of Indian Country without fussing over legal titles; the natives reluctantly gave ground so long as no one was demanding that they sell off their birthright to remain more or less where they had been living for thousands of years. Still, the pattern had been set, as the Puget Sound tribes had allowed themselves to be lulled temporarily into denial of the obvious. By 1853 the commander of the army barracks at Fort Steilacoom noted a tendency he feared was a precursor of trouble ahead: "The practice which exists throughout Oregon Territory of settlers taking from them their small potato patches is clearly wrong and should be stopped."

No restraining hand was lifted, however, by the virtually nonexistent governmental presence in the north portion of the territory while settlers kept coming and taking possession of far more than small potato patches.

BECAUSE THE BULK of the Oregon Territory's white population was clustered along the Willamette River Valley 200 miles south of the new settlements at Puget Sound, the residents up north felt their need for governmental services and protection was being badly neglected as the 1850s unfolded. There were no public buildings in the upper region, and what few roads existed were in dreadful condition much of the year (if passable at all in the rainy and snowy seasons). Postal service was infrequent and unreliable, accurate maps and navigational charts were rarely available, and personal safety, even with a few dozen federal soldiers stationed at Fort Steilacoom and the natives unthreatening, seemed precarious. The territory's financial and political power brokers were at Oregon City, about twenty miles below the Columbia River, and Salem, the territorial capital another thirty miles to the south, where the legislature met. Given these distances and the political reality that the true locus of government oversight of federal territories was in Washington, D.C., it is little wonder the burgeoning settlements on Puget Sound felt themselves isolated and in need of collective self-assertion.

The Oregon Territory, an undulating checkerboard of mountains, rivers, valleys, forests, prairies, and deserts of great scale, all posing formidable natural barriers to travelers, was just too large and unwieldy a political entity for its own good. Those in charge of it tended to favor the concerns of their closest neighbors south of the Columbia River and allotted as little as they could get away with in funds, services, and attention to those living around distant Puget Sound. Feeling orphaned, the latter now began to clamor for their fair share of the public purse. The only solution, the northerners concluded, was to petition Congress to break off their region from the rest of Oregon and designate it a separate territory, able to deal directly with those back east who controlled the federal purse strings.

Early in 1852 settlers north of the Columbia mounted their first organized effort to gain separate territorial status. Nineteen delegates were on hand representing the few thousand whites living between the Columbia River and the nation's northern boundary. On its face, their petition to Congress was laughably premature. Olympia, the most populous settlement on Puget Sound, had many more tree stumps than houses, just a few hundred residents, perpetually muddy streets, and a single saloon with— or so it was said in jest—one keg of beer and three glasses. Hardly a propitious capital for a new U.S. territory. In soliciting Congress, its would-be founders argued that separate territorial status would serve as a catalyst to its growth and swift development. They attached to their congressional petition a request for $100,000 to build a 225-mile-long road through the wilderness from Puget Sound diagonally southeast over the Cascades to the small community at Walla Walla, gateway to Oregon's north country.

The northern frontiersmen felt an urgency to act. For if they delayed too long, the whole Oregon Territory, at the urging of the preponderant population in its southern portion, might soon be accepted into the Union as a full-fledged state, relegating the northland to second-class status. Afterward, Oregon's legislature and citizenry would be unlikely ever to consent to its dismemberment through secession by its northern residents—and the federal Constitution required such acquiescence before a new state could be carved from an old one. To let the northerners go would cost greater Oregon prestige and political clout. Congress, however, was not inclined to rush to judgment. Besides, the more territories the federal government created, the greater the administrative costs and headaches.

The northerners tried again in November 1852, this time with forty-four delegates and increased determination. In reiterating their need for self-rule and public services, the new petition lamented, "Our whole [northern part of the] territory is alive with Indians, who keep up a most provoking and unceasing broil about the lands which they say the 'Bostons' are holding without a proper and legitimate right and title." The second petition was bolstered by support from the southern-controlled Oregon legislature and its nonvoting delegate to Congress. The two regions became political bedfellows because the farmers and developers of the Willamette Valley, their prosperity and influence growing as more and more settlers opted for their region over California, were eager to break the congressional chokehold on their government and handle the natives and other problems as they saw fit by winning statehood at an early date. Their political strategists were aware that Congress was unlikely to accept the Oregon Territory, 25,000 square miles larger than Texas, as a single gargantuan state. Antislavery advocates favored breaking up the region into several free-soil states to counterbalance the politically potent, slaveholding South, which might pursue the same strategy with the outsized state of Texas.* Such imponderables aside, the politi-

---

*Under the Missouri Compromise of 1820, slavery could not be extended into future states or territories below the latitude of 36'30", which corresponded to the southern border of Missouri. But under the 1850 Compromise, slavery was disallowed in California, even though its southern half extended below the 1820 compromise line, and residents in the New Mexico and Utah territories, parts of which extended well north of the 1820 line, were allowed to decide for themselves whether slavery could be practiced within their jurisdictions. When Congress, in 1854, extended this same principle of "popular sovereignty" to allow residents in the Kansas and Nebraska territories, both of which lay entirely north of the Missouri Compromise line, to decide on the legality of slavery within their borders, the South was emboldened while free-soilers grew more adamant that the inhumane practice should not only extend no farther west but be outlawed altogether.

cians at Salem calculated that dividing the Oregon Territory would speed the arrival of statehood for the region below the Columbia—and good riddance to the malcontents up north, who would increasingly compete with them for political sway and the federal services so badly needed by their frontier society. Besides, the reduction of Oregon's bulk to allow the creation of a new territory—and, eventually, a new state—would give citizens along the Pacific coast more political power by increasing the overall size of their representation in Congress and in the electoral college, which chose the President. The split-off of northern Oregon was championed as well by the people in the upper Great Lakes region—the states of Michigan and Wisconsin and the Minnesota Territory—which foresaw Puget Sound as the logical terminus for a prospective northern transcontinental railroad line, to be federally subsidized but facing opposition from equally ardent advocates calling for the route to run across the central or southern tier of the nation.

Thus reinforced, the northern Oregonians, largely Democratic in their party leanings, asked Congress to form a new territory of some 32,000 square miles (roughly the size of Indiana), bounded on the south and east by the curving course of the Columbia River until it touched the forty-ninth parallel, the nation's northern border, and on the west by the Pacific Ocean. They also requested that the federal lawmakers name the new creation the Columbia Territory.

The petitioners had good reason to be hopeful. By the time they submitted their request, the 1852 federal elections had determined that the new occupant of the White House would be the former U.S. Representative and Senator Franklin Pierce of New Hampshire, an obscure, moderate Democrat who favored accommodation with the slaveowning South. Voters also gave his party a strong hand in Congress. The split-up of Oregon sailed through both houses the following March. Somewhat surprisingly, federal legislators, sensitive to southern concern over the potential creation of many new, relatively small states where slavery would be outlawed (and, as a result, antislavery power in the Senate would increase disproportionately), rewarded the petitioners with a boundary line far more generous than they had sought. It followed the Columbia River upstream from the Pacific but only to where it met the forty-sixth parallel, twenty-five miles west of Walla Walla, and then, instead of turning north with the river in keeping with the request by the separatists, it continued east along the parallel to the Continental Divide in western Montana— an expanse that included 40 percent of the superseded Oregon Territory area and amounted to four times the area that the petition had asked for.

Congress balked only at the name the petitioners had chosen. "Columbia Territory" sounded to its members too much like the District of Columbia. Supposedly to avoid confusion, the federal lawmakers, in their infinite wisdom, selected a substitute that honored America's iconic first national hero. They christened the new entity the Washington Territory—not to be mistaken, of course, for the nation's capital. Posterity has confused them ever since. But Oregon's northern secessionists were not picky about what name was given them, so long as they had their sovereignty. That sovereignty, though, was limited. The act creating Washington Territory reserved for Congress, as the Constitution required, the right to appoint and fire (and the responsibility to pay) all its administrative officials, review all acts of its elected legislature, and oversee its relations with the Indians.

As the new territory awaited the arrival of its first governor late in 1853, the tribes there suffered the fourth smallpox epidemic since white men first touched their shores.

3

The Northwest Express

IF ISAAC STEVENS had chosen to reach his job site as soon as possible, he could probably have arranged to travel from the nation's capital to Puget Sound in under three months. But Stevens saw an opportunity to go from coast to coast more deliberately while taking on a mission that could add to his stature even as it hastened the day when Washington Territory could become a land of flourishing enterprise.

The added assignment would entail strenuous effort, denying him the relative comfort of a shipboard voyage and the company of his family, and force him to undertake a hazardous overland trek lasting twice as long. There was no guarantee that he would successfully complete his mission, especially given the limited resources at his disposal. Stevens, though, was a risk-taker—who else would have exchanged the perks of high rank in the peacetime army and the decent regard of his countrymen for the gimlet-eyed scrutiny and countless pitfalls awaiting a keenly ambitious holder of public office?

Besides signing into law the bill creating the new territory, retiring President Fillmore, in one of his final acts in the White House, also approved Congress's appropriation of $150,000 for the War Department to carry out a topographical survey of up to four routes for the construction of a federally subsidized transcontinental railroad line. How better to bind together the newly bicoastal nation, ensure its territorial security, and promote its rapid settlement and economic development? And how better to speed the prospects of his new northwestern domain, Isaac Stevens asked himself, than to help extend the railroad to it? The earlier the northern route was mapped out, the better its chances of being built in preference to routes across rival regions. And who was more ideally qualified to lead the northern railroad survey than Stevens himself on his way west to take over as governor of Washington Territory? Though no frontiersman, he well understood from his fifteen years of military service the engineering need to find the shortest and cheapest route west, with the fewest steep grades, river crossings, and mountain tunnels.

Stevens won the backing of powerful fellow Democrats Stephen Douglas of Illinois, boldest congressional advocate of the northern rail route, originating in Chicago, and Jefferson Davis, former U.S. Senator from Mississippi, Mexican War veteran, and Pierce's incoming Secretary of War. A resolute defender of his region's social arrangements (and a slaveholder himself), Davis much preferred a coast-to-coast railway route, useful for the national defense, that ran through the South, hugged the border with Mexico, and terminated in southern California. But Davis knew Congress wanted to preserve the sectional balance between slaveholding and free-soil states and might in the end approve more than one transcontinental route. Stevens was eager to do the job up north and promised to finish it by year's end, allowing time for a census in Washington Territory to be completed as well, so that the territorial legislature could be organized and he could begin to function as governor.

Directing the northern route survey would put Stevens into contact for the first time with the Native American tribes along the way, who would have to be pacified if the railroad was to go through and if the white settlements that would spring up alongside it were to be safe from attack. This necessity prompted Stevens to file still a third application, so long as he was collecting job titles and concentrating power in his grasp. Since a critical part of his gubernatorial mission would be to coax the Indians of Washington Territory into yielding their homelands by treaty with the U.S. government and accepting confinement on insular reservations, he asked the Department of the Interior's Office of Indian Affairs to appoint him superintendent of relations with the natives—how better to expedite overlapping problems sure to arise in accommodating the needs of both races? With his two additional job requests granted as well, Stevens was anointed commandant of the 250-mile-wide, north-to-south corridor from the crest of the Rockies to the Pacific.

It would be his first role on the national stage, where he had great aspirations. Most who dealt with him agreed that he had a quick mind, courage, and honesty, as well as a hunger to take charge, issue orders, and see to it that they were faithfully executed—and God help any who disobeyed, disappointed, or doubted him. While full of himself and, on occasion, an off-putting self-righteousness, he was faithful in his personal, professional, and ideological allegiances and not prone to disguise them, so he came across on occasion as doggedly partisan and not a little strident. A fellow of stout heart, abundant stamina, and nervous energy, he opted at times for impulsive action over calm reflection. When stymied, he was apt to run short on tact and patience, an unhelpful trait in a frontier setting astir with independent-minded, often contentious settlers and increasingly irritable natives. "Yet in an era of unbounded expansion," wrote Alexandra Harmon, an astute cultural historian and expert on the American Northwest natives, Stevens's skills on becoming governor "may have been precisely what the country needed" on its farthest frontier.

THE MAGNITUDE and complexity of what was officially called the Northern Pacific Railway Exploration seemed to dwarf the resources—human, monetary, and material—that Stevens assembled in his usual painstaking fashion in the late spring of 1853. It was the most serious venture of its sort since the Lewis and Clark exploration of the same general region forty-eight years earlier. The route, with whatever twists and turns were needed to overcome nature's obstacles, would run close to 2,000 miles, from the source of the Mississippi to the shore of Puget Sound. Travel conditions, even during the mildest weather of the year, would be trying, the path uncertain and rarely smooth for long, and the possibility of Indian attacks very real. Stevens was provided with $40,000 to provision and sustain his party of 120 men, among them soldiers, guides, hunters, interpreters, engineers, draftsmen, naturalists, artists, a physician, and a dozen U.S. Army officers reluctantly accepting the command of their newly civilian leader.

Never a trusting delegator, Stevens himself fussed with many of the details to facilitate his caravan's progress: obtaining adequately trained mules and learning how best to pack them, finding material well suited for tent flooring in rough terrain, requisitioning lightweight India-rubber boats to carry men and bulky supplies across streams, making sure their sextants, barometers, and altimeters worked properly, and selecting gifts to bring along as a good-will gesture to whatever Indian bands they met along the way. To complete the mission by year's end, Stevens prudently arranged the deployment of a satellite party at the western end of the projected route, charged with finding a suitable pass through the steep Cascades for the final run to Puget Sound. To undertake that task he enlisted Captain George B. McClellan, his fellow West Pointer and a close friend from their Mexican War combat six years earlier.

Stevens and his party left in mid-June, "sweeping west in a blaze of self-confidence," as the author of *Isaac I. Stevens: Young Man in a Hurry* put it. They clung to the most level ground they could find while they crossed the northern plains of Minnesota, skirting the Black Hills and the worst of the Dakota badlands until they reached the Rockies. There they hunted for an opening through which the future railroad could be threaded. Stevens was awed by the spectacular landscape, with its endless prairie, gentle hills, jutting buttes, the big sky, and all the wild horses. He wrote in his diary:

> About five miles from camp, we ascended the top of a high hill, and for a great distance ahead every square mile seemed to have a herd of buffalo on it. Their number was variously estimated by the members of the party, some as high as half a million. I do not think it is any exaggeration to set it at 200,000. I have heard of the myriads of these animals inhabiting these plains, but I could not realize the truth of these claims until today, when they surpassed anything I could have imagined.

The party was slowed at times by nuisances—mules bedeviled by swarming horseflies, malfunctioning instruments, forest fires that obscured the topography ahead, the need to hunt for fresh food and other supplies not readily at hand in so remote a setting. Perhaps the most wearing element of their journey was the friction sparked by Stevens's own temperament. Like his father, he was not sympathetic toward underperformers and too often curt and needlessly offensive when a daub or two of honey would have quashed resentment toward him, especially among the military men.

The tension may have been unavoidable, for Stevens was incessantly on the job. One member of the party called him "a smart, active, ubiquitous little man, very come-at-able." His hyperactivity led to a recurrence of his groin rupture, causing him stabbing pain, ill humor, and periods of confinement to his wagon that may well have given the rest of the party welcome respite from their leader's demanding regimen. Yet they could only applaud Stevens's selfless devotion to their joint effort when, as the journey lengthened and the cost of everything—food, new mules to replace the exhausted ones, extra laborers—grew and the money ran out, he had to appeal desperately to Secretary of War Davis for an additional $50,000 to keep the underfunded project going. He was grudgingly granted half of his request, and when it, too, was exhausted, Stevens refused to call off the expedition. Instead, as its climactic stage loomed, he had faith that his country would eventually reimburse him if he provided a meticulous accounting of the cost overrun, and he went into personal debt so his party could continue rolling west.

Stevens encountered Indians in ever greater numbers the farther west his party advanced. Every bit the dutiful soldier with marching orders in hand, he seems to have suffered few, if any, pangs about the effects his mission would eventually have on Indian life. In late July, for example, he met with a party of Assiniboines in a cordial parley, where the peace pipe was shared along with bowls of soup "made of buffalo and typsina, a species of turnip, which was rich and greasy but quite palatable," Stevens noted in his diary. After the ceremony an old Indian came toward him and shook his hand and then that of every other member of his party. "His appearance was much in his favor," wrote Stevens, "carrying himself with great dignity. With great fluency, and at times with many gestures, he addressed me substantially as follows:

'My father, you see us now as we are. We are poor. We have but few blankets and little clothing. The Great Father of Life, who made us and gave us these lands to live upon, made the buffalo and other game to afford us sustenance; their meat is our only food; with their skins we clothe ourselves and build our lodges. . . . But I fear we shall soon be deprived of these; starvation and cold will destroy us. The buffalo are fast disappearing, and before many years will be destroyed. As the white man advances, our means of life will grow less. . . .

'My father, we hear that a great road is to be made through our country. We do not know what this is for, we do not understand it, but we think it will drive away the buffalo. We like to see our white brothers; we like to give them the hand of friendship; but we know that, as they come, our game goes back. What are we to do?'

If Stevens was moved by this plaintive speech, he did not admit to it either in his diary or in his response to the Indians listening. Distress was running high among the native peoples over more than the survival of the buffalo; rumors had preceded Stevens's survey party that its coming was the harbinger of the Bostons' seizure of all Indian Country. En route, Stevens tried to sweet-talk the tribesmen he met with scripted compassion and reassurance that the oncoming white settlers were not their enemies and that the Great White Father who occupied the Big Teepee back east had deep concern for their well-being. Stevens told them the road from the Mississippi to the Pacific would not injure the Indians or deprive them of their comforts, and while the railway and the whites who settled along its route would admittedly drive off the buffalo, the tribes "would receive from the President implements of agriculture, and learn to till the soil, so as to obtain food with less labor than now." There was not a glimmer of hope in his remarks that the white man's government would or could try to divert the tide of settlement that was sweeping the natives aside. Rather, in its benevolence, he said, it would station troops between tribes to prevent them from preying on one another. The natives were in greater peril from other native peoples, Stevens argued, than from the Americans. It was a hard sell, especially among the large and excitable Blackfoot nation on the eastern slopes of the Rockies, whose 12,000 members would have to be tamed if the railroad was to be built in that vicinity. But Stevens was received cordially enough and promised to revisit Blackfoot Country to work out a permanent peace treaty.

These early exchanges with the Native Americans apparently strengthened Stevens's confidence in his ability to bend them to his will. He wrote in his diary at one point, "I was much pleased with these Indians, and they seemed to be very favorably inclined towards the whites, and sincere in their professions of friendship." Why that should have been the case, given his mission and the tide of massive dispossession it foreshadowed, he did not speculate. A plausible inference can be drawn, though, from Stevens's writings that he believed himself to be a wily ambassador from an advanced civilization while the natives were gullible primitives naturally inclined to defer to their racial superiors. His reaction to them on the basis of personal contact seemed to oscillate between admiration and revulsion. He was appalled, for example, by their practice of polygamy, noting that some men had as many as six wives and did not cavil at pimping for them when profitable. What he saw in Indian camps he visited was no less distasteful. "They are filthy in the extreme in their habits," he wrote of one tribe, "the women actually eating the vermin out of each other's heads, and out of the robes in which they sleep."

Yet he appreciated the quiet dignity of the chiefs, their readiness to share food and tobacco with white strangers, and the respect accorded their visitors in the form of gifts—at one village Stevens was presented with thirty-two deer and buffalo skins and two robes (presumably de-verminized)—and their donning of ceremonial dress. "On all solemn occasions, when I met the Indians on my route, they were arrayed with the utmost care," Stevens observed, admiring in particular the intricate beadwork on their robes. "My duties in the field did not allow the same attention on my part, and the Indians sometimes complained of this, say-ing, 'We dress up to receive you, and why do you not wear the dress of a chief?' " Stevens's lapse of etiquette in his attire and his politely patron-izing manner of speech might have stemmed from simple cluelessness or been meant to convey a calculated indifference aimed at putting the natives in their place.

The most disappointing—and potentially ruinous—aspect of the rail-way survey effort was the performance on the western end of the route by George McClellan, who would disappoint again, disastrously so, eight years later as commander of the Union's Army of the Potomac. In trying to find a passage through the towering Cascades for the train line, Cap-tain McClellan's party floundered, moving slowly and getting lost. Native guides reported that the most direct route would have required too precipitous a climb, that the weather was too cold in the high mountain passes, and that the usual midwinter snowpack of twenty-five feet or more was too deep to allow the iron horse to operate over its steel roadbed. That McClellan's guides might have dreaded the coming of the railroad as a monstrous intrusion into their homelands and the spearhead of expansive white settlement—and were thus conspiring to dupe the sur-vey party through misinformation—seemed not to have occurred to the gentlemanly army officer. Stevens tried to buck up his friend, exhorting, "We must not be frightened with long tunnels, or enormous snows, but set ourselves to work to overcome them." But McClellan made only a cursory investigation of the likeliest site, accepting his guides' judgment, and failed to discover any alternative route—an outcome the infuriated Stevens would not tolerate. He had not come this far only to be stymied by the back of Mother Nature's hand. Suspecting that the Indian guides were unreliable and, in their hostility to white infiltration, had overstated the cold weather conditions, Stevens sent an order to McClellan to revisit the pass. McClellan declined to undertake the trip. Once snow began to fall, he insisted, it was "positively impracticable to use snowshoes" for the trek, though the natives seemed to do well enough with them. Disgusted, Stevens assigned another officer to make the ascent in January, peak snow season, and his party not only found a route through the mountains but also determined that the snowfall was insufficiently deep to block passage of the projected railway line. It was the end of the mutual regard Stevens and McClellan had once shared.

Discovery of the Cascade passage crowned Stevens's splendid achievement. He may not have endeared himself to the ranks of the survey party, but he surely won their respect. Under his leadership they had avoided natural disasters, Indian raiding parties, serious health problems, hunger, and going broke. They had found that neither the weather nor the terrain was so extreme as to foredoom a northern route for the transcontinental project, and the course he mapped out required construction of just one major tunnel. Stevens, knowledgeable about the cost of materials and labor for big construction projects, estimated the price of building the cross-country railway line at $105 million, not an unthinkable sum, given the scale of the project and the likely long-term commercial rewards to the nation for opening up the Northwest. As a dividend of the survey, his party had gathered much scientific data and anthropological insight into the native culture. Stevens's final report on the journey filled three volumes totaling 1,500 pages.

HIS ARRIVAL in Olympia, the ragamuffin hamlet that served as the capital of Washington Territory, lacked panoply. Word had gone out that the first governor to preside over the region was making his way up from the Columbia River along the muddy track through the Cowlitz River Valley, a six-day slog that ended November 25, 1853. Five months and nineteen days had passed since his party had set out from St. Paul. The journey concluded amidst a downpour that had drenched the eagerly awaited eminence right through his deerskin undershirt. The throng of local notables on hand to greet him at the ramshackle Washington Hotel was momentarily dumbstruck on learning that the small, disheveled, waterlogged figure who strode into the lobby without fanfare had, in fact, been sent there by the President and Congress of the United States.

It did not take long, though, after Stevens filled the place with his commanding voice, for the assembled citizenry to shed their disappointment. "I have come here not as an official for mere station but as a citizen as well as your chief magistrate to do my part toward the development of the resources of this territory," said the new governor, a hint of defiance in his tone for anyone who might confuse his short stature with deficient resolve. "From your hands an imperial domain will descend to your children . . . in the cause of humanity and freedom." His maiden speech struck just the right chord, invoking the spirit of "manifest destiny," as the concept had been labeled eight years earlier by a New York City journalist with strong Democratic Party affiliation. The term may have been freshly minted, but the idea behind it had been in place since the founding of the republic: God had assigned the American people, robust and pure of heart, to spread the gospel of liberty and democracy around the earth—well, certainly across all of North America—and prosperity and happiness would follow. This promise was now echoing with full-throated righteousness at the far end of the continent, and Isaac Stevens meant to see that it was delivered. Those who stood in his way were being put on notice that they did so at their peril.

The next morning Governor Stevens began to inspect his inchoate territory. He found a raw frontier community of just under 4,000 white inhabitants, as its first census shortly revealed. It had no real roads; local travel was most swiftly accomplished by canoe. The only passenger connection to the outside world was a weekly steamer to and from San Francisco. But Washington Territory's prospects were palpable. The lumber business was booming—you could smell it in the air—and homesteaders were arriving every week to grab up and fence off free farmland under the Donation Act, with confidence that the U.S. government would soon certify their title to it after formally extracting it from the Indians.

Tension between the races had been on the rise, Stevens soon learned, ever since the Whitman Massacre and the failure of the Oregon Territory treaties to gain Senate ratification. The natives around Puget Sound, even those well-disposed, or at least cordial, toward the whites, had now come to grasp the difference between the King George men, who had been respectfully doing business and intermarrying with tribal members for the past twenty years, and the Bostons, who had come to displace the Indians from their homelands. For his part, the governor knew that his agenda should begin with dismantling the two most formidable obstacles to swift American settlement of Washington Territory—the Indian tribes' homeland claims and the British bastion, the Hudson's Bay Company's operations at Fort Nisqually.

First, though, Stevens had to organize a government. He was fortunate in the selection of his primary aide, Charles M. Mason, whom he had appointed territorial secretary. Stevens had long been friendly with

Mason's older brother, James, a colleague in the Corps of Engineers and during the Mexican War. Charles, though only twenty-three, brought impressive credentials with him from his hometown of Providence, Rhode Island, where he had graduated from Brown University with academic distinction and worked as a lawyer for several years in the office of the former state attorney general. Mason's low-key personality was the ideal complement to Stevens's; the second-ranking official of Washington Territory was soft-spoken, amiable, and unfailingly courteous, yet at least as brainy as the governor and no less efficient a paper-pusher. Mason quickly gained Stevens's full confidence, to the point where during his frequent extended trips away from Olympia, he did not hesitate to designate the young lawyer as acting governor.

To secure his political base in a strange land, Stevens quickly surrounded himself with a coterie of some thirty settlers, many of whom had become residents since or soon after the Oregon Territory was made official U.S. soil in 1846. Mostly partisan Democrats devoted to the expansionist policies of the American government, they were led by James W. Wiley, editor and publisher of Olympia's weekly newspaper. A lapsed lawyer who came west from Ohio to become a frontier journalist, Wiley launched a sheet he named the *Columbian* in 1852, when he was thirty-two, and used its columns to advocate separate territorial status for northern Oregon. He was one of the leading delegates at the convention that applied to Congress for such a change, and when the breakaway movement succeeded but the requested name of "Columbia Territory" was denied, he rechristened his sheet the *Pioneer.* Wiley was an alcoholic, but friends said he was never a mean drunk or let the bottle sully either his professional performance or his gentlemanly demeanor. A loner with no family, he was said to have a sensitive temperament and generous disposition—except toward the natives. His dislike of Indians was not subtly expressed. Admired for his vigorous writing style, Wiley was praised at his death in 1860 as a journalist who, when "he felt it his duty to attack the acts of individuals . . . cheerfully opened his columns to their defense." Stevens would have no more loyal a booster during his years as governor than Wiley, the territory's leading disseminator of news and shaper of public opinion, and to leave no doubt about his political affiliation, he soon lengthened his paper's name to the *Pioneer and Democrat* and served happily as the governor's unabashedly partisan mouthpiece in print.

In his capacity as superintendent of Indian affairs for the territory,

Stevens picked two men to help him prepare for his treatymaking efforts. To act as Indian agent for the tribes around Puget Sound who were closest to the seat of the territorial government, he chose a burly, full-bearded former Kentuckian, Michael T. Simmons, who had come to Oregon Country as a co-leader of a wagon train in the mid-1840s and established himself financially by opening the first gristmill near the head of Puget Sound. A tough guy, barely literate, Mike Simmons regularly vented his displeasure with the continuing British influence in the region, and had been one of the most vocal leaders of the movement to get the neglected northern portion of Oregon Territory designated a separate federal entity. Simmons was an intimidating presence, well suited to play the second part in Stevens's good-cop/bad-cop approach to the natives.

The governor wisely selected Simmons's polar opposite to provide him with in-depth intelligence about the surrounding Indian population. George Gibbs, three years older than Stevens and far more cultivated, was the offspring of a socially, financially, and politically prominent family with roots in New York and Connecticut. His maternal grandfather had succeeded Alexander Hamilton as Secretary of the Treasury and regaled young Gibbs with his memories of Washington, Jefferson, and other national icons. Gibbs's father was beneficiary of a family fortune from international trade, allowing him to enjoy life as a gentleman farmer across the East River from Manhattan and to gather a world-famous collection of geological specimens that drew George toward a career of scientific and wide-ranging intellectual inquiry. First, though, he tried his hand at the law, earning his degree at Harvard, writing a useful treatise for practitioners, and working for a New York firm. But lawyering failed to satisfy his omnivorous curiosity, and he turned to academic research, which eventually won him appointment as head librarian of the New-York Historical Society. Tiring of the sedentary bookish life, Gibbs headed west in the wake of the Gold Rush, and, hungering not for wealth but for adventure and knowledge of the landscape, its flora and fauna, and the native culture, he was in no rush to reach the Pacific coast. Instead, he honed his skills as a surveyor, cartographer, and ethnologist while gathering zoological specimens for the Smithsonian Institution and filling notebooks with reports on Indian language and customs drawn from many an evening around native campfires.

His travels eventually took Gibbs to the newly organized Oregon Territory, where he served as a U.S. customs official and, again donning his lawyer's hat, drafted half a dozen Indian treaties that the governor imposed on the Willamette Valley tribes and others nearby, only to have them rebuffed by the Senate. His diverse abilities drew him to the attention of George McClellan, who used his linguistic and geographical knowledge to help him map the westernmost leg of the northern railway route. Probably no white man in the Northwest was better informed on Indian life than Gibbs. Stevens, mindful of his own fleeting exposure to tribal folkways, engaged Gibbs's service and asked him to compile data as soon as possible on every aspect of tribal life west of the Cascades. His 200-page report was in the governor's hands by the time Stevens was ready to deal with the natives.

JUST BEFORE heading west in June 1853, Stevens had received a letter of instruction from the new Secretary of State, William L. Marcy, the ablest figure in President Pierce's new cabinet. As the first governor of Washington Territory, Stevens was urged to get rid of the Hudson's Bay Company's Fort Nisqually and its neighboring farms and ranches on the Nisqually Plain as soon as possible by coming to terms of "fair compensation" with William Tolmie, as required by the 1846 U.S.-British pact dividing the Oregon Country. The sooner the British left, American officials thought, the easier it would be to handle the natives and, without the Bay's bolstering friendship and supplies, to pressure them into accepting treaty terms.

Marcy's letter ensured an early confrontation between Stevens and Dr. Tolmie, the governor's only serious rival for power in the region. There is perhaps no better illustration of the striking difference between the two men than their attitudes toward the natives surrounding them.

Casting himself as a white overlord of Olympian stature, Stevens could scarcely allow himself to make the acquaintance of Indians on an individual basis or to be exposed to their culture—familiarizing himself with them as quite human beings would have made displacing them en masse all the more unpleasant a process. The natives' utility, however, did concern him. In a December 26, 1853, letter to George W. Manypenny, commissioner of the U.S. Office of Indian Affairs at the Department of the Interior, Stevens dispassionately reported that the natives around Puget Sound were

> very useful in many ways for transporting persons about the
> Sound in their canoes . . . in chopping wood, plowing, driving

wagons, etc. Some of the women wash clothes well, and in a variety of ways make themselves useful; and if confined on reservations under the direction of efficient agents, I am inclined to think that little objection, if any, would be made by the whites.

That the natives themselves might object to such confinement seems not to have troubled him. Tolmie, by contrast, from his first days among the Nisqually tribe and the neighboring Puyallups, had treated the Indians not as an inferior race good only for exploitation but as fellow occupants of a glorious wilderness, whose unfamiliar ways, compatible with the natural setting, made them the more worthy of respect and emulation.

Consider how the two men reacted when their sleep was disturbed by the Nisquallies' favorite game, the raucous "bone gamble." Sides were chosen at the beginning of the game, during which considerable sums were often waged for correctly guessing—after much body shaking and behind-the-back manipulation of a pair of small, barrel-shaped animal bones—which of the lead player's tightly clenched fists held the bones. The contests lasted long into the night, sometimes for a week of nights, to the constant accompaniment of songs, chants, and beating of sticks against wooden boards in the hope of inducing the hovering spirits to favor one side or the other. To whites within hearing range, the resulting racket proved intolerable at times. Here is how Stevens reacted on one such occasion, according to a letter his wife, Meg, later sent to relatives back east:

> They [the Indians] gamble all day and night, and make night hideous with the constant rapping with a stick upon a dry board, accompanied by a droning noise or chant. The Governor got up from his bed, took a club and went amongst the Indians and told the chief of the tribes that he wouldn't let them disturb the whites, that the first man that opened his lips, he would knock him down & c.
>
> Mr. Stevens has them right under his thumb, they are afraid as death of him, and do just what he tells them.

When apprised of this account years afterward, Tolmie's assistant during this period, Edward Huggins, recalled how Tolmie reacted to a similar incident. Not long after Huggins arrived at Fort Nisqually, a large gathering of natives was camped in the open near the fort and engaged in a bone gamble that continued night after night. "The noise made became almost unbearable, rendering sleep almost impossible to the denizens of the fort," Huggins recounted.

> Dr. Tolmie determined to stop the noisy proceedings and went amongst the gamblers—not with a club as the governor was reported to have done—but emphatically told them they must stop this incessant thumping with sticks, and threatened them with punishment, perhaps drive them from the vicinity of the fort, if they did not desist. . . . I never saw Dr. Tolmie threaten to club Indians.

By using less aggressive methods, the Scottish physician had won the natives' tacit assent to the Bay's requisition of thousands of acres of their homeland for crops and pastures. In return he strongly advocated setting aside most of the region as a hunting preserve for the Nisquallies and their kin, to be left inviolable by white settlement. It was this happy accommodation between the British and the Indians that Stevens was determined to destroy.

The first letter of instruction the governor received from Secretary of State Marcy had advised him that while Bay employees and British subjects in Washington Territory had the right, under the 1846 treaty with Britain, to travel the Columbia River and its tributaries for the purpose of commerce, they were not permitted to trade with either their longtime native customers or American settlers. The practical effect of this policy would have been to close down the Bay's operations before the U.S. government had honored its pledge to pay "fair compensation" for the company's facilities and real estate claims.

Stevens lost little time in letting his British rival Tolmie know that a big wind had blown into the territory. Within a month of his arrival in Olympia, the new American governor sent Tolmie a letter at Fort Nisqually, twenty miles away, underscoring his intention to enforce the policy set down by Marcy. Tolmie wrote back swiftly that no such prohibition on the Bay's commercial activity, denying it access to both its white and native clientele, was included in the 1846 treaty, and, absent reference to an explicit and mutually agreed-upon embargo, Fort Nisqually was entitled to continue its normal operations until an accord was reached with the U.S. government to pay the company for its property. If either side had a grievance, Tolmie went on, it was his. Ever since passage by Congress of the Donation Land Act, he pointedly advised Stevens, American settlers had been encouraged to squat on tribal and Bay lands without holding certified title to them—and were, nevertheless, busily plowing up and planting prairie lands they did not own and stealing, shooting, or driving the Bay's cattle into the woods, all with impunity.

The contest was thus drawn. Stevens was gratified to learn that antipathy toward the Bay and its British employees ran high within the American community. Anglophobia with roots reaching back to the Revolutionary War fed a deep-seated conviction that the British presence, along with all other Old World interlopers, should disappear from North America. More immediate resentment was fed by the Bay's commercial dominance of the region, controlling prices and credit conditions, and its failure to buy their lumber and farm produce for export while holding its American debtors as captive customers. Thus, the Bay and its British masters, it was charged, enjoyed a lopsided advantage in their balance of trade while being permitted to remain on U.S. soil. Men like Mike Simmons and other hardnosed settlers braced Stevens's resolve by arguing that the Bay had even less legitimate claim to title over Indian lands than American squatters who were establishing homesteads as the Donation Land Act had intended them to. Pressing his case, Stevens advised Tolmie that the 1846 Oregon boundary treaty had granted the Bay the right to compensation only for the land it had placed under cultivation as of that year and not for any acreage planted or used for pasture in the subsequent seven years—land that American settlers had as much right to as the Bay, if not more so. Accordingly, Tolmie's request for $450,000 in compensatory payment, Stevens told him, was too high by 50 percent.

While making clear that the U.S. government viewed Fort Nisqually and its subsidiary operations as an intolerable irritant, Isaac Stevens understood that he could not risk an immediate display of overt enmity toward William Tolmie, who was so warmly regarded by the natives. Even if Stevens had had enough police or military force at his disposal for a peremptory shutdown of the Bay's business at Puget Sound, such an action might have stirred an uprising among the Indians, who had come to depend on the British goods and services—and heavily outnumbered the American settlers. Besides, the tiny U.S. Army contingent at Fort Steilacoom was neither answerable to orders from the territorial governor (only to those from the War Department) nor any match for all those Indians if they went on the warpath.

Stevens, then, knew that he would have to try to divide and conquer his prey, not provoke the tribes into bonding in militant resistance that could massacre or frighten away squatters and discourage potential new settlers. The trick would be for him to determine just how hard and how fast he could push the Indians.

4

A Credit to His Race

AMONG ISAAC STEVENS'S CONTEMPORARIES, George Catlin (1796–1872) was one of the rare Americans who troubled to familiarize himself with the ethos of the native people as they were being uprooted by onrushing white settlers and driven west across the Mississippi by government policy. A lawyer-turned-painter, Catlin had set up a studio in Philadelphia as a portraitist. A chance encounter with a delegation of visiting western Indians moved him to dedicate his future artistic labors to, as he put it, "rescuing from oblivion the looks and customs of the vanishing races of native man in America."

Years of travel among them produced more than 600 portraits of prominent Indians and scenes of their habitats and ceremonies, a collection that has been exhibited around the country ever since and, along with Catlin's notebooks, diaries, and letters, marked him as one of the most acute and sensitive admirers of Native American culture. "I love a people," Catlin wrote, "who are honest without laws, who have no jails and no poor-house . . . who never take the name of God in vain [and] who worship God without a Bible . . . who are free from religious animosities . . . who never fought a battle with white men except on their own ground . . . and oh! How I love a people who don't live for the love of money."

Few other white Americans or the British colonists who preceded them ever waxed as ecstatic about the virtuous ways of the race they found already in place on the continent. It would have been awkward to do so and then set about systematically extinguishing their light. Instead, the vast majority of newcomers disdained almost every practice and tenet of the natives' existence. The heart of their cultural disparity was the two races' contradictory perceptions of their physical surroundings. The Indians detected a divine spirituality in every aspect of nature; all of creation, whether animal, vegetable, or mineral, was part of a single web of being and the manifestation of a universal Great Spirit imbuing the entirety with the life force. The earth and everything on it—the oak, the lily, the grizzly bear, the waterfalls, and the mighty mountains no less than humankind—possessed a soul, if not an equal degree of self-awareness, and was to be regarded with reverence. The flora and fauna the Great Spirit had provided might be used to sustain human life, but each species was to be thanked for that sacrifice, and nature was to be disturbed as little as possible. The land and the waters were sacred, not to be fouled. What grew of its own accord could be taken, but never in excess, and whatever agriculture was essential for survival in the cold months had to be minimally invasive; violators were guilty of sacrilege.

To the European and American colonial mentality, such worshipful regard for the natural world reeked of animism, idolatry, superstition, and a pagan perversion of the true Holy Spirit. The whole point of the British settlement of the New World was to possess the land for its utility. The immigrants' mission was to take title to the fecund earth and tame it for domestic purposes—seek out its best growing places, clear them, fell their timber for durable dwellings and fuel, turn the wilderness into fields, plant them and fence them off from neighbors and the natives, and prosper with the smiling approval of God in heaven and His Son, sent to save humanity. The land, in short, was there to serve man, not to be left sacrosanct. The aborigines who disdained intensive agriculture as ungodly work were taken for shirkers, whose Stone Age benightedness and immorality corrupted their view of life. Their minds suffered from arrested development; they had no knowledge of the wheel or locomotion, no written form of communication, no laws, and no shame in their nakedness, dirtiness, polygamy, bodily disfigurements, and other vile habits. Their silence, a high virtue among them, was believed to cloak venomous hostility toward the white Christian arrivals, whom they plotted to waylay at the first opportunity. When the tribesmen dared to resist incursions by the whites and shed their blood, the Indians were accused of evidencing a brutish, treacherous character.

This profound racial confrontation did not abate after the colonists rebelled to form their own nation. George Washington spoke for many of his countrymen when he wrote in 1783 that Indians and wolves were "both beasts of prey, though they differ in shape." A more kindly assessment was offered by Thomas Jefferson, who remarked, "I believe the Indian to be in body and mind equal to the white man." This proved an unpopular sentiment, however, and the politically attuned Jefferson soon amended his appraisal. Yes, the natives were endowed with the capacity to ascend to the white race's level of attainment and become assimilated within it—but only by adopting its cultural matrix.

Essential to this metamorphosis would be correcting the red race's attitude toward the land, which they shrank from actively cultivating but regarded as a hallowed preserve, to be wandered over at will, for hunting and gathering as venerable custom allowed or simply for joyful contemplation. Such footloose practices were deemed unsuitable for a civilized society. Instead, the Indians needed to buckle down within far less expansive territory, where they would work the soil as the Scriptures directed (see Genesis 9:1) and make it flourish. Whites would show them how to rigorously farm their own individual plots and teach them to disavow their quaint notion that the earth abided as the common protectorate of all who dwelled on it yet belonged to none but the Great Spirit. Once the natives reined in their rampant squandering of the earth and properly valued what it might bring forth for their sustenance, there would be plenty of room as well for multitudes of white settlers to live nearby in peace and mutual prosperity.

The elected leaders of the United States thus declared early on the divinely inspired right of their government to impose restrictive measures on the conduct of the aboriginal people. On paper, at least, the Founding Fathers charitably added that any such strictures were not to be imposed tyrannically or unilaterally. The most admired piece of federal legislation drawn up under the Articles of Confederation—the Northwest Ordinance of 1787, shortly adopted under the Constitution as well—clearly asserted Congress's right to extinguish Indian land titles. Where that right derived from was not addressed. But the lawmakers pledged, in Article 3 of the ordinance, that they would not act oppressively in doing so: "The utmost good faith shall always be observed towards the Indians; their lands and property shall never be taken from them without their consent; and, in their property, rights, and liberty, they shall never be invaded or disturbed, unless in just and lawful wars authorized by Congress." What Congress gave with one phrase, it took back with the next, for who was to decide, other than Congress itself, what was a "just and lawful" war?

In order, it was said, to prevent wrongs from being inflicted on the Indians and thus to preserve the peace, the U.S. government began presenting written treaties to the illiterate Indians of the Ohio Valley. They were asked—none too politely—to surrender most of their lands for white settlement in exchange for a token payment and sanctuary beyond future white incursions. The practice was initiated with the Treaty of Greenville (1795), under which the resident tribes, having lost a "just and lawful war" led by General Anthony Wayne, were required to give up a major portion of modern Ohio and Indiana and sixteen other strategic enclaves, including the sites of Detroit and Chicago, for an annual payment of $10,000. The ceded land was not enough, though, and its boundaries were soon breached by white homesteaders without the U.S. government lifting a restraining finger. By 1809 the natives had been separated from 50 million acres of their former homelands

The takeaway grew even more transparent after that. As Americans swept westward during the first half of the nineteenth century, they displayed little patience with the natives who stood in the way while asserting their right of ancestral occupancy. Scholars have estimated that by 1850, the aboriginal population in North America—besieged by the invaders' explosive weaponry, wondrous technology, contemptuous cruelty, and irresistible pathogens, as well as the Indians' own ever-deepening despair—was just one-tenth of what it had been when Columbus first ventured ashore. And the American government, entrusting the mission to avid officials like Isaac Stevens, was doing its best to hurry along that forced march toward virtual annihilation.

MANY AN AMERICAN schoolchild before the Space Age grew up hearing tales—gross distortions as often as not—about the native people who once ruled the unspoiled inner spaces of their continent. Their tribal names had a magical ring, otherworldly and not a little menacing: Iroquois, Algonquin, Narragansett, Mohawk, Shawnee, Winnebago, Chippewa, Cherokee, Choctaw, Chickasaw, Seminole; the Sioux and the Cheyenne, the Ute, the Blackfoot; the Comanche, the Apache and Navajo, and in the Far West, the Nez Perce and the Spokane, the Yakima and the Walla Walla. Some of their legendary chiefs' names have likewise been woven into the tapestry of American memory, usually because of their heroic but doomed defiance of the whites—iconic figures such as Tecumseh, Red Cloud, Crazy Horse, Sitting Bull, Cochise, Geronimo, and Chief Joseph. Among these faded native nations and martyred leaders few were less celebrated, or even less heard of beyond their home precincts, than the Nisqually tribe and its last chief, Leschi.

The heart of the Nisquallies' homeland lay near the southern end of

Puget Sound, scarcely a dozen miles from Governor Stevens's headquarters in Olympia. Because it was the closest of the native nations within his jurisdiction, the Nisqually tribe was the principal object of the first of the treaties Stevens hoped to arrange with all the Indians in the territory. On the strength of the reports from his subordinates, he supposed that the Nisquallies were docile and would readily accept whatever terms the U.S. government offered them.

The Nisquallies had never been numerous, probably totaling at their peak in 1800 or so between 800 and 1,200 members before the white man's pestilence began to strike them. Except for the warm summer months when they camped away from home on food-gathering forays, the Nisquallies lived in thirteen or fourteen villages strung out along both the banks of the river to which they gave their name, or close by its upstream tributaries. This decentralization helped fend off amphibious assaults—at first sight of an enemy, drums of alarm and fleet runners alerted the upriver settlements—and probably eased the spread of contagious disease so deadly in closely packed communities. The Nisqually River, the tribe's binding life force, flowed for roughly eighty miles, running down from the glaciers on the slopes of Mount Rainier and following a serpentine northwesterly course until forking into a broad delta, known as the Nisqually Flats, on reaching Puget Sound, which the surrounding tribes called the Whulge. In its progress seaward, the river cuts through a broad plain of half a million acres once ideally suited to the growth of long bunchgrass that made rich fodder for horses and livestock. Freely roaming this broad, velvety prairie, the natives there were first known as the "Squally-absch," meaning "people of the grass country" in their Salish dialect, which had a guttural cast that struck one white pioneer familiar with their tongue as "a compound of the grumblings of a pig and the clucking of a hen." Modern tribal historians and elders say the name Nisqually also includes the meaning "people of the river," though the double association seems curious. Whatever the precise derivation of their name, anthropologists testify that Nisquallies and their now nameless forebears had been living along their river basin for perhaps 10,000 years before the first white men appeared on their waterways.

The Nisquallies' origins are misty. They may have trekked from Asia over the Siberian-Alaskan land bridge or come, as other northwestern tribes did, in ocean-going canoes that probably island-hopped along the Aleutian chain until they found a gentler climate, paddled up through Juan de Fuca Strait, and debarked at Puget Sound with its idyllic setting.

Tribal lore conjectures as well that the broad-shouldered, short-legged Nisquallies may have originated in Central America, where intense and prolonged drought drove them north in search of more temperate weather and a lush landscape.

Theirs was a family- and village-centered culture. Each village consisted of two or three lodges or longhouses accommodating a few extended families, polygamous units in which the paterfamilias typically had two or three wives of descending seniority and children with each. The wives and offspring tended to be mutually supportive rather than competitive since the Nisqually family was as much an economic as a social unit. Polygamous marriages produced more hands per family to perform the labors essential for group survival.

Politically, each Nisqually village may have had a recognized "headman," but he had little formal authority. The loosely confederated villages rarely appointed a formal tribal council or functioned under a hierarchal leadership. At times, a charismatic chief might emerge, but more often an oligarchy of the more influential village headmen held sway. The Nisquallies, then, were no fonder of autocracy than their neighboring tribes, with whom they regularly intermarried and lived at peace. The closest of them, the Puyallup (pronounced "Pew-allup"), was grouped along the river bearing their name and running roughly parallel to the Nisqually about twenty miles to the northeast. Beyond them was a group of smaller, related bands that came to be known collectively as the Muckleshoots. Across the formidable barrier of the Cascades and southeast toward the Columbia River were the larger and more combative plains tribes, the Klickitats and their relatives, the Yakimas, who in turn were allied at times with the Cayuses, Walla Wallas, and Nez Perces to the east and southeast. Aside from occasional quarrels with the Yakimas, the Nisquallies enjoyed amicable dealings with them all. Periodically, though, a threat arose from the Snoqualmies well up the eastern shore of the Whulge or, far more dreaded, from the Haidas, who swept down the Sound in war canoes from the distant north in quest of slaves, usually women and children, snatched from the peaceable riverside tribes.

The Nisquallies fell into two defined groups. Their "fish people" dwelled along the river and closer to the Sound and lived principally off salmon and shellfish. Their "horse people," whose villages were in the uplands bordering the plains and forests, hunted and gathered as the seasons dictated, developing their equestrian skills. The two groups were bound by the river as well as by appearance, language, dress, domestic arrangements, and ceremonies like the potlatch feasts with gift-giving to all attendees and the solemn rite of thanksgiving to honor the arrival of the salmon, staple of the tribal diet, each spring. The nearness of untainted fresh water invited healthful habits, like frequent bathing at sites segregated by gender and washing of food in the preparation of meals. The women rarely cut their hair, typically letting it trail down their backs in two long braids. They often painted their faces, less for decoration than to protect them from the sun, and tattooed their bodies with the use of gooseberry thorns and charcoal. The women favored skirts of shredded cedar and deerskin blouses, except in warm weather, when they often went topless. The men generally cut their hair to shoulder length, did not decorate their bodies except for combat, and in mild seasons wore next to nothing.

The Nisqually conception of property allowed for the private ownership of slaves, horses, canoes, weaponry, housewares, and shell money, but items made for communal use like lodges, sweat houses for purification rites, and fishing traps were treated as shared holdings. Village land, as well as surrounding and outlying territory, was not considered anybody's private possession but rather a gift of the Great Spirit, like the waters, there to be shared and lived on lightly and respectfully, their natural products available for the personal use of whoever tended them. This is not to say that the Nisquallies were any more tolerant than other tribal groups of acts of trespass within their homeland or more kindly disposed to those who hunted or fished there without permission.

While hardly renowned as warriors, Nisqually tribe members were highly proficient fishermen, hunters, and carpenters. The abundance, pliability, and versatility of the red cedar in their region allowed them to master woodworking—a considerable achievement, considering that the only tools at their disposal were made of stone and bone. Although they did not craft totem poles to honor and propitiate their spirits, as did the tribes farther to the northwest, their canoes were often ornamentally carved, and anthropologists have pointed out the smooth joinery and well-designed interiors of their lodges and longhouses. Nisqually women produced subtly exquisite baskets, woven from coiled cedar thread, marsh reeds, and dried prairie grasses, that were especially treasured as items of trade by tribes east of the Cascades.

Nisquallies did not take their blessings for granted; they heeded and paid homage to the spirits, for the most part benevolent, who they believed were watching over nearly every aspect of their existence. The secret of prospering, not just surviving, in the Nisqually world was to be attuned to its ubiquitous spiritualism. And no member of the tribe had prospered more than Leschi, pride of the Nisquallies and, to whites who had dealt with him, a credit to his race.

WHAT WE KNOW about the life of Leschi is derived chiefly from the written testimony of a dozen or so English-speaking contemporaries, interviews with a handful of fellow natives who knew him, and the oral tradition of the Nisquallies, persisting into the twenty-first century.

There is no reliable graphic rendering done from life of Leschi's appearance, only a few drawings of an indeterminate date by unknown artists, but several people acquainted with him described his looks. His younger tribal friend and later companion-in-arms, Wahelut (called Yelm Jim by the whites), told an interviewer in the 1890s that Leschi was tall, heavily built, and very strong. Tallness, though, is a relative quality, and since the Nisqually physique ran generally to squatness, we may guess that Leschi was of medium height by modern standards. Charles Grainger, a white man who saw him daily near the end of his life, said Leschi was about five-foot-six and had "a very high forehead for an Indian," meaning it had probably not been flattened in infancy, as was often the case among tribes of the region. According to Grainger, Leschi had a strong, square jaw, an aquiline nose, and piercing dark brown eyes that "would look almost through you—a firm but not a savage look." Benjamin Franklin (known as Frank) Shaw, a Washington territorial official who had several extended discussions with him, wrote that the Nisqually stalwart was about six feet tall, 175 pounds, and "a true flat-head." According to late twentieth-century Nisqually tribal historian Cecilia Svinth Carpenter, Leschi had "a tall agile body, strong heavy shoulders," and a face more slender than others in his village. But Carpenter could offer no verifiable authority for her description. Nor did regional historian Murray Morgan, whose engaging book *Puget's Sound: A Narrative of Tacoma and the Southern Sound* states that Leschi was light-skinned and powerfully built, with a thin, straight mouth, short chin, heavy brows, and black hair parted a little to the left and cut straight below the ears. Leschi's third and youngest wife, Mary, who married him when she was a teenager and outlived him by sixty-six years, gave an interview, unearthed by Washington State archivists eighty years after her death, in which she said that Leschi was light-skinned ("almost as white as a Boston man"), had a round face with cheeks often naturally flushed, and was strong with great powers of endurance.

Such conflicting evidence means that the modern investigator in the matter is unavoidably forced to rely a good deal on hearsay and surmise in portraying Leschi and trying to separate legend from facts. That he was a historical presence, though, is certain, and the events in which he was certifiably a central actor are worthy of fresh consideration for what they reveal of the primal racial confrontation between Americans, native and immigrant.

According to Leschi's tribal biographer, the star his people saw rising over the Nisqually Plain on the day of Leschi's birth in early January 1808 was hailed as a portent that the new arrival was destined to become their warrior chief and savior. His native village of Bashelabesh lay midway up the Nisqually basin, thirty miles or so below Puget Sound, on the Mashel River, a tributary that snaked east to west through a broad grassland prairie and provided ideal grazing for his family's large herd of horses. Leschi's father, Yanatco, was a Nisqually; his mother, a Klickitat closely related to Yakima chiefs and ranking braves of that formidable tribe on the far side of the Cascades. His mother's name did not find its way into Nisqually oral history, only the report that she sang well, or at any rate a lot. Her Yakima genes were probably the reason Leschi stood taller than most Nisquallies.

The origin and meaning of his name are unknown. In keeping with tribal convention, Leschi likely chose it himself; it may have belonged to a distant relative, or he may have just liked the sound of it. He had two known siblings, his older half-brother, Quiemuth (pronounced "Kweemuth"), from whom he was said to have been inseparable when they were young, despite the ten-year age gap between them, and a sister who married Leschi's friend and prominent comrade-in-arms, Stahi. The brothers helped tend their father's growing herd of horses, whose value made the family one of the tribe's wealthiest. With their pick of mounts, they became expert riders who roamed widely and hunted skillfully in the game-rich forests bordering the Nisqually Plain. In the warm months the family crossed to the southwest side of the Nisqually to gather roots and berries on Yelm Prairie and fish the heavy summer run of salmon.

After Leschi married, he moved from his home village and settled on land near Muck Creek, another Nisqually tributary, about eighteen miles downstream toward the Sound and a lot closer to the new Hudson's Bay Company establishment at Fort Nisqually, which opened when he was twenty-five. Its nearness offered him opportunities to sell his talents and work product to the King George men, with whom he got on well, thanks to what was said to be his soft-spoken and unabrasive manner. He traded the skins, pelts, meat, and fish he had caught and trimmed, as well as some of the horses his family raised, for the whites' tools, garments, and guns (with which he was said to have become a crack shot). In time, he and Quiemuth, along with other Nisqually men, worked, mainly tending horses, for the Bay's Puget Sound Agricultural Company, the sprawling British farm and ranch operation.

His various forms of livelihood made Leschi prosperous by his tribe's gauge, allowing him to build a substantial cedar house and accumulate a goodly herd of his own horses. By his wife Mary's recollection, the herd may have amounted to as many as 100, though William Tolmie's principal assistant at Fort Nisqually, who dealt with Leschi over several years, doubted that the number ever exceeded 25. According to Nisqually lore, Leschi generously shared the accumulated earnings from his horses, hunting, and employment by the Bay with his tribe in gift-giving at potlatch feasts and by alms to the infirm, aged, and those otherwise needy. Such altruism has traditionally been viewed among many Indian cultures as the noblest form of conduct. "He had a big, good heart," Yelm Jim said of Leschi, and was "kind to all people."

Leschi's generosity extended to his teenage wife, who recalled that "he was always giving me presents . . . and always let me have all the nice clothes I wanted." He would periodically sell off one of his horses at Fort Nisqually and then "bring home a lot of things. We always lived well." He occasionally took Mary on camping and hunting trips, but he was away from home a lot on his distant travels—a mounted wanderer who kept in touch with whites and native communities on both sides of the Cascades. He "never told me anything about his business," said Mary. "I was young, [and] he was rich and had lots of horses, and like a fool I married him. He was old enough to be my father"—a thirty-one-year age gap that may explain why Leschi felt he could not confide in her. He had likely married Mary after his first wife died, and he already had a second wife, older than Mary by a good number of years, with whom he may have been more companionable. His teenage bride was probably the trophy wife of Leschi's middle age, and there is contemporary testimony that he was intoxicated with her charms. By Mary's account, he did not physically or verbally abuse her. She recalled, "I never saw him angry in my life and . . . he never spoke an angry word to me."

Among his other talents, Leschi was, by all accounts, a highly persuasive speaker when he chose to be, in both public and private settings. Frank Shaw, one of the few whites in early Washington Territory days who was fluent in Salish dialects, called Leschi "the greatest orator I ever heard." He may have been as circumspect as he was articulate. According to tribal stories, Leschi was often invited to act as an informal judge and arbitrator, with a knack for smoothing out differences among a people whose contentiousness and family feuds died hard (and continue to smolder in the twenty-first century).

Soon after William Tolmie returned to take charge of Fort Nisqually in 1843, he detected a shrewd intelligence and high trustworthiness in Leschi, whose duties he expanded beyond tending horses and herding cattle. Tolmie seems to have used him as something of a straw boss in his dealings with the Bay's Nisqually and other native employees. On at least one occasion that impressed the Scottish business manager, Leschi and Quiemuth saw to it that a fellow Nisqually workman charged with abusing a non-Indian hand was brought forward to accept his punishment. And there is reason to believe that the brothers rendered valuable service to the Bay's ranching subsidiary by patrolling for native rustlers. Such invaluable cooperation cemented a genuine bond between Tolmie, the Salish-speaking impresario of the biggest commercial enterprise in the territory, and the Nisqually brave. Leschi took to wearing, on selective occasions, white men's clothing bought from the Bay and was noticed from time to time riding with Tolmie in his buggy.

When American settlers began to arrive in the south part of the Whulge in the mid-1840s, Leschi, along with Quiemuth, was as adept at dealing with them as with the Hudson's Bay Company people and gaining their confidence as a "good Indian." Tolmie would later recount, "From the early days the brothers were known for their readiness to assist the whites on all occasions." This impression was reinforced by a less friendly observer, Hazard Stevens, who wrote in 1901 that Leschi was "a chief of unusual intelligence and energy [who] had much to do with the Hudson's Bay Company people at Fort Nisqually, by whom he was much trusted as a guide and hunter, and was supposed to be well affected toward the whites." Prominent among the earliest American settlers in the region was George Bush, a half-black (his mother was Irish) former slave from Missouri who had joined a party of five families in an Oregon-bound wagon train and wound up homesteading in the Nisquallies' terrain. Bush recalled how Leschi brought urgently needed supplies on pack horses to help the settlers during their precarious first days and taught them how to enjoy the unfamiliar types of seafood in which the area abounded. "Leschi was as good a friend as we ever had," Bush added. Another settler, Andrew Bradley, who reached the territory in 1854, never forgot how he tried to lead his cattle across the rushing Puyallup River, misjudged the force of the current, and suddenly found himself, his horse, and his herd all being swept downstream—until Leschi, fortunately nearby, rode to the rescue. It was a favor Bradley would repay a few years later.

On another occasion that won him special plaudits in the white community, Leschi offered to lend and oversee the use of a dozen of his horses as part of an effort by the settlers to build a badly needed road at Naches Pass, the main entry point through the Cascades to the Puget Sound region. On inquiring about the pay rate for this trailblazing project, intended to facilitate white settlement in the Nisqually basin, Leschi was told that it was a volunteer effort without pay for its public-spirited participants. Whether hoping to ingratiate himself with the Americans or to benefit otherwise from increased traffic across the mountains, Leschi agreed to join the undertaking on the same unpaid basis—apparently without suspecting, we are left to assume, that he was helping seal the fate of the native population in his region.

Probably none of the early American settlers near the south end of the Sound was on closer terms with Leschi than the family of James McAllister, a lean, muscular six-footer with little learning and not much to say but viewed in the community as honest, industrious, and, like Leschi, highly skilled as a horseman and hunter. The McAllisters had been members of the same party with George Bush that arrived in 1846 and, according to an 1893 memoir by McAllister's daughter, Sarah M. Hartman, was urged by Leschi to settle in the fertile bottomlands of the Nisqually basin, where the arriving families staked claims near one another about twenty miles below Fort Nisqually. Guided by Leschi, the McAllisters chose a farm site—with no legal title to it—at the convergence of two creeks close to the Nisqually River, where "everything we put in the ground grew," including potatoes that weighed as much as ten pounds. Jim McAllister soon picked up the Nisqually dialect, and his wife, a southern woman "used to negro servants," took in three Indian girls as housemaids. Once the Oregon Land Donation Act went into effect, McAllister filed a claim for 640 free acres, the maximum spread allowed, and proceeded to improve it without concern that the land had not been formally ceded to the U.S. government by Leschi's people. If

Jim's Nisqually friend had raised no objection, why should he? McAllister deemed Leschi a worthy man and friend who frequently visited his home, bringing gifts of meat from his latest hunting trip, perhaps in thanks for McAllister's tutelage on the best method for growing wheat, which Leschi and Quiemuth had begun to plant on the farm they shared a few miles away at Muck Creek.

Leschi became even more entwined with the whites encroaching on his tribal homeland when Charles H. Eaton, a neighboring farmer from Oswego County, New York, and ten years younger than himself, took Leschi's only daughter, Kalakala, as his live-in lover. Her tribal name (meaning "Flying Bird") was a mouthful for Eaton, who chose to call her Jenny. The couple had twin daughters in 1851 and a son two years later, Eaton family documents show, but like a number of white settlers who were enjoying the companionship of native women, Eaton would not dignify her by taking wedding vows in the manner of his own race or hers.

Although tribal members often gained social standing when their daughters married whites, there is ample reason to suspect that Leschi, like other fathers (Indian or otherwise) in his predicament, felt demeaned—and his standing in the native community thus degraded—by Eaton's failure to sanctify the relationship. In February 1854, Washington territorial law officers dragged Eaton into the U.S. District Court in Thurston County, his home jurisdiction, on an indictment that he "did live and cohabit in a state of fornication with an Indian woman, named Jenny, being then and there in an unmarried state, against the peace and dignity of the Territory of Washington." The sole witness mentioned in the indictment was James McAllister, who may have been asked to testify by his friend Leschi, eager to have the white man's government force his daughter's lover to make her a respectable woman. No surviving record of the outcome of the case has been found in the Washington territorial court archives, but Eaton family records show that Charles and Jenny later moved east to Yakima Country and had two more children—evidence suggesting that the fornication charge was dropped after Eaton agreed to marry Jenny. But the underlying Eaton-Leschi tension was not resolved, as events in October 1855 would make clear.

Despite Leschi's skills and accomplishments, he had not been embraced by his tribe as its foremost leader and formally designated chief of the Nisquallies. One likely reason is that the title did not carry the meaning, prestige, or authority among tribal members that were attributed to it by white society used to a hierarchal social structure. For another, the informal title of Nisqually chief did not become vacant until the death of Laghlet in 1849, when Leschi was forty-one. While it was not a heredi-tary title, one of Laghlet's three sons would have been the most likely consensual choice by the headmen of the confederated Nisqually vil-lages. Laghlet's oldest son, the handsome Weymoch ("Fighting Man"), was unfortunately known to be more accomplished as a vagabond lover than a leader or fighter—or much of anything else—and his two brothers were nearly as disreputable. The tribe, evidently, had been getting along well enough without a reigning chief, as it had done for extended periods in the past, and Leschi, secure in his standing both within and outside the tribe, had no need to step forward and campaign for the honorific title. Instead, it would soon be pressed upon him.

FOR A WEST POINT MAN, Isaac Stevens had little fondness for cere-monial spit and polish, much preferring sturdy, unfussy garb suited to a man on the go and partial to fieldwork. But on the last day of February 1854, the governor donned a frock coat to address the first-ever session of Washington Territory's newly chosen legislature.

For the celebratory event, Stevens ginned up his rhetoric and, as he had done less grandly on the day he arrived in Olympia, heralded the lim-itless commercial promise of Washingtonians' land of natural plenty. Through their verdant, variegated countryside, a place of dramatically contrasting vistas, would flow "the highway of the trade of nations." The territory was in urgent need of federal funds to build wagon roads and river crossings that would facilitate new settlement and allow bountiful harvests and products to be delivered to a waiting world. And the rail-road, whose pathway Stevens had just mapped, would come someday soon and exponentially accelerate the development of the Northwest.

But first, the new governor stressed, Indian title to the land had to be formally voided so that settlers' Donation Act claims could be certified. His intention, Stevens made clear, was to obtain title to all the Indian land in the territory excepting only "such portions as are indispensable to their comfort and subsistence." In achieving this goal, the governor reassured the lawmakers, he expected the cooperation of the natives, whom he called "a docile, harmless race, disposed to obey the laws and be good members of the State." He asked the legislature to petition Congress promptly for authority—to be exercised by the governor—to conduct treaty negotiations and survey the whole territory so that tribal reservations could be accurately drawn and white settlement quickly expanded once the treaties were in place. Then, in case anyone doubted his intent to shut down the Hudson's Bay Company, he disparaged Tolmie's enterprise as "a foreign corporation, usurping a large portion of our trade," and charged that its property claims were "so vague and uncertain . . . that they must necessarily give rise to many disputes between the Company and the settlers, and tend to retard the settlement of many portions of the territory." The Bay's right to continue trading with the Indians, the governor added as a reminder to Tolmie of his resolve, was not recognized "and will no longer be allowed." He stopped short, though, of saying if or how he would enforce his edict.

When spring arrived, Stevens appointed his young, well-mannered territorial secretary, Charles Mason, as acting governor, and traveled to Washington, D.C., to meet with his federal superiors and lobby Congress. The capital was caught up in the intensifying fight over slavery, then focused on the two newly created heartland territories of Kansas and Nebraska, whose settlers would be allowed to decide for themselves if the iniquitous practice was to be permitted on their soil. Faced with such overriding distractions, Stevens reapproached a powerful ally he had previously cultivated—Stephen Douglas, another "Little Giant" like himself and architect of the Kansas-Nebraska Act—and won his renewed backing. Though few in Congress were worrying about remote Washington Territory, its governor managed to wangle reimbursement for his personal outlay to complete the Northern Pacific Railway Survey and funding for the construction of primary roads, plus an allocation of $145,000 to conduct treaty council sessions with the natives in his jurisdiction. His spirits lifted, Stevens returned to Puget Sound toward the end of the year, now joined by his wife, their four children, and an Irish nursemaid.

Meg Stevens, a Newport socialite whose husband had spared her the rigors of military outposts, was naturally apprehensive over the family's transcontinental relocation. On first sight of Olympia, the grubby little territorial capital that was her new home, her "heart sank with bitter disappointment," she wrote to her sisters. But she was no hothouse orchid. Meg was soon riding her horse along the shore of Puget Sound and before long quelled her distress over the high price of food and the frequent sight of uncouth natives. She brought a polished grace note to the ball given in her honor, and became the center of the capital's social set, drawn largely from the wives of officers stationed at Fort Steilacoom. She would also form an intellectual bond, and perhaps an emotional one, with Charles Mason, whose wire-framed spectacles gave him a scholarly appearance but did not hide his good looks.

Governor Stevens, his political future on the line, now directed his burning energy toward one goal: persuading the natives to accept treaties—the Indians called such white men's devices "talking papers"— that were tantamount to complete acquiescence. He was determined not to repeat the mistake of his gubernatorial counterpart in the Oregon Territory who had won the cession of 7.5 million acres of tribal land for $200,000 in money and goods, only to have the U.S. Senate fail to ratify the treaties for having granted the natives overly generous reservations. But if he pushed the tribes in his territory too hard, Stevens knew, he risked igniting a violent response that he was nearly powerless to counter in the short run. His basic problem, of course, was the severity of the American government's proposal—it was a demand, really, no matter how blandly worded—and the expectation by the Pierce administration that the Indians would just have to bow to it.

For centuries, millennia actually, the local tribes in Stevens's bailiwick had been used to living well and peaceably off the land, moving about unimpeded, communing with their spirits, heeding the diurnal and seasonal rhythms of nature, and thriving—until the recent arrival of the palefaces. The King George men, at least, had been respectful of the tribes; the Bostons, almost not at all, treating the natives' very presence as an annoyance, if not downright repellent. All around the tribes now were the sights and sounds of white Americans poaching on their homelands, fencing off choice acreage, and wielding rifles that warned the Indians not to interfere. Since the U.S. government had signed the talking paper with the British representatives eight years earlier, all of the land from the Whulge to the natives' revered, snowcapped Tahoma (and far beyond in every direction) was said to be under the sway of the faraway Great White Father. It was he who allowed the Bostons to enter Indian Country. He had sent few soldiers to protect them, restrain them, or drive away the tribes they encountered, but the settlers nevertheless came—and kept on coming. Now here was their first governor, a stumpy princeling with a swagger, whose messengers were beginning to visit tribal villages, urging the Indians to attend council meetings, where they would be expected to give up their right to occupy their long-held portion of the earth and hand it over to the whites—to *sell* them something that belonged only to the Creator! The idea could only have stunned and angered a man like Leschi. Perhaps, though, the whites would prove gen-

erous and make adequate provision for the Nisquallies and their neighbors so all might live side by side in harmony.

Americans, from the beginning and throughout much of their history,
were a warrior people when dealing with those who stood in their path.
Generosity toward the Indians as conceived of by the soldierly Isaac
Stevens meant sparing them from annihilation provided they were properly abject. All he asked in return was full compliance with his orders,
however harsh they might seem to the natives. But could he gain his end
without resort to military force?

Given his minimal exposure to and understanding of the native culture, Stevens relied on a three-man team to prepare the way for his direct
dealing with the tribes. Its heaviest thinker was George Gibbs, whom
Stevens had assigned to report back to him on the location, languages,
membership, and cultural affinities of the tribes in the territory so they
could be compressed compatibly into the fewest and smallest possible
reservations. To add muscle to the team, Gibbs was joined by Mike Simmons, who was not given to mincing words with the natives. Assisting
them was Frank Shaw, then twenty-five and well acquainted with—
though not overly fond of—Indians. Shaw would become Stevens's most
loyal enforcer. He had fought under his father's command in the Cayuse
War after the Whitman Massacre and picked up the Chinook jargon as
well as the more complex Salish languages. Stevens made him a freewheeling special agent in the Indian service and his primary interpreter at
the treaty councils due to begin soon.

The treaty team's mission, undertaken during the autumn of 1854,
was to tour the tribal homelands, advise the natives that the new governor
would soon invite them to powwows to learn about the new living conditions the Great White Father would mercifully offer them, and convince
them why it was in their interest to accept the summons. It was not an
easy sell, even when sweetened by the promise of a feast to be given in
their honor by the governor and the distribution of gifts from him at each
council session. In circuiting the tribal villages, Stevens's three traveling
ambassadors took the position that the governor's purpose was to honor
the tribes, to recognize their long occupancy of the land, and to reward
them with money, useful goods, and the white men's mechanical skills in
fair exchange for their making room for the more advanced and masterful
race. The whites would soon be arriving in overwhelming numbers, with
their firearms, plows, and the terrifying iron horse, building sawmills and
roads, and spreading their deadly diseases. Attempting to challenge this

irresistible wave of settlers would prove disastrous for the natives, for no one could halt the tide of history. How much wiser it would be for the Indians to accept the hand of friendship from the Bostons, along with the places to be reserved for them beyond the reach of white molestation, than to be pointlessly destroyed.

Most of the natives who heard them speak that way told Stevens's missionaries that they would hear out his proposals. At least he was coming among them to talk.

AS STEVENS took up his mission, he was guided by the new treaty-making policy that Congress had lately adopted after forging its great 1850 Compromise. The change invited westward expansion despite the still smoldering dispute over how much American territory would be open to the practice of slavery.

The new prototype for advancing the frontier was the Fort Laramie Treaty of 1851, which, like those before it, offered the Indians—theoretically, anyway—a pair of benefits: protection from extermination or ceaseless abuse by the settlers (provided the natives refrained from scalping and other brutal reprisals against the whites) and instruction in agricultural and other vocational skills and social habits that would allow the Indians to become self-sufficient and eventually assimilable into mainstream America if they so chose. But the Fort Laramie pact scuttled the prior policy of removing the Indians from desirable terrain and shipping them west to far-off, loosely demarcated wilderness regions termed simply "Indian Country." In exiling the natives beyond the pale of civilization, this now discarded policy, according to the thinking of George Manypenny, President Pierce's overseer of Indian affairs, had served only "to confirm [the Indian] in his savage habits and pursuits" and thus exclude him from "the example and influence of the industrious pioneer." Besides, the sudden settlement of the Pacific coast, with its accompanying inland and eastward incursions by whites, was causing a steady contraction of the marginal places to which the natives could be banished.

The new treaties, starting with the one signed at Fort Laramie and others that Manypenny negotiated with tribes west of the Missouri River soon after taking office in 1853, departed from the earlier ones in several notable ways. In return for giving up their ancestral homelands, compliant Indians were to be assigned to small, surveyed reservations, putatively off-limits to whites, and provided with limited welfare benefits;

there would be no further removals to some vaguely demarcated Indian Country. At some future time, furthermore, the reservations might be divided into free family allotments of a "quarter section," or 160 acres, similar to but only half as generous as the Oregon Land Donation Act grants for whites.

If honestly formulated to benefit the Indians, the new treaties were misconceived from the start. Deporting the natives to the poorest, least arable wilderness lands as far as possible from regular contact with white settlers—which was the old removal policy—had been bad enough. Locking them up in tight, bleak, more confined compounds would only exacerbate the racial separation, making it harder, not easier, for the natives to interact with whites, learn their ways, flourish as farmers, and in time meld into the general population. Far from promoting tribal self-sufficiency, moreover, the creation of closely monitored reservations all but guaranteed that the Indians would turn into dependent wards of the federal government after having surrendered their homelands to it. And the eventual creation of family allotments of land within reservations, in order to promote individual initiative in place of what was considered apathetic collectivism, would also lead to a loss of communal solidarity, the foundation of Indian culture. But all such concerns were brushed aside in the new push to solve the Indian question for good.

To his credit, Isaac Stevens was ambivalent about the new policy toward the natives that he was now expected to extend to the nation's northwestern extremity. In September 1854, while still in the nation's capital preparing for his return west to take up in earnest his duties as first governor of Washington Territory, he submitted a plan of action to the Office of Indian Affairs at the U.S. Department of the Interior. In it he outlined a relatively humane approach to the treatymaking process that he was eager to set in motion by year's end. "The great end to be looked to is the gradual civilization of the Indians, and their ultimate incorporation with the people of the Territory," he wrote Manypenny. "It is obviously necessary that a few reservations of good lands should be large enough to give to each Indian a homestead and land sufficient to pasture their [*sic*] animals. . . . The location and extent of these reservations should be adapted to the peculiar wants and habits of the different tribes. Farms should be attached to each reservation."

This approach, in response to urging by the Indian bureau the previous month that he should crowd multiple tribes into as few reservations as possible instead of assigning each to a separate enclave, was a reflection of George Gibbs's thinking. In his report to the governor, who was a neophyte in dealing with the natives, Gibbs had stressed the need for more, not fewer, reservations because he feared that cramming nonhomogeneous tribes onto a single confined tract would promote instability and a spillover of violence affecting adjacent white settlements.

The Gibbs philosophy, however, conflicted with that of Manypenny, who favored the most economically efficient means for carrying out the government's tribal oversight functions. In a reality check on the governor's stated liberal policy preference, Manypenny directed Stevens to consolidate the forty or fifty identifiable tribes and bands within Washington Territory into the lowest possible number of kindred groupings—six or eight would be acceptable—and to assign each amalgamated group the smallest possible reservation. Such deployment would not only minimize the expense of policing and aiding the Indians but also provide all the more land for use by whites. The trouble with trying to apply Manypenny's formula to the smallish tribes west of the Cascades was that they were not separable like peas in a pod but a complex jumble, mobile and widely spread out, organized loosely if at all, and not answerable to any centralized authority—all traits that were likely to make them more unmanageable and balky when corralled. Yet corralling them was about to become Isaac Stevens's all-consuming mission.

The governor delivered his second annual address to the Washington territorial legislature on December 4, 1854. His main message was a plea to the citizenry to "extend to me a hearty and generous support on my efforts to arrange, on a permanent basis, the future of the Indians of the territory. . . . I believe the time has come for their final settlement." From the sound of his words, the arrangement was to be imposed, not negotiated. Stevens did not explain why the nature or the timing of the "final settlement" of the Indian question—a phrase strikingly similar to the euphemism adopted in the next century by Nazi Germany for its extermination of European Jewry—was his and his government's decision to make on their own.

5

Christmas at Medicine Creek

ISAAC STEVENS'S FIRST ORDER of business on returning to Olympia in early December 1854 was to name a formal territorial commission to work out the treaty language and procedures for dealing with the tribes west of the Cascades and closest to the areas of white settlement. The governor, always a demanding boss and hopeful of having the nearby natives under treaty within a month, put pressure on his commissioners to get cracking.

The ablest and most thoughtful of them, George Gibbs, who among his multiple vocations was both a lawyer and a surveyor familiar with the geography of the region, had the key assignment of drafting a treaty text that could serve as the template for the subsequent council sessions Stevens planned to convene. Meanwhile, Mike Simmons, U.S. Indian agent for the Sound, and his junior business associate, Frank Shaw, were to figure out which tribes to meet with in what order and groupings. Because many of them were loosely structured and lacked an acknowledged headman, Simmons and Shaw were assigned, in the course of mingling with the natives as advance men for the treaty councils, to determine who should act as official tribal chiefs, so that Stevens would be able to deal with authority figures instead of an unruly melee.

The level of disrespect that young Shaw harbored toward the natives he was dealing with may be gauged from a reflection he offered in later years:

Personally, I have always believed that there was a great deal of humbug about making any treaties with the Indians. . . . The question was, shall a great country with many resources be turned over to a few Indians to roam over and make a precarious living on, making no use of the soil for timber or other resources, or should it be turned over to the civilized man who could develop it in every direction and make it the abiding place of millions of white people instead of a few hundred Indians.

To have suggested to Shaw that "a great country with many resources" had never been "turned over" to a few roaming Indians—their people had in fact been living there for thousands of years—but was now in the process of being grabbed away from them would likely have struck him as nitpicking. The Americans were on the side of morality and compassion because, according to their government's official rationale, the natives were being liberated from their savagery by being separated from their land.

To begin the treatymaking, Stevens's commission chose the tribes of the south Sound, the ones adjacent to the territorial capital—the Nisquallies, the Puyallups, the Muckleshoots, and the band on little Squaxin Island, a dozen miles north of Olympia at the mouth of Budd Inlet, which marked the southern extremity of the Sound. Explaining why he gave top priority to these tribes, the governor wrote Manypenny, "They form a very considerable portion of the Trade of the Sound. They are good laborers, and are employed in families, vessels, lumberyards, and on farms. They catch most of our fish, supplying not only our people with clams and oysters but salmon to those who cure and export it."

To count the number of Indians who would be affected by the first treaty and to invite them to attend the council session, Simmons and Shaw visited their villages and preached the necessity of compliance. Simmons, whom admirers called "the Daniel Boone of Washington Territory," had been picked by Stevens as his prime Indian agent because he supposedly understood the natives' disposition and was trusted by them. More to the point, they no doubt saw in his strapping physical presence a veiled threat to the Indians' safety if they risked disobedience. Edward Huggins, William Tolmie's assistant at the Hudson's Bay Company's Fort Nisqually emporium, was among those who viewed Simmons as a dubious conduit between the races. He wrote, "I always thought 'twas very unfair to give a man without any education [a] position of great trust and grave importance to the public," especially one like the unlettered Simmons, who "had to depend entirely on the integrity of his aid[e]s to perform his duties." Simmons's level of competence may be gauged by his report to the governor that the population of the tribal bands at the southern end of the Sound totaled exactly 638—an underestimate of 50 to 100 percent, according to head counts that soon followed. The miscalculation likely contributed to Stevens's judgment about the amount of room he ought to set aside for the first tribes whose homelands he was busily planning to appropriate.

Because the Nisquallies were the most numerous tribe among those to be covered by the first treaty, Simmons and Shaw took particular care in determining who among them should be officially recognized as responsible for carrying out the binding terms of the treaty, a formal transaction between sovereign entities. In the Nisqually nation, tribal chief was not an elected position, filled in an orderly fashion; democracy was not an essential element of Indian culture. For the previous five or so years no Nisqually had been even informally recognized as the tribal headman. But the brothers Leschi and Quiemuth, who moved easily between the tribe's "fish people" nearer the Sound and the "horse people" upriver and closer to the prairies, were highly regarded by both tribal members and the whites who had dealt with them. The papers Simmons issued to them commissioned Quiemuth, a full decade older than his half-brother, as chief and Leschi as subchief. Their formal elevation at the behest of the Bostons probably struck the brothers as a pointless exercise, but it served the governor's purpose of capturing the tribe's attention and ensuring a heavy turnout at the council meeting, set for December 24.

The task of fashioning the treaty language had prevented Gibbs from donning his surveyor's cap in time to stake out specific reservation sites for inclusion in the document. Stevens had toyed with the idea of shunting all the tribes on the western side of Washington Territory to the less fertile, semiarid plains on the eastern side of the Cascades, but older settlers, Simmons and Shaw probably among them, dissuaded him by predicting that the affected natives would forcibly resist so traumatizing a transfer. A second idea was to keep the western tribes on their side of the Cascades but to move them all onto a single large reservation about forty miles above Olympia at the head of Hood Canal, a long, hook-shaped inlet on the western side of the Sound. Such an enforced amalgamation of tribes was also seen, by Gibbs especially, as combustible. Bunching a few friendly tribes on several smaller reservations made more sense.

The question of the reservations—how many and where to put them—was paramount at the December 10, 1854, planning session of

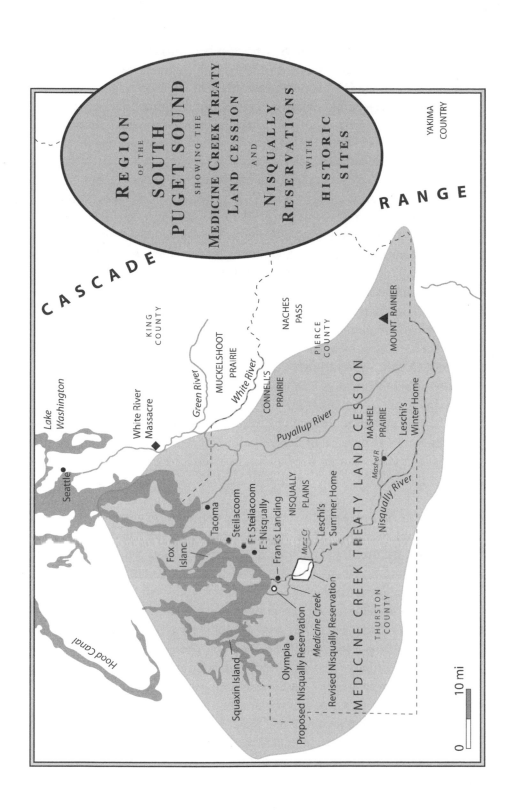

REGION OF THE SOUTH PUGET SOUND SHOWING THE Medicine Creek Treaty Land Cession AND Nisqually RESERVATIONS WITH HISTORIC SITES

YAKIMA COUNTRY

CASCADE RANGE

KING COUNTY

MUCKELSHOOT PRAIRIE

NACHES PASS

PIERCE COUNTY

MOUNT RAINIER

Green River

White River

CONNELL'S PRAIRIE

Puyallup River

MASHEL PRAIRIE

Leschi's Winter Home

Lake Washington

White River Massacre

Seattle

Tacoma

Steilacoom

Ft Steilacoom

Ft Nisqually

Francis Landing

Mud Cr

NISQUALLY PLAINS

Leschi's Summer Home

Mashel R

Nisqually River

Fox Island

Squaxin Island

Olympia

Medicine Creek

Proposed Nisqually Reservation

Revised Nisqually Reservation

MEDICINE CREEK TREATY LAND CESSION

THURSTON COUNTY

Hood Canal

0   10 mi

Stevens's treaty commissioners, who combed through Gibbs's text, intended for all the upcoming treaties. The commission hoped to assign the Indians west of the Cascades to a maximum of ten reservations—and the fewer the better—while diverting them from the immediate vicinity of the white settlements at Olympia, Steilacoom, and Seattle, along the southeastern shore of the Sound, where expanding logging and maritime activity was concentrated.

The minutes of the commissioners' meeting, under the heading of "Probable reserves," begin with these words: "Say three villages, Squawksin, Nisqually, Puyallup. Perhaps all may be removed to Squawksin." The first elliptical sentence may have meant the commissioners were contemplating a separate reservation—but calling them "villages"—for each of the three named tribes. The second sentence may have meant that the tribes could instead be consolidated in a single reservation on Squaxin Island either as an immediate or eventual alternative. But the likelihood is that upon learning just how small the island was—2.16 square miles, meant for close to 2,000 Indians—and unsuitable to settlement, with very little arable land or fresh water, the treaty commissioners dropped the idea. The island would suffice for the small Squaxin tribe itself, but two additional reservations of comparable size, one each for the Nisquallies and Puyallups, were projected on bluffs close to the Sound. Probably because of Stevens's impatience, the commissioners did not have or take the time to pinpoint the sites for these two reservations before the council session began, though their approximate locations were likely set.

There is no evidence to suggest that the contents of the first treaty were shared with the chiefs or any members of the affected tribes in advance of the event. On the contrary, there is evidence that Stevens felt his task would prove easier if the tribes were given neither the time nor the means to grasp fully what was being asked of—and done to—them. How else to account for the unseemly haste the governor insisted upon in scheduling the first council session? Had this been a just negotiation, the Indians would have been entitled to an ample chance to digest all the provisions of the treaty—it was, after all, a transaction of a kind entirely beyond their experience. That Stevens supposed a thorough understanding on the tribes' part would be counterproductive to his mission may be further inferred from his order that the council sessions be conducted not in the natives' own Salish language but in the far more rudimentary Chinook jargon. Salish dialects varied so much from tribe to tribe that regional exchanges were sometimes difficult. Chinook, a half-century-old patois of English, French, and fractured native tongues, was widely used in the Northwest to carry out simple barter or convey travel directions, dietary preferences, or libidinous (even amorous) yearnings. But Chinook was a crude language with an elementary vocabulary of 300 to 500 words—the Salish tongues offered a word selection ten times larger—and was thus incapable of expressing nuances or the abstract social concepts embedded in a document crafted by a Harvard-trained lawyer like Gibbs. Yet Shaw was restricted to Chinook at the treaty conclave with the south Sound tribes. If Stevens had wished to befog the meaning of the treaty he was about to propose—or expand rather than narrow the communication gap between the races—he could not have picked a better way.

THE WEATHER was nasty that Christmastime at the southern end of Puget Sound—rainy and chilly for the three days of Isaac Stevens's all-important first treaty council with the natives.

The place his commissioners had chosen for the session was familiar to the Indians and relatively easy for the territorial officials to reach by water. Fifteen miles east of Olympia and a mile or so from the Sound, the low-lying clearing of about two acres, which the Nisquallies had long used as a meeting ground, was bounded by a clear stream the natives called She-Nah-Nam and a marshy tidal flat. The stream flowed through the alluvial bottomland of the Nisqually basin and ran parallel to the river a half mile away. The Indian name for the narrow waterway signified that historically it had been used by tribal shamans as a sacred retreat to restore their curative powers through immersion in its pure spring waters. The trout there were known to be large and especially delectable. White settlers called the place Medicine Creek. Pioneer James McAllister had a thriving farm right up the way, thanks to Leschi, who had shown him the fertile, convenient site.

Members of the governor's party arrived by schooner and canoe a day in advance to prepare the scene. With Indian assistance, they cleared away the brush at the foot of a small knoll that rose from one end of the council ground, its soaring fir and cedar trees draped with long, straggly strands of moss that formed a gloomy, almost mystical backdrop for the proceedings. Mike Simmons and his helpers put up a large tent on the combed earth to shelter the governor and his commissioners and store the mounds of food brought in for this special potlatch—beef, mutton, deer, elk, geese, ducks, and, of course, the tribes' staple, salmon.

The rest of the Indians started arriving by canoe and horseback on Sunday morning, December 24, and kept streaming in all day—among them entire families, some in colorful ceremonial costume despite the inclement weather. Across the creek from the white officials' tent they set up a makeshift village of huts assembled from cedar mats, and soon the air grew smoky from their campfires. The prows of their beached canoes protruded between the huts, and behind them their tethered horses' whinnies competed with the babble of tribal tongues and the playful shouts of wrestling boys. White observers estimated that about 700 Indians congregated at the site. Gibbs was struck by the size of the throng and, always the ethnographer, by the short, crooked legs of the many half-swaddled infants whose large heads, beady black eyes, and unkempt locks gave them a wild, elfin look.

The proceedings were chronicled by the secretary of the treaty commission, twenty-five-year-old James Doty, son of a former governor of Wisconsin, whose energy and ability had been noticed when he was a member of Stevens's railroad survey party the previous year. Doty carefully logged in the exotic, polysyllabic names of the tribes and bands there assembled, apparently in order of their numbers on hand: Nisqually, Puyallup, Steilacoom, Squawskin [sic], Shomamish, Stehchass, T'Peeksin, Squiaitl, and Sahehwamish. The preamble of the treaty identified them as "tribes and bands of Indians, occupying the lands lying around the head of Puget's Sound and the adjacent inlets, who, for the purpose of this treaty, are to be regarded as one nation." They had thronged the council session in part because the whites, by inviting them to parley, were acknowledging them as longtime possessors of the region. The Bostons, while still relatively few in number, had demonstrated great energy and resourcefulness that suggested their intention to become masters of the territory before long. The tribes thus felt compelled to assemble and hear what fate the whites' regional headman had in mind for them—and to decide what, if anything, they could do about it.

Stevens arrived on Christmas Eve, heading a party of twenty whites that included Hazard, his twelve-year-old boy, excited about witnessing the historic pageant. As the Americans took their places on stools around the long table in front of their tent, there was little about Stevens's appearance to stamp him as their leader. His outfit, as usual, was dictated by practical considerations; he wore a red flannel shirt, dark pants tucked into his old army boots, a long frock coat, and a wide-brimmed black felt hat with a clay pipe stuck in its band. He wore no sash, no saber, no medals, no epaulets, no plumed helmet, or any show of elegance or finery that the natives would have relished as enhancing the theatricality of the ceremonies and honoring their presence. Yet he spoke with a resounding voice as someone who had come not as a beneficent peacemaker eager to bargain in earnest but as the emissary of a conquering race, one who was short on diplomatic finesse and patience.

Indeed, Stevens's expectation, based on reports from Simmons and Shaw and a full measure of his own righteous conviction, was that the tribes' acceptance of his treaty proposal would be a mere formality. Perhaps it was just a pose he struck, urged on him by Simmons and Gibbs, to convey an air of invincibility. His supreme confidence was manifested by the presence in his party of only a single soldier, U.S. Army Lieutenant William A. Slaughter, a popular young member of the small garrison at Fort Steilacoom. The governor's group, moreover, made no show of firearms, probably to emphasize a peaceful intent. No doubt Stevens felt his was the whip hand, so he had no need to flaunt it in front of what he took for an impotent horde. Even so, he must be credited with considerable courage for coming among so large a gathering of natives—then routinely disparaged by many in the white world as "savages"—with such a small and powerless supporting cast yet risking a violent response to his bold proposal to them, one that amounted to an ultimatum. Perhaps his display of raw nerve was intended to awe the primitives. Curiously, several among the treaty commissioners who were on hand remarked that Stevens lacked his usual swagger and even revealed a hint of uncertainty—not surprising in view of all that depended on the outcome of the conclave. His hard-eyed bearing bespoke a man resolute to arrive at a *modus vivendi* without resort to violence.

After an evening of meet-and-greet feasting and interracial hobnobbing intended to ease the Indians' anxieties, the formalities began on Christmas morning. Any attempt to reconstruct what actually occurred that day and the one following is fatally handicapped by a scarcity of documented or equally reliable evidence—and even the documents we have are questionable. A detailed report by treaty commission secretary Doty apparently accompanied the top copy of the treaty text that was transmitted to the Office of Indian Affairs for review and ratification by the Senate. But little remains of Doty's account in the federal archives, only some sketchy minutes, which, other evidence suggests, were sanitized to give the appearance of a frictionless encounter at Medicine Creek. The only book dealing with the event written by a witness to it is Hazard Stevens's adoring biography of his father—and the author, as noted, was only twelve when the treaty council was held. Frank Shaw, the official interpreter on the scene, delivered a spirited address to the Oregon Historical Society about the Medicine Creek proceedings, but it came forty-nine years after the fact, did not attempt to replay any exchanges that may have occurred between the parties, and did not acknowledge the least degree of abrasiveness or disagreement. Seven Indians who claimed to have been there offered at least fragmentary oral recollections of the council during interviews conducted nearly half a century after the event by Ezra Meeker for his valuable 1905 book, *Pioneer Reminiscences of Puget Sound,* and a companion account of Leschi's activities at the treaty council and afterward. The only local newspaper to carry an account of the council meeting, Olympia's weekly *Pioneer and Democrat,* ran just a brief notice that seems to have relied entirely on secondhand sources rather than firsthand reportage. Perhaps the most creditable report offered contemporaneously by a nonwitness came from William Tolmie, who wrote a letter touching on what he understood, from exchanges with a number of those in attendance, to have been the natives' reaction to the treaty. We are left, then, with a collage of fragmentary evidence and can venture no more than a calculated guess about what really happened at Medicine Creek.

It can probably be stated with confidence that the Indians, Leschi and Quiemuth prominent among them, sat in a semicircle in front of the white officials' tent to hear Shaw read out the thirteen articles comprising the Medicine Creek Treaty and explain them, however imperfectly, in Chinook. By one account, Stevens was ill at ease, pacing about with nervous energy as the reading progressed, head down, hands clasped behind him, and listening closely to gauge the Indians' reaction. The tribal chiefs were asked, even as the recitation went on, to draw a rough map of their homelands as they understood them—for inclusion, Shaw explained to them, in a single large map of local Indian Country. It was a project the commissioners could have undertaken themselves in advance of the formal gathering to help them determine the size and site of each reservation to be proposed in the treaty text.

How faithfully did—or could—Shaw translate the treaty from English into Chinook? And how closely did the treaty text he read aloud that day conform to the final version that Stevens transmitted for Senate ratification, especially with regard to the number, size, and specific locales of the reservations to be assigned to the gathered tribes? We have no copy of the original draft to help us determine what changes may have been made in the course of the proceedings. How much of the treaty's meaning did—or could—the listening natives absorb, especially given the novelty of the transaction?

Shaw would later insist that the treaty "was explained slowly by paragraphs, and whenever there was any doubt as to the Indians' understanding it, it was repeated until it was understood by them. It took nearly all day to read and interpret it." But how could Shaw have known if or how well the Indians comprehended what they heard, no matter how many times the sophisticated concepts integral to treatymaking were explained in simple words? Did the Indians fully grasp that, all the other phraseology aside, they were being asked to assent to the surrender of their forefathers' homelands forever? Hazard Stevens's biography of his father claims that the treaty was "carefully explained to them . . . in simple and clear language . . . which nearly all the Indians understood. The Governor was extremely careful to make sure the Indians comprehended every sentence." Hazard must indeed have been an extraordinarily perceptive lad of twelve if he could read the Indians' minds. James Doty made a less sweeping claim in his minutes, reporting that the treaty was "read Section by Section and explained to the Indians by the Interpreter and every opportunity given them to discuss it."

Whether the territorial officials played fair in explaining the treaty to the natives or, if so, the Indians really got it, there are grounds for skepticism based on later remarks by Frank Shaw. He told a historical symposium in Oregon in 1903 that it was really of no importance whether the tribesmen understood the consequence of the legalese being spoon-fed to them at Medicine Creek, because

> there was not a man of note among all the Indians at that council who did not know that they had not a single right that could be maintained by either force of arms or by law. Every one of them recognized that there was no power that could protect them from the encroachment of the white settlers, save and except the Government of the United States . . . [which] had possession of the whole country and could do as they pleased with it.

Shaw's unvarnished words accurately reflected his countrymen's prevailing disdain toward the natives as a breed, disposable at the whim of the superior race. But events would shortly show that, contrary to Shaw's assertion, several men "of note" among his native listeners that Christmas Day believed they had both the right and the power to resist the white encroachment as spelled out in the Medicine Creek Treaty.

If Shaw rendered with proximate accuracy—and truly did his best to explain—the text of the treaty, *assuming what he read them was virtually the same as the version later ratified,* here is what the Indians would have been told:

First and foremost, the treaty was a land deal; there was nothing subtle about Article 1. The nine named tribes and bands were required to "cede, relinquish, and convey to the United States all their right, title, and interest in and to the lands and country occupied by them." Thus, the rough maps of their homelands that the white officials had asked the Indians to draw up during the proceedings would have been little short of weapons for committing territorial suicide. If stated directly and not obfuscated, this demand by the white officials for the unconditional surrender of virtually all Indian Country in the region could not have been lost on Leschi, who, according to at least one native present, soon quit working on his map of the Nisqually lands as requested by the white officials at the outset of the council. The domain the tribes were being asked to abandon stretched from the crest of the Cascades to Puget Sound in a fan-shaped zone that enclosed the entire extent of the Nisqually, Puyallup, and White River basins, totaling—as later calculated by surveyors—some 2.5 million acres or a little under 4,000 square miles of forests, prairies, and rich bottomlands.

In return, Article 2 of the treaty *as ratified* assigned for "the present use" of the tribes, not in perpetuity, three reservations of equal size, each consisting of 1,280 acres or two square miles. Two of them were to be located atop bluffs fronting on the Sound: one for the Nisquallies on a rocky, heavily wooded tract about a mile west of the Nisqually River delta, and one for the Puyallups about twenty miles north and on a similarly timbered and inhospitable site on high ground by the mouth of the Puyallup River in modern-day Tacoma. Little Squaxin Island was designated as the third reservation for the small band of that name who lived there and on the adjacent mainland. For each one of the six square miles set apart for the Indians of the south Sound as their theoretically inviolable havens, they had to relinquish more than 660 square miles to the governor as official representative of the United States. And those six square miles (3,840 acres) assigned to the tribes for their occupancy just happened to be among the least desirable and usable land in the entire region.

The tribes were given one year after Senate ratification to leave their old villages, lodges, and sacred burial grounds and transfer to the reservations. To assist them in paying for the move, the government would contribute a total of $3,250 (but nothing was to be paid for the settlements they were being forced to abandon). Even rendered in primitive Chinook, the appalling inequity of the proposition must have been apparent to the natives.*

Stevens himself soon acknowledged that the tribes were evidently unhappy about the reservations as initially spelled out during the reading of the treaty. In a December 30, 1854, letter to George Manypenny at the Office of Indian Affairs, the governor reported a favorable outcome at Medicine Creek, particularly in view of what he termed certain "disputed points" (his letter did not elaborate on them) that were resolved after the tribes had "in the first instance desired more reserves and larger reserves." This disclosure could have been a reference to hostile Indian response to an initial proposal—a trial balloon, in modern parlance—by the governor to shove all of the tribes onto tiny Squaxin Island, a place without easy access to freshwater fishing, without a prairie for pasturing or exercising their horses, and without open acreage for farming. Yet it is hard to believe that Stevens would have risked making such an extremely punitive proposal, stranding the affected tribes on a speck of an island in return for surrendering virtually all of their homelands to him, and thereby enraging the Indians the moment they heard it—or as soon as the governor's meaning sank in.

---

*A pair of diligent researchers recently suggested that the offer of acreage to the Indians on the first reading of the treaty might have been even stingier than in the final version. In an extensive 2005 article for the *Oregon Historical Quarterly,* SuAnn M. Reddick and Cary C. Collins speculate that little Squaxin Island, by itself, might have been the only site mentioned for a reservation when the text of the treaty was read aloud on Christmas Day. Reddick and Collins base their conjecture on several grounds, the key one being the notes for the December 10 treaty commissioners' meeting in which Squaxin was mentioned as a possible site for a single, consolidated reservation for all the tribes to be affected by the first treaty. The commissioners'—and Stevens's—hope might have been that if the tribes of the south Sound could be persuaded to swallow such harshly restrictive confinement, they would set a pattern for passive compliance that would bode well for the governor's treaty-making with the rest of the natives in his territory. But the mere mention two weeks before the Medicine Creek council session of the possibility of a single island reservation to be prescribed for all the tribes attending is not a sufficient basis for concluding that such a stringent proposal was in fact put forward at the event itself.

We have considerable testimony (discussed below) that some of the listening natives, led by Leschi, did react angrily once the original words of the treaty, as read aloud to them, revealed the severity with which they were to be treated. Writing in the *Oregon Historical Quarterly,* moreover, SuAnn M. Reddick and Cary C. Collins have contended that after witnessing the Indians' reaction, Stevens and his party repaired to their tent to reconsider overnight their offer of a solitary island reservation to accommodate all the tribes on hand. Rather than risking that his whole ambitious treatymaking campaign to pacify all the tribes of Washington Territory might blow up in his face at the very start, the governor probably chose—Reddick and Collins hypothesize—to back off the next morning by offering the tribes three small reservations instead.

Perhaps so. There is no direct evidence, however, that the treaty language as read aloud at Medicine Creek called for restricting the tribes to Squaxin Island alone. Stevens's admission of "disputed points" at the council session might be explained just as plausibly by the natives' immediate rejection of the claustrophobic living conditions they would have had to endure *even if* Stevens had offered them the three small, shabby reservation sites from the start. Consider the fury that Quiemuth and Leschi would surely have felt upon hearing that their tribe was to be penned up on a stony, thickly forested rise overlooking the Sound close to the Nisqually delta and miles downriver from their homes. What would happen to the chiefs' own large herd of horses, the main source of the family's wealth? Or to their homes and farm? Or to their tribesmen living in the villages strung along the river basin? All their dwelling places would have to be abandoned. To relocate on the assigned reservation would mean taking down countless stout trees—and the land remaining was nearly unfarmable, as Stevens's aides would soon discover. Exile to such a place was tantamount to a death sentence. Imposition of such straitened circumstances—whether one shared tiny island or a separate, equally noxious place for the Nisquallies alone—was a total subversion of the spirit of Stevens's memo a few months earlier to the Office of Indian Affairs, proposing large enough reservations with good enough soil for the affected tribes to transform themselves from hunter-gatherers into stable farmers. Hadn't encouragement of such an evolution been declared official U.S. policy?

The governor may have felt that the impact from the drastic reduction in tribal living space he proposed at Medicine Creek would be cushioned to some degree by Article 3 of the treaty. This article, Gibbs's brainstorm, allowed the signatory tribes to continue to "take fish at all usual and accustomed grounds and stations . . . in common with all citizens of the territory" as well as to enjoy "the privilege of hunting, gathering roots and berries, and pasturing their horses on open and unclaimed lands." Even though the Indians' residential space was to be narrowly confined, they were to be free to move about as they had always done for the purpose of feeding themselves and caring for their livestock. Stevens might have hoped this liberating expedient would also serve to relieve the territorial and federal governments of the economic burden of saving the Indians from starvation.

Upon closer parsing of Gibbs's legalese, however, the innocent-sounding conditional phrase tacked on at the end raises doubts. The Indians were free to leave the reservations for food-gathering and pasturing their animals as before—but only "on open and unclaimed lands." Weren't the shortly expected multitudes of new white settlers going to file claims to whatever open lands remained in the region? Wasn't such a prize precisely why they were moving to Washington Territory and why the treaties were being drawn up—to get the Indians off their lands so that Americans could take their place? "Open and unclaimed lands" for tribal fishing, hunting, and pasturage would become a sharply diminishing commodity with each passing year unless the government were to set aside public fishing and hunting areas permanently closed to white settlements. No such provision was mentioned in the treaty, so as a practical matter, exile of the Nisquallies to a barren and remote bluff along the Sound would cut them off from their normal, easy sources of nourishment, distance them from work sites where they could earn the white man's welcome wages, and generally hasten the prospect of their decline.

OTHER SECTIONS of the treaty served only to compound the one-sidedness of the document. Article 6, for example, gave the President the power to remove the signatory tribes from their new reservations "to such other place or places as he may deem fit, on remunerating them for their improvements and the expenses of their removal." Or he could displace the tribes who agreed to the treaty by consolidating them with other friendly and compliant tribes. Or he could, at his sole discretion, break up the reservations, or any part thereof, by ordering the land to be surveyed into lots and then assigned to "such individuals or families as willing to avail themselves of the privilege" of settling on them permanently—just like white homesteaders.

By granting the Great White Father such unilateral power to dislocate treaty tribes even after they had already surrendered their ancestral lands, Article 6 served to make the Nisquallies and the neighboring natives permanently displaced persons, completely at the mercy of an alien power. The seemingly favorable part of the article—the provision that individual Indian families might be given the chance to own and operate farms within their reservation—sprang from the assumption that tribesmen could readily turn themselves into capable farmers prepared to deal with a complex of financial burdens (including property taxes and credit obligations) or lose their land to foreclosure. These gifts of privatized property, moreover, would have the not-incidental effect of breaking down the communal mind-set that sustained tribal cohesion and identity. In short, here was yet another method for white authorities to undermine Indian culture, but it had the virtue of appearing to motivate tribesmen to determine their own individual fates—the ultimate hallmark of the American ethos.

The Medicine Creek Treaty also insisted that the tribes acknowledge their dependence on the U.S. government, promise to be friendly to American citizens and "commit no depredations" against their property, and deliver Indian lawbreakers to white law enforcement officers. Additionally, the Indians were to abjure the use or sale of "ardent spirits" on their reservations, free their slaves, trade only within U.S. borders, and behave peacefully toward other tribes, submitting any irresoluble quarrels with them to arbitration by white officials.

A few drops of honey were added to the brew of hemlock the natives were being asked to swallow. The treaty specified they were to be paid a total of $32,500 (or a little more than one penny per surrendered acre), doled out over a twenty-year period. But in fact no cash was to be involved. Payment was to be made in tools and other practical goods of equivalent value, selected by the government, apparently on a take-it-or-leave-it basis since no remedy was cited in case the Indians felt they were sent useless junk. To advance the vocational training of the tribes, the treaty promised to operate for the same twenty-year period a free agricultural and industrial school as well as a carpentry shop and blacksmithy, with a skilled craftsman to run each, and an agronomist and a physician. If the government failed to honor this pledge, the tribes were provided with no recourse for this delinquency, either.

Isaac Stevens, a man of avowed rectitude, proposed in the name of his government—and on one of the two holiest days of the Christian calendar—an arrangement that transparently victimized a peaceable, innocent people. And he shamelessly insisted, in his formal remarks to his victims the following day at Medicine Creek, that by his swindle he was performing a humanitarian act. For all his religious upbringing, we know that Stevens was not an overtly devout man (how else to explain scheduling the council meeting on Christmas Day?), so he cannot, at least, be accused of false piety. But at Medicine Creek, Stevens engaged in arrant turpitude.

Perhaps in his heart Stevens considered Indians the wretched and doomed refuse of the human species, unworthy of being dealt with in an upright fashion. Perhaps in his heart he felt, as Simmons and Shaw had told the Indians, that the treaty was the only hope for them to spare themselves from the onslaught of white settlers—as if the U.S. government were not complicit in licensing the great westward movement of its people. Most likely, Stevens had satisfied himself that he was merely doing his job, even if it meant cynically going through the motions of earnest bargaining. Good soldiers followed orders, and the governor of Washington Territory was still very much the good soldier, undertaking his mission with unwavering zeal. Degradation of the natives through a coerced treaty, a bloodless form of warfare, was a tactical exercise, not a moral one, for career patriots like Stevens, whose quest for personal advancement fused seamlessly with his nation's drive for expansive hegemony.

But what of the objects of Stevens's pursuit? Did the Indians present at Medicine Creek actually line up like sheep to place their marks of assent on the document? Or might the territorial officials—despite their insistence to the contrary—have committed blatant fraud by falsely or selectively translating for the natives what the treaty said? Or, worse yet, were some or many of the Indian marks of endorsement simply forged?

If posterity is to credit the word of the only contemporary journal to report on the event, J. W. Wiley's *Pioneer and Democrat,* "great pains were taken to express the provisions of the treaty, and the Indians were entirely satisfied," according to the December 30, 1854, issue of the weekly paper. In all likelihood, though, editor Wiley did not attend the council proceedings amid such inclement weather and at the height of the yuletide. His paper's cursory 200-word article was probably based on whatever Wiley gleaned afterward from white officials on hand. Treaty commission secretary Doty likely shared his minutes with Wiley; these stated baldly that "there were no objections made" by the Indians. Frank Shaw, in his 1903 address and memoir on the event, stated that all the leading Indians on hand complied because they were resigned to the white race's supremacy. Hazard Stevens's biography of his father offered no hint of any rancor or dissent that may have surfaced at the treaty council. Gibbs and Simmons, in letters to Stevens soon after the council adjourned, reported encounters with Puyallup tribe members expressing unhappiness with the reservations they had been granted. But both his aides assured Stevens they had told the Indian malcontents that they had had ample opportunity to object to the proposed terms but, having failed to do so, were now bound to abide by their commitment.

What, then, is posterity to make of Stevens's concession, in his official correspondence with the head of the U.S. Indian bureau, that there were "disputed points" in the early stages of the treaty talks and that the tribes requested larger and better reservations than had been offered? Somebody was lying. To determine what really may have occurred at the treaty council that Christmastime, we must consider testimony from those outside the governor's tight-knit circle. Collectively it suggests Stevens encountered a very thorny patch at Medicine Creek.

THE EVIDENCE we have that there was sharp conflict at the treaty council centers on the role of Leschi, whom Stevens's subordinates had urged him to designate as subchief of the Nisquallies for purposes of the Medicine Creek proceedings. His name (spelled phonetically as "Leshhigh" by Doty) appears third on the list of the Indian signers at the end of the treaty; each of them has a cross alongside his name to signify assent. Why, though, from what we know or have been told of Leschi's character and prowess, would he have willingly—or even unwillingly and in anger—made his mark and accepted the crushing terms of the treaty?

Did he, in fact, sign the treaty? Is it possible that Leschi signed it without understanding the contractually binding nature of the treaty? Might he have supposed that signing it was not a sacred vow but merely a gesture of courtesy to please the governor? Written agreements, of course, were not among the illiterate natives' folkways. Leschi, though, was almost surely the most knowledgeable member of his tribe about the dealings of the whites. He traded regularly with them, was said to be unfailingly honorable in fulfilling his business commitments, and for a dozen years had been on close terms with the leading commercial figure

in the region, William Tolmie, who spoke his language and in all likelihood instructed him about the importance of paper documents and
records in the transactions of the King George men and the Bostons.

It is possible, of course, despite his many transactions across the
racial barrier, that Leschi really did not comprehend at first all that was
being asked of his people and how little they were being recompensed.
Terms of the treaty may have been repeatedly explained to him and his
fellow tribesmen, but were they accurately and thoroughly understood?
Were the size and location of the reservations spelled out and pinpointed
on a map for the Indians? Was it made clear exactly what a reservation
was—that is, a place of confinement—and that the tribes would no longer
be permitted to wander at will over the landscape? Did they fathom that
they were getting pitifully little in return for their compliance? It is hard
to accept that Leschi, a man of considerable intelligence and articulation,
did not grasp what was going on and that the central purpose of the treaty
was to require the natives to stand aside for the settlers.

If Leschi truly understood the gravity of the treaty and its likely consequences, did he lack the courage to defy Stevens's demands? Or perhaps, as Frank Shaw later contended, Leschi felt he had no choice—that
to resist would prove fruitless because the white settlers were about to
engulf his race and would treat his people still more mercilessly for their
defiance. Yet the terms of the Medicine Creek Treaty were on their face
so uncharitable, so inequitable, that it strains belief that a self-respecting
and (by his culture's standards) highly accomplished man like Leschi
would not at least have protested the treaty terms and asked for more generous ones. And if he and his people were denied them, why would he
have gone ahead and made a mark beside his name on the treaty instead
of turning his back on the mean-spirited little governor? Would he have
feared that the whites might slay him on the spot? Not likely. Surely the
Nisqually nation's honor required of him and his brother some gesture of
defiance. And the most cogent explanation would seem to be that Leschi
made one and never agreed to the treaty at Medicine Creek. So we are left
with a blanket denial from the whites on hand of any such display of
resistance, while Indian testimony, as we will now find, attests to it. Alas,
we have no surviving statement attributable to Leschi disavowing his
mark on the treaty.

The principal authority for much of the unofficial and unsworn testimony on Indian objections at the treaty council, Ezra Meeker (1830–
1928), was one of the most colorful characters in the history of

Washington Territory and the state it was to become. A native Ohioan transplanted as a boy to Indiana, Meeker set out for the Far West in 1852, when he was twenty-two, along with his wife, Eliza Jane, brother Oliver, and some 5,000 other hardy souls traveling the Oregon Trail by wagon train that year. Upon reaching Puget Sound, the Meeker party explored the region by canoe for the perfect Donation Land Act claim and finally staked out a farm east of Steilacoom. Meeker's fortunes gyrated for several decades while he ran a general store and operated as a wholesale merchandiser—businesses that grew more lucrative once the Bay's Fort Nisqually ceased operation—and became a civic leader. His principal commercial success came as a large-scale grower of hops, which thrived in that moist, mild climate and yielded flowers that when dried were in worldwide demand as a beer flavoring. Meeker's earnings allowed him and his wife to travel abroad and to put up a seventeen-room Italianate mansion regarded as the grandest private dwelling in Washington State's pioneer era (it is still there, undergoing restoration as a museum). In his later years, sporting a patriarchal beard and his old frontier garb, he turned into an ardent booster of the Great Northwest, devoted to preserving the memory of the Oregon Trail with permanent markers as he hitched up his lovingly restored prairie schooner and reversed his original trek by traveling west to east across the entire nation and visiting Theodore Roosevelt at the White House. Along the way he hawked copies of his previously cited 1905 memoir, *Pioneer Reminiscences of Puget Sound,* and its companion narrative on the life of Leschi, bound together in a single volume. In his last years he took to the newfangled medium called radio, recounting his pathfinder days for listeners in the Jazz Age.

Despite the half-century interval between the events at Medicine Creek and the appearance of his book—and allowing for the inevitable erosion of his memory—Meeker's lively account of Leschi's confrontation with Stevens merits respect for its extensive investigative reporting. His findings left him highly critical of the governor's conduct, so much so that Stevens's otherwise evenhanded biographer, Kent Richards, did not even acknowledge the existence of Meeker's book and, like other Stevens admirers, chose to dismiss Meeker as a publicity hound who was baselessly besmirching the reputation of a national hero more than forty years in his grave. Such disparagement of Meeker's volume does not detract from its value or substantiate charges that the author's judgment was poisoned by animus toward Stevens. The reasons for Meeker's disapproval are amply stated.

Meeker contends that Leschi did not make the mark next to his name at the bottom of the Medicine Creek Treaty, would never have submitted to such an oppressive arrangement for his people, and probably was not even on hand when the treaty was presented to the natives for their endorsement on the morning of December 26. Meeker states that he interviewed five Indians who said they were at the scene, all of whom agreed that Leschi defied Stevens during the treaty council. The five witnesses ranged in age from their seventies to over ninety when interviewed, but their unanimity suggests senility had not invalidated their collective memory.

The most persuasive account given to Meeker came from Nisqually tribal member John Hiton, long friendly with whites and considered an upstanding and truthful man, whose family had lived in the same place for generations. Hiton's name appears among the treaty signers. He gains further credibility from his remarks that, while he admired Leschi, he did not agree with him about resisting the treaty, believing instead that it was futile to oppose the will of the white man's government, and did not join Leschi's subsequent campaign against it. He told Meeker that Leschi stood before Stevens, denounced the treaty for stripping his tribe of its ancestral lands, and said that if he "could not get his home, he would fight, and that the governor then told him it was fight, for the treaty paper would not be changed. Leschi then took the paper out of his pocket that the governor had given him to be subchief and tore it up before the Governor's eyes, stamped on the pieces and left the treaty ground, and never came back to it again." Meeker added that he visited with Hiton a second time in order to see if his memory of the event remained constant; it did—and was bolstered by his wife's concurrence that Leschi did not place his mark on the treaty and left the council grounds in a rage. It is not clear from Meeker's account whether Leschi's reputed actions occurred on Christmas Day or the next morning, after Stevens may have weighed Leschi's grievances overnight and declined to adjust the treaty—or did so, but not enough to placate him and other Indian objectors.

An equally vivid picture is etched by Meeker's interview with Shanewa, also known as Tyee Dick, who was over ninety at the time and died not long after their three-hour session, during which, Meeker assured his readers, he went over Dick's story repeatedly to test his memory. By Dick's account, Leschi refused to sign the treaty and told his tribal brethren, "If you sign that paper, I will go away, but I will come back and get what I want," apparently signifying that he would make a fight of it. Dick admitted that he himself signed the treaty because "John Hiton made a speech. This was the second day [it is unclear whether he was referring to December 25 or 26, since the Indians arrived December 24 but no business was transacted that day]. Hiton, he said we sign the treaty, and then we make farms all the same as white man." At which point Dick said that Stevens and his party all took off their hats and cheered, and the Indians began to sign. But Dick held back, he added, until Indian agent Mike Simmons "come and patted me on the back and told me, 'That's a good fellow, Dick—you go and sign, and I will see you are treated right and well taken care of.' I knew Simmons and thought him good man, and signed."

Dick had second thoughts, however, and said he began to feel like a fool for having signed, presumably because he had not grasped the sever-ity of the treaty's terms any more than Hiton had if he believed the reser-vations as defined in the treaty would provide enough land to "make farms the same as white man." Meeker asked Dick if the Indians truly understood the terms and was told, "No, I don't think any of the Indians did understand. Why should they agree to give up all the good land, and that was what we found afterwards the treaty read." Hiton had said that he, for one, understood that the Nisqually reservation on the Sound was "no good, all stones, all big timber, up on bluff, nobody [could] live there—nobody live there now." Then why did Dick think Hiton had signed? "Whites get big guns, lots of ammunition. [If we] kill off all sol-diers, more come. Better sign and get something some other way." Dick, yielding to Mike Simmons's heavy hand on his back, signed but soon recanted and joined Leschi's resistance effort.

Palalla, another of Meeker's native witnesses, claimed that Leschi had torn up the paper that appointed him subchief—"I saw him do it, and then I knew he would fight." Palalla and his three sons also joined Leschi's insurgency. The old brave Steilacoom, after whom the fort and town had been named, met with Meeker at the Medicine Creek council site and recalled how Leschi, taller and stockier than Stevens, had stood ten feet from him and insisted, " 'We want some of the bottom land [alongside the river] so our people can learn to farm, and some of the prairie where we can pasture our horses, and we want some land along this creek so our people may come in from the Sound and camp.' But the governor said, 'No, you can have that land over there' [pointing to the high timberland beyond the creek and overlooking the Sound]. Leschi says, 'We won't take that land,' and the Governor says, 'You must,' " at which point

Leschi reportedly said, "We will fight," and tore up his commission as subchief.

Not all of Meeker's informants were natives. White settler L. F. Thompson, who at the time of the Medicine Creek council lived two miles from the site on the Pierce County (eastern) side of the Nisqually River and was a member of the first Washington territorial legislature, told Meeker that right after the session ended "the Indians came to me and said that Leschi would not sign the treaty. . . . [They told me] M. T. (Mike) Simmons told Leschi if he did not sign it, he would sign it for him. From what the Indians told me at the time, I am positive that Leschi never signed the treaty."

On January 12, 1858, Leschi's most powerful white ally, William Tolmie, lately retired from running the Bay's operations at Puget Sound, wrote to Stevens's successor as governor of Washington Territory, Fayette McMullin, pleading with him to spare the Nisqually chief an unjust fate. "Leschi, I have learned from both whites and Indians who were present at the treaty meeting," Tolmie testified, "protested vehemently there against the reservation originally appointed for the Nisquallies . . . on Nisqually Bay [the part of Puget Sound extending from the Nisqually River delta]."* Tolmie added that he did not discuss the matter with Leschi until the following July, when the Nisqually chieftain came by "to state his grievance and ask my advice." Leschi made no mention, Tolmie said, that he had stalked out of the council meeting and failed to sign the treaty. As noted earlier, there appears to be no evidence—despite Meeker's assertion that "we have the testimony of Leschi himself that he did not sign the treaty"—that Leschi ever denied signing. Nor has evidence surfaced that any of the Indians whose names and marks appear on the treaties arranged by Stevens ever claimed that their consent was fraudulently inserted in the documents.

There is more evidence, though, that Leschi rejected the Medicine Creek Treaty on the spot and, when his complaint was not heeded, walked away from the council meeting. One contemporary American source supporting this contention was a U.S. Army officer, German-born Lieutenant August V. Kautz, a West Point graduate, a Mexican War veteran, and a combatant in several skirmishes to subdue native uprisings

---

*Tolmie's use of the words "the reservation originally appointed for the Nisquallies" and placement of it on the shore of the Sound close by the river delta throws into further doubt the Reddick-Collins speculation that Stevens had at first offered Squaxin Island as the sole reservation for all the tribes convened at Medicine Creek.

across Washington Territory. Wounded in combat with the Indians, Kautz
was assigned to Fort Steilacoom, where he was named quartermaster and
performed other administrative duties. While there, Kautz, later a Union
general in the Civil War, heard a report, which he relayed to Governor
McMullin, from one of Leschi's tribesmen, Kanasket, who said he was at
the Medicine Creek council and "cognizant of the miserable piece of fir
timber that was given to the Nisquallies. He saw how Leschi was spurned
when he spoke up and protested. They [apparently referring to the whites
in Stevens's party but perhaps to some of his fellow Indians as well] told
him to go away. 'You are half Klickitat [Leschi's mother's tribe, which
was not part of the treaty], you have nothing to say.' "

Among latter-day whites who offered evidence that Leschi had vocif-
erously opposed the treaty at Medicine Creek was James Wickersham,
who had come to the Puget Sound region from Illinois while a teenager in
the 1870s, practiced law, and at the age of twenty-seven was elected
municipal probate judge for the booming railroad town of Tacoma. Wickersham, later a member of the Washington State House of Representatives before being appointed federal district judge for the territory of
Alaska, wrote a paper presented to the Tacoma Academy of Science in
October 1893 in which he reported on a visit he had made to the
Nisqually reservation in August of the previous year, in the course of
which he met Quiemuth's son, George Leschi (who had taken his uncle's
name to help perpetuate his memory). Through George he was introduced to a Nisqually elder named Buyachlt, called Luke by the whites.
Luke said he was at Medicine Creek and took an active part in the meeting, though his name is not among the treaty signers. Some Indians present would not sign, Luke told Wickersham, because the reservations
offered them failed to include prairie grasslands. Instead, Luke claimed,
they were offered a steamer, a sawmill, cattle, horses, mules, sheep, dogs,
and 100 cooking stoves—the kind of inducement that Simmons or someone else in the Stevens party might have hinted at, though no such sweet-
eners were mentioned in the treaty itself. At any rate, Leschi, Quiemuth,
and their brother-in-law, Stahi, among others, departed from the council
grounds, according to Luke, without having signed the treaty.

In 1917, a dozen years after Meeker's book appeared, the Smithsonian Institution sent Arthur Ballard, a field researcher from its National
Anthropological Archives, to conduct interviews at the Nisqually reservation. He talked with, among others, Charlie Martin, better known as
Nisqually Charlie, who came from the same Mashel River neighborhood

where Leschi made his home and farmed. Well into his eighties at the time, Charlie was said to have described the outcome at Medicine Creek this way: "When our parley with the Bostons was seen to be fruitless and it was made plain that there would be no agreement . . . Leschi and his brother and the other chiefs, I with them, got up and left. Leschi did not sign the treaty, and Quiemuth did not. Neither did the others." The last survivor to attend the Medicine Creek council and have his memories of it recorded was a Puyallup tribe member known as Wapato John, who was deposed in a 1927 federal court case, *Duwamish et al. Indians v. U.S.,* dealing with a land title dispute. John said he had been brought to the treaty session by his father, Hinuk, and saw him sign the treaty—his name is among the signatories listed—but added, "The one they call[ed] the head chief, Leschi, didn't sign the treaty."*

This considerable body of testimony constitutes the unstated answer to the rhetorical question Meeker's book poses in light of Leschi's reported intelligence and high standing in both the native and white communities:

Is it at all possible that as shrewd a businessman as Leschi had proved himself to be, would sign away his home, and agree to give up everything, and in company with four or five hundred Indians go upon a reservation of two section[s] (1,280 acres) of heavy timberland bordering on the salt water, where the soil was sterile, the timber so dense he could not even build a home without great labor of clearing off the tall giant trees likely to crush it, and finally where no pasturage existed on the reservation or even anywhere near it where he could keep his herds? . . .

To my mind the fact is abundantly proven that the Indians strenuously objected to have all their land taken from them save a small area of heavily timbered upland, totally unfit for cultivation; that the Governor stubbornly refused to give way an inch, but insisted that they must submit to his will, and that not only did Leschi not sign the treaty, but many others whose names are attached as signers did not sign, or give their assent.

*Although his older brother had been designated by the whites as the head chief for the purpose of conducting the Medicine Creek treaty council, Leschi was the more assertive of the two and soon afterward emerged as the ranking Nisqually leader, probably explaining why the speaker remembered him as "head chief."

Among modern-day Nisquallies, Meeker's assessment is taken for gospel. Tribal historian Cecilia S. Carpenter, in her 2002 book, *The Nisqually, My People,* states flatly, "Leschi refused to sign and left the treaty grounds in protest." Among nontribal commentators there is more caution. Professor Charles Wilkinson of the University of Colorado, a leading scholar on Native American law and history and the development of the West, writes in his 2000 book, *Messages from Frank's Landing: An Account of Salmon, Treaties and the Indian Way,* that Leschi "may have refused to sign the treaty altogether." Murray Morgan, in *Puget's Sound,* is careful to attribute Leschi's reported refusal to Indian sources and claims.

According to his much later account of the treaty proceedings, Frank Shaw said Leschi, on one unspecified occasion (whether during or shortly after the council session is unclear), asked that all of Pierce County and part of adjacent King County be reserved as Indian Country while the natives would clear out of Thurston County, surrounding the territorial capital at Olympia, and move away from the white settlements west of the Nisqually River. "This was out of the question," Shaw recounted without saying why. But if Leschi did voice such territorial ambitions during the treaty council and Stevens refused to budge, the Nisqually's angry leave-taking might indeed have forced the governor's hand. Reddick and Collins write:

> Christmas Day ended badly for both parties to the council. The Americans . . . regrouped, hoping to find a way to pacify the Indi-ans and satisfy the government's mandate to establish as few reser-vations as possible. . . . [T]hey would now need to find other small parcels of unclaimed land where the Nisqually, Puyallup and oth-ers could live. . . .
>
> Probably during the course of discussions that evening, two small rectangles were drawn on a rough tracing Stevens had made of a Charles Wilkes map of Puget Sound, indicating some new proposed sites.

Perhaps. But nobody who was there, native or white, testified, orally or in writing, that Stevens changed the treaty terms in this fashion. The absence of such evidence may stem from the governor's wish to cloak any admission of pliability on his part as a treaty negotiator. Or it may mean simply that Reddick and Collins, while thorough examiners of the record, have here taken an unjustifiable leap of imagination.

About all we may safely venture, then, is that James Doty's "official" minutes of the treaty proceedings were probably accurate in stating that after the document was read to the Indians on Christmas Day—we dare not say "*explained* to the Indians" since those are conclusory words—"at the evening session of the Commission, the draft of the proposed Treaty was read, and after a full discussion of the provisions by the gentlemen present . . . it was ordered to be endorsed" for signing the next morning. There is no hint here of whether the text had been altered to provide more liberal reservations for the tribes.

THE DREARY weather had not relented when the parties reconvened around nine o'clock on the morning of December 26 to hear Isaac Stevens address them. His words, as reported in his son's biography of him, were meant to sound like a verbatim transcript as set down by treaty secretary Doty, but they may have been an amalgam that included remarks delivered by the governor the day before when first greeting the assemblage. Or they may have been otherwise doctored after the fact. In any event, Hazard Stevens reported the number of natives congregated in front of the council tent as 650, about 50 fewer than the day before—inviting the inference that those missing might have joined Leschi in an angry walkout on Christmas Day.

"This is a great day for you and for us, a day of peace and friendship between you and the whites for all time to come," Stevens is said to have begun his upbeat remarks. "We went through this country last year [during the railroad route survey], learned your numbers and saw your wants. We felt much for you, and went to the Great Father [i.e., the not-so-great Franklin Pierce] to tell him what we had seen. The Great Father felt for his children. He pitied them, and he has sent me here today to express these feelings, and to make a treaty for your benefit."

This was the standard rhetoric of the age, infantilizing the native race as retarded, sunk in misery, and desperate for rescue by white charity. Stevens, at Medicine Creek and subsequent council sessions, proved himself a virtuoso in the art of racist condescension. He could have harbored little doubt about who would benefit from the treaty and who would suffer, so the governor was a master of hypocrisy as well. His son's biography insists Stevens felt genuine anguish for the plight of the natives. If so, he must have convinced himself that by imposing egregiously unfair treaties on the Indians and confining them in grim havens, he was nonetheless sparing them a still worse fate at the hands of his relentless countrymen. Stevens's speech went on:

> The Great Father has many white children who come here, some to build mills, some to make farms, and some to fish; the Great Father wishes you to learn to farm, and your children to go to a good school; and he now wants me to make a bargain with you, in which you will sell your lands, and in return be provided with all these things. You will have certain lands set apart for your homes, and receive yearly payments of blankets, axes, etc. All this is written down in this paper which will be read to you. If it is good you will sign it, and I will then send it to the Great Father.

These words leave the impression that the treaty had not already been read to the tribes the previous day, as Doty's minutes plainly state. A possible explanation is that Stevens had made no formal remarks of greeting and exhortation prior to Shaw's translation aloud of the treaty text on Christmas Day, perhaps framing it as a tentative agreement, pending the Indians' response. Most plausibly, Stevens and Leschi had their confrontation on Christmas Day, the governor refused to relent, the Nisqually chief and his retinue walked out, and Stevens held fast overnight, hoping that with the malcontents now off the premises, those remaining would not prove troublesome, so the deal could be sealed.

After the treaty was reread, Stevens, according to his son's version, told his listeners to decide if they were now satisfied, and if so, to come forward and place a mark beside their names, after which they would receive gifts—the lure that had probably drawn many to the council site—and more the following summer.* If they objected to the proposition, they should say so. "The Indians had some discussion," Hazard wrote, "and Governor Stevens then put the question, 'Are you ready? If so, I will sign it.' There were no objections, and the treaty was then signed."

The document, as forwarded to the U.S. Interior Department, listed sixty-two Indians' names with marks beside them—whether placed there by them or somebody else afterward, history will never know—and

---

*According to several Indian reports, many of the natives attending the Medicine Creek council expressed disappointment over the meager gifts distributed to them after the signing ceremony—bolts of calico cloth and jugs of blackstrap molasses.

twenty American signers, young Hazard Stevens at the bottom. His book makes no mention of any dissidents having spoken up on either day; Doty's minutes also assert, "There were no objections made," but whether he was referring only to the Tuesday morning reading or the first reading on Monday as well is unclear. These avowals of a friction-free conclusion to the treaty council were echoed by Frank Shaw in his 1903 address to the Oregon Historical Society. The interlude of nearly half a century may have dimmed his powers of recall; as he retold it, the reading aloud, discussion, and signing of the treaty all seem to have occurred on the same day—he made no allowance for any overnight reflection by both sides. "There was no compulsion or persuasion necessary, as they all seemed anxious to sign it," Shaw asserted. "I stood by the whole time and saw each Indian make his mark." When Ezra Meeker, whose book on Leschi had not yet been published, sharply challenged Shaw's account by writing a letter to the *Seattle Post-Intelligencer,* Shaw replied that "there is not one word of truth" in Meeker's assertion, adding: "I know that Leschi did not commit any of the ruffianly acts referred to . . . on that day or any other day. On the contrary, Leschi acted like a gentleman the whole time that the treaty was being made."

If we reject Shaw's account—as well as Doty's, Hazard Stevens's, and the weekly *Pioneer and Democrat*'s—that all the Indians listed on the treaty endorsed it, and instead we accept the sizable body of Indian and other testimony to the contrary, we are forced to conclude that Leschi's mark and those of others on the document were forged. Shaw and both Stevens biographers dismiss such a possibility as scandalous and totally at odds with the governor's honorable character. Nobody, however, including Meeker, ever accused Stevens himself of having perpetrated such a fraud; any of his aides could have done the dirty deed out of his presence—and at least one of them, Mike Simmons, as noted earlier, was said to have told Leschi that if he failed to make his mark, Simmons would make it for him.

Forgery of some of the Indians' marks on the treaty is a real possibility if we take into account evidence that the maps accompanying the treaty when signed on December 26 probably did not show the true sites of the Nisqually and Puyallup reservations. The maps were almost certainly altered between the signing and Stevens's dispatch of the treaty to Washington, D.C., several days later in his rush to have the deal wrapped up in order to serve as the model for all the treaties he hoped would soon follow.

On the evening of December 27, treaty draftsman George Gibbs, in his other role as official surveyor for the commission, chartered a schooner with Frank Shaw as his companion to sail from the Nisqually delta northwestward up the Sound to inspect and lay out the reservation site for the Nisquallies as loosely referred to in the treaty. According to Reddick and Collins, citing a December 29 letter Gibbs sent to Stevens, the two treaty commissioners were buffeted by a howling storm and forced to carry out their assignment with only a hurriedly drawn, fifteen-year-old map left over from the U.S. Navy's Wilkes expedition along the Sound. They appealed to Stevens to send a newer one from the governor's office in Olympia, but none was sent in time to guide them, so "they struggled through the forest that covered a rocky bluff on an unclaimed parcel" deemed suitable for the Nisqually reservation. Only then and there did the pair of treaty commissioners learn that in order for the two-square-mile reservation tract to include any "good ground," the swampy surface would have to be drained—and even then, the rear of the parcel would still be "horrible," as Gibbs advised Stevens without arguing against the site. When Gibbs and Shaw continued northeasterly along the Sound shoreline to survey the promised Puyallup reservation site, they had to shift it in order not to impinge on already existing claims, and what they settled on was, like the wretched Nisqually site, located at the crest of a heavily wooded hill and miles from any prairie. Still, it would serve Stevens's purpose. Both locations was penciled in on the map Gibbs and Shaw were carrying as the affected tribes' woeful new homelands. There is no indication that the map was shown to the Indians before it was dispatched to the Interior Department with the implication that the two tribes were aware of the assigned sites and accepted their fate.

Even if Leschi had not remonstrated against the treaty at the council session, Stevens learned no later than a few days after the signing ceremony that the Nisqually leaders were registering their objection in unmistakable terms. To attempt to mollify them, the governor dispatched Frank Shaw, who, in a written statement on March 11, 1893, cited by Meeker, recalled:

Two or three days after the treaty was made I rode over to Nisqually and met Leschi and Stahi, and they were very much dissatisfied and they complained very much. I told them if anything was wrong it would be fixed by the Government. They were very much excited and accused me of deceiving them. I denied it and told them that I had told them just what the Governor said [in the treaty]. They tried to get a new treaty. They asked me to report their dissatisfaction to the Governor. I told the Governor, but the treaty [had been] sent off to Washington. The Governor promised to get them other reservations.

Why, though, if Leschi had really placed his mark on the treaty, would Stevens have quickly agreed to satisfy the Nisqually chief's objections instead of pointing out to him that, having given his consent at Medicine Creek, he was now obliged to stick to the provisions of the pact? Gibbs and Simmons, according to their separate letters to Stevens in the aftermath of the council session, had said precisely that to Puyallup complainants who had attended the proceedings at Medicine Creek.

If Shaw was not being inventive in his 1893 account, perhaps his memory was playing tricks on him so many years after the event—and it did not improve with age. In his 1904 statement in the *Post-Intelligencer,* Shaw placed the date for his post-treaty meeting with the Nisquallies not very soon after the council session but two months later, and he contended that Stevens, unlike at Medicine Creek, was now entirely open-minded about satisfying their complaint: "As a matter of fact, the Indians could have had . . . any other good reservations without fighting, because I told them so, by authority of Gov. Stevens, in a visit to Leschi, Stahi and others on the Nisqually river in the latter part of February, 1855." He continued:

> At this interview I discovered for the first time evidence of dissatisfaction on the part of the Indians, as they said they had been in consultations with certain white men who told them that Gov. Stevens did not intend to abide by the terms of the treaty, and that they were being laughed at by the white men for being so foolish as to sign the treaty. I [replied] if any mistake had been made the government would make everything right when it was found out.
>
> I then advised them to go home . . . that the government did not intend to see them injured in any way, notwithstanding what these white men had told them. They promised to do so, and would wait and see what the government would do.
>
> I reported the condition of affairs to the Governor, and he promised to do what he could to make everything satisfactory.

Meanwhile, the treaty had been sent East, and before any recommendation could reach Washington the treaty was confirmed.

This 1904 account only muddies the waters. For if Stevens had told Shaw to promise the Nisquallies that "the government would make everything right," why didn't Stevens act with alacrity to rectify matters after Shaw learned firsthand that Leschi's tribe found the reservation assigned to it to be odious and intolerable? The most likely explanation is that it would have been politically awkward, if not disastrous, for Stevens to have forwarded an immediately revised version of his very first treaty, especially if the proposed alteration provided more generous reservations for the disgruntled tribes. At any rate, there is no confirming documentation that Stevens or any of his lieutenants ever promised Leschi a more generous reservation for his tribe in the wake of the treaty council. The governor, with Shaw supporting him, may have wished to convey the impression that they were fair-spirited and willing to compromise with Leschi, when the truth was that he had no such intention. In pretending otherwise, Stevens and Shaw may have been trying to cast Leschi as the real instigator of any impending conflict, a hothead too impatient to wait for the governor to satisfy his grievance and in blind denial that the Indians' day was done.

SURPRISINGLY, GIVEN the great distance and travel time involved, the U.S. Senate unanimously ratified the Treaty of Medicine Creek just a little over two months after it left Olympia—on March 3, 1855, the final day of the Thirty-third Congress. Great White Father Pierce proclaimed it the law of the land the following month.

It was a time of seething intersectional rancor among Americans over the continuing, indeed still expanding enslavement of the black race in their country—an issue arousing the deepest emotions on both sides of the question. Almost no one, by contrast, seemed to be troubled by the harsh treatment and steadily declining condition of the red race. Stevens and his treaty commissioners shared their countrymen's indifference— or outright hostility—toward the well-being of the Native Americans and acted with cold-blooded inhumanity toward the south Sound tribes. After the text of the one-sided treaty had been drawn up in the weeks before the Christmas parley at Medicine Creek, his fellow commissioners asked Frank Shaw, in his role as official interpreter at the imminent event, whether he could really prevail upon the attending tribes to accept the pact. "Yes, I can get the Indians to sign their death warrant," he later recalled replying to them.

Shaw, however, adamantly insisted that, far from serving as instruments of a brutal subjugation, he and his associates at Medicine Creek— and American nation-builders at hundreds of treaty councils like it—were acting with compassion toward the red race. The moral obtuseness behind such a rationalization is clear in Shaw's ultimate expression of it in his virtually genocidal 1903 remarks, delivered at a time when the American frontier had all but vanished and his generation approached the grave:

> I further confess that I was one of the men who believed in allowing the Anglo-Saxon race to take up the burdens that the Indians were incapable of carrying. . . . I can not see wherein the Indian has been injured. He had lived in this country for ages, and had not made much more impression upon it than a good-sized colony of beavers. He now has his home. He has been paid for all his rights, and has no real reason to complain, unless it be that he is no longer considered a savage. . . . And we who have been in this country from the first inception of the new order of things are beginning to see the fruition of our hopes; and as we are nearing our last sleep we will ever pray that this American civilization may not stop until it penetrates every nook and corner of this continent.

Isaac Stevens did not bother explaining himself in any such fashion or with fretting over fine points of morality when dealing with the natives. His purpose in coming to Washington Territory had been to accumulate political credit and advance his aspiration for ever-higher posts of command and access to the levers of power. "I was highly gratified with the result," he wrote George Manypenny in transmitting the Medicine Creek Treaty to the federal government. He forcefully defended his assignment of three reservations to the signatory tribes by noting that none would interfere with already filed land claims or slow down future white settlement. The reason, he might have added, was that the scraps of land tossed to the Indians were so undesirable that no whites would want them.

To further justify himself, Stevens told Manypenny that because the treaty's Article 6 allowed the President to move or consolidate reservation sites whenever it suited the U.S. government, the governor planned eventually to move the Medicine Creek Treaty tribes onto a single, consolidated reservation, perhaps as early as that summer of 1855. In other words, Stevens and his staff had not only dispossessed the Indians at Medicine Creek of all but a miserable fraction of their lands but had also deceived them into believing that the three reservations granted to them would provide irreducible havens where they could maintain their tribal identities in perpetuity.

6

Blood in the Autumn Air

Howsoever discordant a note Leschi may have sounded at Medicine Creek or sullen an irritant he was proving in the aftermath of that first treaty council, Isaac Stevens rated the event a great triumph. As a commander, albeit a civilian one, he relished the sense of empowerment he had never enjoyed before. Down deep, he remained very much a soldier. As a treatymaker, he was soon back at work, directing what amounted to a military campaign for territorial conquest.

Two weeks into 1855, the governor resumed his effort to pry the Indians' homelands from the 8,500 or so natives on the western side of Washington Territory. Treatymaking without benefit of an armed entourage or ceremonial flourishes seemed only to heighten the challenge for him. This time he traveled by steamer fifty miles up the eastern shore of Puget Sound to Point Elliott, near the village of Seattle. There Stevens's task was to persuade a mélange of fifteen small tribes, totaling about 5,000 members, to sign over to the government of the United States 10,000 square miles of their ancestral lands—from the Puyallup River north to the forty-ninth parallel, the national boundary, and from the ridge of the Cascade Range west to the middle of the Sound.

In his opening remarks at Point Elliott, Stevens again patronized his listeners as "my children." He regaled the natives with a tale he claimed to have told the Great White Father of America about how "I had traveled six moons in reaching this country and had never found an Indian who would not give me food, raiment, and animals to forward me and mine to the great country of the West . . . and they took me to their lodges and offered me all they had." He then prevailed upon the Great Father, he said, to favor the western tribes with homes (as if they had none), schools where their children could learn to read (as if they had not survived for millennia without that ability), and ample opportunity "to catch fish in the waters and get roots and berries back in the mountains . . . [and] to become a happy and prosperous community" (as if they were not already enjoying the bountiful gifts of nature). He then said, nonsensically, "We thank you that you have been so kind to all the white children of the Great Father who have come here from the East," and these same children, out of gratitude, "have always told you you would be paid for your lands, and we are now here to buy them." In short, the whites were repaying the natives for their generosity of spirit by unburdening them of their territory for a token gratuity.

The token in this case consisted of one 6-mile-square reservation at Tulalip Bay on the Sound twenty-five miles north of Seattle, to be shared by most of the tribes, and three small reservations, the same size as those offered at Medicine Creek—1,280 acres each—for the outlying bands. That amounted to 42 square miles of reservation land to be set aside for the Indians from the 10,000 square miles they were being asked to hand over for settlement by whites. In addition, the tribes would receive $150,000 worth of tools and supplies deliverable over twenty years, pending their peaceable conduct, and the same services as provided for in the Medicine Creek Treaty. The minutes of the Point Elliott proceedings record no Indian objections to this arrangement. Several of the chiefs present did have something to say, however, and their words are instructive to anyone who would detect dishonor in the Indians' apparent abjectness.

We can only imagine Stevens's satisfaction upon hearing the remarks of the most venerable among the headmen at Point Elliott—Sealth, chief of the Duwamish tribe, whose sad eyes had watched the coming of the white settlers and the spread of their ravaging diseases among the natives. Their collective effect had eroded the old man's will to fight back and riddled him with a despairing fatalism. "I look upon you as my father," Sealth (called Seattle by the settlers) began his seemingly obsequious reply to the little governor who was half his age. "All the Indians have the same good feeling toward you, and will send it on the paper to the Great Father. All of them . . . rejoice that he has sent you to take care of them." What followed this reported gush of patently false flattery were words that have won a place in the annals of heart-wringing Indian oratory, though their authenticity has been questioned by historians:

It matters little where we will pass the remnant of our days—they will not be many. The Indian's night promises to be dark . . . he will prepare stolidly to meet his doom, as does the wounded doe at the steps of the approaching hunter.

A few more moons, a few more winters—and not one of the descendants of the mighty hosts that moved over this broad land will be left. Once my people lived in happy homes and felt protected by the Great Spirit. Soon none will remain to mourn over the graves of a people once more powerful and hopeful than yours.

But why should I mourn at the untimely fate of my people? Tribe follows tribe, and nation follows nation, like the waves of the sea. It is the order of nature, and regret is useless. Your time of decay may be distant—but it will surely come, for even the white man . . . cannot be exempt from the common destiny. We may be brothers after all. We will see.

More surprising but hardly less submissive was the response of the combative Patkamin, chief of the Snoqualmies, a small tribe feared for the prowess of its warriors. It was Pat's pride that had led to an outburst of violence at Fort Nisqually in 1849. His antiwhite hostility intensified the following year when his brother was hanged at Fort Steilacoom for having reportedly murdered an American soldier. Someone of Pat's vengeful nature might have been expected to resist any attempt by white officials to seize the Snoqualmies' homeland. Pat, though, had traveled by steamer in 1852 from Seattle to San Francisco to assess what he took for an advanced example of the white man's civilization. What he confronted—the sheer number of people, the size of their ships and their buildings, the bustle and tumult of their daily activities in the heyday of the Gold Rush—stunned him; he had seen the future unfolding, and it did not belong to his tribe or his race. Their only hope for survival was accommodation, he felt. "Today I understood your heart as soon as you spoke," Pat told Stevens at Point Elliott in mid-January 1855. "It is good that we should give you our real feelings today. We want everything as you have said. . . . Such is the feeling of all the Indians. Our hearts are with the whites." The degrading words of the vanquished drew three cheers from the victors' party.

Discontent lurked, however, among the more distant tribes of the upper White River region who resented the mandated transfer far from their homeland in the deep forest to a coastal reservation to be shared with the sharp-elbowed Snoqualmies. The White River tribes' grievance, unlike Leschi's, remained covert, and Stevens, believing he had won another rich prize using only words as his weapons, pushed on through the stormy January weather. But at his next stop, to deal with 1,200 or so natives occupying some 3,000 square miles between the western shore of the Sound and the Olympic Mountains, the governor drew a less welcoming response.

The tribes and bands covered by the Treaty of Point No Point were offered a single six-square-mile reservation at the mouth of the Skokomish River, which emptied into the Sound about thirty-five miles north of Olympia. The price was $60,000 in goods, to be dispensed over the usual twenty-year period, plus $6,000 to improve the reservation. After Stevens offered his now practiced words of fulsome benevolence, a tribal elder rose and told him off:

> I wish to speak my mind about selling the land. Great chief, what shall we eat if we do so? Our only food is berries, deer, and salmon. Where, then, shall we find these? I don't want to sign away all my land. Take half of it, and let us keep the rest. I am afraid that I shall become destitute and perish for want of food. I don't like the place you have chosen for us to live on. I am not ready to sign that paper.

Another brave arose and said, "I do not want to leave my old home and my burying ground. I am afraid I shall die if I do." Then the head chief of the Skokomish, an old man, stood and said, "I do not want to sell my land because it is valuable. The whites pay a great deal for a small piece, and they get money by selling the sticks [timber]. Formerly the Indians slept, but the whites came among them and woke them up, and we now know that the lands are worth much."

A member of the Clallam band had a different complaint: he did not want to live on the same reservation with the Skokomish people. The Clallam chief, improbably known among the whites as the Duke of York, was a more neighborly and compliant sort, asserting:

> I have heard the paper read, and since I have understood Governor Stevens, particularly since I have been told I can look for food where I please, and not in one place only. Formerly the Indians were bad toward each other, but Governor Stevens has made them

agree to be friends. Before the whites came, we were always poor; since then we have earned money, and got blankets and clothing. I hope the governor will tell the whites not to abuse the Indians, as many are in the habit of doing, ordering them to go away, and knocking them down.

Others sided with the Clallam chief, allowing Stevens and his aides to pass the night among the natives to press the case for compliance. The treaty provided for housing, the governor said falsely, and the continued right to gather food as before—also untrue, strictly speaking—along with schooling and medical assistance and a prohibition against firewater. The Great Father was good to his children, Stevens assured his presumed infantile audience, and had no wish to steal their lands. This deceit proved potent. The next day saw the reluctant natives arrive bearing a white flag. "My heart is white," said the Duke of York, having won over the dissidents and waving his ensign, "so are those of my people, and we will never stain it with blood."

Stevens's next prey, the 600-member Makah tribe at Neah Bay at the northwest corner of the Olympic Peninsula, had a similarly narrow notion of freedom. Theirs was a forbidding landscape of rocky, sterile soil, with an annual rainfall in excess of 100 inches; their orientation was entirely seaward. So long as the U.S. officials allowed their bold sailors and whalers to venture fifty or more miles into the Pacific to provide sustenance for the tribe, the Makahs were willing to accept a small reservation and the governor's $30,000 of goods.

Stevens's powers of persuasion ran out when he wound up his treaty-making swing trying to entice the Quinault and Chehalis tribes in the sparsely settled southwest corner of his territory to accept reservation life. They objected to the whites' selection of some among them to serve as chiefs for negotiating a treaty—all tribal members were equal, they insisted, and chiefs were honored for their bravery and physical skill, not for political conjuring. Nor did they want to be told with whom they had to share a reservation or how much of their land they had to give up without a reason to the predatory whites. It was too wide a gap for Stevens to bridge with verbal voodoo—and no military might at his disposal. He would have to tend to the holdouts later.

Still, it had been a triumphal six-week tour. The nervy, smooth-talking governor had dispossessed the natives of 20,000 square miles without firing a shot. In return, the Indians were given nine reservations totaling about 93 square miles and promised $300,000 in hardware over the next two decades and a few vocational services. The U.S. government was subject to no penalties if it welshed on any of its promises.

Most people in Olympia were impressed by the energy, resolve, and speed with which their territorial governor had acted. Neither he nor they, though, were sensitive to the extent and depth of the rancor his words and deeds left behind. Stevens's haste and want of caution had "utterly precluded the possibility of any knowledge of the tribes or their wants, suitableness of their reservations or consultation with their head men," Ezra Meeker wrote in his long study of Leschi, and argued that the treaties were an ultimatum, not a negotiated agreement. Even Stevens biographer Kent Richards was critical of his subject's razzle-dazzle diplomacy, noting that "despite Stevens's constant assertion to the contrary, the Indians were not his children, and he did not always understand (or try to appreciate) their desires—or their best interests."

NONE OF THE TREATIES Stevens had extracted from the tribes of western Washington Territory that winter, aside from the Medicine Creek agreement, was ratified by the U.S. Senate that year. Yet the governor was so confident of eventual approval of all his handiwork that, almost immediately upon learning his first treaty had been unanimously certified, he published an announcement in the *Pioneer and Democrat*. It proudly defined the areas ceded in all four treaties, listed the small reservation areas that were closed to occupancy by white citizens, and suggested that "settlers may take action accordingly in locating claims" throughout the rest of the region west of the Cascades.

A more prudent policy would have been to confirm earlier Donation Act land claims only within the region covered by the ratified Medicine Creek Treaty and to restrict new settlements in the rest of the territory west of the Cascades until the Senate had acted. But Stevens was feeling his oats. He now sent an advance team of aides over the mountains to begin arranging treaty councils with the more populous and formidable "horse" tribes of his territory's eastern plains—the Yakimas under their chief, Kamiakin, and their satellites, the Klickitats and Palouses. Farther east lived the Walla Wallas under their sachem, Peopeomoxmox (Yellow Bird), and their allies, the Umatilla and Cayuse bands, who overlapped into Oregon Territory, and the Nez Perce, whose country reached into modern Idaho.

To these larger tribes, each with a sizable contingent of warriors, Stevens's agents went beyond soft blandishments in urging acceptance of the governor's imminent proposals. The land long occupied by these tribes had for the past eight years been proclaimed the rightful possession of the U.S. government, which now intended it to be settled. Those Indian nations that resisted the Americans' claim of territorial sovereignty would have to be disciplined, broken up, and, if necessary, destroyed, and their lands taken without compensation. No pretense was made of historical, legal, or moral justification for this decree of wholesale dispossession; there was only the pragmatic appeal by Stevens's men that the approaching treaty councils would provide the natives with their last and best hope to strike a deal and ensure their survival against the imminent flood tide of white settlers.

In retrospect, Stevens's strategy seems daring and unduly provocative. He was denying the tribes time to let his hard-edged reasoning sink in, likely because he feared they might use a protracted delay to organize coordinated intertribal resistance, uncommon among the native peoples but by no means unthinkable. Stevens was proceeding aggressively, moreover, without military support or the immediate prospect of any. In fact, the U.S. Army commander for the Pacific coast region, General John Wool, based at Benicia on the northern end of San Francisco Bay, had so few troops at his disposal that he favored a go-slow settlement policy and was outspoken in his belief that white settlers, in their eagerness to displace the natives, were the ones who ignited most of the violence along the frontier. It was precisely this land-hungry breed, of course, whose interests Stevens had been sent west to serve. As he had just done with Leschi and then at Point Elliott with the tribes of the upper White River, the governor would now miscalculate the will of the tribes east of the Cascades to resist him, treaty or no treaty.

WHILE STEVENS was spinning his web of treaties westward and had begun preparing to spread his dragnet east of the mountains as well with the arrival of warmer weather, Leschi was almost certainly not languishing at his Muck Creek home, just waiting for Mike Simmons and his confederates to round up the south Sound Indians for deposit at their stark reservations. At the least, Leschi was moving among Nisqually villages and neighboring ones, pointing out their options so long as the governor lacked the troops and firepower to banish the tribes forcibly.

It was during this interlude that word began to spread across the region of Leschi's sudden transformation from "good Indian," placid and deferential to the white community, to prideful patriot and firebrand, like a native Paul Revere, riding through the night to spread the alarm that the settlers were coming to dispossess every Indian in sight. Some reports had Leschi shadowing Stevens's traveling entourage, secretly counseling the tribes on whom the treaty treatment was about to be imposed in order to stiffen their resistance. Wherever he went, the Nisqually agitator was said to carry a shocking message to every tribe in Washington Territory about the dire consequences of yielding to Stevens's treaty overtures. According, for example, to Clinton A. Snowden's *History of Washington,* Leschi told any Indians he spoke with that Stevens intended to herd all the tribes in his domain onto steamers in the Sound that would bear them away to Polakly Illahe, the land of eternal darkness, "where no rays from the sun ever penetrated . . . where the sting of an insect killed like the stroke of a spear, and the streams were foul and muddy, so that no living thing could drink of the waters." To avoid so horrific a fate, according to this story of Leschi's wide-ranging propaganda tour, he urged all Indians to rise up while the whites were still few in number and force them to back off and thus discourage others from coming. A. J. Splawn (1845– 1917), who lived among the Yakimas, wrote a tome about Chief Kamiakin, his people, and their allies. In it, Splawn noted: "Leschi was to the Puget Sound Indians as Kamiakin was to the tribes east of the mountains. Like an iron man, he sped from tribe to tribe, night and day continuing his harangue about the wrongs inflicted on the red man by the white."

Neither Splawn nor any other chronicler has cited reliable sources for this colorful depiction of Leschi as bringer of dire warnings and passionate pleader for united resistance to white deviltry. By all accounts, though, he had the time, means, motive, and oratorical skills to have done so. His world was coming apart around him, shattering any illusions about the intentions of white settlers. Their new governor was a lethal enemy who had to be stopped before he subjugated all the tribes. William Tolmie and other whites who were acquainted with Leschi noted that he spent much of that springtime on horseback, circuiting among the tribes of the Sound or traveling over mile-high Naches Pass to meet with powerful Yakima leaders, his own relatives among them, and other tribal stalwarts east of the Cascades, where Stevens was expected to host a multitribal parley in June. Almost surely he conferred at length with Kamiakin, the tall, muscular supreme chief of the Yakimas, along with

Leschi's cousin, Owhi, a Yakima subchief, and his son, Qualchan, among their nation's foremost warriors. Leschi's mission, some reports suggested, was to enlist the support of the eastern plains tribes if he had to go on the warpath against Stevens in case the governor failed to provide more generous reservations to the Medicine Creek Treaty tribes. Other reports said that Kamiakin and Owhi had to buck up the weak-kneed Leschi's courage—he had not, after all, been a warrior, a role hard to take up suddenly in one's mid-forties. The tribes of the eastern plains, moreover, needed him now to forge an alliance of braves west of the mountains who could serve as an effective first line of resistance if Stevens should harness military might in his campaign to dispossess all the natives of his territory.

George Gibbs, perhaps better informed about Indian affairs than any other American in Washington Territory, said that Leschi at the time was "a busy intriguer and a great traveler, and was the principal agent in the matter [of tribal resistance] on the Sound side [of the Cascades]. All that summer rumors came in of the Indians' intention to break out." Conflict was in the air.

ALTHOUGH STEVENS was canny enough to know that the presence of blue-uniformed soldiers in his diplomatic party at the Walla Walla treaty council set for late May might alarm the natives, they themselves arrived at the big powwow with an impressive show of military strength—about 1,800 warriors in all. By some estimates as many as 5,000 Indians camped in the vicinity of the two-week-long conclave. The Yakimas and their close allies, including fourteen tribal groups speaking three different languages, were reluctant to attend and sent word they would not accept gifts from white officials with obvious ulterior motives. Without them, the treaty outlook seemed dim, but after Stevens waited anxiously for five days, the Yakima delegation arrived. The governor's main hope for a friendly meeting and favorable outcome rested on the Nez Perces, who were anything but reluctant participants. A striking cavalcade of 1,000 or so of their mounted warriors in ceremonial gear thundered onto the council grounds with a rider in the vanguard hoisting an American flag that had been presented to the tribe by army officers hoping to rally the Nez Perces to the whites' side in the Cayuse War after the Whitman Massacre. Helen Hunt Jackson, author of *A Century of Dishonor,* a well-regarded nineteenth-century account of the plight of Native Americans, called the Nez Perces "the richest, noblest, and most gentle" of Indian peoples as well as the most industrious. Their amicable relationship with the whites had begun during the Lewis and Clark expedition, and by trying to enlist them fifty years later as willing treaty signatories, Stevens hoped to use and reward them as exemplars of orderly submission to U.S. authority.

The governor's ranking colleague among his official party of thirty-five was Joel Palmer, superintendent of Indian affairs for Oregon Territory, on hand because sizable segments of the attending tribes' land spilled over the white man's arbitrary boundaries. Palmer opened the Walla Walla council session by assuring his listeners, stacked forty deep in an arc surrounding him, "We do not come here to scare you or to drive you away, but we came here to talk to you like men." White settlers would soon be arriving "like grasshoppers on the plains," he noted, and, without bothering to tell the natives just why it was that they should make way for this consuming swarm, added, "If we enter into a treaty now, we can select a good country for you, but if we wait until the country is filled up with whites, where will we find such a place?"

Stevens followed with a two-hour plea that was somewhat less patronizing and rather more reasoning than the remarks he had delivered at the treaty councils with the smaller, more docile western tribes. No doubt the white race had brought unintended misfortune to the natives, he said, but it had also brought many blessings to Indian Country that had much improved its inhabitants' lives—horses, for example, that allowed much swifter and more comfortable travel; guns for easier hunting and self-protection; cattle as a dependable source of meat to replace the buffalo; wheat, potatoes, and other crops so that farming could end their need to roam over vast lands to hunt and gather; metal tools and implements for building, cooking, and sewing; and cotton and other fabrics that were softer and more comfortable to wear than animal hides and shredded cedar bark. So, too, would reservation living improve the natives' quality of life, the governor argued without explaining how.

It was not an easy sell. His pitch failed to acknowledge the destructive impact of white settlement on native freedom and folkways, and Stevens needed to disperse his aides among the tribes to deliver a sobering argument of the sort that old Chief Seattle had readily conceded five months earlier. The Great Spirit, or the Creator, or the Changer—by whatever name the tribes referred to the designer and overseer of the world—had never told the Indians that the lands they had so long occupied were destined to remain theirs forever. The Indians did not hold their territory by entitlement, only by good fortune that had left their sway unchallenged for many centuries. But now their period of dominion was at an end, for a more powerful and advanced civilization had come to replace theirs. Only by accepting the governor's benevolent treaties could they salvage at least a remnant of their ancestral way of life—and the sooner they did that, the better their chances of avoiding utter doom. Not surprisingly, a good deal of grumbling greeted their visitors' announcement that the Great Spirit no longer favored his tribal people and that the Great Father of the whites had now taken charge of their world.

For days Stevens faced a level of intransigence that tested his mettle as had no prior challenge in his career. He remained calmer than was his custom, letting disgruntled tribal leaders vent their unhappiness, then responded by alternately lecturing, cajoling, exhibiting his own brand of anger, and trying to play off the tribes against one another so they would not coalesce in solid opposition to his treaty demands. Finally, he saw he had no choice but to grant the eastern tribes far more generous reservations than the meager ones he had imposed on the western side of the Cascades. His concession stemmed in part from the larger membership and bolder character of the tribes attending and in part from the more arid nature of the terrain, making it less alluring to whites, except in regions like the Walla Walla Valley, ideal for growing fruit.

For his perseverance Stevens came away from the Walla Walla council with the ceded title to approximately 47,000 square miles of former Indian Country. He was so carried away with his success that on June 23, 1855, just twelve days after the three Walla Walla pacts with the various tribal groups were signed, Stevens's treaty commissioners ran an announcement in Washington and Oregon territorial newspapers declaring that "the country embraced in these cessions . . . is open to settlement." This further invitation to Stevens's countrymen to file claims to the freshly liberated tribal lands—title to which could not be legally granted to any settler until Senate ratification of the Walla Walla treaties (not accomplished, as it turned out, for another four years)—was a betrayal of the promise that the now bristling Kamiakin thought he had won from the governor not to rush the displacement of the natives.

As a result of Stevens's self-congratulatory impulse to declare open season on tribal lands all across Washington Territory, white settlers soon began trickling into the Yakima, Walla Walla, and Umatilla valleys. The trickle grew over that summer when gold was found in the Colville region of northeast Washington about twenty-five miles below the boundary with British America. It was hardly a mother lode comparable to the California bonanza, but it was promising enough to lure fortune-seekers from all directions. The shortest route to Colville for hopeful white prospectors was to trespass across Yakima land, now sanctioned by Isaac Stevens as open country. A violent response by the natives was inevitable.

The governor had less luck at his final treaty stopover en route back to Olympia to take up his long-neglected administrative duties. The Spokane tribe and its related bands in the eastern central sector of Washington Territory repulsed Stevens's honeyed professions of paternal concern, telling him flat out that they were not as stupid as he supposed, and wanted no part of any treaty that locked them up on a reservation. The best the travel-weary governor could extract from the Spokanes was a pledge not to join the Yakimas or any other tribe that might choose to rain havoc on the U.S. government or white settlers. In return, Stevens issued a prohibition against white settlement north of the Snake River, leaving Spokane Country free of encroachment for the time being.

Even so, within a single year Isaac Stevens had, on paper at least, pacified an immense swath of the American Northwest and to date bloodlessly wrested formal title to 100,000 square miles occupied from time immemorial by tribes he had convinced that it was pointless to resist him. The price he paid was a token two cents an acre, payable over twenty years in goods, not cash. The natives were relegated to a dozen reservations occupying less than one-tenth of the land they gave up without a fight—and most of what they were left with was the poorest terrain in the territory.

Stevens's feat was, by cold calculation, a remarkable exercise of steely will, driven by patriotism, racism, and a generous application of hokum. Could he have chosen more humane means and yet achieved the purpose of the treaties—to thoroughly marginalize the natives? Would a more judicious, charitable, and gradual process have provoked less resentment and avoided bloodshed? No one can say, any more than we can know whether Stevens might have genuinely believed that protracting or otherwise trying to soften the blow would only have made things worse.

It is tempting in retrospect to make villains of authority figures who in their own time were accorded respect for acting in ways unacceptable to succeeding generations. In Stevens's case, modern commentators may be inclined to overlook the realities all too apparent to his aides and contemporaries. George Gibbs faulted Stevens for providing inadequate reservations for the Puget Sound tribes and, in the case of those gathered at the Walla Walla council, for "cramming a treaty down their throats in a hurry." Yet Gibbs, who participated in the process, did not attribute the outbreak of warfare on both sides of the Cacades that followed Stevens's treatymaking campaign to heartlessness or impetuosity on the governor's part. "Much is due," Gibbs would write soon afterward, "to the natural struggle between the hostile races for the sovereignty of the soil." The war's origin was simply "the unwillingness of the Indians to have their lands intruded upon." Frank Shaw echoed this view, expressing it with blame-the-victim disingenuousness. The real cause of the violence so soon after the treaties, he wrote, was that "these Indians saw all the country being taken up and their privileges curtailed from year to year. At length, they imagined their condition was becoming worse all the time." Imagined?

Stevens's arch-critic, Ezra Meeker, saw events in a different light: "The making of the Medicine Creek and Point Elliott treaties was the sole cause of the war that followed . . . that drove the pioneers from their homes [and] the Indians either into hiding, the war camp . . . and more demoralizing, dependent pauper-making camps to be fed by the government." The opposite argument was made by Hazard Stevens, who held that in permanently pacifying so large an area, his father had "frustrated the well-planned efforts of the hostile Indians to bring about a universal outbreak, and saved the infant settlements from complete annihilation at the hands of the treacherous savages." One wishes the younger Stevens had provided some evidence of those "well-planned efforts" by the Indians. And did he take all who chose to fight in defense of land they had occupied for ages to be "treacherous savages," or just those who opposed American invaders? Only a son devoted to beatifying his father could assert, as Hazard did, that Stevens's policy "was one of great beneficence to the Indians, jealously protected their interests, and provided for their improvement and eventual civilization, while at the same time it opened the country for settlement by the whites." Stevens's more reflective biographer, Kent Richards, conceded that "despite Stevens's constant assertion to the contrary, the Indians were not his children, and he did not understand (or try to appreciate) their desires—or their best interests."

. . .

AS THE GOVERNOR kept chalking up his list of signed treaties, however abrasively extracted, he assumed each would be carried out without
resistance by the tribes, thereby ensuring the accelerated settlement of
the territory. That the Senate would approve his land deals as soon as it
reconvened later in the year, he had no reason to doubt. After that the
tribes would have no legitimate basis on which to lodge a protest, and
their dispossession could proceed in an orderly fashion, each tribe exiled
to its reservation—by armed escort if necessary. Resistance, though,
seemed unlikely, particularly west of the Cascades. The treaty tribes living there were not warrior nations. Only a territory-wide uprising would
pose a serious military peril, but from earliest colonial days the Indians
throughout North America had failed to mass their might and sustain the
effort to repulse the whites besetting them. The governor probably lost
little sleep over a few disgruntled chiefs like Leschi.

Even if the governor had been chastened by the fervor of Leschi's
objections and been willing to concede that he had dealt too harshly with
the tribes at Medicine Creek, it was now too late to alter that agreement.
Its ratification by the Senate had given it a political finality all but impossible to undo. Moreover, if Stevens adjusted the Nisqually and Puyallup
reservations to placate Leschi, he would be sending a message to every
other tribe that all the subsequent treaties were open to renegotiation.

The bind Leschi's tribe was in did not immobilize him or stunt his
efforts. By his calculation, the Nisquallies had been dealt the worst hand
of any of the treaty tribes and most deserved to have the inequity
redressed. Rumors about his newborn fanaticism aside, Leschi was
surely no madman, preaching extermination of the whites; there is no
evidence of such a murderous impulse in him. While he recognized, no
less than Chief Seattle, Patkamin, and the Duke of York among the tribal
leaders west of the Cascades, that the whites were too numerous and
powerful to be driven away for good, Leschi still hoped they might be
persuaded to leave a large enough portion of Indian Country untram-
meled so the tribes might sustain their basic lifestyle. As the treaties were
activated, though, they did no such thing. Only spirited objection to them
might change Stevens's thinking and that of his government, and so at
first Leschi had chosen to resist verbally—he was an orator, not a warrior,
so his words took the form of a plea, not a threat. But with each passing
month of 1855 and each new treaty agreed to, Leschi must have increasingly understood that winning a more generous deal for his people from
Stevens was not going to be achieved by words alone. His only recourse

was to shock the whites through an armed resistance movement by the south Sound tribes, united with their more combative relatives and allies east of the mountains.

To his credit, though, Leschi did not give up on Stevens for the first nine months of 1855.

He shared his deep concern about the Nisquallies' unsatisfactory reservation with apparently trustworthy whites like his friend James McAllister and his former employer, William Tolmie. One Sunday morning in July, Leschi confided to Tolmie, still the Hudson's Bay Company boss at Fort Nisqually, that he had begun to fear for his personal safety. Leschi's long absences from the region while he was consorting with Yakima and other tribal leaders across the territory were being noticed, and he had heard rumors, he told Tolmie, that the authorities might soon arrest and even hang him as a threat to the peace and ship off his tribe and its neighbors to the dreaded land of never-ending night. Tolmie urged Leschi to bring his grievance to the acting governor, young Charles Mason, while Stevens was away on his treatymaking drive, even though Mason lacked the authority to adjust the Nisqually reservation. Ezra Meeker writes that Mason had hired Leschi and Quiemuth that summer to serve as guides and interpreters on a trip Mason made to try to quell the growing anger among the tribes of the upper White River over their expected removal to the distant reservation on the Sound that the Point Elliott Treaty required them to share with the Snoqualmies. No doubt the two Nisqually brother-chiefs gave Mason an earful about their own problems and the improved reservation that Frank Shaw told them Stevens had promised but not yet delivered on.

Stevens, if we accept his word for it in a May 5, 1856, letter to U.S. Indian Affairs Commissioner Manypenny, had not forgotten his promise to adjust the Nisqually reservation. The governor wrote that sometime the previous summer he had sent Shaw to meet with Leschi "and received from him and his people a most ready assent to the proposition"— namely, that the Nisquallies would share a newly created reservation with the previously treaty-resistant Upper Chehalis tribe to their south, providing plenty of pastureland for their horses. The new reservation did not materialize, Stevens claimed, due to circumstances that might never have arisen if he had actually offered the substantially improved reservation and, on its acceptance, formalized it in a timely fashion.

There is some reason to doubt Stevens was being honest in his recounting to Manypenny of how Shaw's meeting with Leschi unfolded.

Shaw himself retold the story in his *Post-Intelligencer* statement of January 31, 1904:

> Met these Indians again—Leschi, Stahi, Quiemuth, Tanaskut and others—at Connell's prairie in the fall of 1855, and asked them again to say where they would like to have their reservation located, but they did not want to talk; and I knew then that they had been consulting with a delegation of Yakimas. I advised them to be careful about listening to the Yakimas for they would get them into trouble, and they (the Yakimas) would run away and leave them to do the fighting, if there was any. They pretended to be pleased with what I said, but I knew better than to believe them, and I mounted my horse . . . and made tracks for Steilacoom, where I reported the situation to the officers.

Even if we grant a margin of imprecision due to a faded memory, Shaw's version is substantially at odds with Stevens's letter to Manypenny. Shaw's date is off by one whole season, there is no mention in it of an offer of a larger reservation to be shared with the Upper Chehalis tribe, and the Nisqually response is totally different in the two versions. It is impossible to determine whether either man was telling the truth, or each was trying to make the shoe fit but in different ways, or if any offer was ever made. And the underlying question remains without an answer: If Leschi had signed the Medicine Creek Treaty in the first place, why would Stevens have been willing to renegotiate, given the chain reaction such a step could easily have set off with the rest of the treaty tribes? Logically, Stevens might have been so inclined only if Leschi had *not* signed, because the governor, even with the Medicine Creek Treaty ratified, did not want a popular native leader at liberty, preaching resistance to white oppression. There is no doubt, though, that Stevens was aware of the Nisquallies' profound unhappiness.

When Stevens prematurely declared most of Washington Territory open to white settlement before any of the treaties besides the Medicine Creek pact had won Senate approval, he spurred the influx of gold-seekers into the northeastern sector of his jurisdiction. Their increasing numbers led to the separate murders of eight whites, three of them from Olympia, on their way to the Colville mines in the late summer of 1855. Most were stragglers picked off on Yakima land that Chief Kamiakin considered inviolable until the treaties were officially certified and in effect.

Little outrage was expressed at first as reports of the scattered killings filtered into Olympia. The slain men, like most whites in the region, knew the risks of trespasssing on land still part of Indian Country until it was formally ceded to the U.S. government under ratified treaties. The murder and mutilation of prominent federal Indian agent Andrew J. Bolon in Yakima Country was a different matter.

A large, rawboned redhead and member of the Washington territorial legislature, Bolon had been dispatched to investigate the wave of violent deaths on Yakima land. The barrel-chested official, well known and little loved among Kamiakin's people, reportedly attended a campfire council in Kamiakin's village and promised reprisals by U.S. forces unless the bloodshed ended. On his ride back to the army post at The Dalles, Bolon was reportedly shot, stabbed, and, for good measure, cremated—by whom was not disclosed, although Yakima leaders put out word that a foolhardy young brave, hoping to win prestige within his tribe for doing in so notable a Boston, had invited the traveling Bolon to share his campfire site and slit his throat after the flames ebbed. In blaming a rogue youth, the Yakima elders tried to signal U.S. and territorial authorities that the slaying was not ordered or countenanced by Kamiakin, but the Yakimas were sending Stevens a message all the same.

Their excuse was unacceptable. A pathogen of fear had been planted in the white community. If Andy Bolon, representing the sovereign might of white America, could be cut down with impunity, who anywhere in Washington Territory was safe from Indian savagery? In late September, 47 U.S. Army soldiers led by Lieutenant William Slaughter marched out of Fort Steilacoom headed for Naches Pass and a rendezvous with a contingent of 102 soldiers, towing a good-sized howitzer, that left its barracks at Fort Dalles on the Columbia River a week later; their mission was to find and kill Yakima warriors. The inexperienced and ill-trained force from Fort Dalles, under the command of Major Granville Haller, was closer to hostile Indian Country and engaged the natives before Slaughter's troops could arrive. The Yakimas, unwilling to accept punishment for the deaths of Bolon and the eight intruding would-be gold miners, mustered 1,500 warriors—or more, by some accounts, including Haller's.

At first, the badly outnumbered U.S. soldiers held their own, but after three exhausting days of assaults, the Americans pulled back, with five dead and seventeen wounded, and were lucky to avoid annihilation during their hasty twenty-five-mile retreat. The Yakimas captured the cannon and a famous victory that drew cries of joy all across Indian Country. Haller won only a tongue-lashing from regional army commander General Wool for recklessly endangering his men. Slaughter, advised of Haller's rout and the Yakimas' greatly superior numbers, turned back and made camp in the Cascades uplands to await reinforcements from Puget Sound.

Alarm and outrage over the temerity of the Yakimas surged through the white settlements and was registered in the *Pioneer and Democrat,* which called for bloody vengeance against the barbarians: "We trust they will be rubbed out—blotted from existence as a tribe." Some voices of dissent were heard, however, like that of the *Puget Sound Courier,* a Whig sheet issued in Steilacoom, which attributed the vehemence of the Yakimas' response to the harshness of the treaties imposed by the territory's Democratic governor. Whatever their opinion, white settlers on the whole felt a dire need for protection. The 350 or so regular army men posted across the Northwest were far too few to quell the natives if they refused to surrender their lands and move to where they had been told. Accordingly, Acting Governor Mason tried to ease incipient panic among the settlers by issuing a call on October 14 for the formation of two companies* of volunteer militiamen under territorial, not federal, jurisdiction, one company to be based at or near Olympia, the other 100 miles to the south at Fort Vancouver on the Columbia. With the harvest now in or nearly so, the farmers and mechanics who made up the bulk of the territory's population quickly answered Mason's call and, alongside the U.S. regulars, provided a measure of reassurance in case the Yakimas chose to press their numerical advantage by trying to maul the white settlements around Puget Sound.

A MORE IMMEDIATE threat to the western side of the territory was now perceived in the person of Leschi. His movements among the nearby and less violent tribes between the Sound and the mountains were increasingly believed to be aimed at sowing discontent and organizing armed resistance to the treaties. Having made no secret of his feelings and openly petitioned territorial officials to deal more fairly with tribal grievances, Leschi was a marked man.

---

*A company with a full complement at the time consisted of eighty-five soldiers, seventy-four of them privates and eleven officers, though many operated with fewer active members.

Local concern grew when, in early October, a Hudson's Bay Company employee rode to Fort Steilacoom to report that Leschi was drilling Indian braves on neighboring Muckleshoot Prairie in what looked like military maneuvers. That the Nisqually chief would have engaged in such provocative action within easy view of white eyes seems curious at first—unless the point of it was to signal Stevens and the entire white community that if his grievance continued to be ignored, the Sound tribes, like the Yakimas, would actively—and violently, if required—resist enforcement of the treaties.

Acting Governor Mason could not have been surprised, then, when he received an urgent note written on October 16 by taciturn settler James McAllister. His friendship with Leschi had become strained after the Medicine Creek Treaty and reached a critical point when, as McAllister's daughter, Sarah, recalled,

> Leschi came to our house, bringing both of his wives. . . . He told us that he was going to fight; father and mother both tried to persuade him to remain neutral, and really thought they had done so. The women talked and cried together. He told father that if he would remain on the farm and not join the army, he should not be hurt or his property destroyed.
>
> Leschi said, "I will never raise a hand against you or yours, but if you join the army, I cannot be responsible for whatever others may do, for the Indians are going to fight." And I firmly believe he would have done as he said.

At first McAllister seems to have taken Leschi's threat as bravado, perhaps intended to be relayed to Mason and Stevens and thereby intimidate them into expediting the promised new reservation for his tribe. Sarah remembered how her father had dismissed the Nisquallies' prowess as warriors by boasting, "I could come and drive these Indians like sheep—they will not hurt anything." But by mid-October, McAllister had grown concerned. Sarah recalled how her family heard blood-curdling war whoops in the night coming from the nearby Nisqually council ground at Medicine Creek. McAllister now wrote to Mason:

> From the most reliable Indians that we have in this country, we have information and are satisfied that Leschi, a sub-chief and half Clickatat is and has been doing all that he could possibly do to

unite the Indians of this country to raise against the whites in a hostile manner and has had some join in with him already.

Sir, I am of the opinion that he should be attended to as soon as convenient for fear that he might do something bad. Let his arrangements be stopped at once.

Your attention to the above will be exceedingly appreciated by the people of Nisqually Bottoms. For further information, call, and I am at your service.

Mason, hoping to avoid violence and keep open the chance that Stevens, who was still traveling east of the Cascades, might yet create a more liberal Nisqually reservation, invited Leschi to meet with him in his office. It was nearly ten months now since he had first sent word to Stevens, complaining about the inadequacy of the Nisqually reservation, and in the interim the governor had managed to parley with virtually every other tribe in Washington Territory—but not Leschi's. Under the Medicine Creek terms, the Nisquallies had one year's grace after Senate ratification of their treaty to leave behind their villages, so the passage of time was weighing on Leschi. By the end of the coming winter, if not before, Mike Simmons would begin rounding up the Nisquallies and escorting them, at gunpoint if necessary, to their new "home" on the rocky bluff beside the Sound. Perhaps Leschi's last chance to prevail upon Stevens was to try speaking forthrightly to the governor's intelligent young surrogate, with whom he was already acquainted.

Urged by Tolmie and joined by Quiemuth and, according to some reports, a Catholic priest, Leschi accepted Mason's invitation to meet at the governor's office on October 22. The low-key, nonconfrontational Mason asked Leschi to give Stevens a chance to resolve the question of the Nisqually reservation once he returned from his heavy duties on the road. Leschi reaffirmed his friendly feelings for whites in general and great reluctance to break the peace. Mason seized on those sentiments and urged the Nisqually half-brothers to bring their families from the countryside to Olympia, where the government would provide them food and shelter and they could thus demonstrate their peaceful intentions until the reservation question could finally be resolved. The suggestion sounded reasonable enough, and Mason made no threats about the consequences should the Nisqually chiefs decline his proposal.

If Leschi, Quiemuth, and their supporters had been deceived at Medicine Creek—the evidence remains inconclusive—they were not about to be gulled a second time. Mason's invitation was transparently intended to inveigle the Nisqually headmen into voluntary confinement under constant surveillance inside the white authorities' headquarters. The two chiefs and their families could then easily be detained or held as hostages in the event of a Yakima assault. Leschi, having restated his tribe's grievance, reportedly promised, at the least, to think over Mason's proposal to protect him and Quiemuth while keeping them at bay. Mason would later claim that the brothers had agreed to return with their families within a few days.

Whatever Leschi's intentions, Mason was now importuned by army officials to supplement his earlier call to raise two militia companies by summoning four additional units. The acting governor promptly complied, issuing an explanatory proclamation that he was doing so "in order to make fully secure the lives and property of our inhabitants from any incursions or outbreaks [by] the Indians." The territory was officially mobilizing for warfare, although all the recent bloodshed had occurred on what was still Yakima land and was directed at white civilians and soldiers who, from the natives' perspective, had no business being there until the Walla Walla council treaties were certified by the Senate.

Among the four new companies of volunteer militiamen was one incongruously placed under the captaincy of Leschi's son-in-law, Charles Eaton. Second in command of "Eaton's Rangers" was newly commissioned Lieutenant Jim McAllister, who had not been dissuaded by Leschi's promise not to harm him, his family, and their farm if he declined to take up arms against the Indians. Eaton's company joined with regular U.S. Army troops under the command of Captain Maurice Maloney to form a 240-man force headed for Yakima Country to avenge the blows dealt to Haller's short-lived expedition. That this was a combat mission and unmistakably an act of war was evident from an October 23 letter sent by Second Lieutenant John Nugen of the Olympia militia to Mason that reported, "The Volunteer Company got off in fine order at 2 p.m. yesterday—the men in fine spirits and apparently with a determination of taking the Scalp of every Red-skin who may be so unfortunate as to fall in their way."

Miffed by Leschi's failure to give himself up after two days, Mason called on Captain Eaton to form a detachment of nineteen of his rangers, with himself at their head, to apprehend the Nisqually half-brothers at their Muck Creek farm twenty miles away and bring them back to Olympia. None of the rangers missed the irony that it was Leschi's son-in-law who was being dispatched to bring him in. Perhaps Mason reasoned that, as a relative, Eaton would have a better chance than any other white man in the territory of persuading Leschi to accept Mason's offer of benign confinement as a privileged prisoner. Or perhaps Eaton relished the assignment because there was lingering bad blood between them over Leschi's having resorted to the white man's judicial system to force him into marrying his daughter instead of retaining her as his concubine. Or maybe Eaton just didn't like his father-in-law—it has been known to happen.

When Eaton's party arrived at Leschi's farm, they found a plow left standing in mid-furrow on his wheat field, a herd of horses left untended on the adjacent pasture, and no sign of the brothers. On the chance they were off on some nearby errand, Eaton's men hid in neighboring woods for two days before deciding the brothers had been tipped off, possibly by Eaton's wife, Jenny/Kalakala, who was no doubt torn between love for her husband and filial devotion to her father. As a consolation prize, Eaton seized fifteen of Leschi's horses, brought them back to Fort Steilacoom, and rejoined Captain Maloney's main force as it moved east to Yakima Country.

7

The Territory in Dread

ALTHOUGH NO BLOOD HAD YET been shed by either side west of the Cascades, few supposed the region would be spared for long once American soldiers had taken the field against the tribes on the eastern plains of Washington Territory. Leschi, foremost among the western Indian militants, had anticipated the moment. While showing patience, and loath to initiate hostilities, he had sown the seeds of insurgency by enlisting the staunchest of his tribal brethren—and their nearest neighbors—in his cause. By holding warlike drills within easy surveillance of white officials, he had still been hoping to gain concessions. Covertly, the native militants, whether under direct orders from Leschi or, more likely, by consensual action, had begun to prepare a place of refuge in the deep forest beyond the Puyallup River. The secluded uplands between the White and Green rivers, seventy or so miles northeast of Olympia, offered an ideal haven, only a two-day ride from their villages along the Nisqually and close by the most traveled trail to the Naches Pass through the Cascades, gateway to Yakima Country and the eastern side of the territory.

When Leschi left his meeting in Olympia with Charles Mason and considered his next step, he could not have known how many potential resistance fighters had taken to the woods or might soon be lured to their ranks, away from the comforts and comradery at home. He may have been reluctant, moreover, to assume active command of even a loosely organized force of unpracticed warriors so long as there was any hope of reconciliation with Stevens. Besides, there were too many imponderables for him to have acted precipitously. Could he attract recruits from other tribes? How long would their weaponry and supplies hold out if the Indians were actively pursued by white soldiers? How mighty a force would the enemy muster?

Leschi had never been a warrior, or certainly not a combatant for any protracted period, but he was a skilled horseman and hunter, a keen marksman, and thoroughly at home in the woods. If necessary, he knew he could inflict damage on the whites—a prospect he did not relish after so many years of living amicably with them. But now, with Mason trying to entrap him, he felt he had only one option.

He tarried at his farm near the Mashel River probably just long enough to gather essential supplies. Whether alerted surreptitiously or not by his daughter that he was officially a fugitive, Leschi sprang onto the sturdiest mount in his herd and headed northeast with a party of five, including his young wife, Mary, and, in all likelihood, Quiemuth. On their first night of flight, they camped in the woods about five miles from their farm while Leschi weighed his immediate options. If there was a plan for him to rendezvous with a corps of resistance fighters just waiting for him to assert his command, he did not confide it to Mary, who later recalled, "I didn't know there was to be a war—Leschi never told me anything about it. If I had known there was to be a war, I wouldn't have gone."

"I did not intend to make war on this [western] side of the mountains," Leschi reportedly told a tribesman named Packwood Charlie a year or two later.* But when he reached the White River, he encountered a group of warriors from the Muckleshoots and other backcountry bands who were as incensed over the provisions of the Point Elliott Treaty forcing their removal to the Sound as Leschi was over the harsh Medicine Creek pact. These angry Indians, led by chiefs Kitsap and Nelson, were "nearly all for war," Leschi contended, "and it was they who persuaded me into it." He told the same story to William Tolmie, who a few years later wrote that Leschi "seems to have lingered in uncertainty to

---

*The Leschi quotation comes from the files of the Tahoma Research Service, the business name of Nisqually tribal historian Cecilia Carpenter's book publishing enterprise, and is included in the archives of the Washington State Historical Society under the title "Leschi Confession to Packwood Charlie." A footnote states that Leschi's statement was taken down by his son-in-law, Charles Eaton, who may have listened to the exchange, "in '55 and [not 'or'] '56" and was apparently found and typed up by Eaton's daughter, Mary Alice Hubbard, on September 29, 1915. I cite this document because there are so few recorded instances of Leschi's purported words; this one, at least, comes from a relative, but its authenticity is fragile.

the last, and to have gone off . . . under the strong impulse of fear for his personal safety." The Nisqually brothers, Tolmie added, "intended going direct from Nisqually to the Yakima country, where they had numerous relatives, but were induced to remain [west of the mountains] by the threats of chiefs . . . there to follow and assassinate them if they persisted in going on."

Leschi may well have been disingenuous in claiming he had just wandered into an insurrectionist hotbed and been talked—or browbeaten—into taking charge of a spontaneously assembled force of combatants. It is far more probable that he had taken the lead in forging an alliance with likeminded braves who had acclaimed Leschi their war-chief-in-waiting and, by prearrangement, recruited to their camp a force of several hundred Nisquallies, Puyallups, and Muckleshoots. The first order of business of Leschi's high command was to determine how their little migrant army could operate most effectively.

Leschi likely understood that Stevens's unresponsiveness to the Nisquallies' complaint over their reservation was traceable in large part to his perception that the scattered, poorly armed, and generally submissive natives of the Sound posed little military threat to the nearby white settlements. If so, the governor was making a risky calculation—one that suited Leschi's designs. Customary Indian warfare differed sharply from the European and American practice. Tribes rarely engaged in pitched, sustained, directly confrontational clashes on a battlefield, where tactical maneuvers and massive firepower were usually decisive. Nor did Indian combatants visit mass destruction on their enemies or engage in permanent occupation of alien territory. Their warring typically took the form of short, surprise attacks mounted for maximum shock value and a limited purpose, such as avenging a killing or repaying a perceived insult or breach of honor. Then they would withdraw, having reminded their victims that the attackers were to be trifled with only at great peril. Tribes thus rarely "won" a war in the white sense of the word. Victory for Leschi would not require massive carnage or driving whites into the sea; his goal would be far more limited—to force Stevens into treating the tribes equitably.

To teach Stevens an effective lesson would, of course, require well-armed—and necessarily lethal—harassment of the white soldiers on a sustained basis. But as Leschi, Quiemuth, Stahi, Kitsap, Nelson, and their highly mobile band of warriors reckoned, the enemy force was light in number, heavy of tread, lodged in widely dispersed strongholds, and vulnerable in the field because of their long, exposed supply lines. And they made ideal targets for guerrilla attacks by Indian marksmen who knew the terrain intimately, were used to braving the elements and living off the land, and could damage and discomfit the white community out of all proportion to the size of their force. This form of combat, relying on covert positioning, accurate riflery, and feints to lure the enemy into exhausting chases across a natural obstacle course, had been used with notable success by George Washington's ragtag army against the British; the American revolutionaries had, of course, learned the technique from the Indians.

The Nisqually high command, however, was divided over whether to direct Indian wrath solely against the whites' military ranks. Should they assail only armed soldiers who were clearly on combat maneuvers, or should they subject all whites, including unarmed male civilians and others who were incapable of defending themselves—women, children, the aged, and infirm—to terror tactics? Leschi, according to a number of sources, strongly opposed the latter strategy, arguing that it would be taken for savagery and serve only to double white efforts to destroy the natives. His tribal adversaries, mostly but by no means all young hotheads like Leschi's nephew, Sluggia, argued that in a race war there could be no "innocent" whites—that their children were tomorrow's relentless usurpers of Indian Country and their women gave birth to them, so the more their blood flowed, the more likely they would be terrified into curtailing their oppressive ways. Both sides in Leschi's camp would soon make their case on the warpath.

Leschi positioned his men midway along the direct route from the Sound to Naches Pass in the Cascades, a seventy-mile corridor that Captain Maurice Maloney's relief column had lately traversed to join up with Lieutenant Slaughter's smaller force and go Yakima-hunting. The narrow wagon road cut through forests and around marshes before coming to a mile-wide pasture about twenty-five miles due east of Olympia, where Leschi pitched his base camp in the woods at its edge. The place was called Connell's Prairie after a former army man who had completed his posting at Fort Steilacoom, filed a 320-acre Donation Act claim to the spot, built a cabin on it, and lately volunteered to serve with Eaton's Rangers. For Leschi the area made an ideal encampment: there was plenty of grass on Connell's Prairie for his horses and livestock, fallen timber and thick underbrush everywhere for shelter and cover, and fresh water and a glut of salmon in the White River just to their east. The river allowed easy access and escape by canoe. Best of all, it was a fine spot for spying on and interrupting white troops moving in either direction.

Michael Connell himself, a young bachelor of Irish extraction, had been part of a militia unit drawn from Eaton's Rangers as they moved east from Olympia, according to the October 30 *Pioneer and Democrat,* "in quest of the whereabouts of Leschi, who, it was apprehended, had for some time been preparing his band for active hostilities against the settlements. Leschi is an Indian of more than ordinary power. . . . He has some good, substantial houses at his place and to all appearances . . . he might live there comfortably." Already he was being transformed into a charismatic presence by whites as well as his own people.

His days of living comfortably, though, were over. Eaton's party, on its way to catch up with Maloney's main force after having failed to grab Leschi at his farm, divided into two, with Jim McAllister in charge of a reconnaissance crew that crossed the Puyallup River and pushed toward a reported encampment of roughly 500 natives, including women and children, who appeared to be up to nothing more sinister than fishing on the White River. Guessing that Leschi might be presiding over these Indians, who were congregated a dozen miles away, McAllister asked Eaton if he might approach the group and try to beguile his old friend Leschi— assuming he was there—into giving himself up and renouncing all thought of violence against the whites. Eaton allowed him to take along Connell, whose cabin stood in the immediate vicinity, and two native guides on the risky mission and made McAllister promise to return by nightfall rather than expose himself to attack in the dark. "I will return," McAllister promised, "if I'm alive." Leschi and his men, attuned to the whites' footfall on the autumn leaves littering the forest floor, were lying in wait. As the rangy McAllister approached along the military road not far from Connell's Prairie, a Nisqually named Toopapyti drew a bead on him but then hesitated. Leschi glared at the brave, who whispered that McAllister was a friend of his. Steeling himself, Leschi told Toopapyti that he, too, was a friend of the settler-turned-Indian-hunter, but if Toopapyti didn't pull the trigger fast, Leschi would kill him first and then turn his rifle on McAllister.

The shot rang out, and then another, and the farmer from Medicine Creek fell dead, the first fatality in the fighting west of the mountains; Connell was dropped by the third bullet. Leschi, as part of his later statement to Packwood Charlie, acknowledged, "I was engaged in the murder of McAllister, but Towapite [*sic*] shot McAllister with two balls." McAllister had survived just eleven days after betraying Leschi in his letter to Mason. The rest of Eaton's soldiers escaped with their lives by taking cover in an abandoned Indian longhouse that absorbed a night-long riddling from Indian rifles. For Leschi, it must have been a bittersweet baptism by gunfire.

BY ANY STANDARD, the slayings of McAllister and Connell were legitimate acts of military combat. By Leschi's standard, what happened the next day, Sunday, October 28, 1855, fifteen or so miles farther north along the White River Valley, was an unpardonable atrocity committed against innocent white civilians by warriors under his loose command but evidently out of his control. He would nonetheless be blamed for the crime throughout Washington Territory.

The insubordinate element in Leschi's camp, chafing under his edict to attack only enemy combatants, went on the prowl among the few scattered white dwellings along the last bend of the White River before it runs north to the Sound near Seattle. There they fell first upon the three-room house occupied by farmer Harvey Jones, his wife, and their three small children. The family had settled there two years earlier and done very well for itself. Their spread boasted 2,500 fruit trees, 11 cows, 9 hogs, and a substantial wagon. Their good fortune allowed them to afford a hired man, who was breakfasting with Mrs. Jones and the children that Sunday morning around eight o'clock. Mr. Jones lay in bed, suffering from a pleurisy attack.

A strange shuffling noise that usually signaled an unannounced visit by friendly local Indians drew Mrs. Jones to the door. She opened it narrowly and was confronted by the barrel of a rifle wielded by a decidedly unfriendly native. She had the presence to slam the door shut and shovel the children out of sight, but the adult residents of the cabin, taken by surprise and defenseless, were quickly done in. When later found, Mrs. Jones had been fatally shot and disfigured with an ax. Bedridden Mr. Jones had been set on fire where he lay—along with the rest of the cottage. The hired man was brought down with a bullet in his back 150 yards from the house. Miraculously—or because of Leschi's dictum against extreme cruelty—the three children escaped unharmed into the surrounding woods. The seven-year-old boy, John King (who bore the last name of his mother's first husband), led away his four-year-old half-sister, who understood what was happening, and two-year-old half-brother, whom

John had to restrain from crying out as they stumbled through the forest. Eventually the children fell into the hands of a friendly Indian who escorted them to safety.

Fifty years afterward, heroic big brother John composed an account of the traumatic event for Ezra Meeker to insert in his book on Leschi. It included this affecting passage about how the children wandered back to their charred home after the assailants had vanished:

> As I was passing along I unexpectedly came upon my mother, prostrate upon the ground, some hundred feet or so southwest from the remains of our dwelling. She was yet alive. I do not know how or when she came there, nor what was the nature of her injuries. She was pleased to know we were yet safe, but chided me for my delay in making my escape. She told me I must take the children and go to Mr. Thomas's. . . . I did not want to leave her, but she told me it was best—that she could not live, and that I might save the children and myself. I wanted to remain. She explained that if the Indians came back they would probably kill us all, and that I must go. With a sad heart and a courage inspired by mother's charge of responsibility, I made the attempt to do as she bade me. I never saw her again.

The raiders had moved on to kill William Brannon, his wife, and infant son and then still another couple farther downriver, taking their four-year-old son as a hostage.

News of what became instantly known as the White River Massacre, with all the grisly details about its eight peaceable victims, raced across the territory and left tremulous all who had not previously understood the depth of resentment among the natives over the pending disposession of their homelands. Fearful that the catastrophe was the harbinger of a wave of blood-letting about to engulf the territory, Acting Governor Mason ordered the emergency construction of hermetic blockhouses in the towns along the Sound, near army posts, and at strategic locales in the countryside to shelter the civilian population. Soon most of the settler families, especially those in which the man or men of the house had volunteered for the militia, collected their household necessities and a domestic animal or two, temporarily abandoned their homes and farms—hoping the Indians would not devastate them in their absence—and crowded into the blockhouses and every other available refuge as if all of white Washington were under siege. At the same time Mike Simmons, his fellow Indian agents, and their deputies began rounding up the 4,000 or so natives west of the mountains who had not gone off to evade forceful removal to their reservations. In part to ensure the Indians' safety from itchy white trigger fingers, in part to keep the natives from acting up, the bulk of the tribal population was moved to temporary internment camps set up on three small islands at the south end of the Sound.

The surge of dread coursing through the collective white psyche was reflected, as well as fed, by the incendiary language in the *Pioneer and Democrat,* which in its November 16 issue carried what its editor called "a horrid recital of the massacre of women and children on White River, by a lot of fiends under the command of Leschi, Nelson, and others." In fact, neither the newspaper nor posterity ever uncovered firm evidence that Leschi had joined in or approved of the mayhem at White River, but as by far the best-known native among the suddenly rampant renegades, he would thereafter be personally linked to every Indian assault against soldiers patrolling anywhere near the south Sound and every outrage inflicted upon any white civilians.*

Nisqually tradition continues to hold that Leschi was a humane warrior who denounced the White River killings as terror tactics hurtful to the Indian cause and thereby earned fierce enmity among those guerrillas who disagreed. Majority support for this view may be inferred from the absence of any further multiple atrocities against white noncombatants over the remainder of the Indian uprising.[†] The Nisqually chief apparently lacked sufficient power to have prevented the barbaric episode at White River, but having tasted the spilled blood of white noncombatants, its perpetrators were evidently willing thereafter to abide by Leschi's command.

.   .   .

*The next year a jury in King County, where the White River Massacre occurred near the border with Pierce County, went so far as to return a murder indictment against Leschi alone for having killed Harvey Jones, even though ten other Indians were named as well—including Nelson, Kitsap, Leschi's brother, and their nephew, Sluggia—as members of the raiding party. Leschi was never made to stand trial, though, likely due to insufficient evidence against him.

[†]A cryptic portion of Leschi's so-called confession to Packwood Charlie suggests that he may well have accompanied the perpetrators to the vicinity of the White River Massacre "but [I] took no part in the murder[s]."

FARTHER EAST in the forested upcountry and western slopes of the Cascades, Captain Maurice Maloney weighed his options after his forces had lately met up with Slaughter's smaller band of U.S. Army regulars. Militiaman William Tidd, a soft-spoken carpenter by trade and owner of reputedly the fastest horse in the territory, had just arrived from Fort Steilacoom with an express message. The troops due to arrive from The Dalles and join Maloney's men in an attack on the bristling Yakimas might not appear for another week or ten days. Meanwhile, his soldiers were rapidly using up their supplies, and the rainy season enveloped them, turning the landscape into mud and making it all the harder to send supplies to that remote setting. Without the reinforcements from the south, an advance on the Yakimas seemed very risky. Maloney's scouts reported there were between 2,000 and 3,000 Yakima and Klickitat warriors, ten times as many as his own force, strung out along the Naches River Valley and ready to ambush his men at any turn. And if he waited while provisions dwindled, the snows would soon come to the mountain passes, blocking his return route and dooming his soldiers to death by freezing.

Reluctantly, Maloney decided to lead his men back west to their base on the Sound and return to take on the Yakimas in the spring. To advise his commander at Fort Steilacoom of his tactical retreat, Maloney sent Tidd galloping back across the territory as part of a seven-man express party that included a surgeon, Dr. Matthew Burns, a zealous veteran of service with British forces in India, and three militiamen well known around Olympia. Most prominent among them was Maloney's aide-de-camp, Abram Benton Moses, a native of South Carolina and veteran of the war with Mexico who had come west to serve as a deputy sheriff of booming San Francisco and migrated to the Puget Sound region. After a term as sheriff of Thurston County, the core area of Washington Territory's white population, Moses had lately become customs inspector for the Port of Nisqually before volunteering for the militia. One of his colleagues in Tidd's express party was Joseph Miles, recently elected justice of the peace for Olympia while continuing to work on the construction of the first territorial capitol building. They were joined on Tidd's mission by Antonio B. Rabbeson, who had succeeded Moses as sheriff of Thurston County. A longtime sidekick and sometime business associate of Mike Simmons, Tony Rabbeson had become part of the tight coterie of political musclemen Isaac Stevens had drawn within his orbit.

All was going well for the first fifty miles of the Tidd party's fleet ride back toward Steilacoom until the overcast midafternoon of October 31, when they came upon the large band of Leschi's braves at Connell's Prairie, a short distance from where McAllister and Connell had been ambushed a few days earlier. The express riders knew nothing of that, or about how Eaton's Rangers had withstood an all-night assault not far from there, or about the White River Massacre a few hours' ride to the north just the day before.

For the moment, Moses and his fellow riders were lucky that Leschi's lookouts had been posted on the western side of the Indian encampment, where a fresh contingent of soldiers replacing Eaton's shot-up unit was expected to appear heading east from Fort Steilacoom. The express party, coming the other way, thus took the natives' camp by surprise. Upon being greeted amicably by Leschi and his confederates, the militiamen saw no evidence the Indians were gathered for any reason other than the one they gave: to fish the nearby White River. One of the soldiers was even escorted from the wagon road at the prairie's edge to the nearby Indian campground after asking if he might purchase a pair of moccasins. Rabbeson noticed that some of the braves who had met them now slipped away.

The white troopers' mood darkened when they spotted the charred remains of Michael Connell's cabin and asked how it had happened; the Indians professed ignorance. The Americans were now alert to their peril. Dr. Burns impulsively grabbed the gun of one of the young braves, thinking he was Leschi and threatening to shoot the startled youth dead— not the wisest move under the circumstances. Rabbeson, who had known Leschi for years and purchased deer meat from him, restrained Burns and told him of his error, calming the scene, but prudence dictated that the express party now resume its journey with alacrity. Remounting, the soldiers headed down the narrow wagon road as it dipped through a swampy thicket that surrounded them with tall firs, fallen timbers, and heavy brush.

They had not proceeded more than half to three-quarters of a mile into this shadowy stretch when a volley of musket fire from the woods strafed them. Joe Miles fell from his horse with a fatal bullet wound in his neck. He told his comrades he was done for and urged them to hurry away. Abram Moses, too, was soon hit by a ball passing through the left side of his back and out his chest just beneath the heart. Despite the severity of the wound, he was able to remain mounted for a time as the others dragged Miles off the road and into cover, hoping the Indians would not find and mutilate him, and then rode off to escape further deadly fire.

After they galloped several more harrowing miles over rough terrain, Moses had lost too much blood to go on. His companions carried him off into the brush, as they had Miles, covered him with their overcoats, and promised to return as soon as possible. The five survivors rode on with pounding hearts until they ascended a bluff where they were pinned down in a firefight and then hand-to-hand struggle with Indian assailants, four of whom they managed to shoot or stab before the rest fled, with a crazed Dr. Burns chasing them into the wilds and howling that he would kill them all. His colleagues were sure they had seen the last of him. Then, as promised, they rode back to where Moses lay, realized they could do nothing to save him, and bid him a poignant farewell.

For the next three days and nights, all cold and rainy, the four surviving troopers proceeded on foot and off the road to escape detection until they could stagger back to the safety of Fort Steilacoom. The bodies of Miles and Moses were soon recovered and buried near Olympia on a bleak November morn.

Their obituaries appeared in the November 9 issue of the *Pioneer and Democrat,* along with a letter from Tony Rabbeson describing the express party's travail. His unit, Rabbeson wrote, had come unexpectedly upon some 150 Indians at Connell's Prairie and "conversed with their main chief, Leschi"—the only time his name was mentioned in the militiaman's extensive write-up; no other Indian among those they had run into was named. Rabbeson recounted how, after leaving the natives behind, the soldiers took the road down through a "deep, muddy swamp. There we received a murderous fire—from those very same Indians, who had secreted themselves in ambush—from behind us." How, toward the end of an overcast autumn afternoon and while riding rapidly along a narrow dirt road through a shaded thicket, Rabbeson and his companions could have determined who their hidden attackers were is a mystery. But Rabbeson's letter clearly implied that the Americans recognized their assailants as "those very same Indians" with whom their party had conversed up on the prairie a short time before—an improbable claim unless the attack was made at point-blank range. The letter in the newspaper did not say that, however. It said the shots came "from behind us," making identification of the triggermen yet more improbable unless the Indians had come out from cover, and why would they have done that—to make better targets of themselves? At any rate, Rabbeson's letter did not identify Leschi as one of the shooters. The question of who they were would soon be revisited.*

DURING THE FIRST HALF of November, Maloney's retreating troops suffered the indignity of trying to engage an enemy that used the wilderness to maximum advantage. Leschi's warriors were adept at leading their foe on wearying hide-and-seek chases that forced the white soldiers to pick their way through thorny woodlands and ford ice-cold rivers and streams as winter began to grip the uplands.

Maloney's officers tried to mask their frustration with field reports back to Fort Steilacoom and Mason that contained more bravado than truth. A combined force of about 100 regulars and militiamen under Lieutenant Slaughter, for example, pursued part of Leschi's scrambling band across the Puyallup River and up along the White River to a point not far from where the massacre of civilians had occurred. Exploiting the natural camouflage of shaggy woods that sloped up from the far riverbank, the Indians looked down on their trackers and delivered a torrent of whoops, catcalls, and bullets as they prevented a twelve-man crew from chopping down a tree for a log bridge over the rushing current. For six hours the whites fired at anything that moved, including bits of cloth at the end of sticks held aloft to attract their fire and exhaust their ammunition. At dusk the natives slipped away. Reporting the encounter to Adjutant General James Tilton, commander of the Washington territorial militia, Lieutenant Jared Hurd claimed there was "no doubt" that between twenty-five and thirty Indians had been killed while only one U.S. soldier was wounded in the thigh—surely a wishful tally since the natives almost always removed their fallen brethren from the battlefield.

Slaughter's men continued to chase their nimble prey to the Green River, a tributary of the White, taking casualties as they plodded on, mostly uphill, without ever knowing what damage, if any, they were inflicting. None of this prevented another field officer with Maloney's forces, Captain Gilmore Hays, from writing to Mason on November 11:

*Rabbeson's letter was accompanied in the same paper by a shorter one from Dr. Matthew Burns, contradicting reports that he had been killed after charging into the woods to chase the express party's Indian assailants. He claimed to have shot and killed seven natives "with my own hands," while suffering only "a skin wound in the forehead from a buckshot." He conceded that "my feet are badly hurt" because he had to discard his shoes and that he lost his horse ("shot in the kidneys"), his instruments, and medicine case.

"The Indians are whipped—they will never rally again. Their plan will be to ambush, fire and then run—my men have proven that they fear no danger—they are ready to fight under any circumstances." In truth, it was Maloney's expeditionary forces that had been stung during their eleven-day trek back to Fort Steilacoom, arriving with thirteen dead and six wounded.

The natives remained at large, lithe phantoms, always on the move and impervious to the cold, drenching rainfall and autumn mists that would lift on rare occasion to reveal snow-topped Tahoma (Mount Rainier) looming above the wild landscape like a great guardian spirit of the surrounding tribes. Left behind in the forest in the hope of bloodying any Indian encampment they might uncover was the brainy Lieutenant Slaughter and his unit.* Neither his spirited leadership nor the tactics he had learned at West Point were of much use in that often torturous theater of combat, which J. A. Eckrom, in his lively account of the Puget Sound Indian War, called "a numbing blur of marches across prairies, wet forests and bone-chilling streams. One day was much like another, and the foe was seldom seen as more than a rustling in the brush or a threatening shadow in the night."

On one of those nights in late November the enemy made off with forty of Slaughter's horses, further reducing his men's morale and increasing their exposure to furtive attack. Yet he kept his men on the move, reinforced by a fresh detachment of Captain Hays's volunteers. During the first week of December, after struggling through a downpour and closing on a band of hostile wraiths, Slaughter's unit camped for the night. He and his fellow officers took shelter in a root house to dry off and plan the next day's maneuvers. The light cast by the fireplace, where their clothes were drying and dinner was cooking, silhouetted Slaughter and another officer conversing in the doorway of the little structure. A single shot rang out through the darkness—plainly the guards posted on the perimeter of the shelter, probably hungry and with their chattering teeth the only perceptible sound, had been less than vigilant—and Slaughter fell dead. Before the long night ambush ended, three other soldiers in the company were also killed. Slaughter's wife, Mary, a bright light in the Steilacoom community, had been visiting at the governor's quarters in Olympia with Stevens's wife, Meg, when the news arrived of her husband's death.

---

*Slaughter's personable manner had earned him assignment as the only army officer to accompany Stevens's treaty commissioners at Medicine Creek.

The whole white community, civilian as well as military, went into instant mourning over the loss of so luminous a young leader. The thirty members of the Washington legislature, which was then sitting, passed a resolution of grief and tribute and then adjourned to attend Slaughter's funeral, along with every other territorial official. The welter of disheartening news, including reports of scattered raids by Indians torching settlers' barns bulging with lately harvested grain, quickened the flow of civilians from the exposed countryside into the hastily built blockhouses that nearly every able-bodied pioneer had taken a hand in raising. Meant to be tightly sealed bastions and thus little ventilated, the blockhouses were soon filled beyond capacity and smelled that way. In the daytime, town streets were a magnet for the refugees, especially in the two villages that had become the thriving rival hubs of the white population.

At Olympia, where the legislature had outgrown its original quarters on the ground floor of the Gold Bar restaurant and then the wooden Masonic Hall, the first territorial capitol building was taking shape as the centerpiece of the community, by then equipped with a three-story hotel and a livery stable for 100 mounts. When the legislature was not gathered in Olympia, Steilacoom, twenty miles up the Sound along the rutted Nisqually Road, was the busier town. Pushed by locals as the future Gotham of the Northwest, Steilacoom owed its prosperity to a wharf that accommodated deep-keel ships and to its adjacency to the army and Hudson's Bay Company posts. It had already grown into a cluster of seventy homes, six stores, three hotels, three sawmills, two smithies, two bowling alleys, a gristmill, a billiard parlor and connected saloon (or the other way around), a school open daily, a church, a tailor, a cabinetmaker, and a print shop, where the weekly *Courier* was run off. Fear now overhung the usually bustling town.

In the continuing absence of Governor Stevens, whose return from contentious treatymaking with the distant Blackfoot and Spokane nations had been delayed by threats from and skirmishes with the no-less-cranky Yakimas, Mason addressed the December opening of the legislature by trying to reassure the nervous white community. The army and militia, he claimed not very convincingly, were keeping the natives in line, and settlers who had fled their farms for the temporary safety in numbers afforded by the towns and blockhouses would be able to return to their homes in time for spring planting. Everyone knew Mason was whistling in the dark.

It was evident that the Indians were in control of the whole countryside outside the white settlements. To travel anywhere in the territory without a military escort—or even with one, as Stevens had discovered— was to risk one's neck. True, Leschi's warriors west of the Cascades were hardly an overwhelming force, probably never in excess of 300 at any given time. They lacked a disciplined chain of command and intertribal coordination. They carried mostly old muskets that were no match for the white soldiers' modern rifles. Yet under Leschi's direction they were besting their adversaries. Logistically they were running rings around the Bostons because they knew every pathway and shortcut through the forest. They knew where it was easiest to cross waterways, and they knew how to come and go swiftly and silently by light, portable canoes. Their rain-repellent hoods and capes woven of shredded cedar bark made them look like shaggy creatures from the wild but kept them a lot drier than their pursuers. If their ranks had been stouter, their rifles more accurate, and ammunition plentiful, Leschi's braves might have been tempted to storm Fort Steilacoom, torch the nearby town, and lay waste the little territorial capital of Olympia in the misguided hope of gaining a substantially more generous allocation of land from the U.S. authorities.

So uneasiness ran like a contagion among the 5,000 Americans in Washington Territory, and Leschi's name was whispered with fear around many a fireplace as the coldest, gloomiest winter any of the settlers could recall descended on the troubled landscape.

AN OBJECTIVE assessment of the military situation at the time was offered by Isaac L. Sterret, commander of the U.S.S. *Decatur,* a gunship berthed at Seattle while undergoing repairs. Sterret wrote to Secretary of War Jefferson Davis on December 5: "The valor and prowess of the Indians has been greatly underrated. . . . [T]he whole military resources of the Territory are totally inadequate to conduct the war with success, even to afford protection to the settlers." Isaac Stevens, in transit but apprised of the disconcerting success of Leschi's guerrilla tactics west of the Cascades, shared Sterret's judgment. The governor also continued to believe that the suddenly dire Indian problem was the result not of oppressive and relentless treatymaking on his part but of the tribes' treachery in forsaking their solemn vows to uphold the written agreements.

The problem of low manpower was especially apparent east of the mountains, where Stevens was encamped near Walla Walla on December 28 when he addressed a haughty letter to General Wool, Pacific coast regional commander of U.S. Army forces, who was based in California, accusing him of shirking his duty by leaving pacification to "the citizen soldiery [i.e., the volunteer militias] alone to fight the battles and gain the victories." This was an unpardonable slight to the army regulars from Fort Steilacoom and other barracks who had already fought and died in Indian combat. Stevens compounded his slur by going on to recommend "that you will urge forward your preparations with all possible dispatch. Get all your disposable force in this valley in January, establish a large depot camp here, occupy Fort Walla Walla and the Yakima country, and be ready in February to take the field." Then, as a civilian territorial official presuming to direct the top U.S. Army officer in their part of the nation, he outlined his own sweeping "plan of campaign" for the Snake River region in eastern Washington Territory.

General Wool, understandably, did not relish being dictated to by a former brevet major. Arriving at Fort Vancouver in southernmost Washington Territory, he assessed the situation, decided that a winter campaign against the Indians would be disastrous, ordered forts to be built in the Yakima and Walla Walla valleys—a sop to Stevens, perhaps, but strategically useful—and conveniently forgot to answer the governor's letter until February. In his reply, Wool reiterated his outspoken view that Indian misconduct was generally set off by white settlers' abuses, and in the belief that volunteer militias were prone to turn into unbridled vigilantes eager to bash any redskin within reach, he called for all actions against the Indians to be carried out solely by regular army troops.

An appalling confirmation of Wool's worst fears about the excesses of territorial militiamen occurred in early December when the Walla Walla chief, Peopeomoxmox, tried to improve race relations in his region. Peo, who had shown a cautious and conciliatory hand the previous June at the Walla Walla treaty council, subsequently proved unable—or unwilling, according to white squatters in the region—to prevent Indian looting and livestock-rustling directed against settlers still without legal title to the land they occupied. The Oregon militia had taken the field to curtail robberies by the Walla Wallas, and to avoid a bloodbath, Peo, accompanied by forty warriors, approached the militia camp under a flag of truce. With five braves at his side, Peo was ushered to the militia commander's quarters to work out a *modus vivendi.* The white commander demanded, as a precondition for any deal, that Peo turn over his tribe's livestock in repayment for the stolen head and their firearms as a preventive against further violence against the settlers. When Peo objected that he had already struck treaty terms with Stevens and was not about to humor a headstrong militia officer, he and his bodyguards were arrested and confined. After he failed to reappear, the rest of Peo's party began skirmishing with the militiamen at the edge of their camp. That evening the chief, objecting to being tied up, was shot to death in a scuffle. Peo's captors then scalped him, skinned the rest of him, pickled his ears in a jar of alcohol, and brought selected body parts with them to display at a boozy celebration in Portland.

The atrocity, which General Wool denounced as soon as he heard about it, sent precisely the wrong signal to the Indians: whether they behaved in a friendly or hostile fashion, were submissive or resistant, rational or intemperate, they would be abused by the whites once they had the upper hand. Stevens would later upbraid Wool for wasting his sympathy on Peo by contending that the chief had been out to subvert the Walla Walla Treaty ever since it was signed and, prior to his detainment, was planning to attack the governor's entourage before it crossed the Cascades on its way back to Olympia—a charge he did not substantiate.

What Stevens had failed to grasp, along with his policymaking superiors in Washington, D.C., was that pressuring the natives to make their mark on a piece of paper—no matter how onerous its provisions—was no substitute for genuine engagement with the Indians' needs if their existence was to be sustained with a modicum of dignity. Stevens would always deny that his strong-arm approach, like the settlers' disdain for Indian rights, had inflamed red-white relations—an evasion of responsibility characteristically expressed by the *Pioneer and Democrat* in its December 7, 1855, edition: "This war has been contemplated by the Indians from two to three years, long before a treaty was spoken of with them." White self-righteousness did not allow admission of who the real aggressor was; how much more convenient to blame the victim.

As he neared Puget Sound on his return march, Stevens's wrath overflowed. In a December 22 letter to Manypenny, he wrote:

> My plan is to make no treaty whatever with the tribes now in arms; to do away entirely with the reservations guaranteed to them; to make a summary example of all the leading spirits, and to place as a conquered people, under the surveillance of troops, the remains of those tribes on reservations selected by the President, and on such terms as the Government in its justice and mercy now vouchsafe to me.

So much for any promise he may have made to Leschi to liberalize the reservations provided for in the Medicine Creek Treaty. The Nisqually chief had rejected its terms and spoken angrily of his intention to resist them, but he had taken no overt action to do so until he was branded a fugitive, was chased into the woods, and had to transform himself into a guerrilla fighter—all of which Stevens now claimed as justification for treating him and his tribe as a "conquered people." That Leschi and the Yakimas, far from being conquered, had in fact taken the upper hand during the first two months of their armed resistance failed to impress Stevens or compel him to deal fairly with the Nisquallies or their neighboring tribes. Disdainful of thus dignifying a backward race, the governor, a proud West Point graduate and daring combatant in the Mexican War, had not yet begun to fight.

8

An Impressive Performance

IT WAS A WINTER of both rich satisfaction and high anxiety for
Leschi. His success at hectoring soldiers in the upriver woods
between the Sound and the Cascades and the Yakima-led militancy
on the eastern plains had traumatized the whites all across Washington
Territory, but he knew that these assertions of Indian anger and strength
would not stymie the enemy for long. The settlers, taking shelter for the
winter, would await the spring warming, the arrival of U.S. Army reinforcements, and the return of Isaac Stevens from his wandering campaign
of treatymaking, which had thus far won the whites neither peace nor
security.

Leschi, meanwhile, could hardly afford to rest on his laurels. It was
taking all his powers of endurance to sustain the fight and all of his leadership skills to hold together his corps of inexperienced warriors—and
particularly to restrain his younger braves from the use of terrorism as an
equalizing weapon. Since there were no soldiers in the field to target, the
days without combat passed slowly for the native fighters. Away from
their familiar surroundings, they suffered from the dropping temperature
and dwindling food, supplies, and morale. Leschi's recruits began to slip
away in the face of these privations. To make their situation still more
precarious, the Nisqually-led coalition could no longer rely on their best
friend among the whites, William Tolmie. As the Hudson's Bay Company's chief officer on the Sound, he was compelled to sell weaponry and
supplies to the soldiers while denying them to the natives who desperately needed them to survive in the wilderness long enough to bring Isaac
Stevens to the bargaining table. Had Tolmie continued to deal with the
Indians, the governor would surely have shut down Fort Nisqually and

suspended compensation talks with the Bay for the takeover of its property. Given the circumstances, Leschi chose to take a daring gamble at the outset of the new year.

Most of the noncombatant Nisquallies whom Mike Simmons had rounded up in the fall were transported to a five-mile-long island they called Bu-ta-u, after a legendary tribal princess, and known to whites as Fox Island, about a dozen miles above Olympia. The island, an ideal lookout post from which to detect northern tribal marauders, had long been frequented by Nisquallies, who came there to gather clams and oysters in its rocky tidelands, snare the plentiful ducks and pheasants, and fish in its salmon streams. But once transformed into a detention center, Fox Island lost its charm. There was no room for pasturage or horseback-riding, the housing and clothing provided by the territorial government were in short supply, and because most of the tribe's ablest hunters and fishers were off with Leschi's fighters, the 1,000 or so internees were dependent on white man's food, grudgingly shipped in to sustain the overcrowded encampment. Sickness was soon rampant. While their white warden, John Swan, previously a Sound fisherman, was well known to and liked by the natives, he could do little to gloss over what Fox Island had become—a prison camp.

On the afternoon of January 5, 1856, Leschi brought a fleet of six war canoes, manned by thirty-three armed braves, onto the pebbly shore in front of Swan's cabin on the north end of Fox Island. Swan, the sole white guardian of the island, was relieved when Leschi approached peacefully, saluted, promised that no harm would come to him, and said he had come on a diplomatic, not military, mission.

Once the two men were seated, Leschi asked Swan to convey a message to the white authorities: his people were not fighters by nature and had taken up arms only because they had been misled at Medicine Creek into accepting a hellish reservation; they wanted no more than enough space to live as they were accustomed. It was the same point Leschi had made to other prominent whites—Mason, Tolmie, McAllister, and Shaw among others—to no avail. His tribesmen and their allies had grown tired of the war; they were sick, cold, and hungry, said Leschi, and in view of Stevens's continuing absence, they would gladly talk peace and reconciliation with any U.S. Indian agent but Simmons, for whom he harbored a "deadly hatred," as Swan recounted their conversation a few days later to the *Puget Sound Courier*. Mindful of the horrified response by the white community to the White River Massacre, which he always claimed to have counseled against, Leschi insisted to Swan that the braves under his command did not attack innocent or helpless civilians—it was *cultus* (bad) Indians who had committed the atrocity.

The timing of Leschi's extended hand of peace coincided with several trying considerations on the whites' side as well. The three-month enlistment period for which most of the volunteer militiamen had signed up when Acting Governor Mason first issued his call was about to expire, and the expectation of further sacrifice by these amateur soldiers was daunting. Furthermore, most settlers had fled to safety, and their confinement in blockhouses or behind barricades while their farms and stock stood untended was naturally producing tension and irritability. An opportunity for rapprochement was at hand.

Swan, of course, was not empowered to negotiate with Leschi, and so, whether earnestly or duplicitously, he persuaded Leschi to let him send a messenger to Fort Steilacoom, just six miles away, to ask if Captain Erasmus Keyes, the commanding officer, might parley with the Nisqually chief or arrange for an Indian agent other than Simmons to do so, pending the return of the governor, who was expected shortly. The messenger was also told to report that Leschi's party had no harmful intentions, so any armed effort to rescue Swan or to capture the beached warriors would be ill-advised. Keyes, though also powerless to negotiate with Leschi, thought he had been handed a perfect opportunity to seize the insurgents' principal leader and break their resistance effort. He sent an urgent request to nearby Fort Nisqually to borrow the *Beaver,* the Bay's clunky old paddle-wheel steamer, long since stripped of its guns and now in service mostly as a cargo carrier. Tolmie had little choice but to agree, and Keyes made overnight preparations to dispatch an expeditionary force under Captain Maurice Maloney, still smarting from the punishment his forces had endured at the hands of Leschi's warriors.

Soon after the *Beaver* set out at sunup, Maloney, who knew nothing about amphibious operations, realized that he and Keyes had brought only one rowboat for landing the troops. If they came ashore a single boatload of five men at a time, Leschi's armed warriors would pounce on them. While the ship drew as close to shore as it dared in the hope the native raiders would take to their canoes and approach within range of the army sharpshooters on board, Leschi bided his time so long as no gunfire was directed shoreward. After a while, Swan was allowed to row to the

Beaver to learn if the U.S. Army was willing to advance peace arrangements. Told that Maloney had no such instructions, and urged to remain on board lest he be held as a hostage (or worse) on his return to shore, Swan said he had given his word to Leschi that he would return—and did so. A messenger was sent back to Fort Steilacoom to ask for further guidance.

When Swan's ensuing day-long shuttle diplomacy between the *Beaver* and shore yielded no progress, Leschi tended to the second purpose of his mission, to enlist fresh recruits for his guerrilla band from among those marooned on Fox Island. He may have enticed as many as two dozen—accounts differ—before his canoes slipped away undetected at night after thirty hours onshore. In his wake many whites questioned the sincerity of Leschi's peace feeler and suspected it was just a cover for his real purpose, luring reinforcements from their island prison. The *Courier,* though, was impressed, remarking, "It is in vain that we look for a parallel case of bravery in the annals of Indian warfare . . . which proves to us we have sadly underrated the courage and daring of the Indians on the Sound." Captain Keyes seemed to have been left in a wait-and-see mode by Leschi's gesture, suggesting in a letter to the acting governor a few days later that "forward movement at this time [by either regular army or volunteer troops] would not hasten the termination of the war, but might and probably would, induce the hostiles to recommence their depredations."

Any hope of a peaceful, negotiated settlement of Leschi's grievance was dashed at once by Isaac Stevens on his return to Olympia two weeks later after having spent most of the year on the road, treatymaking in Indian Country. He interpreted Leschi's foray at Fox Island not as a brave, daring, and sincere gesture of conciliation but as a confession of the rebels' weakness due to waning manpower, firepower, and willpower. Now was the time to press the attack on the renegades, not to relent.

Within a week of his return, the governor addressed a packed session of the Washington territorial legislature, whose members he told—to "deafening cheers," according to the account in the *Pioneer and Democrat*—that "the war shall be prosecuted until the last hostile Indian is exterminated." Far from altering the Nisqually and Puyallup reservations, the governor cried fiercely, "Let the blow be struck where it is deserved," and promised that "nothing but death is a mete punishment for their perfidy—their lives only should pay the forfeit." The tribes at war had to surrender unconditionally "to the justice, leniency, and mercy of our government. The guilty ones shall suffer, and the remainder placed on reservations under the eye of the military."*

Stevens chose to view the violent resistance under Leschi's banner as an act of personal betrayal against a white dignitary (i.e., his august self), not to be forgiven lightly—or at all. Resolved to cut down the hostile Indians with or without the help of the U.S. Army, the governor now issued a new call for militiamen to replace those whose enlistment periods were about to expire. He asked for six companies, and that the new volunteers as well as those willing to stay on agree to a six-month enlistment period, long enough, he felt, to eradicate the Indian menace during the coming season of fair weather. As if trying to relive his military career while serving as the highest civilian official of his territory, Stevens now took to signing correspondence with militia officers as "governor and commander-in-chief."

By inflating his personal power, Stevens was casting himself more firmly as an adversary of Major General John Wool, the U.S. Pacific coast commander. An old warhorse and a decorated veteran of many a campaign dating back to the War of 1812, Wool strongly disapproved of civilians serving as volunteer soldiers, answerable only to state or territorial authorities who were not professional military men. He considered militia enlistees little better than vigilantes, generally ill-trained and poorly disciplined, who posed a greater threat to the peace than irritable Indians did and who often took their empowerment as a license to kill, plunder, and profiteer. As second-ranking officer in the U.S. Army, Wool, like his sole superior, General Winfield Scott, had an outsized ego, but he

---

*Among those besides Leschi who may have regretted Stevens's return to Olympia to take active charge of the warfare against the Indians was the governor's wife, Meg. In a chatty letter dated February 1, 1856, to her sister, Mary Howard, back in New England, Meg expressed her keen enthusiasm for Charles Mason, the young territorial secretary serving as Stevens's stand-in. On getting back to the capital, the governor sent Mason off to Washington, D.C., for no particular errand but perhaps because of what he may have sensed in the relationship between Meg and Mason. As she told her sister, "You can't imagine what a loss Mason is to me. For . . . months we have been together most of the time. Walked and rode together and he has been full of kindness and little attentions. I never knew a young man that I liked so well. If he heard me express a wish for anything he would get it for me. Then he has a fine intellectual taste and is highly educated. He took as much interest in me as I did in him. I expect you will think I am running on at a furious rate for a married woman concerning a young man but you can understand the tie between us when you consider how few people in this country I had any sort of sympathy with. . . . I am wild as a hawk. . . . I was never so well or happy in my life as now." Mason died in Olympia three years later at the age of twenty-nine.

was no witless blowhard. Even now, past seventy, Wool maintained his reputation as honest, public-spirited, and highly professsional. He was no one for a former brevet major to try to order about, as Stevens discovered when in early February Wool got around to answering his cheeky December letter demanding an instant show of force against the Indians in the Walla Walla Valley.

"I have neither the resources of a Territory nor the Treasury of the United States at my command," Wool replied to Stevens with disdain, characterizing the natives' sporadic display of violence as a brushfire that he had no intention of fanning into a full-scale conflagration. Indians rarely became active hostiles unless provoked, Wool remonstrated, and those in arms west of the Cascades should be effectively isolated in the countryside while army units and territorial militia confined their efforts to protecting the settlements. Wool promised to combat the Indians "with all the vigor, promptness and efficiency I am master of . . . without wasting unnecessarily the means and resources at my disposal by untimely and unproductive expeditions." The general confidently expected the war could be brought to a close within a few months "provided the extermination of the Indians, which I do not approve of, is not insisted upon . . . and the volunteers are withdrawn from the Walla Walla country." The Fort Steilacoom garrison was being strengthened and would soon reach 400 men, "sufficient to bring to terms the 200 warriors" in the Puget Sound region. In short, Stevens should shut up and let the professional soldiers do their job.

The governor, his own considerable hubris swelling by the day and no longer constrained by the military's chain of command, reacted to the rebuke by going over Wool's head—as well as that of army boss Scott, whom Stevens had previously offended by insufficiently buttering him up in his book on the Mexican War—and writing directly to Secretary of War Jefferson Davis to urge Wool's dismissal from his high post.

A FEW DAYS after the governor's avowal to the territorial legislators that every last hostile Indian would be done away with, the objects of his wrath sent him a bloodcurdling message of their own by assaulting the maritime village of Seattle, midway up the Sound's east coast. The settlement, with fewer than 100 permanent white residents and nearly as many friendly natives living alongside or close by, was ringed by a rise of thick woodlands that left the town isolated on its inland side, vulnerable to attack. Seattle residents had erected a pair of blockhouses after the White River Massacre and kept a watchful eye on the surrounding forest.

In January 1856, at an Indian encampment thrown up on the shore of Lake Washington, separated from nearby Seattle by the heavy forest, warriors from numerous tribes assembled, including a contingent of 100 or so Yakimas and Klickitats who had crossed the mountains under their warrior chieftains, Owhi and his son, Qualchan, Leschi's uncle and cousin, to help the western tribes take a more aggressive stance against the whites. The Indian gathering place for the raid came to be referred to as Leschi's camp.

Just who thought up and who led the impending raid on Seattle has never been firmly established, any more than the number of attackers, estimated unreliably by chroniclers of the event at between 150 and 1,000 Indians. Leschi, daring and seemingly ubiquitous as the leader of the native uprising on the Sound, is generally credited with having masterminded the venture, even though he explicitly denied it and evidence of his participation is sketchy at best. Strategically it was a promising idea from the Indian perspective, no matter who was responsible for hatching it. Seattle appeared to be a ripe fruit to pluck because it was small and well removed from the main white settlements at the head of the Sound. For the tribal warriors the village also hosted a prize well worth risking their necks for: the sixteen-gun sloop-of-war U.S.S. *Decatur,* which had been undergoing repairs for several months and looked like a sitting duck with its stores of weapons, ammunition, and food, all badly needed by the natives, not to mention the ship's cannons, which they hoped to remove and turn against white fortresses.

As the Indians pondered their plan of attack, though, they failed to take several important factors into account. For one thing, the *Decatur*'s repairs were nearly completed, the ship was now back in the water, and its shipboard contingent of ninety U.S. marines was in place and available to defend the settlement. So were most of the seventy-two militiamen from the region who had just been mustered out of service but not yet dispersed. Tactically, moreover, the natives had no experience when it came to assailing a well-defended settlement. Their old smoothbore muskets lacked range and accuracy, hand-to-hand combat against whites with bayonets and revolvers was a frightening prospect, and the natives were entirely unprepared for the ferocious cannonfire aimed their way.

Early in the morning of January 26, rifle shots from the forested hillside behind the village began to pepper the cabins below, setting off a hurried exodus to the residents' prearranged shelters. They had been tipped off by an Indian friendly to them who drifted in and out of the encampment on Lake Washington. Had the attackers drawn closer before firing or owned more accurate rifles, they might have turned Seattle's streets into a shooting gallery and exacted a heavy toll on the citizenry. By the time the sporadic gunfire intensified into a steady barrage, though, the villagers had made it safely to cover; only two of them were picked off fatally, and nine others were wounded.

Unwilling to charge the better-trained and well-armed defenders of the port and storm the warship with its prized supplies, the raiders clung to the fringe of the settlement, where they torched and looted a few of the buildings. For the most part, they were kept in check by sporadic cannon-fire from the *Decatur*'s batteries, aimed more or less blindly toward the timbered slope where most of the attackers remained hidden. Howls of dismay and indignation greeted each long-distance volley falling on them from the sky, and cries of lamentation went up when any of the missiles drew blood. How many casualties white gunnery inflicted was never determined since, as usual, the natives took their dead and injured with them on leaving the battleground. After the day-long fight, with a break for lunch by both sides, the attackers slipped away, regrouped by a swampy stand of willow on the west shore of Lake Washington, and then vanished into the night after having caused relatively little physical damage.

The psychological impact of the raid on the white community was quite another matter. That the Indians had come so near to the settlement was doubly stunning because Governor Stevens had visited Seattle only a few days earlier in an effort to allay residents' fears over a rumored assault on their village. "I believe that the cities of New York and San Francisco will as soon be attacked by the Indians as the town of Seattle," he had declaimed. Thus the undertaking may be said to have served its purpose for the Indians. Word of the raid particularly frightened settlers who had previously been reluctant to abandon their homesteads for refuge in blockhouses and other temporary havens. Enlistments in the new militia units Stevens had called for jumped. Around Olympia and Steilacoom, deep regret was expressed over the shaping role in the bold attack attributed to Leschi, until lately the most trusted and admired of his people.

But was Leschi really involved in the notorious raid and, if so, to what extent? The Nisqually chief would deny soon afterward that he had taken part in the raid, but most historians have dismissed Leschi's denial. The well-regarded Hubert Howe Bancroft, in his 1890 *History of Washington, Idaho and Montana, 1845–1889,* stated that a parley was held by Leschi, Owhi, and other leaders—no place or date was given or source provided for the report—"in which the plan was arranged for an immediate attack on the town." The plan called for "the 'friendly' Indians to prevent the escape of the people to the ships in the bay, while the warriors assembled to the number of more than a thousand in the woods which covered the hills back of town made the assault." No mention was made of Leschi's role once the shooting began. In his 1922 *History of Oregon,* Charles Henry Carey wrote that "a considerable number of hostiles led by Leschi of the Nisquallies and Owhi of the Upper Yakimas attacked Seattle and poured hot fire into the town all day." No source was given. Clinton Snowden's 1909 *History of Washington* went so far as to say, "A few days after the battle Leschi sent word to Captain Gansevoorst [recently installed skipper of the *Decatur*] that he would return in another month and destroy the town"—again, no source was provided for this bit of bravado, out of keeping with almost all other accounts of Leschi's deportment. A. J. Splawn, a cattle rancher who spent fifty years among the Yakima people recording their history, touched on the Seattle raid in his 500-page, 1917 biography titled *Kamiakin: Last Hero of the Yakimas.* Splawn wrote that in January 1856, Kamiakin's subchief, Owhi of the Upper Yakimas, received a message from Leschi "asking that a band of warriors be sent him to aid in his contemplated attack on Seattle." Splawn concurs that Leschi's uncle Owhi brought along his son Qualchan, one of his tribe's best warriors, to lead a band of 100 braves over the mountains to Leschi's camp near Lake Washington; he added that "Qualchan told the Nisqually leaders that he disapproved of their plan of attack," but provided no details about their disagreement. When the attack failed, "Qualchan and his braves returned to the Kittitas valley," just east of the Cascades.

The closest thing to hard evidence placing Leschi at Seattle is the testimony, however sketchy, recorded at a special U.S. military commission hearing convened at Seattle on May 15, 1856, to settle, among other issues, who the perpetrators were. An Indian named Clackem testified he had spent time at Leschi's base camp near the upper White River, where he had been detained as a suspected informer. He had not wanted to join Leschi's party of fifty warriors hauling eight canoes on the trip to Seattle, but went just the same; he did not say whether he himself joined the raiders or saw Leschi among them. "Old Mose," eager like others among the tribal witnesses to ingratiate himself with his examiners and avoid punishment, said he had sent his son to Seattle to warn the whites of the imminent raid. In answer to a direct query as to whether he saw Leschi among the warriors there, he said: "I suppose I saw him, but did not recognize him." Another native witness, Sklinsum, confirmed having seen Clackem at Leschi's White River camp, but when asked if Leschi was among the raiders who arrived on the western side of Lake Washington, he said, "I think he was." A brave called Bob said he heard that Leschi was around but did not actually see him. Another Indian, Bruream, testified, "I first saw Leschi at the lake. They [not explicitly naming Leschi] made me come with them to Seattle. They gave me some beef."

With no stronger evidence than this, newspapers and other popular accounts of the event routinely cite Leschi as the raid's instigator and spearhead, and his alleged role has been memorialized by the white community, which now refers to the upscale lakeside Seattle neighborhood where the Indians reassembled after the raid as Leschi Park. Thus do legends sprout. Today's Nisquallies are of two minds about the raid and whether Leschi inspired it. Tribal shaman Jim McCloud, prideful about the cheeky assertiveness if not the outcome of the mission, says that Leschi "camped there, organized it—and was behind it." But one should not ask or expect a shaman to provide documentary evidence. Nisqually tribal historian Cecilia Carpenter, who gathered an archive that occupied much of her home in the Parkland section of Tacoma before her death in 2010, doubted that Leschi was at Seattle, but her opinion as well rested more on supposition than hard evidence.

THE BATTLE OF SEATTLE—a shooting spree more than a military engagement—was the high-water mark of the Indian resistance movement west of the mountains. While the raid inflicted only small losses in life and property on the whites, it was a far more aggressive statement of the natives' burning resentment than the earlier game of hide-and-seek they had been playing to lure their pursuers into woodland ambushes. But the raid did not affect the balance of power, which now began to shift away from Leschi's ragged little army.

The failure of the Seattle incursion to garner fresh weaponry and supplies—the attackers must have spent a considerable portion of their remaining "gun food" on the unavailing raid—stood in marked contrast to the condition of their foes, growing more numerous and fearsome. Patkamin, believing that Indian defiance of the white man was doomed, now brought his band of seventy-five Snoqualmie warriors over to Stevens's side, hoping in return to extract favorable treatment for his tribe. The addition of Pat's braves to others who had already gone over to the settlers' side to save their skins meant that Leschi now faced as many Indian enemies in the field as he retained in his own ranks. Worse still for his military outlook was the arrival of a new, astute commander of the regular army garrison at Fort Steilacoom, along with several hundred more troops.

Lieutenant Colonel Silas Casey of the Ninth U.S. Infantry division had graduated from West Point a dozen years before Stevens, earned battle scars in the Mexican War, and fought Indians on two coasts—the Seminoles in Florida and the Coquilles in Oregon—and elsewhere in between. Having learned the natives' ways of war by use of speed and stealth, he would soon turn them against Leschi's ambushers. Possessor of a lucid military mind and a deft pen, Casey later wrote a two-volume treatise on infantry tactics that became a standard guide for U.S. Army troops during the Civil War.

Friendly and cooperative with Stevens on the surface, the tough-minded Casey put up with little guff from the governor, whom he took for an ambitious intriguer out to crush the straggly Indians and gain glory for it. "It will afford me pleasure to cooperate with the force [of militiamen] you are [going] about raising," he wrote Stevens soon after his arrival at Puget Sound. Since he shared the views of his superior, General Wool, about the troublemaking tendencies of undisciplined volunteer soldiers, Casey added, "As my small rations are limited I shall not be justified in opening them to you." Translation: *Please leave the fighting to us, Governor.*

Aware of the growing size and improving skill of the white forces likely to be thrown against his as soon as warmer weather arrived, Leschi tried again to reach out for a negotiated peace, now that Stevens was back in Olympia. For an intermediary he selected a neighbor, John McLeod, one of a group of former employees of the Bay's Puget Sound Agricultural Company who were of British, Gaelic, or French descent but had become naturalized American citizens, married Indian women or those of mixed blood, and established their own farms along Muck Creek, not far from Tolmie's domain. A thirty-four-year-old ex-sheepherder, McLeod was locally renowned as a prodigious drinker, a Bible-wielding moralizer, and fiercely independent. When promised by Leschi, just as Jim McAllister had been, that he and his partly Indian family would not be harmed if they stayed on their land and did not side with the white soldiers once the fighting began, McLeod—along with most of his Muck Creek neighbors—chose not to abandon their farms and join the white flight to the blockhouses and stockaded forts and towns.

A week after the Seattle raid, Leschi and fifteen of his warriors paid a clandestine visit to McLeod. According to an account in the *Courier,* Leschi wanted McLeod to deliver a message to the new commander at Fort Steilacoom, who he hoped might be more receptive to it than Isaac Stevens, with his insistence on the Indians' unconditional submission. The gist of Leschi's message was similar to what he had told John Swan at Fox Island a month earlier about the natives' desire to end the war. In the interim, though, had come the Seattle raid, which, whether or not under Leschi's command, had served to let white officials know that the Indian resistance was still capable of disturbing the peace and delaying the expansion of white settlement. Speaking to McLeod with what the newspaper termed "savage earnestness," Leschi assailed Stevens and

accused him of having deceived them at the [Medicine Creek] treaty, and said he would like to have two pieces of paper taken, on one to be written the wrongs done by the Indians; on the other the wrong the whites have inflicted upon them. Let these two papers, said he, be taken to the Great Chief, and let him decide who is the most to blame—the Indian who has had his lands taken from him, or the white man who has deceived him?

Leschi ended his message for Casey by insisting that neither he nor his warriors had taken part in the Battle of Seattle. In a further effort to show his good faith, he also asked the Fort Steilacoom commander to dispatch John Swan, lately retired from his post as warden on Fox Island, to visit the Indian guerrillas' hideout deep in the forest between the White and Green rivers in order to observe his people's condition and to hear them express firsthand their desire to coexist amicably with the whites. Casey, probably without clearing the mission with Stevens, urged Swan to take up the offer by Leschi; at the least, Swan could bring back useful intelligence about Leschi's capacity to continue waging war.

After a stay of a day and two nights at the remote Indian war camp, a ring of twenty log cabins arranged for maximum protection beside the

Green River, Swan returned and reported to Casey on the bleak conditions and signs of discord among the 150 or so braves gathered there. "Leschi is anxious for peace," the *Courier* said Swan had concluded, "but he wishes a guarantee that his people will receive no punishment, and that a new reservation shall be set apart for their use. He fears that if his people lay down their arms private citizens may take their lives for what they have done in war."

Stevens offered no receptivity to Leschi's terms and almost surely interpreted his plea and straitened circumstances as further proof of the Indians' growing desperation in the face of an expected all-out assault by white soldiers. Leschi's vulnerability was revealed ten days after Swan's stay when the Nisqually leader received other visitors, distinctly unwelcome ones. Baited with an offer from white officials of twenty dollars for the head of any of Leschi's warriors and eighty dollars for the chief's, Patkamin's Snoqualmie braves made their way to Leschi's secluded camp. Outnumbered by the defenders, Pat's men used the cover of darkness to surround Leschi's compound but were detected by the Nisqually sentries. According to an account in the *Pioneer and Democrat,* the two chiefs loudly exchanged insults through the night air, each promising to own the other's head once daylight came. After withstanding ten hours of steady gunfire, which grew more intense and destructive as Pat's marauders crept closer, Leschi's men ran for it at dawn. They splashed across the Green River or clung to logs to stay afloat, but lost at least nine braves and perhaps twice that many; the attackers, far fewer. It was Leschi's first real defeat since he had taken up arms, and ironically it was inflicted by those of his own race.

As Leschi tried to regroup his forces, in part by urgently seeking reinforcements from his Yakima and Klickitat relatives beyond the mountains, Silas Casey moved out from Fort Steilacoom with 250 trained army regulars, determined to flush out pockets of Indian resistance with short, swift jabs. Meanwhile, Stevens was dispatching his volunteer units in every direction to inflict all possible pain on any natives at liberty (instead of being inside their assigned internment camps) and to build forts, blockhouses, and ferry landings ever deeper in Indian Country for easier pursuit of their quarry. Stevens was unmoved by advice from Office of Indian Affairs Commissioner Manypenny urging him to "avoid vindictive and unnecessary bloodshed" and to bear in mind that Indians "who were criminal may be treated with magnanimity after laying down arms."

With a total force of nearly 700 regulars, volunteers, and friendlies scouring the countryside as it burst into bloom, the governor insisted it was no time to exercise restraint or to act charitably. In a snarling March 9 reply to Manypenny, Stevens delved into fantasy to make his case. The Indians were on the rampage, he wrote, threatening "entirely unprotected" settlements, targeting supply trains, inciting hostility among friendlies by "wiles and falsehoods"—all requiring that the white community be saved from "the treacherous and ferocious Indians who have barbarously murdered men, women and children and laid waste nearly two entire counties . . . and whilst they shall be made unconditionally to surrender and their leaders to be made to suffer death, the Indians generally shall be dealt with in a spirit of humanity and kindness."

It was a rant by a once self-possessed man who had allowed his pride, wounded by his own misjudgments, to turn him delusional, bordering on the pathological. The wrong he had done the tribes, more acute in some cases than others, was nothing in his mind when compared to the way they had wronged him by disavowing his treaties with them. How dare they defy him! In deep denial of his contribution to the outbreak of hostilities, Stevens would take it out on the Indians' collective hides and, in the process, become an out-of-control avenger. His fulminating letter to Manypenny was awash with distortions. The Indian resistance fighters had not laid waste much of anything, let alone "two entire counties" or Seattle, and their barbarous killing spree of civilians on the White River was four months in the past and had not been repeated. Meanwhile, as he neglected to mention to the head of the Indian bureau, militiamen had slain and mutilated a revered Indian chief, Peopeomoxmox, and his guards who had come to parley under a flag of truce.

Stevens's letter also disclosed a troubling unfamiliarity with basic human psychology. Did he really think the way to end the fighting was to promise a death sentence to every rebel Indian leader? If anything, it would guarantee their diehard resistance. And when did the governor suppose he had ever shown the natives "a spirit of humanity and kindness" that might have encouraged them to place their fate in his hands by surrendering to him unconditionally?

LESCHI'S GRAVEST problem from the first had been the meager support given his struggle of defiance by the tribes west of the Cascades, few of whose members were willing to stand up to Isaac Stevens. Most, like old Chief Seattle, had resigned themselves to a stiflingly confined existence as the whites dictated. And the stouter-hearted plains tribes led by the Yakimas' Chief Kamiakin were disinclined to throw in with Leschi's nearly exhausted guerrilla campaign.

To blunt the eastward surge of the white soldiers, Leschi had to gamble now by trying to bloody the troops newly based at barracks on Connell's Prairie. On the evening of March 9, he positioned about 150 braves, the bulk of his thinning ranks, on a heavily wooded hillside overlooking a narrow road from the prairie down to the nearby White River, where army engineers were constructing a ferry landing and adjacent fortification. Given their advantage in numbers, firing from cover on higher ground, and the element of surprise, Leschi's braves seemed poised for a major victory.

But the Indians were overanxious. As a column of volunteers proceeded single file down the road early the next morning on their way to help the engineers by the river, a native rifleman opened fire prematurely. The whites in the lead scrambled for cover while those in the rear raced back to camp to summon reinforcements.

As the two-hour firefight grew in fury, the attackers' lurking women spurred on their braves with thunderous drumbeats intended as well to unnerve the whites. The Indians, though, were unwilling to press their early advantage by breaking from cover and charging down on the soldiers. New militia units, responding quickly to the reported ambush, were able to prevent the attackers from encircling the poorly positioned column of militiamen. The longer the battle lasted, the better the volunteers coordinated their movements to deflect the full brunt of the enemy fusillade. Still, they were firing uphill, and their officers saw that the only way to dislodge their assailants from their hiding places was to engage them hand to hand. But as Major Gilmore Hays later described the action:

> It was deemed too dangerous to charge them in front. Capt. Rabbeson was ordered to take a few men and join Capt. Swindell to make a flank movement to the right and charge the enemy in his rear.*
>
> This they succeeded doing in the same gallant manner, that

---

*The heroic Captain Rabbeson was the same Tony Rabbeson who had barely escaped with his life only a few miles away the previous October as a member of the Tidd express party, whose ambush by Leschi's men he described in the *Pioneer and Democrat* soon after.

they had done at an early hour during the fight. Simultaneous with this movement, Captain Hennes and Capt. White charged them from the front. The Indians were routed, put to flight, and pursued for a mile or more along the trail . . . covered with blood. It is believed that not less than twenty-five or thirty were killed dead on the field, and many wounded—they were seen carrying off their wounded and dead from the time the fight commenced until its termination. . . .

I regard the victory of this day as complete—a grand triumph. The Indians had together their whole force. They picked their ground. They brought on the attack without being seen by our own troops. They exceeded us in numbers nearly if not two to one, and we whipped and drove them before us.

The celebratory spirit among the volunteers was echoed in a reply to Hays from his commanding officer, General James Tilton, at militia headquarters: "The morale of the enemy being now broken by the shock it has received from the blow lately inflicted by the Central Battalion, following so rapidly the defeat of the enemy lately sustained from the U.S. regulars under the gallant Col. Casey of the 9th Infantry, it is confidently expected that these savages will be speedily annihilated and driven over the Cascades."

Indian morale was further depressed by events that soon occurred near Seattle, north of Leschi's theater of operation. There a force of Duwamish rebels and their allies rejected an order to disband by officers from two arriving U.S. Navy ships. The result was an assault on their terrain by marines who killed or wounded nearly half of the 120 natives. The Puget Sound Indian War was over; only the militant tribes east of the Cascades remained an unspent force. And thanks to the policy adopted by Colonel George Wright, in charge of army operations there, of not forcing the plains tribes to submit so long as they stayed off the warpath and did not commit individual acts of violence against whites, sustained combat appeared to be all but over.

Given the forces ranged against him, likely only to grow in size, Leschi now had three options. He could surrender himself and his men unconditionally in the hope that Stevens's call for vengeance would be tempered by recognition that the insurgency had been the final spasm of protest from a people fearful that their whole way of life was doomed. Alternatively, Leschi could divide up his people and allow them to disperse into the countryside, perhaps to reassemble sometime in the future, but essentially quitting the fight with little to show for their effort. Or he could retreat over the mountains and seek refuge with the Yakimas and their relatives for a time, waiting for Stevens to retire or to be removed from his post and praying that his replacement would prove forgiving—and maybe even grant his tribe a more generous reservation.

Leschi chose the third course, trying to hold together his hungry and ill-clad cohort as it dragged through the late-winter snows and over the mountains in flight. Yet he could take solace even in travail, considering the long odds that had militated against his success. For the fact was, as historian Alexandra Harmon has pointed out, Leschi's little army "had demonstrated impressive powers. They had terrified settlers, avenged some injuries, and forced Americans to acknowledge their pride and strength." But Isaac Stevens was not among them.

LIEUTENANT COLONEL CASEY, commander of Fort Steilacoom, was satisfied that the Indian resistance west of the mountains was ended but remained fearful that roaming militiamen might reignite trouble. He wrote to Stevens a few days after the volunteers' victory at Connell's Prairie—admittedly their finest hour in the war—and advised that his own command of army regulars had "a sufficient number of troops to protect this frontier without the aid of those now in the service of the Territory." The governor replied that to withdraw his militia would leave the settlements "open to attacks by marauding Indians, and at the very moment when our troops are prepared to strike a blow, and perhaps the decisive blow."

Stevens may not yet have realized that his men had already struck the decisive blow and that there were no "marauding Indians" west of the mountains for white soldiers to engage. Nor would he admit that Colonel Wright was in a strong position in the Naches Valley, past the Cascades, to deal with further outbreaks of Indian violence. Perhaps hungry for plaudits over his performance as warmaker as well as treatymaker, the governor certainly seemed to be relishing the role of self-appointed commander-in-chief of his civilian army too much to give it up. Writing to Secretary of War Davis in disparagement of Casey's pointed invitation to him to stop playing soldier, Stevens insisted, "Our safety lies in two things: 1st. To carry the war against the hostiles with the full force of the Territory, and to bring them to unconditional submission; and 2nd. To give no cause of offense to the friendly Indians in our midst." Stevens then appealed to Davis as a former Indian fighter himself, aware of the natives' expectation that white troops would "not be withdrawn till they have accomplished the object for which they were sent into the field. We must push forward and do the work we have undertaken, else the Indian will say HE has driven us from the field." In other words, butcher the lot of them so none is left to call you weakling.

So long as he was at it, Stevens stepped up his effort to vilify General Wool by telling Davis that if the tribes in his region were to be subdued, the War Department had better recognize "the necessity of removing from the command of the Department of the Pacific, a man who has by his acts, so far as this Territory is concerned, shown an utter incapacity."

Their loathing was mutual. In an April 4, 1856, letter, two weeks after Stevens's outburst against him, Wool wrote to his superiors in the capital that if the governor were not so "anxious for a long and expensive war and the barbarous determination . . . to exterminate the Indians, I would soon put an end to the Indian war."

Behind Stevens's vehemence in pressing to continue all-out war was a self-deluding spitefulness that he revealed in his March 21 letter to Davis:

> Perhaps the most melancholy feature of the war is, that the Indians who have taken the lead in murdering our men, our women and children, were those who received the most favors from the Whites, and were held by them in the most consideration. Many cases have occurred of Indians killing their friends and benefactors. Are you surprised that a general distrust of all Indians pervades in the public mind . . . ?

Here again, he was trafficking in mendacity. In fact, the number of women and children who were murdered by the Indians in Washington Territory since the war began could be counted on the fingers of one hand. And there were no cases of Indians killing their "friends and benefactors" except in combat. And what exactly were all those alleged "favors" and many forms of "consideration" that the governor believed the whites had showered on the likes of Leschi that had not been reciprocated many times over? Stevens was unwittingly saying, with Leschi foremost in his mind, that here was a mere Indian whom some whites had actually treated well, as if he were approximately human, yet this barbarian had had the temerity to respond in strenuous self-defense when the white community demanded virtually all of his people's land.

Not only did Stevens decline to deactivate his militiamen as urged by the army, but now he spurred his volunteers to a new level of death-dealing by issuing his unit commanders a license making explicit what until then had been only a tacit understanding: any natives not already residing in an internment camp or among an officially approved band of friendlies, like Patkamin's warriors, were legitimate targets. "All Indians found in your field of operations . . . are to be considered as enemies."

One of the governor's militia units, the Washington Mounted Rifles, commanded by Hamilton Jordan Goss Maxon, used this new license to kill with particular viciousness. Maxon, forty-three at the time and characterized by one contemporary commentator as a fellow of "jolly disposition," beneath which lay "a low cunning and brutal instinct . . . with a stomach entirely out of proportion to his brains," was a native Virginian who had traveled up the Oregon Trail with his wife and three children in 1845 before settling in what became Washington Territory. He made his mark on the frontier operating a sawmill and fighting in the Cayuse War.

Early in April, Maxon's unit was sent to answer a complaint that Indians along the upper Nisqually River had been stealing horses and cattle from white farms. With fifty-five mounted militiamen riding behind him, Maxon had traveled thirty miles up the Nisqually basin to where the swift-running Mashel River joined it from the east, close to Leschi's birthplace village. There Maxon's marauders scouted out an encampment of forty to fifty Nisquallies, mostly women, children, and old men, trying to hide out from the war and avoid internment. When found, they were fishing and otherwise peacefully engaged. Maxon would later tell the *Pioneer and Democrat* that his scouts had found several members of the band slaughtering horses taken from white farms and that gunshots had been aimed in his soldiers' direction before they retaliated. His claimed provocation was not supported by the extensive field notes of the episode recorded by Private A. J. Kane or by a white civilian witness at the scene, Robert Thompson, who operated the supply wagons servicing the militia horsemen.

Maxon's party dismounted, crept close toward one of the several groups the Nisquallies had divided themselves into for safety, and pounced, setting off a great tumult as the Indians tried to flee toward the river. The soldiers shot at everything that moved, starting with the slow and decrepit, and chased the fleeter victims into the water, which soon ran red with their blood. Some infants had their skulls dashed on the rocks, according to the oral tribal rendition of the massacre, which was said to have taken about thirty Indian lives. Kane's notes said that only eight of the Indians were cut down but acknowledged that few prisoners were captured, implying that the volunteers were on a killing spree. Thompson estimated that fifteen to seventeen natives were killed, noting that there were almost no able-bodied men among Maxon's prey.

The *Pioneer and Democrat* wrote up the slaughter as if it were a great victory, headlining its account "Southern Battalion Right Side Up: Complete Surprise on an Indian Encampment," and credited Maxon's account that the Indians had fired first—almost certainly the last thing that the defenseless Nisquallies would have done. At the least, the death toll of the atrocity equaled that of the White River Massacre and was probably twice or three times as high.

It was precisely the kind of mindlessly vindictive bloodshed that Manypenny had urged Stevens to avoid, and it bore the mark of the untethered vigilantism Wool and Casey feared from the militiamen. By contrast, a regular army unit under Lieutenant August Kautz came upon another Nisqually group in the same general area soon after the Maxon abomination and, without violence, took the seven men and sixteen women and children into custody and marched them back to Fort Steilacoom, to be held for internment until transfer to a reservation.

Maxon got promoted to major for his accomplishment.

9

The Wages of Zealotry

ISAAC STEVENS'S BOUNDLESS FURY over Leschi's rebellion, even after it had been quelled, and his seething resentment toward the settlers in Washington Territory not in full accord with his relentless crackdown on the Indians now drove the governor to a sequence of extreme measures that imperiled his career of genuine, if checkered, accomplishment. This time, Hamilton Maxon served as the instigator of the governor's rashness rather than merely his genocidal instrument in the field.

As Maxon's volunteers continued their mounted manhunt crisscrossing Pierce County from the foothills of Mount Rainier to the Sound, rumors reached them that the colony of farmers and stock-raisers along Muck Creek, about a dozen miles south of Steilacoom, had been siding with the Indian resistance by offering Leschi's warriors food, supplies, overnight shelter, and information about the white soldiers' movements. The Muck Creek people, who, as noted earlier, were mostly foreign-born men married to native women and formerly employed by the British-owned Hudson's Bay Company, were allegedly promised, in return for their hospitality, that they would be left to farm unmolested by tribal rebels.

This reported grant of immunity struck Maxon as all the more incriminating when added to the Muck Creek residents' claim of neutrality, their unwillingness to serve in the militia, and their refusal to take refuge with most of the white community. These attitudes seemed to belie the farmers' insistence that they had not willfully harbored Leschi's fighters and had given them only enough supplies and comfort to deter their uninvited visitors from turning on them. It did not much matter to Maxon that other white settlers had similarly remained on their homesteads and did not join the fight against the natives—that may have made them cowards and shirkers but not traitors.

Maxon told Stevens it was pointless to try to wage all-out war on the Indians so long as these obviously anti-American intriguers at Muck Creek were allowed to remain on their land and help the enemy every way they could. Frankly, he added, his volunteers were threatening to lay down their arms and go home unless these Indian-lovers were arrested and detained.

Stevens bought Maxon's argument and in early March, without any hard evidence in hand or the other requisites of due process of law, ordered a dozen Muck Creek families taken into custody and held indefinitely. Explaining this gross abridgement of liberty to the territorial legislature, the governor railed against "so-called neutrals, who remained on their claims unmolested, when our patriotic citizens were compelled to live in blockhouses." That no citizens had been *compelled* to live in blockhouses or anywhere else made the denunciation just another instance of Stevens's indulgence in self-justifying demagoguery. "There is no such thing, in my humble judgment, as neutrality in an Indian war," he said, "and whoever can remain on his claim unmolested is an ally of the enemy and must be dealt with as such." So much for the hallowed American presumption of innocence; suspicion was reason enough to hound dissenters.

Five of the Muck Creek farmers, including the irrepressible John McLeod, escaped after several weeks of confinement and returned to their farms, only to be recaptured, labeled prisoners of war, and told they would be tried for treason—a capital crime—not by a civil court but by a five-man military tribunal chosen by Stevens. In asking Colonel Casey to confine the prisoners in the Fort Steilacoom brig, the governor explained that "we have reason to believe, from their immunity from disaster, that [the accused] have been giving aid and comfort to the enemy."

The Muck Creek Five hired a pair of prominent Steilacoom lawyers, who, since the civil courts were not then in session, hurried up the Sound to the Whidbey Island residence of Judge Francis Chenoweth of Washington Territory's Third Judicial District and convinced him to issue a writ of habeas corpus freeing the prisoners pending an arraignment proceeding. The next day, April 4, 1856, Stevens decreed martial law in Pierce County, suspending all functions of civil government, including the courts. In an accompanying statement, he sought to justify this radical measure by tarring the prisoners as "evil-disposed persons" who had been at liberty while the Indian war was being actively prosecuted "throughout nearly the whole of the said [Pierce] county . . . with great injury to the public"—a gross distortion of the extent and consequences of the combat. Casey knew as much and tried to check Stevens's misguided zealotry by expressing doubt that his proclamation of martial law "can relieve me from the obligation to obey the requisition of the civil authority"—that is, the writ to free the prisoners—and asked for permission to be relieved of their charge.

Judge Chenoweth had just fallen ill but was well enough to issue a scathing denunciation of Stevens's "monstrous assumption of arbitrary powers" in a letter to the Muck Creek Five's lawyers. Since the territorial courts were fully operational, wrote the judge, "it is difficult to conceive the necessity for so extraordinary a proceeding [i.e., the martial law decree], and the lives and interests of the people would seem to be a sufficient guarantee, that they could not but feel a deep and lively concern in the prompt arrest and punishment of traitors." Stevens's decree, the judge added, "shows no necessity whatever for taking the law into his own hands. He does not even indicate that there was the slightest difficulty in prosecuting to final judgment and execution of these 'evil disposed persons.'"

With Chenoweth bedridden and sidelined, the issue hung in abeyance—and the captives stayed in jail—until early May, when Pierce County's regular court term was due to open. Chenoweth's lingering illness forced onto the stage his senior colleague, Edward Lander, who served as both the presiding judge of the neighboring Second Judicial District, centered in Thurston County, and chief justice of Washington Territory's Supreme Court, its appellate tribunal. Lander's dedication to the anti-Indian cause could not have been doubted by Stevens. Having volunteered to serve as captain in the militia company active in the Seattle region, the judge had to absent himself from his temporary military assignment to come to Steilacoom, where Chenoweth normally held forth. A scholarly, Harvard-trained lawyer who had practiced in Massachusetts, Lander displayed a magisterial presence on the bench, with a girth that matched his massive dignity and a lacerating gaze known to intimidate even the most practiced advocates who came before him. Stevens sent Frank Shaw, by then a colonel in the militia, to ask the territory's ranking judge to delay the start of his court's term so that the governor's declaration of martial law could not be challenged. Pointing out it was his sworn duty to hold court, Lander wrote to Stevens that he was fearful of "an imminent collision between civil and military authorities" and politely asked him to rescind his martial law decree, "especially as the present conditions of the county seem not to require it as strongly as before." But Stevens would not draw back.

With the governor's gauntlet waving under his nose, Judge Lander responded by ordering every able-bodied male over sixteen in the county to attend court the next day and function as a *posse comitatus* to protect the integrity of civil law. Shaw in turn ordered twenty armed men in territorial uniform to accompany him into the courtroom, telling them to empty it if the judge gaveled the chamber into session. About thirty citizens, a number of them lawyers, braved the threat of violence in order to defend the court and civil rule over martial law. Among the lawyers was George Gibbs, who was well acquainted with Shaw from their work together on the Medicine Creek Treaty and other labors in Stevens's behalf.

"What do you aim to do to the judge, Frank?" Gibbs reportedly asked the militia colonel at their confrontation in court.

"I'm going to arrest him and take him to the fort," Shaw told him.

"You can't do that," the lawyer cautioned.

"The hell I can't," Shaw replied.

As his soldiers lined up, rifles at the ready and doubly menacing within the confines of so small a chamber, Shaw's resolve could not be doubted. Fearful that blood was about to flow, Judge Lander begged his protectors not to unsheathe their weapons or otherwise intervene as he submitted at gunpoint, allowing himself, his clerk, and the court's records to be taken to the governor's lair in Olympia.

In Steilacoom, where sentiment strongly favored Whig politics over the governor's Democratic ties, there was shock over the thuggish tactics that shut down the court. A torchlight parade and street rally were held that same night to protest Stevens's alleged flouting of the Constitution, which ordained in Article 1, Section 9 that the issuance of habeas corpus writs "should not be suspended unless when, in cases of rebellion or invasion, the public safety may require it." A resolution of outrage was drawn up, with Gibbs as its principal author, signed by Whigs and Democrats alike, and sent to territorial newspapers. To underscore the gravity of the perceived offense, the protesters also crafted a petition to President Pierce, attacking the governor for "flagrant usurpation of power" and the conduct of a despot. If there were legitimate charges to be lodged against the Muck Creek farmers, the petitioners asserted, they had to be heard and considered by a jury of the accused's peers, not in a star chamber proceeding of the governor's creation—Anglo-American jurisprudence had decreed as much since the signing of the Magna Carta 641 years earlier.

Not altogether indifferent to public opinion (or the scrutiny of federal officials in Washington, D.C.), Stevens drew up an anonymous rebuttal to his critics and had it published in the local press. The essence of his defense was that he had indeed acted in a time of rebellion by the natives, which threatened the public safety; witness that "whole families had been inhumanely massacred; alarm and consternation pervaded the whole territory . . . a majority of citizens [were] in arms, actively pursuing the enemy." His rationale ignored the reality that west of the Cascades, no Indian warriors had been detected for two months prior to Stevens's imposition of martial law. It was true, though, that the Indians had not heeded the governor's demand for unconditional surrender, and a sizable number of tribes remained hostile, if militarily inactive, on the eastern plains. Arguably, there was still a war on.

But the rest of Stevens's self-defense revealed the degree of fanaticism that seemed to have routed his better instincts. Without offering evidence, he insisted that the Muck Creek Five had been "acting as spies," giving the Indians supplies, and "in every way furnishing them aid and comfort." He claimed that if the habeas corpus writ had been complied with, the result "would have been to paralyze the military in their exertions to end the war, and to send into their midst a band of Indian spies."*

---

*In another display of his growing tendency to indulge in self-justification no matter how casual its acquaintance with the truth, Stevens had written two days earlier, in his annual report to U.S. Indian Commissioner Manypenny: "It is here to be remarked that the reservations both of the Nisqually and Puyallup tribes were selected by them and agreed to by me. On an examination of them, they were found to be different from what they were represented to me by the Indians and both Col. Shaw and Col. Simmons had assured the Indians, that they were unquestionably to have the benefit of that provision of the treaty, which provided for change of the reservation, when their good and the public advantage required it." There is no known evidence that (1) either tribe chose and then prevailed upon Stevens to grant them the two tiny, stony, heavily wooded reservations on high ground above the Sound cited in the treaty—the very cause for Leschi's having taken up arms against him—or that (2) Shaw and Simmons told the tribes they "were unquestionably to have the benefit" of the treaty article allowing a change of reservation sites. Shaw's version, discussed earlier, was a vague promise without a time frame. And any such change of reservation was not ensured by the Indians' requesting it for their benefit, as Stevens intimated, but was possible only upon the President's approval.

Even some of the governor's firmest adherents were now quietly expressing concern over his draconian methods to restore domestic tranquility after it had already returned.

When Stevens gave no ground, Gibbs and several others among the governor's close former associates now unloaded on him. In a May 11 letter, authored principally by Gibbs, to Secretary of State William Marcy, the ranking member and War Secretary Davis's principal adversary in the Pierce cabinet, the governor's detractors vilified him as—a bit redundantly—"a diminutive Napoleon" who was "actuated by arrogant and unbridled love of power that unfits him for any trust in which life or liberty are concerned." His actions, they wrote, required Stevens's superiors to determine "whether a public servant shall be allowed to overrule the law . . . at his sole and absolute discretion . . . or whether the law of the land is to control him." Then came the crushing charge that Isaac Stevens was a drunkard: "Of naturally arrogant and domineering character, of overweening ambition, and even unscrupulous of the means requisite to effect his objects, he has been further inflamed by the immoderate use of ardent spirits, and in his fits of intoxication knows no bounds to his language or to his actions [as] almost everyone who has had official connection with him is aware."

When the previously unpublicized letter was disclosed by the *Pioneer and Democrat* the following spring, the paper trivialized the drinking charge as standard political calumny and sneered at its author, Gibbs, for his failure "to risk his precious neck in the field of danger in the late . . . Indian war." Gibbs returned the fire by amplifying the charge in the June 5, 1857, issue of the new *Washington Republican,* stating that Stevens had exhibited himself while drunk at numerous "important public functions," including speeches at Portland, Vancouver, and Steilacoom, the last of which Gibbs said he had personally witnessed. Worse still, the governor was charged with making an inebriated display of himself at treaty councils with the south Sound, Nez Perce, Spokane, and Blackfoot tribes, "bringing his official status in contempt with the Indians, destroying his influence over them, and endangering the peace of the territory." The governor's unfitness for office was further revealed by "his vulgar and indecent abuse of prisoners at Olympia . . . [and] when swaggering in the barrooms of Portland, he swore that, by G-d, he would crush every one who had opposed his martial law." Gibbs was neither sued for libel nor challenged to a duel over his scathing revelations.

The confrontation between the chief executive and the chief justice of

Washington Territory, meanwhile, grew hotter still when Lander was released from custody after a few days and returned to Olympia to preside over the opening of the Second District Court term in Thurston County, his home jurisdiction, on May 14. Stevens, anticipating the judge, had decreed martial law there as well as in neighboring Pierce County. Lander's first order of business was to issue a bench warrant summoning the governor to appear before him to explain why he had disregarded Judge Chenoweth's habeas corpus writ to free the Muck Creek prisoners pending legal action against them.

In response, Stevens plunged still deeper into lawlessness. The U.S. territorial marshal assigned to serve the summons on the governor found the door to Stevens's office barred by as many as a dozen—accounts vary as to the exact number—of his bulkiest loyalists among the militiamen, including Adjutant General James Tilton and Tony Rabbeson, lately a hero in the rout of Leschi's braves at Connell's Prairie. When the marshal tried to force the issue, a fistfight broke out, with Stevens himself, an old scrapper from his West Point days, reportedly part of the scuffle, and the summons went unserved. Compounding their malfeasance, the militiamen then marched to the house that served part-time as Lander's court and, finding that the judge had barricaded himself in his clerk's room, broke down the door and for the second time in eight days hauled away the chief justice of the territory. Told by his captors that his freedom would be restored if he agreed not to hold court or issue any more writs or warrants while martial law remained in place, Lander replied that he intended to carry out his duty and that the governor should do likewise. His defiance landed him in the territorial jail at Camp Montgomery, the militia headquarters, in a cell alongside the Muck Creek Five.

The law remained hostage to the governor's runaway behavior until the following week, when Judge Chenoweth, his health restored, returned to his courtroom in Steilacoom and denounced Stevens for his continuing usurpation of executive power. Upon learning the governor had instructed Shaw that the Muck Creek prisoners must "at all hazards" be tried by the commission of five militiamen (including Hamilton Maxon) whom Stevens had appointed at Camp Montgomery, Chenoweth defied the martial law decree and issued a fresh habeas corpus writ ordering Shaw to produce the prisoners in his courtroom. Stevens then deepened the predicament he had dug for himself by ordering Maxon to send thirty volunteers and arrest the judge if he reopened court on May 24. As Lander had done, Chenoweth called on the law-abiding citizenry to protect his courtroom, asking the Pierce County sheriff to round up enough man-power to form a defense posse. Then the judge took the added precaution of enlisting the help of Colonel Casey of nearby Fort Steilacoom, who agreed to position U.S. Army troops a mile from the courthouse, ready to intercede at the first outburst of violence. The showdown between law and order and tyrannical will was at hand.

Between fifty and sixty armed citizens had mustered in front of the courthouse when a force of thirty volunteers approached under the lead-ership of a young lieutenant whom Maxon had delegated to command them. As the militiamen neared, they were met by Casey, who had come alone to advise the officer that if his men used force to drive off the civil-ian guardsmen and arrest the judge, a force of army regulars was close at hand and under orders to stop them. In a display of discretion that proba-bly spared Isaac Stevens from dire consequences if his martial law fiasco had resulted in spilled blood, the lieutenant ordered his men to stand down and sent an express message to the governor, saying, "I shall make no forcible effort to arrest the Judge until I receive further orders from [Major] Maxon or some higher authority." No such order ever came. Stevens's fury had been checked.

The crisis unraveled quickly now. The military tribunal the governor had appointed to try the Muck Creek Five for treason declined to hear the case on the ground that it was a civil matter over which a militia had no jurisdiction. Chenoweth's habeas corpus writ was served at Camp Mont-gomery, the prisoners were brought to the county courthouse, and after the district prosecutor decided that the allegations against them were a hodgepodge of rumors and strained innuendo, the treason charges were dropped. On May 28, Stevens ended his protracted tantrum by rescinding the martial law decree.

The damage to his standing and reputation was severe. Letters protesting his conduct began to appear in *The New York Times* and other leading papers, attracting the nation's attention. In July, Judge Lander issued a warrant for Stevens's arrest on a contempt-of-court charge for having refused to accept the summons and explain why he had ignored Judge Chenoweth's original habeas corpus writ. Stevens momentarily submitted and appeared before Lander, but when the judge found him guilty and fined him a token fifty dollars to establish the principle that no official, even a governor, could flout the law with impunity, the unchas-tened despot *manqué* balked. He invoked the powers of his office to par-don himself temporarily until President Pierce had had an opportunity to

Isaac I. Stevens, as U.S. Army brigadier general ca. 1861 (left), and after serving as first governor of Washington Territory (above)

Leschi, last chief of the Nisquallies (below), painted after his death, and his half-brother Quiemuth (lower right), drawn in 1855

Enemies of Stevens:
author Ezra Meeker (below),
Hudson's Bay Company manager of
Fort Nisqually, William F. Tolmie
(right), and George Gibbs (lower right),
who drafted the
Medicine Creek Treaty

Key Stevens aides (clockwise from upper left): translator B. F. Shaw, territorial secretary Charles Mason, U.S. Indian agent Michael Simmons, and trial witness Antonio Rabbeson

Above: The tallest peak in the Cascade Range, 14,410-foot Mount Rainier, called Tahoma or Tacobet by Puget Sound tribes, painted in 1854 by John Mix Stanley

First Washington Territory capitol in Olympia, begun ca. 1855

Nineteenth-century Nisqually basket of coiled cedar and prairie grass

U.S. Army officers favoring justice for Leschi (clockwise from upper left):
Lieut. August Kautz, Lieut. Col. Silas Casey, Maj. Gen. John Wool,
and Maj. George Wright

Principal figures in Leschi's trials (clockwise from upper left):
Chief Justice Edward Lander, Judge Francis Chenoweth, attorney Frank Clark,
and Governor Fayette McMullin

Nisqually council chairwoman Cynthia Iyall speaking at a tribal event in 2009

Shapers of the Historical Court of Justice for Leschi (clockwise from left): Nisqually historian Cecilia Carpenter, Chief Justice Gerry Alexander, and attorney John Ladenburg

Nisqually rebirth: a new tribal youth and community center (above)
and the interior of Red Wind Casino (below), which houses
975 slot machines

review the entire matter. For a moment it appeared as if Stevens was about to bring down the pillars of jurisprudence upon his head, but his friends stepped in and paid the fine for him.

Stevens learned how far his star had fallen when he received a letter dated September 12 from Secretary of State Marcy, advising him of President Pierce's opinion of the governor's martial law misadventure. The President "has not been able to find in the case you have presented a justification for that extreme measure," Marcy reported, adding,

> It is quite certain that nothing but direful necessity, involving the probable overthrow of the civil government, could be alleged as any sort of excuse for superseding that government temporarily and substituting in its place an arbitrary, military rule. . . . While the President does not bring into question the motives by which you were actuated, he is induced, by an imperative sense of duty, to express his distinct disapproval of your conduct so far as respects the proclamation of martial law. . . . [I]t can never be excusable when the object in resorting to martial law was to act against the existing Government of the country or to supersede its functionaries in the discharge of their proper duties. The latter seem to have been the principal grounds you had for proclaiming martial law.

Yet Pierce was reluctant to remove from office a loyal supporter who had played a useful role in gaining him the White House. If Stevens's misconduct did not cost him his job, it earned him the rebuke of the two legislative bodies empowering him. The territorial legislature, favorable toward Stevens's overall performance in office, voted to reprimand him for having imposed martial law, and in January the U.S. Senate, yet to ratify any of his treaties after the one concluded at Medicine Creek, registered its "strongest condemnation" of his conduct.

Had Leschi been advised, as well he might have been, about the nature and extent of the reprimand his arch-nemesis had just been dealt, he could have justifiably taken satisfaction in the part he himself had played in driving the haughty governor toward frenetic self-destruction.

IN LATE MARCH 1856, a few weeks after the fighting had ended west of the Cascades with Leschi's retreat from Connell's Prairie, the militant southeastern tribes of Washington Territory delivered the bloodiest blow of the war in an attack on the white settlements along the Cascades Rapids on the Columbia River, near the army depot on the Oregon shore at The Dalles. Fourteen American civilians and three soldiers were killed and twelve wounded before troops arrived to drive off the raiders. The toll shocked General Wool into ordering a serious show of force, composed of about 500 soldiers, in the Yakima and Walla Walla valleys to quash further violence.

The new army initiative was led by Colonel George Wright, regarded as smart, tough, and tactful enough to cope with the captious Isaac Stevens. A West Point graduate, Wright was a thirty-year veteran of the Mexican and Indian wars with an exemplary combat record. After hunting down and hanging a number of the perpetrators of the Cascades Rapids atrocity, Wright chose a nonconfrontational mode of pacifying the Indians in his vast theater of operations: if the tribes would remain peaceable, he would discourage—if not forbid—white settlement in the region east of the mountains and north of the Columbia River so long as the Walla Walla council treaties remained unratified. He won peace pledges from the Yakimas and their allies, vows that Stevens would not credit.

Wright's strategy was repugnant to Stevens, of course. Keeping Yakima Country and beyond an Indian preserve, the governor argued, would only perpetuate the natives' savage condition, undercut treaty terms aimed at civilizing them, and, worst of all, allow the Indians to retain millions of acres of arable land coveted by white settlers. So he goaded Wright regularly, writing him, for example, on May 8, even in the midst of his martial law woes, that "my information in regard to the Indians on the Walla Walla and Snake River is that they are determined to prosecute the war." Skeptical of every aspect of Wright's policy, the governor grumbled to Indian commissioner Manypenny, "The point now is to exercise vigilance to prevent hostile bands [from] approaching the settlements. . . . Excesses and outrages must be met with a firm hand."

By mid-June, with the martial law tempest petering out, Stevens picked up his war cudgel anew and handed it to Frank Shaw, ordering him to lead 200 volunteers across the Cascades to kill Indians, never mind that George Wright did not need or want such a provocative presence. The governor wrote Wright on June 18 that Shaw's troops were on the way and instructed the veteran army officer, "The Walla Walla valley must be occupied immediately to prevent the extension of the war to the interior." Stevens added that he would happily take charge of any formerly hostile Indians who had "changed their condition," but then said he trusted that Wright shared his view "as to terms which should be allowed the Indians, viz: unconditional submission, and the rendering up the murderers and instigators of the war for punishment." In case Wright failed to grasp whom Stevens had most in mind, he closed: "I will . . . respectfully put you on guard in reference to Leschi, Nelson, Kitsap, and Quiemuth from the Sound and suggest that no arrangement be made which shall save their necks from the Executioner."

The governor's ardor for heaping vengeance on the Nisqually chief in particular was still more pointedly expressed in a letter he sent at about the same time to Sidney S. Ford Jr., the new U.S. Indian agent for the Sound and warden at the Fox Island internment camp, where hundreds of Nisquallies remained, including refugees who had lately come straggling back from the now stilled war zone. "It is necessary to procure a guide who knows the position of Leschi," Stevens instructed Ford. "If any of your Indians can be procured, promise fifty blankets to the man who will lead a party of soldiers to [Leschi's] camp." Fifty blankets was enough to make any Indian rich; Leschi now had a high bounty on his head.

Why did the chief of the Nisquallies continue to rank first on Stevens's hate list? The governor's fevered resolve to punish Leschi seemed to go beyond just an understandable desire for revenge against him for having been instrumental in the Indian uprising and the events that culminated in Stevens's disastrous decision to decree martial law. The pursuit of Leschi for his faithless defiance of the whites' dictates was now becoming Stevens's consuming obsession. Could it have been the result of a psychological blockage against admitting, even if only to himself, that he might have precipitated Leschi's actions by preying on a people unschooled in the transactional devices of the white world? For if the governor had done wrong at Medicine Creek, then Leschi must have been right to oppose him—a syllogism likely unacceptable to Stevens's rigid mental apparatus.

But why the need not just to punish and defame the Nisqually but to liquidate him? Why invest such passion vilifying Leschi as a criminal and murderer instead of recognizing him as a patriot among his own people who had been vanquished in a cause that was noble in their own eyes? In his unremitting rage, Stevens refused to dignify his antagonist in any way. As his biographer Kent Richards reflects, Stevens was convinced that the Medicine Creek tribes had willingly placed themselves under his paternal authority, "so to him their subsequent rebellion was a blatant breach of faith"—and had to be severely punished. Fair enough, perhaps, until we recall that after the treaty council Stevens himself repeatedly acknowledged, in various official reports and in the words of his principal aide, Frank Shaw, that the reservations he had awarded to the Nisquallies and the neighboring Puyallups were improper, that Leschi therefore had a legitimate beef, and that he would redress the natives' grievance— a promise that, if it had been honored in a timely fashion, would very likely have prevented the Indians' armed resistance to the treaty.

To testify to his own purity of heart and thus the legitimacy of his actions against Leschi, Stevens seemed compelled to paint his tormentors as low characters who had won the whites' favor and then betrayed them. Leschi, he wrote in a May 31, 1856, letter to Manypenny, was "familiarly known to most of our Citizens, had in part adopted the habits & usages of civilized life, was a good farmer and expert hunter, and believed to be an honest man." Yet he and his tribal brethren, "in direct violation of their Solemn word, commenced the war by the massacre of an entire settlement"—a crime Leschi was never connected with by anything beyond hearsay.

Perhaps the real root of Stevens's need to dissemble and denigrate the Indian combatants in general, and Leschi in particular, was repugnance toward the very notion that primitive natives could qualify as real soldiers. For him the concept of military honor, as enshrined at West Point and drawn from centuries of European and classical tradition, seems not to have been applicable to the red race, a scruffy and degraded order of creatures, no matter that they were fighting to preserve their homelands, sacred traditions, and dignity as human beings. They did not rate treatment under the rights and practices of war as adhered to by godly people and civilized nations. Capture an Indian commander who had fought as his fellow savages had fought for millennia, and you could arraign him as a common criminal—if you cared to bother—and then, for the ultimate humiliation, hang him as a brutal killer. Honorable soldiers, deserving of chivalric respect, were, by definition, white.

The kindest, and perhaps fairest, explanation of why Stevens targeted Leschi above all the other native guerrillas is that the Nisqually chief was a charismatic figure, a luminous presence across the territory. As Shanna Stevenson of the Washington State Historical Society suggests, "It was important to isolate and extinguish him as a potential force to reignite Indian discontent." Stevens's private obsession may well have coincided with a public purpose he deemed essential to the future tranquility of Washington Territory. However parsed, there was only one solution by Stevens's reckoning: Leschi had to die. Others, especially U.S. Army officers, came to the opposite conclusion: persecution of the Indians' pre-eminent chief after the fighting had ended would serve only to stir his people to a new round of retributive violence.

STEVENS'S OBSTINATE conviction that the militant tribes east of the mountains would behave themselves only after having been thoroughly whipped in battle—a view entirely at odds with the approach favored by General Wool and Colonel Wright—was now dramatized by the totally uncalled-for intrusion of Frank Shaw's militia raiders into the Walla Walla area, on the lookout for any Indians they chose to identify as hostile.

Shaw's 200-man force encountered no Yakimas or Klickitats to engage—a good thing, perhaps, given those tribes' fighting prowess. So Shaw continued southeastward, crossing the Columbia into Oregon Territory, with the permission of its governor, until he reached the valley of the Grande Ronde River. There, on July 17, 1856, his scouts came upon an encampment of some 500 Cayuses and other Indians, mostly women and children, gathering edible roots and revealing no mischievous intent.

A few of the Cayuse men rode out to meet Shaw's scouts and advised them that there were no warriors in their camp. Shaw would later claim that one member of the Cayuse party dangled a white man's scalp in front of the militiamen and promised that they would meet a similar fate if they harassed the village. Whatever the truth, Shaw advanced, and the Cayuses scattered before his troops, taking cover in the brush along the riverbanks. Shaw sniffed an ambush in the making and charged. The defenseless prey was slaughtered; at least sixty Indians were killed—no figure was reported for the wounded. The rampant attackers burned down 120 of the natives' lodges, destroyed their stores of food, stole some of their 200 horses, and slew the rest. Shaw lost four men; four others were wounded.

Thus, the combined Indian massacres at White River and Cascades Rapids were repaid at least three times over by the atrocities committed by Stevens's militiamen under Maxon at the Mashel River and Shaw at the Grande Ronde. James Tilton, commanding general of the volunteer militiamen, wrote Shaw, "We were all delighted with the report of your brilliant success." Stevens pointedly told the combat-wary Colonel Wright and his regulars that Shaw's men had delivered a "severe blow" to the natives, and then crowed to Jefferson Davis, "The Walla Walla expedition has been completely successful."

SATISFIED THAT Shaw's actions at the Grande Ronde was the coup de grâce that would end further armed resistance to his treaties, Stevens now began to disband his militia corps and to fulfill his promise to adjust the harsh reservations assigned to the tribes at the Medicine Creek council. He did so even though none of the Indian groups who had engaged in combat had surrendered to him unconditionally, as the governor had demanded. Many individual warriors had simply cast aside their weapons, declined to join Leschi's withering band in its refuge on the far side of the Cascades, and drifted back west toward the Sound to await the ultimate determination of the site and dimensions of their reservations.

Stevens, still dismissing any thoughts that he might have wronged the treaty tribes at Medicine Creek, now made a gala occasion of his abrupt about-face, garlanding himself in sweet magnanimity. To witness the rite of reconciliation, he invited Silas Casey and William Tolmie, the two most powerful men at Puget Sound after himself. The proceedings were held on August 4 in the form of a treaty council at a place where it was easiest to assemble tribal members—Fox Island, still in use as an internment camp for upward of 500 Nisquallies, Puyallups, and members of other tribes. Indicative of the overcrowded and otherwise debilitating conditions on the island, about 100 of the internees had died of tuberculosis and other diseases. Among those not attending but decidedly in the thoughts of those present—especially of Stevens himself, as his remarks would soon reveal—was Leschi, who was still at large, much to the governor's chagrin.

Sidney Ford, Fox Island warden as well as territorial Indian agent for the Sound region, spoke first, offering comments intended to leave no doubt in the minds of those assembled who the transgressors had been in the lately concluded hostilities. He and his fellow white officials had come to the island, he said,

> ready and willing to forgive the cruelty and injustice which many of you have manifested during the past year to those whose pledges of friendship have never been violated. . . . The very men

who but a few months since, you [referring to the former warriors among them] sought to kill are here today offering you land, offering you their aid and encouragement, in cultivating your farms and building your houses, offering to feed and clothe you until you have advanced far enough to feed and clothe yourselves. . . . These same offers were made long ago, and Leschi understood these offers. . . . Then why did you go to war? Why did you take up arms against the whites?

Not only did Ford's harangue wildly overstate what the original treaty had promised to its signatories, but it also failed to concede in any way that they were flagrantly confiscatory and that the tiny reservations provided for their survival were barren and imprisoning. Stevens then offered his listeners a far-from-contrite rendition of his world-turned-upside-down view that the treaty troubles were all their fault.

The governor began by expressing his sorrow that the settlers and natives had gone to war, his gladness that peace had returned, and his reassurance of concern for the Indians' welfare—else why would he have come among them that day? He went on to rewrite history for an audience that knew better but was powerless to object. The reservations set out at Medicine Creek, Stevens declaimed, "were suggested by yourselves. I had them surveyed and found them not good. I sent word to Leschi [and] all the Indians that the reserves should be changed." But Stevens failed to explain why he had not done so over the intervening nineteen months. He now agreed, however, to reassign the Nisquallies and Puyallups to "a large reservation" for each of them along their ancestral rivers and create a separate new one for the Muckleshoots in the White and Green upriver highlands, thereby addressing the grievance of those bands over the Point Elliott Treaty.

Even while acting belatedly to ease the cruelty of the Medicine Creek reservations, Stevens could not resist delivering a diatribe against Leschi that displayed the depth of his obsession with him. The previous Christmas, he said, Leschi had come to the very island where they were now gathered—he had done so two weeks later than that, actually—"and took off half your people." That would have meant Leschi stole away with several hundred warriors in his six canoes, which already held thirty-three warriors. At most, a dozen or two internees made their escape with the canoe raiders. This sort of contempt for factual accuracy had by then become habitual with Stevens. "And Leschi, honest Leschi—where is he now?" he taunted. "East of the mountains with a handful of men. I do not say that Leschi meant wrong. I say he did not know what was for his own interest." If Leschi had indeed been merely misguided, why had Stevens vowed to execute him?

Finally, Stevens tried to portray Leschi as too impatient for his and his people's good. The governor claimed to have sent Shaw to see him in April 1855—about the time word had reached Stevens that the Senate had ratified the Medicine Creek Treaty—to assure the Nisquallies their reservation would be improved at some point; he did not say when. But Leschi had not trusted Stevens's pledge, so "your land became a war ground. . . . I do not speak this to punish Leschi." It was all the Nisquallies' fault, he implied, because "we had [the reservations] surveyed and found them unsuitable for you." In fact, George Gibbs had told him so just days after the treaty council ended, and yet Stevens did not alter the reservations. Instead, he quickly sent off the treaty text and accompanying maps, explicitly showing the terrible reservation sites, to Washington, D.C., for Senate approval. "We sent you word accordingly," he said of his intended remedial action, yet "half of you go to war saying you are not satisfied. . . . How do I know by past experience what course you will pursue in the future?" Stevens asked. What his audience knew was that it had taken fierce armed resistance, even if finally unsuccessful, by Leschi to force Stevens to act at long last.

The unapologetic governor agreed that August day to provide the Nisquallies, in place of 2 virtually uninhabitable square miles on a bluff above the Sound, a new reservation of 7.5 square miles of fertile bottomland and adjacent prairie that straddled the Nisqually River for about 4 miles from where Muck Creek joined it and ran northwesterly to a point close to the estuary at the Sound. The reservation, carved from the core of the tribe's homeland, allowed its members good cropland, a fine stretch of the river for salmon-fishing, and suitable terrain to pasture their horses and other livestock and gather roots and bulbs. The Puyallups were given a more generous reservation of 36 square miles to replace the earlier one that was just as small and bad as the Nisquallies'. Some of the newly assigned land surrounded the mouth of the Puyallup River and some extended inland for pasturing. It was likely no accident that Stevens had more generously rewarded the tribe whose chief had not bedeviled him for the better part of two years. At any rate, the two tribes between them received 43.5 square miles of reservation land from the suddenly forthcoming governor and in return had ceded the United States some 4,000 square miles of ancestral Indian Country.

Why did Stevens, with the renegade Indians on their knees before him, now yield just enough for the Nisquallies and Puyallups to salvage a modest haven on their native ground? Why, after tribal resistance had been shattered in the Sound region, had Stevens acted in a way that seemed to reward Leschi and his warriors for their effrontery in challenging him and his hateful treaty?

Rather than having been stricken with an acute case of kindness, Stevens may have acted for two plausible and expedient reasons. The bulk of the land composing the new Nisqually reservation, 3,300 out of its 4,700 acres, had been used for a dozen years to pasture the vast herds of sheep, other livestock, and horses belonging to the Bay's Puget Sound Agricultural Company. So nearly two-thirds of the acreage now earmarked for Leschi's tribe was part of the disputed property claim for which the British government was seeking compensation from the United States as provided for in their 1846 Oregon Treaty. It was no small matter to Tolmie, who, sympathetic to the Nisqually grievance, protested after the Fox Island council that Stevens was generously giving the Indians land that was not yet his, or his government's, to dispose of. It was Britain's land, by right of use. Stevens's sudden largesse became further suspect after he made clear to the interned Nisquallies at Fox Island and those returnees camped for their protection near Fort Steilacoom that they would not be allowed to occupy their new reservation until their fugitive chief surrendered or was otherwise handed over to the governor. In short, Stevens was dangling the lure of more and better land to force Leschi to give himself up for the sake of his people or to encourage them to betray him to the governor.

Stevens's official explanation for his actions, spelled out in a letter to Manypenny three weeks after the Fox Island concessions, was that "humanity and sound policy required that no delay should occur . . . in establishing these Indians on reservations, suitable to their wants and where they could be contented," where all tribal members would be welcome "with the exception of certain leaders and murderers." He took full responsibility for this step, although it was at odds with the official U.S. Indian policy of granting the fewest and smallest reservations possible, because he felt it was "essential to preserving the relations of confidence and good will which now exists . . . by acts, which will show to the Indians, that they live under a fatherly and merciful government." Yes, but why hadn't he taken this fatherly and merciful step during the nine months preceding the outbreak of the fighting and thus averted it?

Several historians with extensive knowledge of the region, including

Charles Wilkinson and Cecilia Carpenter, believe Stevens was under heavy pressure from his government superiors back east to relent, especially after his despotic imposition of martial law. We know that General Wool was urging the War Department to get Stevens sacked for his vengeful and provocative attitude toward the Indians and that Stevens himself was expecting a formal reprimand, if not outright firing, after his martial law fiasco. But there is no documentary evidence that Stevens was directed by federal overseers to revise the miserable Medicine Creek reservations. Perhaps he believed that his actions—if not his words—at Fox Island would mollify his critics.

Even while acting to alleviate Indian discontent west of the Cascades, Stevens remained at odds with the efforts of General Wool and Colonel Wright to keep the tribes east of the mountains off the warpath. To regain the initiative as master of his federal domain, Stevens summoned a second Walla Walla council for September. Its agenda was to confirm and reinforce the three treaties the eastern tribes had reluctantly signed the year before but the Senate had not ratified, technically leaving a great expanse of Indian Country afloat in no-man's-land.

Many chiefs refused to attend the council session Stevens had called, and those who did come wanted to know what would be done to punish his militiamen for inflicting atrocities on peaceful Indian civilians like those at the Mashel and Grande Ronde rivers. Little was accomplished at the council, and the governor's exiting party might have been overwhelmed by hovering young Yakima and Walla Walla warriors if it had not been escorted by a guard of thirty Nez Perces. As he returned to Olympia, frustrated by his failure to force the eastern militants to bend to his will, he shifted his attention to disposing of the one lingering irritant among the Indians of the Sound. He had to get Leschi.

PART II

The Trials of Leschi

10

Judgment Day—and Night

A S SUMMER FLOODED the Kittitas Valley with wildflowers, birdsong, and all the fruits of nature that his beleaguered Nisqually band required for their sustenance on the eastern edge of the Cascades, the fugitive Leschi was in a deep quandary.

This was his forty-eighth and probably unhappiest summer. His liberty was no more than an uneasy respite from the defeat his forces had suffered in late winter. His own—and his people's—future remained darkly clouded. Leschi had lost his home, his large herd of horses, his flourishing farm, and his status as headman of his tribe. He was now branded an official outlaw by decree of Governor Stevens and a refugee in the upper Yakima Country at the sufferance of that tribe—their tolerable guest but one, he feared, who was rapidly wearing out his welcome.

Leschi pined most for his adored young wife, Mary, who was somewhere back home, upriver from Puget Sound, likely in hiding lest she be taken hostage to force her husband to give himself up. According to a later reminiscence of Letitia Huggins, wife of William Tolmie's chief aide at Fort Nisqually and a woman of mixed European and Indian ancestry who had known Mary in their teenage years, "Leschi took her as his wife not long before the war broke out. . . . [P]oor devil, he was infatuated with her, and we are firmly impressed with the idea that if it hadn't been for the mad feeling of devotion he . . . could easily have gotten away, and [by remaining] amongst friends east of the mountains, lived a life of safety."

All too aware of Stevens's insistence that only his capture and punishment would ensure permanent peace in western Washington Territory, Leschi calculated that his best hope for salvation was Colonel George

Wright, still commander of the U.S. Ninth Infantry forces bivouacked along the Naches Valley within a day's ride of the Nisqually fugitives' encampment. In early June, accompanied by twenty unarmed warriors and their families, Leschi risked face-to-face contact with Wright— "without any agency on my part," as the colonel later reported. Most of the Nisqually party struck Wright as poor, horseless, and "desirous of returning to the Sound, provided they can do so safely." He found the guerrilla leader to be of a mind "decidedly for peace" and "perfectly willing to go wherever I say." Wright did not want any of the Nisquallies or their allies in Leschi's remnant to return to the Sound due to concern that their arrival might lead to a renewal of the fighting. Instead, the colonel promised not to infringe on the Nisqually band's liberty or otherwise punish them so long as they made no trouble. He urged Leschi to sheathe his weapons and sit tight, just as he had counseled the Yakimas and their allies. "The assurances I gave to all the chiefs who submitted, including Leschi, were full and complete, so far as the military authorities were concerned, as to their personal safety."

It was a few weeks later when Wright received the stiff note, cited earlier, from Stevens regarding the Indian refugees, their leaders in particular, demanding that "no arrangement be made which will save their necks from the Executioner." But the colonel had a more humane agenda and would not break faith with Leschi. Wright, a professional soldier of high character and dispassionate judgment, explained his sharp difference with the vengeful Stevens in a letter the following year:

> That they [the Indians] had committed acts which among civilized people might be regarded as murders, I doubted not, but knowing their peculiar habits and modes of warfare, and that they regarded the indiscriminate killing of men, women, and children as a legitimate preceding [sic], and the natural result of hostilities, I certainly expected it to be so regarded by our people. When we looked at the number of Indians killed by our people, many of them perfectly friendly . . . it must be confessed that it is hard to say which side has the advantage. . . . [U]nfortunately our hands are stained with innocent blood, and the perpetrators are free. Let impartial justice be meted out to both parties, or cast oblivion over all.

He also relayed that wish to his associate in command at Fort Steilacoom, Silas Casey, who he knew shared his distaste for Isaac Stevens's vehemence toward the Indians. Alerting Casey of his pledge to protect the refugees under Leschi's care, Wright wrote that the Nisqually leaders "may have been guilty of some great atrocities during the war, but I have never been able to obtain any reliable information on the subject. If they have committed murders of men, women, and children, I suppose they regard that as legitimate warfare with them." The best way to deal with these exiles, he now proposed, shifting his earlier stance, would be to return them to their reservation, provided "the superintendent of Indian affairs [i.e., Stevens] will receive them, and guaranty their safety." He asked Casey to pursue the matter with the governor.

Wright's hope that Stevens might relent was soon quenched. He again called on Wright to grab Leschi even if he came into the army post under a flag of truce. The colonel replied that he had already promised Leschi and his band safe passage back to the Sound. In October Wright further irritated Stevens by suggesting, "In the present unsettled state of Indian relations it would be unwise to seize [the pacified native chiefs] and send them to trial."

Probably convinced by now that the U.S. Army harbored more hostility toward him than toward any of the native tribes, Stevens revealed the depth of his monomania over alleged Indian savagery—and his indifference to the atrocities against native noncombatants committed by his own militiamen. The native warriors no longer active but still at large, he told Casey, "are notorious murderers" whose barbarous acts had been perpetrated "under circumstances of treachery and blood thirstiness almost beyond example." In his own mind, Stevens inflated the White River Massacre a hundredfold. In fact, no such incidents had been repeated within Leschi's sphere of influence. "I am convinced," the governor nevertheless concluded his screed, "that men guilty of such acts should at least stand trial, and if convicted, [be] punished." He had all but hammered a LESCHI WANTED—DEAD OR ALIVE poster to the door of the new capitol.

Once the welcome news circulated of Stevens's concession of more habitable reservations for the Medicine Creek Treaty tribes, more of Leschi's followers began to drift west toward their tribal homeland. Most of them regrouped around Fort Steilacoom, where they counted on Casey's garrison for protection from white harassment that Colonel Wright had promised them as they awaited permission to resume a semblance of their old lives along the Nisqually basin on the newly designated reservation. Leschi, though wary of the possible consequences, soon joined the returnees but chose to remain out of white sight.

In a risky departure from his underground existence, Leschi slipped into Fort Nisqually to visit his friend William Tolmie and beseech him to plead his case with the U.S. authorities. According to some Indians who recognized Leschi at the Hudson's Bay Company post and reported his presence to the *Pioneer and Democrat,* the Nisqually chief was "in very destitute condition (being very nearly naked) and applied to Dr. Tolmie for ammunition, for the purpose, as he averred, of killing game."

In writing later of their meeting, Tolmie confirmed that Leschi was indeed in a bedraggled state but was also at pains to impress upon him the earnestness of his vow to make no further trouble for any whites. "[H]e desired me to acquaint the Americans, that if they needed that reassurance, he would cut off his right hand in proof of his intention never to fight them again." Tolmie counseled Leschi to place himself under Casey's personal protection—and Leschi was willing, "but that officer considered it most prudent that Leschi should, for a time, remain in the woods, as prejudice ran high against him." Stevens had managed to whip up a hatred for Leschi across Washington Territory that left its settlers thirsting for an Indian scapegoat for the war.

By late October, with more than 100 displaced Nisquallies squatting just outside his post, Casey decided that his soldiers had better things to do than stand protective guard indefinitely over the Indians. He wrote Stevens, asserting, "Inasmuch as the hostilities have ceased in this district, I do not consider that it is my province to take care of these Indians," but because territorial officers had refused to carry out that function, which he took to be their duty, Casey had been doing so "to prevent any disturbance that might ensue"—a none-too-veiled reference to potential molestation of the unarmed natives by white assailants. Then, directly confronting the governor's recalcitrance, Casey ventured: "Permit me to say . . . that if the Indians are treated with kindness and justice, and lawless men restrained from violence against them, there will be no danger of any outbreak on their part."

Stevens did not relish being lectured by an apparently weak-kneed, native-loving officer. In his reply to Casey, he made clear that he intended to keep holding the Nisqually refugees hostage until he had Leschi in his grasp. The Indians whom Casey referred to, the governor replied, "are not in that condition of submission which makes it safe to incorporate them with the friendly Indians, nor will they be in that condition till the known murderers of that band are arrested for trial." Meanwhile, Stevens said, "we shall at all times be exposed to renewal of the war and its scenes of death and devastation." He added that "recent information" had reached him to the effect that Leschi was "endeavoring to raise a force to prosecute the war anew." To bear witness that neither the white populace of the territory nor its governor were persecutors of the natives, Stevens expressed doubt that "any country or age has afforded an example of the kindness and justice which has been shown towards the Indians by the suffering inhabitants of the Sound, during the recent troubles . . . but they complain, and have a right to complain, if Indians, whose hands are steeped in blood of the innocent, go unwhipped of justice."

As their epistolary duel went on, Stevens offered Casey his rationale for denying Leschi the status of a legitimate military combatant. The Indian operations on the Sound, he wrote, "have been from the beginning . . . those of murderers and outlaws—no tribe as such having broken into hostility—and they are therefore entitled to none of the rights of war." In other words, because Leschi had not assembled his whole tribe and formally polled it to see if they supported his armed defiance of the governor and then, with a democratically determined majority in favor, sent him a formal declaration of war tied with a silk ribbon, the insurgency was not an authentic expression of the Nisquallies' sovereign will. But, of course, Charles Mason, serving as acting governor, had not polled the people of Washington Territory or gone to its legislature to authorize the creation of a militia and the lethal pursuit of the aroused Indians. Rather, he had acted as the appointed leader of the territory, even as Leschi was acting as the Nisqually leader, a position to which Stevens himself had assigned him.

Casey had no patience for scoring such debating points against the governor. Instead, he made sure he had the backing of his commanding officer, General Wool, to whom he passed along his doubts about Stevens's intelligence report that Leschi was up to no good. Casey registered his own belief that the Indians had no wish "to break out again unless they are driven to it." He also questioned Stevens's claim that the guerrillas failed to qualify as legitimate warriors, and therefore whether the Indians the governor had asked him to seize "can be convicted of any murders, if a fair chance is given them . . . Leschi, in particular, I have always understood, opposed them." Then Casey touched upon the issue that would determine whether Leschi would be given a "fair chance" if caught and put on trial:

> Whether Colonel Wright did or did not exceed his authority in receiving and making peace with [Leschi's band], it is not my intention to discuss; but of one thing I am quite sure, that after

peace had been made with Indians without such conditions, to hold them accountable as murderers for acts committed in the war, is certainly inaugurating a new policy in the general government, and should receive the assent, at least, of the highest executive officer of the republic.

Without awaiting a formal blessing from Wool, who he knew was constantly on the move about his vast Pacific coast theater of operations, Casey capped his confrontation with Stevens by writing him that "it would be bad policy, if not bad faith"—presumably by the governor and Casey alike—to overturn Wright's decision to grant protection to the Nisquallies and their chiefs. He wrote, "Now with due deference to you, sir, I would suggest that the better way would be to consider that we have been at war, and now, we are at peace." Then Casey closed defiantly:

> To be sure they have killed some of the people, but that is incident to the war. Most of those who committed murders have been killed, and the Indians have suffered much.
>
> You say that some of the Indians who killed whites are still at large; it may be so, but are there not whites at large who have wantonly murdered innocent Indians in this district?
>
> For the reasons above mentioned I cannot assist in arresting the men whom you have named, but I will submit the matter to the general commanding the department in the Pacific.

Wool backed Casey and denounced Stevens for his apparent determination to renew the Indian war: "His removal from the office [of governor] alone can prevent it."

Stevens's hunger for Leschi's hide would not abate. But Casey did not budge, either. He responded at one point to the governor's latest request for him to hunt down Leschi by promising to refer the matter to his superiors. In another thumb of his nose, the commandant of Fort Steilacoom made clear that he felt Stevens was dishonoring the rights of soldiers engaged in warfare by trying to vilify a legitimate enemy combatant as a murderer: "In all ordinary cases I should have no hesitation in complying with the requisition of the Superintendent of Indian Affairs [i.e., Stevens], but this is a case in which, in my opinion, the rights and usages of war are somewhat involved, and in consequence I consider myself and military superiors the proper persons to judge in the matter."

General Wool weighed in with the strongest possible endorsement of Casey's position. In a message forwarded to Casey by the general's adjutant, once again expressing regret over Stevens's "vindictive spirit," Wool directed "that you will not fail to give protection, if necessary, to Leschi and all other Indians peaceably inclined to the whites." Should the governor attempt to renew war on the Sound, "you will resist to the extent of your power," and if Stevens's volunteers returned to the fray, "they should be arrested, disarmed and sent home" by Casey's regulars. Wool then forwarded a copy of the Casey-Stevens exchange to the U.S. Army's New York headquarters, "approving his [Casey's] course in refusing to surrender for trial Leschi and others, demanded by Governor Stevens." Wool's letter carried a pregnant postscript of endorsement. It read: "I concur fully in the views of Major General Wool and Lieutenant Colonel Casey as expressed within. Respectfully submitted, Winfield Scott." General Scott remained the highest-ranking member of the U.S. Army (and evidently still not an admirer of Stevens).

So Leschi, though likely unaware of it, enjoyed at every level the respect of an American army that regarded him as an honorable—and deactivated—foe in a lost cause. But that regard could not keep the Nisqually chief from entanglement in the web of his venomous enemy.

SILAS CASEY'S refusal, now fully authorized by his superiors, to turn Leschi over to Stevens for trial was somewhat academic since the tribal leader was not within the army's custody. In all likelihood, the prized fugitive, for whose capture (or information leading to it) whites were being offered a $500 reward (and Indians fifty blankets), was living in the woods close to his deserted home and cropland near Muck Creek.

Stevens, adjusting to the circumstances, now moved on his own by making use of the territory's judicial system, which he had lately so grossly abused. On November 3, the day after Casey's latest and most spirited rebuff to Stevens, a grand jury was summoned to sit in the territory's Third Judicial District at Steilacoom to consider a charge against Leschi for the ambush murder one year earlier of Colonel Abram B. Moses. A member of William Tidd's express party, Moses had been killed, as described earlier, along with militia colleague Joseph Miles in the swamp just below Connell's Prairie. The prosecutor's charge—and the subsequent indictment—said that Leschi "with malice aforethought . . . did discharge and shoot off his gun" at Moses, inflicting a wound six inches deep and a half inch wide, from which Moses "then and there instantly died."

In fact, none of Moses's compatriots in the express party had reported seeing Leschi fire at Moses or that the wounded officer had died on the spot. But the factual misstatements were the least of it; the indictment proceeding against Leschi taken as a whole was a mockery of legal codes and practices, even for that rough-hewn frontier setting.

To begin with, there was the timing of the grand jury proceeding. Why was it brought against Leschi *in absentia* if not to speed his trial after his anticipated arrest? And since Leschi was not yet a prisoner, almost certainly no legal representative had been appointed by the court to protect his rights—at least there is no documented evidence of such an appointment. And even the most incompetent practitioner in the territory would likely have objected to the seating on the grand jury—and his selection as its foreman—of Antonio Rabbeson.

Rabbeson, as we have seen, had worked his way into the Praetorian guard of two-fisted cronies who surrounded Isaac Stevens. He had been among the gang of henchmen guarding the governor's office to fend off service of a subpoena by a territorial marshal during the martial law crisis. And he had risen to captain in Stevens's volunteer corps during the war against Leschi's guerrillas and played a key role in turning the Nisquallies' last stand at Connell's Prairie into a rout. The decision by the territorial court to allow Rabbeson to be impaneled on and chosen foreman of the grand jury summoned to weigh an indictment of Leschi even before he was in custody all but demanded invocation of Section 46 of the Laws of Washington Territory, passed in 1854: "Challenges to individual grand jurors may be made . . . for reason of want of qualification to sit as such juror, such as would render him unable to sit impartially and without prejudice"—language that on its face should have disqualified Tony Rabbeson from sitting on the jury, especially as its foreman. But there was no one to make the challenge on Leschi's behalf.

Equally outrageous, according to what scanty evidence we have of the proceedings of that jury, Rabbeson was the principal witness and one of only two people to come before it and testify against Leschi; the other was Dr. Matthew Burns, the volatile surgeon who was a member of the seven-man express party that was ambushed at Connell's Prairie—and his veracity was highly suspect even among his fellow militiamen (see footnote on page 140). Rabbeson was permitted, in other words, to testify and then weigh his own evidence as he voted, with the rest of the jury, to indict Leschi for murder. Accordingly, we may reasonably infer that the territorial prosecutor, J. S. Smith, chose not to introduce into evidence Rabbeson's long, firsthand report in the *Pioneer and Democrat,* appearing a few weeks after the deaths of Moses and Miles, which failed to name any of the Indians who had fired on the ambush victims. Rabbeson's published account stated he had been too far away from the scene to witness the shooting. He had written, as we have seen, that Leschi was among the Indian leaders who met the express party in a peaceable exchange up on the prairie shortly before the ambush attack, but did not place the Nisqually chief or any other specific Indian among Moses's assailants. Now, though, in testimony before the grand jury, Stevens's pawn—and deadly instrument of the governor's craze for vengeance—had evidently embellished his story in order to implicate Leschi.

Beyond all else, the question remains whether the rules and procedures of the civil code permitted the charge of murder to be lodged against a legitimate combatant who killed enemy combatants in time of war. Even if Leschi had shot and killed Moses, the episode occurred in the early stages of an armed conflict (though there had been no formal declaration of war by either side). Undeniably, U.S. Army regulars and officially inducted territorial volunteers had been on a deadly hunt for defiant native warriors on both sides of the Cascades for nearly a month prior to the ambush at Connell's Prairie. The engagement was no mere police action by civilian authorities against a gang of thieves or frivolous disturbers of the peace; the Indian uprising was the expression, through force of arms, of a profound social grievance by the Medicine Creek tribes.

How, then, could the civil courts of law be used to prosecute soldiers—whatever their nationality or race and whether marching in array across an open battlefield or attacking by stealth from cover—as murderers when they were engaging in exactly the grisly task they had been sent to do: take their enemies' lives? Fighting wars is a nasty sort of business, to be sure, but one which almost all societies have sanctioned as a legitimate and honorable endeavor. Indeed, history overflows with examples of ghastly slaughter in combat with little if any regard for ethics. War has never been a morally defensible alternative to rational conflict resolution; war is a way of forcibly gaining advantage over others by whatever means may be required. Killing disarmed prisoners of war, for example, while no doubt reprehensible, has been recognized throughout much of recorded history as a right or privilege of the victors—the fewer enemy survivors, the slimmer the chance for them to rise again in retributive acts. At the time of Leschi's indictment, the killing of armed and active enemy combatants had never been considered murder, which was universally understood to mean the unlawful taking of another's life, usually with malicious intent. Murder was a *personal* act while war was a sanctioned, impersonal group activity, usually to advance a governing authority's policies or interests, that freed its participants from individual responsibility for the taking of enemy lives. How, then, could Leschi be tried as a murderer for engaging in combat in order to save his people's homeland and birthright?

Unfortunately for Leschi, in 1856—when the murder charge was formally filed against him—there were no globally recognized laws, codes, compacts, covenants, or rules for waging war or defining its misconduct as a crime. Various commentators had touched upon the subject, but by the mid-nineteenth century only one had produced a systematic compilation forming a body of general principles patterned on past practices— the prodigious Dutch scholar, jurist, and philosopher Hugo Grotius (1583–1645). He had studied with some of the foremost thinkers of the northern European Enlightenment and gone on to create trailblazing works of encyclopedic range that laid the foundations of international law. Coming of age in the midst of Holland's eighty-year struggle for independence from Spanish royalist tyranny and the Thirty Years' War between Europe's Catholic and Protestant states, Grotius struggled to extract order from turmoil in his most enduring work, *De Jure Belli ac Pacis* (*The Rights of War and Peace*). Begun when he was a political prisoner and published while he was in exile in Paris in 1625, it is a massive, three-volume effort to define a broad moral consensus governing warfare. Throughout the Christian world, he said, he had observed

> a lack of restraint in relation to war, such as even barbarous races should be ashamed of; I observed that men rush to arms for slight causes, or no cause at all, and that when arms have once been taken up there is no longer any respect for law, divine or human; it is as if, in accordance with a general decree, frenzy had openly been let loose for the committing of all crimes.

At the time of Leschi's indictment, there was no more authoritative guidance on the nature of his alleged crime than volume 3 of Grotius's masterwork, in which chapter 4 is titled "The Right of Killing Enemies in a Solemn War and of Other Hostilities Committed Against the Person of the Enemy." His deductions on the subject were drawn almost entirely from ancient and classical sources, starting with the Bible and including Greek and Roman historians, playwrights, and philosophers, as well as Christian theologians. His basic finding boiled down to this: "it is lawful for one enemy to hurt another, both in person and goods, not only for him that makes war on a just account, and does it within those bounds which are prescribed by the laws of Nature . . . but on both sides, and without distinction; so that *he cannot be punished as a murderer, or a thief, tho' he be taken in another prince's domain*" (emphasis added). Nor did Grotius believe that this so-called right of arms was predicated on a formal declaration of war, which he dismissed as "often no more than mere ceremony."

Among Grotius's biblical sources was Epistles 95, which states, "Things, which would be punished with death, had they been done in secret and by private authority, are commended when done by generals of armies. It is a crime when a private person is guilty of homicide, but when it is done by public authority, it is called a virtue." Pithier was Euripides' proverb, "The blood of an enemy doth not stain the man who kills him." Thus, while Greeks did not customarily wash, drink, or worship with a man who had killed another, Grotius noted, "it was lawful to do it with him that in war had slain his enemy; and frequently to kill is called the Right of War." Plato was invoked for his contention that, "according to ancient law, founded upon the Oracle at Delphos, those, who had killed an enemy in war, ought not to be looked upon as defiled; no more than if they had killed a friend without design in some public exercise."

If there was no historical or consensual precedent, then, for pressing a murder charge against Leschi for acting as a legitimate combatant, there was still Stevens's contention that the Nisqually chief had been an *illegitimate* combatant because his tribe had not, *as a tribe,* gone to war against the whites. By this rationale Leschi was merely a rowdy leader who had rounded up a gang of troublemakers for the purpose of defying the terms of the Medicine Creek Treaty. His forces were just a bunch of irregulars, not warriors officially sanctioned by their own people at a tribal council to do battle against the white authorities. These Indian malcontents had therefore engaged in a criminal insurgency, according to Stevens's reckoning, and should be put on trial. It was a flimsy argument. By most accounts, Leschi had enlisted 100 or more Nisqually braves to fight alongside him—probably a majority of the hardy adult males within the tribal membership; women and children would not have had a say in the matter. As much to the point, Stevens himself, through his aides, had anointed Leschi and Quiemuth as official Nisqually spokesmen at the Medicine Creek council and their names were listed among the first signatories of the treaty, so the brothers were on record as, in effect, heads of their quasi-sovereign nation. Otherwise, what had been the point of the whole treatymaking exercise and their appointment as Nisqually chiefs? Therefore, their prompt disavowal of the treaty for having been deceitfully pressed upon them established a just cause for the brothers to have led those in their tribe who chose to follow them into war against the United States. Leschi, then, could hardly be dismissed as a two-bit thug; he was a political and military leader highly esteemed in both the Indian and white communities before the fighting had begun.

Even if Leschi qualified as a soldier of sorts, though, Stevens was still free to fall back on the U.S. Supreme Court–approved designation of the native peoples as wards of the federal government, not as independent nations—thus turning the governor's whole treatymaking campaign into nothing more than a ceremonial exercise. Rebellious Indians like Leschi, under this line of argument, were not foreign nationals but perpetrators of civil war—criminal insurgents and disturbers of the peace acting outside the law.*

Rather than ruling as a matter of law whether Leschi could be tried on a murder charge in a civil proceeding in Washington Territory's Third Judicial District, Judge Francis Chenoweth, who presided over that jurisdiction, allowed the grand jury to hear the prosecutor's case and, once it returned the indictment, to let the trial jury decide whether the defendant

---

*An instructive analogy may be drawn between Stevens's treatment of Leschi and the George W. Bush administration's view of how to deal with captives during the Iraq War. In an August 12, 2006, op-ed article in *The New York Times,* Timothy William Waters challenged the Bush position that anyone who killed a U.S. soldier fighting in Iraq ought to be prosecuted if captured: "But killing American soldiers in Iraq is an act of war, not a crime, and the U.S. is wrong to oppose amnesty for the insurgents there." Waters pointed out that amnesty would not apply to prisoners accused of war crimes, and he distinguished between insurgents and terrorists (like those who kill innocent noncombatants, as happened in the 9/11 destruction of the World Trade Center towers, though Waters does not cite them specifically). The insurgents in Iraq were "the one group that resembles a normal fighting force . . . There is an organized insurgency in Iraq. We're at war, and so are they. When our soldiers kill in combat, they are not committing a crime. The same logic should apply to Iraqis." Isaac Stevens argued that Leschi's guerrilla movement was not an organized insurgency, making him into a terrorist and criminal.

was a legitimate combatant or a vicious criminal who presumably was targeting American soldiers as a result of some personal pathology. Chenoweth also declined to interfere with the impaneling and testimony of Tony Rabbeson. It would seem that the judge had decided to bury the hatchet with Stevens, a fellow Democrat, who had abused him and the basic concept of the rule of law by arbitrarily imposing martial law the previous spring.

NO WHITE MAN tracked Leschi down. His Judas was his sister's boy, Sluggia, whom he had raised almost as a son along with his own two daughters. Nisqually oral tradition portrays Leschi's nephew as a shiftless and untrustworthy young fellow and an avid but reckless player of the "bone gamble" and other games of chance, who had more than once clashed with his uncle. Sluggia reportedly found Leschi's teenage wife, Mary, irresistible, and she, put off by some of her much older husband's less than companionable habits—his constant comings and goings were rarely explained—returned her young admirer's affection. For a time, probably when Leschi was chasing all over the territory to gather allies for resisting Stevens, Mary went off to live with Sluggia but soon realized that he could not provide for her well-being a fraction as well as her wealthy husband. She contritely applied for his forgiveness, and Leschi took her back and apparently did not punish his nephew for partaking of the family's forbidden fruit.

Sluggia was sullen over Mary's rejection of him and jealous of the reunited couple. Still, he was consoled by his uncle's tolerance, attended the Medicine Creek council as a Nisqually in good standing, put his mark on the treaty—unless some white official did so for him—and was among the younger braves who joined Leschi's insurgency in eastern Pierce County. But soon he was at odds again with Leschi over the chief's edict that his men should not terrorize innocent white civilians. To Sluggia and a sometimes mutinous portion of Leschi's younger recruits, there was no such thing as innocent whites so long as their race was depriving the natives of their homelands. Leschi's friend Yelm Jim would tell author Ezra Meeker forty years later that Sluggia had quarreled bitterly with his uncle because "Leschi wouldn't allow him to kill [white] women and children during the war."

Whether motivated by resentment of his uncle's antiterrorist policy, the promised reward of fifty blankets, or, most likely, the hope of rekindling his amorous relationship with Mary after Leschi was out of the picture, Sluggia found his way to the chief's hidden camp in the upper Nisqually basin on November 13, 1856. He was probably accompanied by several confederates who, on his arrival, waited in the shadows. Apparently retaining enough of his all-too-trusting uncle's affection to be given a hearing, Sluggia told Leschi he had been assured by white officials that the Nisqually chief would be treated fairly if he surrendered himself. In all likelihood, Leschi was dubious and probably suspicious of why his nephew was acting as an intermediary with the American authorities. Whatever actually transpired between them, the *Pioneer and Democrat* reported not long afterward, Sluggia managed to decoy his uncle into bidding him farewell at the edge of the campsite, where his henchmen lurked, and "they pounced upon, bound him and placed [Leschi] on one of the horses" for delivery to Steilacoom. There, U.S. Indian agent (and Stevens devotee) Sidney Ford, probably forewarned of the abduction plot, took custody of the prisoner.

The next day, Leschi was transferred under close guard to Stevens's home, where the two men confronted each other for the first time since their initial meeting at Medicine Creek nearly two years earlier. The governor was no doubt delighted by the sight of his pinioned prey, whose subversive resistance to his domineering will had finally been shattered. The Nisqually chief had fought him with valor but few resources to save his tribe's existence, and now his captor was determined that the prisoner should play no future role in it.

"It came down to this," wrote Ezra Meeker in his *Pioneer Reminiscences of Puget Sound:* "If Leschi was proven guilty then Stevens would be vindicated. . . . If Leschi and [his] compatriots were not proven ruthless savages, murderers and criminals, what would become of all those official reports from Governor Stevens going forward with regularity to Washington [D.C.]? . . . Leschi must be proven guilty or else Stevens would be discredited, and the contention of the regular army officers proven." How fair a trial, then, could Leschi have been given when the chief executive of the territory would likely find his career in ruins if the Indian was let off?

HAVING JUST completed the autumn session of his territorial district court in Steilacoom, Judge Chenoweth was headed to his home in the northern sector of Puget Sound when an express rider overtook him with a message from the governor. Would the judge please turn around and reopen his court in a special session for an immediate trial of the already indicted Leschi?

The judge obliged the governor. The trial was set for November 17, allowing the defendant's two court-assigned lawyers just a few days to prepare their case. With this peremptory scheduling added to the irregularities of the grand jury proceedings, the trial already had the unmistakable whiff of a kangaroo court about it.

Francis Chenoweth, at thirty-seven a year younger than Isaac Stevens, was the classic kind of frontier go-getter. He had migrated west seven years earlier after growing up in Ohio and coming of age in Wisconsin, where he was admitted to the bar at age twenty-two. He married an Iowa woman with whom he would have eight children and arrived in the Columbia River basin, where the family settled in the new community of Cascades, alongside the Columbia's lower set of rapids. The location presented an impassable barrier for settlers headed downstream to the Willamette Valley farm country on the south or north up the Cowlitz Valley—and thus an ideal spot for Chenoweth to open a store servicing travelers who had to debark for a five-mile portage around the rapids and might as well lay in fresh supplies. After two lucrative years, Chenoweth launched a still more profitable enterprise, a wooden tramway bearing mule-driven flatcars over a flimsy but serviceable track. It was a less arduous way for travelers to move all their earthly goods past the rapids. At a cargo rate of seventy-five cents per hundredweight, practically extortionate given the short distance the tramway covered, the freight hauling enriched its owners but earned their customers' hearty resentment.

Chenoweth eventually sold his business interests and turned his hand to law and politics. In 1852 he entered the Oregon Territory legislature and before long was playing an active role in the movement to split off the northern counties to form the new territory created in 1853. Upon entering the Washington legislature, he rose meteorically to become Speaker of the House of Representatives, where his talents and personality shone—in 1854 the *Pioneer and Democrat* called him "one of the most agreeable men living"—and in short order he was tapped to become associate justice of the territorial Supreme Court. The position required him to double as trial judge for the Third Judicial District, stretching from Pierce County north around the Sound as far as the U.S. boundary with British Columbia.

While Chenoweth could have been in little doubt about how Stevens wished the Leschi trial to turn out, the verdict would, of course, rest with the trial jury, and most people in the territory had reason to suppose that the outcome was foregone. Leschi's only real hope was that the pool of potential jurors in Pierce County, notwithstanding the grand jury's indictment, might yield at least a few citizens fairer-minded than Tony Rabbeson, whose testimony would form the core of the prosecution's case. The Steilacoom region, after all, was home to the U.S. Army post under Silas Casey's command and the still considerable commercial and agricultural operations of the Hudson's Bay Company under William Tolmie. Some county residents in both places, civilian and military alike, viewed the governor as a provocative tormentor of the normally placid local Indians. Politically, too, they tended toward Whiggery, not Stevens's Democratic Party. Here Leschi's motives for going to war were well understood and, if not embraced at either the army barracks or the big British trading post at Fort Nisqually, at least respected. Even so, would Pierce County jurors stand up to Washington Territory's prevailing phobic complex toward the Indians?

The proceedings in the small courtroom attracted keen interest throughout the territory but not, alas, the attendance of its leading journalist, James Wiley, editor of the *Pioneer and Democrat,* then the only paper operating in the region since the pro-Whig *Puget Sound Courier* had ceased publishing the previous May. Wiley's absence was especially unfortunate for posterity because the court clerk's notes on the trial, along with other court and Pierce County records, were destroyed by fire in April 1859, leaving only two unsatisfactory accounts of the trial.

The shabby piece of secondhand reportage that the *Pioneer and Democrat* did manage to run was much like its earlier threadbare account of the Medicine Creek treaty council. Published eleven days after the one-day trial of November 17, the article reads as if it had been stitched together so as to give the least possible offense to Stevens. Editor Wiley, a notorious boozer, may have been indisposed on the day of the trial, or remarkably lazy, or just indifferent to his readers' expectation of an eyewitness account of the life-or-death trial of the man who was, according to the opening paragraph of the paper's write-up, "the accredited leader and ruling spirit among the hostile Indians in the war on this side of the mountains."

The paper began its report by stressing the supposed fairness of Leschi's treatment in court. "Both sides, we are told, were ably

argued"—"we are told" signifying the writer's absence from the scene—
"and no disposition was manifested to take undue advantage of the prisoner by opposing counsel." Instead of focusing on how well or badly the
prosecution presented its case, the article dwelled on the purported weakness of the defense. The only evidence offered that was favorable to
Leschi, said the paper, was given by William Tolmie as a character witness, testifying that before the war "Leschi was, and always had been, a
good Indian, friendly to the Bostons," and by Sluggia, hoping he could
make amends to his uncle for having betrayed him. According to
Leschi's nephew, who claimed to have been at the Connell's Prairie
ambush site where Moses and Miles were killed, Leschi was not present
but on the far side of the Cascades. Sluggia's testimony, "we believe,"
said the newspaper report, "had little weight with the jury, as it is well
known that he (Leschi) was in Olympia on the 27th and 28th of October,
and those murders were committed on the 31st of the month." But the
article erred in claiming that Leschi had been seen in the territorial capital on the days it mentioned. In fact, the Nisqually chief had last been
seen in Olympia in Acting Governor Mason's office on October 22, so he
would have had sufficient time to ride over the mountains to where Sluggia had placed him the day of the ambush. Moreover, by referring to the
deaths of the two armed militiamen, who were on a combat mission, as
"murders," the paper was refusing, like Stevens, to concede that the time-
honored "right of war" (i.e., to kill an enemy in combat without later risk
of prosecution for homicide) could be applied to Indians.

Not one of the sixteen witnesses who testified against Leschi, the
paper went on, "expressed a doubt as to the guilt of the prisoner as
charged." The only one whose testimony the article bothered to cite was
"A. B. Rabbeson, esq.," whose evidence was "conclusive and to the
point." This was the same Tony Rabbeson whose article in the same
newspaper describing the same incident a year earlier had mentioned
Leschi's name only once, as being among the Indians who met the Tidd
express party on the prairie shortly before the ambush occurred. Now in
court, according to the *Pioneer and Democrat,* Rabbeson said

he saw Leschi and Quiemuth and another Indian issue from the
brush and take a position on the road in front of him, at a distance
of not to exceed thirty-five or forty feet; that then and there Leschi
deliberately leveled his gun at him [presumably Rabbeson] and
fired; that immediately afterward either Quiemuth or the other

Indian fired; that he had known Leschi for years, and could not be mistaken in identifying him. This is precisely what Mr. Rabbeson has stated on all occasions from first to last since the murderous encounter the party to which he belonged received from the hostile Indians over one year ago.

In fact, his courtroom testimony as reported was (1) remarkably *unlike* what Rabbeson had earlier stated in print and (2) certainly not "conclusive and to the point." Rabbeson never said on the stand (or at least the paper did not report it) that he saw Leschi and his compatriots shoot Moses and Miles or that Rabbeson was told as much by any of his fellow volunteers. All he said was that Leschi had fired at *him,* not at Moses or Miles, from close enough range for Rabbeson to have recognized him.

The incompetence of the paper's report was suggested by its failure even to mention the substance of Judge Chenoweth's charge to the jury, which would shortly prove the focus of its deliberations. The jury was sequestered around 7:00 p.m., but despite the expectations of those thronging the candlelit little courtroom and gathered outside, no verdict was forthcoming. The jurors reappeared after about three hours to report they could not agree and wished to be excused. Chenoweth sent them back to reconsider the matter. Shortly before midnight the jurors returned to the courtroom and advised the judge that they were still deadlocked, forcing Chenoweth to declare a hung jury and remand Leschi to the brig at Fort Steilacoom to await retrial.

The temper of the community may be inferred from the *Pioneer and Democrat*'s shocked comment at the close of its write-up:

> The failure of the jury to agree upon a verdict, with the character of the evidence before them, we are informed, created general surprise. The attorneys for the prisoner expressed no doubt but he would be convicted, and merely labored to discharge a duty imposed upon them professionally, and Judge Chenoweth is said to have been astonished when, on concluding his charge, he was informed that it was necessary to clear the court room, expecting that a verdict of guilty would be pronounced from the jury box.

The paper speculated that in the view of some, a guilty verdict would have emerged if the jury had been forced to continue deliberating past midnight, while "others are inclined to think that repugnance to capital punishment had something to do in preventing an agreement." As if to stir up public sentiment in favor of a more satisfactory outcome at the retrial, the article concluded, "We learn that there are a number of other indictments found against [Leschi]—one by the grand jury of King county, for having been engaged in the massacre of the families on White river last fall or winter."

Nearly half a century would elapse before the world could read a more revealing report of the trial. The new account was almost as skewed as the original one in the *Pioneer and Democrat*—but in favor of the defendant in this case. The 1905 account was part of a book, *Pioneer Reminiscences of Puget Sound,* written by one of the two jurors at the Leschi trial who held out against a guilty verdict—Ezra Meeker. He drew on a wide range of historical documents and undertook considerable reportorial legwork (see Chapter 5).

Meeker was twenty-five at the time of the Leschi trial, having lived in Pierce County for four years since coming west from Indiana, where he grew up on a farm and had the benefit of just six months of formal education. After struggling up the Oregon Trail, Meeker, his wife, their new baby, and Ezra's older brother, Oliver, settled on a Donation Land Act claim below the modern city of Tacoma and got along well with the nearby natives, who he found reciprocated the Meekers' kindness. By nature Meeker believed strongly in the rights of minorities, and for his time and place he was notably free of prejudice against the Indians. Still, he was no sentimentalist on that subject. "We are apt to look upon the native race as indolent, filthy, and worthless," he would later write in his study of Leschi, appended to *Pioneer Reminiscences*. "And so they are, many of them." But over his lifetime, Meeker went on, he had encountered many natives who were industrious, clean, and honest. As a class, however, he had been forced to conclude, Indians were "without ambition, without mental capacity to embrace a real civilized life and without keen perception to quickly grasp the new problems incident to higher culture."

What troubled Meeker far more was the hypocrisy his government displayed in its dealings with the Indians. His lament applied with particular force to Isaac Stevens's treatment of tribal people, "acknowledging their ownership of the soil on the one hand while grasping it firmly with the other; when making professions of peace, when under prevailing conditions there could be no peace and finally professing the desire to have them adopt the habits of civilized life while driving them into conditions to make such a life impossible."

At the outbreak of Leschi's armed resistance, Meeker did not elect to join the militia to hunt down and punish the Indians for venting their grievance against Stevens's treaty and all the white settlers who stood to benefit from it. Instead, the Meeker family took refuge in Steilacoom, where Ezra helped build a blockhouse and opened a general store that was more or less successful until the Civil War. In 1862 he turned to growing hops of a quality and on a scale that in time would gain him a fortune. But on November 17, 1856, Ezra Meeker was just another young settler plucked by chance to decide Leschi's fate.

In his often absorbing 257-page account of Leschi's struggles, Meeker devoted only 7-plus pages to the first trial, the one in which he himself took part, and recounted mostly from memory, given the absence of court records and the few other documentary sources. Yet the event seems to have left an indelible impression on him, as did almost everything else having to do with Leschi. He was grieved by the prejudicial atmosphere he had detected outside the courtroom; the prisoner, he thought, had been convicted before the trial began. "For months and months Leschi's name had been a household word"—and not a nice one, presumably. "With the partisans of Stevens the story of his guilt had been told on every street corner, in every hotel or before the camp fire," Meeker wrote, "until it was generally believed he was the monster murderer he was charged to be . . . [with the] false accusation told and retold a thousand times."

For all of that, Leschi appeared to Meeker, as he studied him from the jury box, to be somewhat hopeful as the trial got under way. "I shall never forget his searching as he glanced over the jury with seeming contentment as he knew several of them." His hair was long and his appearance haggard, hardly a surprise under the circumstances, but Meeker thought he detected a glow to the Indian's cheeks that suggested underlying good health. Leschi's anxiety level was no doubt lowered by the presence beside him of William Tolmie, who, at risk of antagonizing many in the white community, had agreed to serve as his native friend's interpreter at the trial and contributed to his defense fund.

Short on details of the trial, Meeker's book nonetheless offered three important revelations. First, but the least fleshed out, was what Meeker termed "the now-unquestioned fact of the perjury of the chief, and, in fact, the only witness" against Leschi—Tony Rabbeson. In sharp contrast to the *Pioneer and Democrat*'s account, Meeker wrote: "He was a too willing witness to the truth, and had not been on the witness stand for five minutes [before] the guilt of perjury showed so plainly reflected in his eyes that no one really believed he was telling the truth." A subjective impression, certainly, and unsupported by any specific, demonstrable falsehoods. Of far more importance was Meeker's vivid recollection of Judge Chenoweth's charge to the jury.

Under Washington's territorial statutes, Chenoweth had the power, without need of a motion by the defense, to suspend the proceedings before the case ever reached the jury. The judge could have called the case off if he had found "no legal authority in the grand jury to inquire into the offense charged, by reason of its not being within the jurisdiction of the court," or if "the facts as stated in the indictment do not constitute a crime or misdemeanor." Either of these reasons could have been cited by Chenoweth as ground for tossing out the case. He could have ruled, as a matter of law, that because Leschi had been a legitimate combatant in a conflict validated by the mobilization and field maneuvers of U.S. Army regulars and territorial militiamen starting a month before Moses and Miles had been killed, the Nisqually chief could not be charged with murder for killing an enemy in wartime—any more than Moses and Miles could have been so charged, had they shot Leschi. But the politically attuned Chenoweth chose instead to leave the question up to the jury as a finding of fact.

Leschi's lawyers, while no novices, seem to have been less than aggressive in mounting his defense. Before the trial began they apparently failed to file a motion to dismiss the case on the ground that the judge should have thrown out the murder indictment as a matter of prevailing law instead of allowing the jury to hear the arguments. Nor, apparently, did the defense team, at the trial's end, request that the judge instruct the jury to return a directed acquittal on the ground that the prosecution had failed to prove Leschi was anything other than a lawful combatant. But without any prod from the defense, Judge Chenoweth now unexpectedly reversed his pattern of conducting the case—much to Leschi's benefit. The court instructed the jury, as Meeker recounted, "that if the deed was done as an act of war the prisoner could not be held answerable to the civil law."

Chenoweth then went even further in bolstering Leschi's chances by indicating to the jurors what constituted a condition of war. "His meaning appears vivid in my mind almost as if his words had been spoken but yesterday," wrote Meeker. A declaration of war consisted of acts as well as words, Chenoweth reportedly told the jurors, and "in Indian warfare a formal declaration was never expected and that with civilized nations often omitted." Acts of war frequently preceded formal declarations and "in such cases shielded the person from individual responsibility, and if we found, at the time Moses was killed, a state of war existed between our Government and the Indian tribes as such, then the prisoner could not be held; otherwise, even if [Leschi was] proven only an accessory [i.e., had not committed the act himself but actively aided and abetted it], we must bring in a verdict of guilty."

Inside the jury room Leschi had two staunch champions, Meeker and William M. Kincaid, "far past middle age" and thus the oldest member of the panel, whom Meeker described as a man "of sterling character . . . and deep convictions." Affectionately known as Father Kincaid, he was a devout Christian "who never had contentious relations with his neighbors or questioned their political or religious convictions . . . [and] did not have an enemy in the whole settlement. . . . [N]othing on earth could swerve him from the path of duty as he saw it."

The debate among the jurors was intense and, according to Meeker, marked by trepidation because "it was well known what the feeling on the outside was for vengeance." The case to spare the defendant, initially favored by four of the jurors, rested on three points: (1) There was undoubtedly a war going on between the Indians and the whites at the time of the Moses killing, and "the U.S. government acknowledged the fact by sending organized troops against them." (2) Leschi and his warriors had "committed no depredations or acts of war prior to the date Acting Governor Mason had sent the Eaton Rangers to make war on them." And (3) Moses himself had been armed and on military duty as part of that war effort. The key counterargument against extending the so-called right of war to Leschi was the one Stevens had repeatedly invoked—that Leschi and his band did not represent the prevailing view of their tribe, which "as such" had not gone to war against U.S. forces, making Leschi no better than a marauding wildcat.

Meeker argued in his book, as he may have in the jury room, that the Medicine Creek Treaty had not been made with any of the tribes *as such,* since they had no procedural means to ratify the pact by majority vote or some other way; rather, the treaty was made with representative chiefs, headmen, and elders *as individuals.* And it was as individuals, not by conscription or a tribal ballot, that a considerable number of braves had embraced Leschi's decision to resist by arms the whites' enforcement of the treaty. The insurgents might have been found to be an *informal* assemblage of manpower, but that hardly disqualified them as lawful combatants when they began to fight in behalf of a legitimate tribal cause.

The jury split eight to four for conviction as the balloting began. Over the next several hours the minority may have lost one of its members, but the holdouts, especially Meeker and Kincaid, were unbending in their support of Leschi's innocence; to them he was a patriot and freedom-fighter for his people, not a murderer. The wearying evening debate after a long day in court induced frayed tempers among the jurors, leading them to abandon hope of attaining unanimity. Judge Chenoweth, however, issued an "instruction that we *must* agree. What a travesty this on justice, to pen up men and make them perjure themselves to agree."

They tried again as hot words flew among them "almost to the point of intimidation," and one or possibly two men among the Leschi advocates defected. Only Meeker and Kincaid held fast, the latter declaring, "I will never vote to condemn that man." Meeker added admiringly, "He was firm as the rocks at the bottom of the sea. Kincaid finally ceased to contend with words and sat with head bowed as if in prayer, his only response a slow shake of the head to the importunities of other jurors."

The vote remained ten for conviction, two for acquittal, until the end.

WORD OF LESCHI'S abduction and hastily arranged trial quickly reached his half-brother and steadfast companion, Quiemuth, who was probably sharing his encampment or lying low nearby. Right after Leschi had been taken, Stevens—if we credit a letter he wrote to Indian Commissioner Manypenny—sent word to Quiemuth "to come in, surrender himself, and submit to his trial." The governor did not explain what the charges were against him.

Why Quiemuth yielded to the governor's siren song is unknown. Perhaps he was promised a fair hearing by the white authorities. And almost certainly he hoped his acquiescence would deflect some of the rampant hostility in the white community away from his more renowned—and notorious—brother, to whom he was still greatly devoted. Was Quiemuth naively trusting of whatever reassurances he may have been given by the Little White Father? Perhaps the governor, who in August had rewarded the displaced Nisquallies with a better reservation site in the heart of their homeland, was now moved to kindness and prone to leniency.

Whatever prompted him, Quiemuth contacted a prominent white neighbor and fierce Stevens admirer, James Longmire, to escort him to Olympia. It was a sound choice. Longmire was known to be nursing a sizable grudge toward the Indians generally for the loss of many of his horses. Who better than Longmire to safeguard him against hateful settlers who might otherwise have shot Quiemuth on sight or dangled him from the nearest stout-branched tree? They were joined by two younger whites and Quiemuth's niece, Betsy, when they set out for Stevens's home the same day Leschi's trial was unfolding. To avoid detection, they rode through the chill, rainy night and reached the governor's residence around two in the morning.

In all likelihood, Stevens was wide awake at that hour, awaiting word of the outcome of the Leschi trial. The news of the hung jury might have arrived only a short while before Quiemuth's party reined up outside his door, and would probably have left him out of sorts. Yet, according to Longmire's account of the episode, Stevens was cordial, perhaps cheered by the sight of the consolation prize he had been handed in the immediate wake of his disappointment over the non-verdict by the Leschi jury.

Stevens reportedly offered food and a peace pipe of tobacco to Quiemuth, gave instructions that the voluntary prisoner not be bound, and moved his party into the governor's private office, where a fresh fire was lighted and talk ensued. Longmire recalled that Quiemuth, pleased by his reception, praised Stevens as a good man who he knew would not harm him—perhaps a shrewd plea for forgiveness or a challenge to the white overlord to continue his display of Christian charity toward the Nisqually people, their subdued chiefs included.

After a while, Stevens had blankets brought and suggested that Quiemuth's party get a few hours of sleep on his office floor before the captive was escorted to Fort Steilacoom, preferably before dawn broke and word could circulate that the Indian war leader was in custody—and within gunshot range. As a precaution, the governor locked the front door to his office but left the side door unsecured, either forgetfully or perhaps to allow his unexpected guests direct access to the nearby outhouse. Is it possible that Stevens intentionally provided this easy side entry into his office so that Quiemuth might be attended to on the spot and not allowed to escape his ultimate punishment, as his brother might yet manage? Possible but improbable.

"Father sent a man over to the stable to get horses to transfer Quiemuth to Fort Steilacoom to be held for trial," Hazard Stevens wrote his grandmother two days afterward. "The man told the hostler and so it came out." U.S. Indian agent Sidney Ford wrote to the governor the following week that a Frenchman named Osha, who had ridden into town with the Quiemuth party, made a beeline for the Hotel Washington, "got them up and told them he had brought in Quiemuth." Soon much of Olympia was apprised of the twin events involving the infamous fraternal chiefs of the Nisquallies—the Steilacoom jury's failure to convict Leschi and his brother's presence right there in town and in the governor's custody. The capital turned into a tinderbox of fury. Among those most aroused was Joseph Bunton (or Bunting; accounts differ), son-in-law of the late James McAllister, who had been ambushed by Leschi's renegades at the outset of the war against the Indians. Stevens later described Bunton as "a very quiet, industrious young man . . . [who] always sustained an excellent character. But the whole [McAllister] family seem bent to have revenge on the Indians who killed the husband and father."

In a community that small, word quickly spread that Bunton was part of a group of men who, soon after the governor retired around 4:30 a.m. on November 18, slipped through the unlocked side door to his office and into the dimly lighted room where Quiemuth and his party slumbered. In the scuffle that followed, one of the young white men guarding Quiemuth sprang up and tried to deflect the lead assailant's gun, but amid the darkness and frenzy, he neither prevented the weapon's discharge nor recognized (so he said) the determined intruder. The bullet went through Quiemuth's hand, according to the coroner's report, and lodged in his chest. As the victim struggled to his feet, he was stabbed in the heart by a knife with a very fine blade and fell dead. The assassins fled, unpursued.

Hazard awakened his father with the news around 5:15, and according to Longmire, who had been in the room, the governor was more enraged than he had ever seen him, bellowing that the murder of a notorious Indian leader under his roof would hand his outspoken critic, General Wool, "a club" over him. The site of the killing, Stevens wrote Manypenny, gave "a certain character of ferocity and lawlessness to the transaction which words can not extenuate. It has been to me a great sorrow." His grief, if genuine, seems to have been manifested less over the slaying of the prostrate Indian chief than the embarrassment of his appearing complicit in the foul deed or powerless to have prevented it.

Hearing reports in the morning that Bunton had been Quiemuth's killer, Stevens pressed charges against him. But no one in the territory would step forward and identify the murderer. "Strange as it may appear," the governor explained to his superiors at the U.S. Indian Commission, "evidence enough was not elicited to warrant the magistrate to bind [Bunton] over for trial, and he was accordingly discharged."

The meaning of such an appalling act of lawless retribution, carried out with impunity, was not lost on the tribes of Puget Sound. "My Indians feel very much dissatisfied concerning the death of Quiemuth," Sidney Ford advised the governor. By the natives' reckoning, Quiemuth's savage murder more than avenged Abram Moses's death, whoever had been responsible for it. In the wake of this latest act of white injustice, Leschi's retrial ought now to be dropped. But Isaac Stevens was not ruled by magnanimity. Indeed, notwithstanding his show of regret that Quiemuth had been done away with so crudely, his announced plan to bring the leaders of the Indian uprising to justice as he conceived it was working out well. That the Nisqually brothers' entrapment had been engineered by Stevens himself is strongly suggested by his November 21 letter to Commissioner Manypenny, reporting that since Fort Steilacoom commandant Casey "had no disposition to comply with my requisitions" to hunt down and turn over the two fugitive tribal leaders, "I have resorted to other methods, which have resulted in [their] apprehension"—and in Quiemuth's murder, which he failed to point out. Stevens's mind was fixed: the more dangerous of the Nisqually brother chiefs would be retried in a few months as scheduled.

I I

With Malice Aforethought

W HILE HE WAITED FOR the whites' baffling legal machinations to determine his fate, Leschi languished in the guardhouse at Fort Steilacoom, his universe reduced to a thirty-one-by-twenty-six–foot indoor corral. For a man like him, who had passed his life roaming the wilderness amid some of the most sublime scenery on earth, his confinement must have seemed a living death. Yet he was not entirely bereft of hope.

For one thing, his jailers, under orders from the upstanding Lieutenant Colonel Silas Casey, tendered Leschi an almost chivalrous regard as a legitimate prisoner of war who had fought well in a forlorn cause. To a man, Casey's soldiers thought Leschi no more deserving of conviction and punishment as a murderer than they themselves would have been for carrying out their sworn duty to kill Nisqually tribesmen while they were on the warpath. Casey, moreover, may have asked himself whether, in holding Leschi prisoner at Stevens's request on a charge that mocked the military profession, he was not violating the pledge of safety that Colonel George Wright had granted the Indian leader—a promise endorsed by Wright's superiors all the way up the army's chain of command. Why not grant the Nisqually chief asylum at the army post until the nation's chief executive could rule on whether Leschi should be set at liberty as an honorable defeated foe or submitted to the mercies of frontier justice? If Casey was tempted to lock horns with Stevens for a final time over the Nisqually chief, he kept the idea to himself. Meanwhile, he insisted that his captive not be mistreated while held at the army post.

Leschi was still more fortunate that his daily oversight had been assigned to the post quartermaster, twenty-six-year-old Lieutenant

August Kautz, a German immigrant who had done well enough as a volunteer in the Mexican War to win an appointment to West Point. Assigned to Steilacoom in 1853, Kautz was enchanted by the surrounding landscape, invested in local real estate, and ingratiated himself with members of both races in the vicinity. One of his early assignments had been to investigate the illicit sale of liquor to the Indians by both soldiers and civilians—a frequent cause of trouble. In the process, the personable lieutenant learned a good deal about the tribal life and culture of the Nisquallies. He fell in love with one of them—Quiemuth's daughter, whom he called Kitty—and married her. The outbreak of hostilities naturally caused him anguish, but he had no choice other than going to war against his wife's people. When Lieutenant William Slaughter was slain in the early weeks of combat, Kautz stepped into his role as one of the top young field officers and conducted himself well. In the final battle west of the Cascades, at Connell's Prairie in early March 1856, Kautz suffered a leg wound and was confined to less strenuous duties at the fort, including the care of his wife's imprisoned uncle.

Under Kautz's benign custodianship, Leschi was permitted frequent visits from friends, facilitating preparations for his defense at the retrial, set for March 1857. The senior member of his two-man legal team, William H. Wallace, had co-represented Leschi at his first trial. A solid citizen of Steilacoom, Wallace was an experienced practitioner in his mid-forties and had been among the group of lawyers who denounced Stevens for decreeing martial law. For the retrial Wallace was joined by a former member of the Pierce County prosecutor's office who had assisted in the case brought against Leschi—precocious Frank Clark, lately turned twenty-three and regarded as energetic, smart, and a bit flamboyant. An upstate New Yorker, Clark had studied law at an academy in Lowell, Massachusetts, before making his way to Puget Sound while still a teenager. With legal talent in short supply in that pioneer era, Clark soon established himself as an able attorney, frequently jousting in court with Wallace and men far more seasoned than himself. He would take on any case that came his way and drove some of those he bested in court to accuse him of unscrupulous conduct in behalf of dubious clients. The Wallace-Clark team yielded to none in their dislike of Isaac Stevens, perhaps their driving motivation in taking on Leschi's defense.

In contrast to Leschi's unconscionably hurried first trial, his lawyers had more than three months to prepare for the retrial. Although no reliable records or extensive accounts of the first trial have survived, it appears that the defense team enlisted additional witnesses to challenge Tony Rabbeson's account of the ambush at Connell's Prairie. They had less luck in enticing any of Leschi's tribesmen or allies to come forward and vouch for his whereabouts when Moses and Miles were killed. Wallace and Clark also concluded they could not risk asking Leschi himself to offer an alibi. Once called to the witness stand, he would likely have been riddled with questions intended to confuse, mock, and impeach him. Moreover, he would have been committing perjury if he had claimed that the Indian encampment on the prairie was not under his command and that the ambushers had not been stationed in the swamp beside the wagon road at his directive—tantamount to admitting responsibility for Moses's death, leave aside whether it constituted murder. His defenders pondered other ways to bolster his case. Kautz, supposedly the Nisqually chief's watchdog, took the lead in trying to fashion new evidence casting doubt on Rabbeson's story that Leschi was among the shooters at the ambush site even if he had not fired the actual bullet that took Moses's life.

Despite the wintry weather and soggy terrain, Kautz, the faithful Dr. William Tolmie, and at least one member (possibly William Tidd) of the seven-man express party that had been ambushed below Connell's Prairie on October 31, 1856, revisited the scene with surveying equipment in their packs. They measured the distance from the spot on the prairie where the militiamen had paused in a friendly encounter with a group of Indians—Leschi among them, according to Rabbeson—to the approximate spot down the road where Moses was shot after the soldiers had resumed their ride toward Steilacoom. Using surveyor's chains, Kautz's group came up with a distance of 4,488 feet. The mounted expressmen, even if proceeding cautiously along the narrow road as it dipped through the low-lying marshes, would likely have covered that stretch of less than a mile in five to ten minutes. To have positioned themselves under cover beside the road where the ambush occurred, Leschi's party would have had to scurry through the woods a good deal faster than the militiamen while remaining out of their sight and earshot—not an impossibility since the natives presumably knew the terrain well and any possible shortcut to beat their prey to the ambush site.

Extensive investigation of the area, however, revealed to Kautz and his colleagues that there was no shorter way to reach the ambush site, only an Indian trail that looped around the wagon road, and it was very rough going—a man on foot would probably have had an easier time negotiating it than one on a nervously stepping horse. But even a mounted rider traveling the back trail that shadowed the wagon road would have had to cover, according to the measurement by Kautz and Tolmie, 6,900 feet—more than half a mile farther, over tangled terrain, than the militiamen's route. It seemed a logistical impossibility, and a finding that must have cheered Leschi's lawyers.

Another development encouraged them as well: the outcome of the trial of Winyea, a native warrior who had given himself up over the summer and been indicted for participating in the Connell's Prairie ambush by the same grand jury that found against Leschi. There are no surviving records of the trial proceedings, only scattered references to it in the press and the testimony of witnesses at the two Leschi trials, but we do know Winyea was acquitted despite testimony by Rabbeson. Because the defendant was hardly a well-known figure like Leschi in the white settlements, the testimony identifying him as a participant or present at or near the ambush site must have lacked credibility even to a jury primed to exact vengeance on a native foolhardy enough to have submitted himself to its judgment.

These sanguine omens were outweighed, unhappily for Leschi, by a pair of developments affecting the level of impartiality he and his attorneys could expect at the pending retrial.

The first setback, which may well have been engineered by the governor, was a shift of the trial venue from Steilacoom in Pierce County, a nexus of anti-Stevens sentiment, to Olympia in neighboring Thurston County, where Stevens held sway over the territory's political machinery. The switch had been neatly managed in a way that made it hard to prove Leschi had been administratively victimized.

Congress, as an economy move, had just approved a new rule for the administration of justice in U.S. territories: federal district courts could now sit at only one location per judicial district, of which there were three in Washington Territory. In December, a few weeks after the first Leschi trial, the territorial legislature redrew the judicial map, transferring Pierce County from the Third to the Second District and, with the approval of the three district judges, designated Olympia as the one permitted site for the court to sit. This was a heavy blow to Leschi's chances. Few potential jurors in the vicinity of Olympia shared the fair-mindedness of Ezra Meeker and Father Kincaid in their tolerance toward the Indians. The realignment of the judicial districts might not have been undertaken explicitly to victimize Leschi, but there seems to have been no other reason, in view of the sparse population remaining in the Third District once Pierce County was subtracted from it.

Even more potentially prejudicial to Leschi's case as a result of the redistricting was the change in the presiding jurist at the retrial. Edward Lander, chief justice of Washington Territory, whom Stevens had arrested and detained twice during his martial law debacle—acts that one might suppose had soured the judge on the governor and left him disinclined to take his side in the Leschi matter—was in charge of the Second District trial court.

But Lander had much in common with Stevens. A year older than the governor, he had grown up in Salem, north of Boston and only fifteen miles or so from Stevens's hometown. After earning his bachelor's, master's, and law degrees from Harvard and practicing locally for a few years, Lander performed well as district attorney in Indiana. Commissioned as an army officer during the Mexican War, he saw no action and returned to Indiana, where his magisterial bearing and formidable bulk served him well as a state judge and won him appointment in 1853 as Washington Territory's first chief justice. His keen juridical aptitude made him an invaluable member of the commission that drafted the territory's legal code.

Lander, for all his high professional standing, was frustrated that he had not been given a chance to display his manliness on a battlefield, so he jumped at the chance to leave the bench temporarily right after the Indian raid on Seattle to serve as captain, the top-ranking officer, of Company A of the Washington Territory Foot Volunteers. It was one of the militia cadres that Stevens summoned in his crusade to exterminate hostile Indians within his jurisdiction. Lander's company, consisting of a dozen officers and forty-four privates, served in the Puget Sound Indian War for six months beginning January 29, though Lander was forced to absent himself temporarily in an effort to check Stevens's decree of martial law.

Thus, when Leschi was retried in March 1857, the court was presided over by a judge who had taken active part in the forces marshaled to do battle against the Indian guerrillas, of whom the defendant was the leader, charged with having murdered one of Lander's fellow militiamen. In keeping with both the letter and spirit of the very statutes that he had helped draft, Lander could have been declared ineligible to preside over the case. Under modern legal ethics, he would almost surely have had to recuse himself from acting as judge at Leschi's retrial. But in that frontier

society he did no such thing. Leschi's lawyers, no doubt fearful of antagonizing Lander, did not challenge him or call for his replacement.

FAR MORE DOCUMENTATION has survived from the second Leschi
trial than the first. We have many of the legal papers submitted to the
court, the clerk's notes on the testimony, accounts of the proceedings in
two newspapers, the *Pioneer and Democrat* as well as the new *Washington Republican* (of the opposite political persuasion), and a long article
by Elwood Evans, a contemporary lawyer and regional historian who
later served as territorial secretary. What is missing is a verbatim transcript of the testimony, and in the case of Antonio Rabbeson, the key witness against Leschi, we have only a disjointed, stream-of-consciousness
rendition, with none of his words directly quoted. The sequence of the
events he described is at times muddled beyond deciphering. Yet it was
Rabbeson's words *alone* on which the prosecutors' case relied.

The retrial was held on March 18, 1857, with a large but orderly
crowd attending. Stevens may well have been on hand, and we are told he
arranged for two of the leading tribal chiefs in the Puget Sound region—
Seattle and Patkamin, both opposed to Leschi's insurrection—to witness
how fairly the white authorities rendered justice to the natives. In all likelihood, William Tolmie, who again bore witness to Leschi's good character, served once more as his interpreter, as he had at the first trial.

The prosecution opened with its strongest, indeed its only, card.
According to Ezra Meeker's book on Leschi, Rabbeson answered his
questioners in a more careful way than he had at the first trial. But there is
no basis for believing Meeker was on hand for the retrial, so he probably
depended on the notes by the court clerk that formed the basis of the
newspaper accounts and Evans's article and commentary. A ragged blend
of first- and third-person narrative, Rabbeson's testimony as reported
began with the statement that he and his fellow militiamen

> in Connell's prairie met a party of Indians—had a long conversa-
> tion—several minutes talking with them—there were several that I
> knew personally—none that I knew the names of at the time—
> after we left Connell's prairie came on three-fourths of a mile to a
> mile—struck a swamp—after we had got into the swamp—four
> were in the swamp some 150 yards, three of us near the edge of the
> swamp when we received a volley—when the firing commenced. I

looked behind me to see if any one was killed—I discovered Mr. Miles off his horse—I rode back to assist Mr. Miles, and assisted him across the swamp out of gunshot—while I was assisting Mr. Miles, holding his horse, three Indians stepped out—two of the three fired—I then rode on three or four miles, overtook the balance of my company, and there found Mr. Moses was wounded, and I believe he was dying at the time—Mr. Moses was left some 50 or 100 yards off of the road.

Rabbeson soon amended and elaborated on his choppy narrative, but he never said that he was present when the fatal shots were fired at Miles and Moses and never claimed to see who fired them. Nor did he initially identify the three Indians who he said "stepped out" while he was holding Miles's horse, two of them firing—presumably at Rabbeson—and apparently doing him no damage because he said he rode on another three or four miles, evidently unpursued by the Indians who had stepped into his path. Rabbeson continued, dwelling on Moses's injury:

I saw a wound somewhere about the left breast—he told me at the time that he was shot through the back—Mr. Moses did not tell me when he received the wound—Mr. M. was aware that he was dying—I don't know how long I rode from swamp to where I overtook—rode fast—was left alone—Mr. Moses was 100 to 150 yards ahead of me when volley was fired in the swamp—I took one of the Indians who came out to be Quiemuth—the other Leschi, prisoner at the bar—third did not know—Leschi was one who fired towards me—I had been more or less acquainted with him for ten years—had seen him very frequently before that time.

Rabbeson's testimony now bogged down in a series of contradictory claims. He said Moses had not told him when he was shot, yet he also said Moses was 100 to 150 yards ahead of him when the volley was fired in the swamp, suggesting Rabbeson might have covered the distance in a moment or two and aided the wounded Moses. This second statement did not accord with his opening account of how he had ridden three or four miles more before he overtook the rest of his party and learned that Moses had been gravely injured. The allegation that Leschi was in the swamp and among the Indians involved in the ambush was the critical piece of testimony against him, despite the fact that he had been indicted for killing Moses, not simply serving as an accomplice. Rabbeson went on by doubling back to the beginning:

> In Connell's prairie we saw a party of Indians—among them Leschi—he said he supposed the house of Connell was burned by accident. . . . Leschi was friendly—some three-quarters of a mile from the swamp—the wagon road is three-quarters of a mile, and the trail three or four hundred yards—we traveled the road—it was a large party of Indians we met on the prairie—left Leschi on the prairie—this swamp is in Pierce county—it was either the 30th or 31st of October, 1855—the three Indians were from 30 to 50 feet distant—so close they didn't think it worth while to take sight— quite a number of guns fired after that—some on high ground— heard no guns except around there.

His story changed with each new recitation. Now he was saying that Leschi was among the Indians his party had encountered on the prairie, though earlier he had said he had recognized some of the Indians but did not know their names "at the time." By his own account, though, he had been acquainted with Leschi for ten years and must have known his name; he certainly did not learn it only subsequent to the ambush. Rabbeson then spoke of "the trail" being 300 or 400 yards—what trail was that? Did he mean a trail through the woods that served as an alternative, off-road path from the prairie to the ambush site where Miles was shot? If so, how did he know there was such a trail and what its length was? Lieutenant Kautz had lately searched that very terrain and found that the only trail running from the prairie to the ambush site was nearly half a mile longer than the wagon road between the same two points. And if Leschi, his brother, and a third native had stepped in front of Rabbeson and fired at him from such close range (by Rabbeson's account, they did not even bother to take aim), why did all of their shots miss him? Leschi was known to be a keen hunter and marksman. A fortunate escape, indeed, from his three alleged Indian assailants.

The longer Rabbeson testified, the more he dwelled on his connection with Leschi, who, he said, "has been around my house often . . . been at my house to sell meat—several Indians I know as well—lived within six or seven miles—did not often encamp on my prairie—I did not know his name—for ten years called him old man and Stub." Rabbeson said he went to see Tolmie after the ambush: "I described him—the Indian's clothes—Dr. Tolmie said from my description of the clothes that it was Leschi, as he had sold him clothes but not his hat." That sequence in the identification process would shortly be challenged.

The court clerk's notes and newspaper reports relying on them did not mention any other witnesses who substantiated Rabbeson's story, but did indicate a quite different version offered by another member of his express party, Andrew J. Bradley, who had known Leschi since arriving in the region in the spring of 1854. Leschi had helped rescue Bradley's herd of cattle as it was being swept away by a swift current while crossing the Puyallup River. Bradley told the court that he knew Leschi well but did not place him at either Connell's Prairie when the militia party first ran into the Indians or afterward in the swamp. After leaving the natives on the prairie,

> I was the first to ride on—perhaps 50 or 75 yards in the swamp when we were fired upon—I looked around, saw Miles and Rabbeson in back of me—tried to see Indians—could not because of smoke rising from their guns . . . we rode on one-and-a-half to two miles when Mr. Moses said he was wounded and should fall off his horse—I stopped my horse—he fell towards me as I came up—I caught him and carried him off the road—said he was shot through just below the heart—I had just got up the hill some 50 or 75 yards, when Rabbeson and Tidd rode up, and said Mr. Miles was killed—Mr. Moses then asked us for some water—all he said was to Mr. Rabbeson and myself, who were the last to leave him— he said, "Boys, save yourselves, and if any of you are saved, remember me."—said he wouldn't live—then left him, and in two days and nights got to Steilacoom—I could not say how many Indians on horseback when we first came up—they got out of the way—I have recognized the place spoken of—I did not see Leschi there.

Bradley added that it was a cloudy day, and the encounter with the Indians was "towards sunset—about fifteen or twenty minutes after we left them were fired on . . . I was near enough to recognize them," but he said none of the shooters was Leschi. On further questioning, Bradley again drove home the point: when his party first met the natives, "I saw Rabbeson talking with Indians, two men on horseback—neither of them was Leschi—the question he asked the Indians was, as to the people living in the vicinity." Was it possible that Bradley could have survived his party's harrowing experience, lasting several days deep in Indian Country, and during the course of their escape not heard from any of his colleagues, Rabbeson included, that Leschi had been among their assailants? Was Bradley, for all the seeming clarity, consistency, and affecting detail in his testimony, lying to protect his friend Leschi?

Another of Rabbeson's militia colleagues, A. J. Simmons, according to the clerk's notes, seemed to confirm Leschi's absence. Simmons told the court: "Me and Mr. Rabbeson had a conversation one day going from Mr. Smith's to camp Montgomery [headquarters of the territorial volunteers]—I asked him if he saw Indians in the swamp—understood him to say he did not know any of them—was not close enough to distinguish—he said nothing of his acquaintance with Leschi at that time or any other time."

The defense lawyers then introduced a number of character witnesses to vouch for Leschi as friendly and industrious. Foremost among these was Tolmie, who said he had known Leschi since 1833 and that he "never knew him to be unfriendly until July, 1855, when I knew him to be dissatisfied about the treaties about the reservations." He added that he

> heard Mr. Rabbeson's testimony—Rabbeson came [to Fort Nisqually] on his way in [from Connell's Prairie], and gave a very detailed narrative of everything—said there was shouting and noise when they rode up to the Indians . . . said he knew several Indians by sight—I then described Leschi and a coat—said he thought that was Leschi—question made about a hat—Mr. Rabbeson described Indian—said Leschi lately at [his] place with felt hat like it.

Thus, in Tolmie's telling, it was he who first described Leschi's clothing, and then Rabbeson said yes, that was what Leschi was wearing—the opposite order from Rabbeson's account. To incriminate the Nisqually chief by placing him at the ambush site, Rabbeson could simply have been agreeing that Leschi was wearing whatever garb Tolmie had just described to him.

Two government officials then offered testimony intended by Leschi's lawyers to help persuade the jury that he was not a murderous outlaw. Charles Mason confirmed that while serving as acting governor of the territory in October 1855, he had issued two proclamations, the first on the fourteenth of the month, requesting residents to form two volunteer militia units to quell unrest among the native people—a call to arms in response to recent combat engagements, particularly the September rout of Major Haller's regular army forces east of the Cascades. Mason's testimony thus established that armed territorial combatants had been officially summoned more than two weeks before the Connell's Prairie ambush and that Eaton's Rangers had been sent into the field to apprehend Leschi more than a week before the Moses incident. In short, there was a war on, and even if Leschi was at or near the ambush site, he was by then a legitimate combatant against white soldiers out to get him, so he could not, under the all but universally understood "rule of war," be charged with murder for slaying an enemy soldier.*

The defense lawyers then produced John Swan, who had been serving as an Indian agent and warden at the Fox Island internment camp when Leschi and his party of thirty-three braves arrived by canoe in January 1856 to ask him to convey the Indians' wish to reach peace terms with white officials. Swan stressed that for the thirty-six hours he had been held by Leschi's men, he was not molested or tied up.

The closest any testimony came to supporting Rabbeson's placement of Leschi at the ambush site served to cast as much doubt on Rabbeson's words as to strengthen them. Israel H. Wright said that he had been a juror at the trial of Winyea, charged with the same crime as Leschi but acquitted, and that he recalled Rabbeson's testimony that he had seen Leschi "and he had a scar on his forehead—he saw him at one place at the edge of the swamp—said he saw him on the prairie, Connell's prairie." Other jurors from the Winyea trial offered conflicting memories of whether Rabbeson had identified Leschi by such a scar, but the court clerk's notes made no mention of whether the lawyers from either side at the retrial pointed to the defendant sitting right in front of the jury and called attention to such a scar—or its absence. No surviving description of Leschi makes mention of a prominent scar on his forehead.

---

*In the relatively few cases where the idea is discussed in the literature of military justice, the term "rule of war" is used interchangeably with "right of war" and "law of war." All mean the same thing—that wars are about intentionally killing the enemy, and combatants who do so are to be exempt from the charge of murder by civilian authorities.

. . .

UP TO THIS POINT, Leschi's lawyers would seem to have mounted a reasonably creditable effort in his defense. But they had not been willing to risk putting Leschi on the stand to provide an alibi for his activities on the afternoon in question, and nobody else had come forward to place him somewhere other than at Connell's Prairie when the killings occurred. There were, furthermore, three curious omissions on the defense's part, perhaps all of them intentional yet all worthy of note.

First, why hadn't Wallace or Clark, in cross-examining Rabbeson, asked him why the article he wrote for the *Pioneer and Democrat* just a few weeks after the Connell's Prairie ambush failed to mention Leschi as having been among the natives who shot at his party in the swamp—an accusation he leveled at the two trials, long after the event? Leschi's team may have desisted because Rabbeson could have replied that the article was written in haste and, at any rate, he had named Leschi as one of the Indians his party had initially encountered on the prairie.

Why, though, didn't the defense team make use, in the course of the retrial, of the recent discovery by Lieutenant Gus Kautz and William Tolmie that the Indian trail from Connell's Prairie to the ambush site was nearly half again as long as the wagon road traveled by the mounted militiamen and that it ran through more tangled terrain? These factors would presumably have made it impossible for Leschi and his colleagues to reach the ambush spot ahead of the soldiers. Since Rabbeson had stated that the Indian trail was the much shorter route, disclosure of the precise measurements on a map of the Connell's Prairie area drawn especially for the defense by Kautz, a well-regarded regular U.S. Army officer, might have damaged Rabbeson's credibility.

The problem for the defense was likely the fuzziness of the chronology and other details of the encounter with the Indians on the prairie. How long did the "friendly" exchange with them last? Had some of the natives perhaps slipped away in the course of the conversation and headed down the trail to the swamp? Was Leschi himself still on the prairie to bid farewell when the soldiers rode off down the wagon road, or might he, too, have ducked away as soon as the militiamen's attention was distracted? Bradley's testimony, moreover, estimated the time elapsed between the soldiers' leavetaking on the prairie and the first ambush shots to have been "fifteen or twenty minutes," more than sufficient for some of the Indians who had met the express party on the prairie to have taken the longer back trail and been in place to carry out the ambush. So the Kautz map could have been rebutted as evidence proving nothing beyond Rabbeson's incompetence as a geographer.

The third omission by the defense team, however, is harder to understand, even with the benefit of hindsight. At the close of testimony, and before each side delivered its summation, the court invited counsel to submit in writing any special instructions or points they wished the judge to cite or emphasize in his charge to the jury. In view of Judge Chenoweth's charge at the first trial that Leschi could not be convicted of murder in a civil court if the jury considered him a legitimate combatant fighting for his people in time of war, Wallace and Clark ought logically to have asked for the same directive from Judge Lander, clearly a less sympathetic judge and far more unlikely to be generous to Leschi in framing the case for the jury.

Yet there is no record that the defense asked for such an instruction. If it had, though, the prosecution might well have responded that there was no statutory basis for any "right of war" or "law of war" defense, that it was not a legal precept or construct but only a historical conceit steeped in outmoded notions of knightly valor. Besides, the prosecution could have added, the defense was trying to have it both ways by arguing that Leschi had not committed or been complicit in the killing of Moses while also claiming that even if he had been involved, he could not be held personally responsible.

The defense team might also have asked the judge to tell the jury they could convict Leschi on the lesser charge of second-degree murder, that innocence or a death sentence were not their only choices. The statutory definition of first-degree murder applied to "every person who shall purposely and of deliberate and premeditated malice" kill another and as a result "shall suffer death." A person who "shall purposely and maliciously, but without deliberation and premeditation, kill another . . . shall be deemed guilty of murder in the second degree and upon conviction thereof shall be imprisoned." It would have been hard for the prosecution to claim that Leschi had, with deliberation and premeditation, planned the ambush of the express party, which had come upon them by surprise. Killing in wartime was generally a random business, not directed at specific individuals but at the enemy as an undifferentiated mass.

In the end, Leschi's lawyers placed their trust in Judge Lander's merciful reading of the strictures of justice. Contemporary legal commentator Elwood Evans called Lander's charge to the jury "brief, able, clear and impartial." To find Leschi guilty, Lander told the jury, it "must believe the defendant was present, aiding, abetting, assisting or encouraging the commission of the offense charged." Under territorial statute, the distinction between principals and accessories had been done away with, the bench asserted. "All who were present tendering assistance, became principals, and if the jury believed from the testimony that Leschi was present, so assisting, they must find him guilty of murder." But if the jury members had any doubt about the evidence as to "the presence of Leschi on the occasion referred to, the prisoner must have the benefit of it." Lander, however, glaringly failed to follow Chenoweth's lead in instructing that lawful combatants could not be convicted of murder for killing in wartime.

The whole case thus came down to whether the jurors chose to believe Rabbeson; there was no corroborative evidence whatever in support of his jumbled testimony. The fate of the accused was turned over to the panel at 11:00 p.m. The jurors sat through the night, taking far longer in their deliberations than the Leschi-haters could countenance. Unlike the jury in the first trial, this one included no stouthearted adherents of the defendant's side. The jurors reappeared in court at 10:30 the next morning and declared their unanimous belief that Leschi had had a hand in the death of Abram Benton Moses and—never mind the reasons for his participation—must die for it.

The judge set the execution for June 10 at Steilacoom, Pierce County's principal settlement. Lander refused a defense motion filed the next day to reopen the case in light of the Kautz map purporting to show that Leschi could not have been the killer or shooter. If the exhibit had any persuasive evidentiary value, said the judge, it ought to have been submitted in a timely fashion, during the course of the trial. Submitting it the day after seemed to have been no more than a desperate ploy.

"LESCHI REBELLED against bad treaty," Chief Seattle's biographer Eva Anderson quoted the old sachem as commenting after witnessing the trial firsthand. "White man gives Leschi's people new treaty [at Fox Island]. White man must know, in his heart, that first treaty was unfair— or why give new treaty?" The Nisqually chief had been justified in his defiance of the white authorities, Seattle was saying, and the governor could not stomach the rebuke, so Leschi had to pay the ultimate price.

Stevens saw only vindication of his own firm hand in dealing with the Indians. Reporting to U.S. Indian Commissioner Manypenny soon after the Leschi retrial, the governor insisted that the judicial proceedings had gone off with "solemnity and fairness" and that the defendant "had all the aids to make his case good, which a[ny] white man had," so the accused "was most ably defended"—a highly questionable claim.

Leschi's lawyers now pursued their last judicial remedy, an appeal to the territorial Supreme Court. In asking that the jury's finding be vacated, the defense attorneys argued that the venue of the trial had been unconstitutionally changed to the defendant's detriment, that the preponderance of the testimony ran counter to the guilty verdict, and that the judge had failed to inform the jury that it might convict the defendant on a lesser charge than first-degree murder, among other contentions. But in retrospect it is unfathomable why Leschi's defense team, with nothing to lose now that the jury had spoken, did not raise the "rule of war" issue in its appeal as a basis for tossing out the whole case, just as Judge Chenoweth had pointedly cited that option to the first jury and Judge Lander had ignored it.

The prospect of a favorable outcome of the appeal was dim at best. The Supreme Court, the sole appellate tribunal in the territory, was composed of the same three judges, sitting *en banc,* who had presided over cases individually in their own judicial districts. There was no disinterested, independent review apparatus, so the appeal would be heard by Chief Justice Lander, reviewing his own rulings as Judge Lander at the retrial; by Associate Justice Chenoweth, who had presided as Judge Chenoweth at the first trial; and by Associate Justice Obadiah L. McFadden, presiding judge of the First Judicial District. Since there was zero chance that Lander would vote to reverse himself, Leschi's lawyers could only hope that Chenoweth, on hearing the appeal, might part company with Lander for having ignored the "rule of war" issue, and that perhaps McFadden, who held forth in the southern tier of Washington Territory, was less in thrall to Stevens's influence and more willing to see Leschi's life spared. According to Ezra Meeker's book, however, McFadden was a supporter of Stevens's martial law decree and therefore unlikely to part company with the governor on his Indian policy.

The Supreme Court was not due to reconvene until December. Stevens, with his prized prisoner condemned to die and under military surveillance, was content to let the justice system play itself out; to have acted otherwise would be to have branded himself a brutish subverter of the law—his persecution of the Muck Creek Five and the murder of Quiemuth under his roof had been bad enough. Leschi would linger in prison nine months before his appeal could be heard.

The Nisqually chief's conviction marked the virtual fulfillment of Stevens's primary objective in assuming the governorship: subjugation of the native tribes and seizure of title to the bulk of their homelands, so that white settlement could proceed apace and the lush region opened for economic harvesting. Yet Washington Territory had still not been entirely pacified as 1857 unfolded. The eastern tribes continued to erupt in irregular displays of violence as the U.S. Senate dallied with the ratification of the treaties Stevens had rammed through after the Medicine Creek council session. For his excessive zeal in the treatymaking campaign, resulting in open warfare, and the martial law outrage, Congress stripped Stevens of his appointment as commissioner of Indian affairs and assigned the added responsibility to the Indian commissioner for Oregon Territory.

Having fallen from grace with federal officials and fearful of imminent dismissal as governor of Washington, Stevens might well have chosen to resign from public office and cast his lot with the white settlers of the territory as a business, political, and social leader. Instead he took just the opposite course. He devoted most of 1857 to campaigning for the elective two-year post as Washington Territory's lone delegate to Congress, which would allow him to return to the nation's capital and try to restore his reputation.

The campaign proved stressful, even though Stevens's opponent, while able, was little known and ungifted as a stump orator. A cadre of anti-Stevens lawyers, including Leschi's defenders William Wallace and Frank Clark, spoke out in speeches against the governor's bullying and blustering ways, and George Gibbs's detailed charges of Stevens's bouts of public drunkenness were grist for the local press. Stevens's steadfast advocate, the *Pioneer and Democrat,* railed against his detractors as "beneath the contempt of patriotic men." The governor retained the admiration of the white yeomanry of the territory, many of whose members had joined his militia to quell the native insurgency and formed his core of political support. In the September balloting, Stevens won his first race for office with 65 percent of the vote. He and his family soon boarded a steamer for San Francisco, and by December he was in Washington, D.C., in time for the opening of Congress. The governor's chair in Olympia was handed to Fayette McMullin, an ex-congressman from Virginia, who strongly favored the continuation of slavery in places it had been lawfully practiced. There was little reason to suppose that the new governor would be inclined to deal generously with nonwhites.

Still, Leschi's partisans were not without hope. McMullin, at least, did not harbor Stevens's rabid animus toward the Nisqually chief and might be open to a plea to pardon him if the territorial Supreme Court turned down his appeal. Over the summer Wallace obtained a helpful letter from Colonel George Wright, still commanding U.S. forces east of the Cascades, who confirmed that Leschi had been granted virtual amnesty—or at least a firm pledge of protection that should have prevented his seizure by white civil authorities to try him as a common criminal. Hoping to arm the defense lawyers with ammunition for an eventual appeal for clemency, Wright wrote,

> It is hard to make an Indian understand the difference between civil and military power, as administered in our country; when restored to friendship by the military, they look upon that as sufficient.
>
> Under all the circumstances of the case, I sincerely hope that Leschi will not be made to suffer death, even if convicted by the stern mandates of our code. I most earnestly pray that the pardoning power may be interposed, and Leschi saved from the gallows.

There was, too, at least a possibility that Leschi's own people might contrive, under the averted gaze of sympathetic officers at Fort Steilacoom, to rescue him from confinement. But such an insult to the whites' governmental apparatus would likely have been met with a resumption of violence against the Indians and a sustained manhunt for Leschi; he would become an eternal wanderer, estranged forever from his homeland. Suicide, rumors around Steilacoom had it, was the despondent chief's more likely form of escape from his living entombment.

Leschi must have taken bittersweet solace from a piece of news reaching him in October: he had outlived Sluggia. For betraying his uncle, Sluggia had become an outcast among the Nisquallies and the special target of vengeance for Leschi's loyal follower Wahelut (Yelm Jim). Not much older than Sluggia, Wahelut was a warrior of fortitude, a bit on the sullen side, a bachelor without family ties—and thus free to pursue the assassin's role. He tracked down Sluggia, shot him to death, and rolled his body off the edge of a bluff in the Nisqually basin. Almost everyone in Indian Country knew of and approved the killing. White officials, too, likely knew who the revenge killer was but chose not to pursue him on the ground that it was intratribal business.*

WHEN WASHINGTON TERRITORY'S Supreme Court heard Leschi's appeal on December 16, 1857, Chief Justice Edward Lander was not present. He had been called away from the territory on a pressing but unidentified matter—or so he said. His absence could only be deemed fortunate for Leschi's cause, leaving the decision up to Justices Chenoweth and McFadden. Any hope, though, that Justice McFadden, who had served ably in the state legislature and on the Court of Common Pleas in his native Pennsylvania before moving west, would prove receptive to Leschi's appeal was thoroughly demolished by almost the first words of the opinion of the court that he delivered the day after the oral argument had been conducted.

The ruling, which ran some 7,000 words and was carefully footnoted, could not have been crafted overnight. The opinion rejected all the pleas in the appellant's brief, and whatever the contending lawyers said in person before the two-judge court evidently carried no weight with Justice McFadden. The prejudicial language in the opening paragraph of the court's opinion—Chenoweth signed on to McFadden's decision—signaled what was coming:

> The case comes before us, on a writ of error to the Second Judicial District. The prisoner has occupied a position of influence, as one of a band of Indians, who, in connection with other tribes, sacrificed the lives of so many of our citizens, in the war so cruelly waged against our people, on the waters of Puget Sound.

---

*Wahelut was captured several years later and charged with the March 2, 1856, killing of a prominent white settler, William White, who had been walking down a road alongside a cart carrying his wife and a woman friend when they were set upon by an Indian band emerging from the woods. Wahelut was tried but acquitted for lack of firm evidence. He survived another fifty years and provided a valuable interview for Ezra Meeker's book about Leschi and the Medicine Creek Treaty, which bears a mark beside Wahelut's name. An Indian school named in his honor has been in operation at Frank's Landing, a few miles north of the Nisqually Reservation, since the mid-1970s.

The words were injudiciously, unmistakably accusatory. They implied that the Indians had exacted a ghastly toll without justification while displaying savagery unmatched by their white foes. Accentuating this series of distortions, the text continued:

> It speaks volumes for our people that, notwithstanding the spirit of indignation and revenge, so natural to the human heart, incited by the ruthless massacre of their families, that [*sic*] at the trial of the accused, deliberate impartiality has been manifested at every stage of the proceedings.

One may wonder whether it was "deliberate impartiality" that permitted Judge Lander, a commanding officer in the territorial militia that fought against Leschi, to preside over his retrial. Was it impartiality that prompted the judge to omit any mention to the jurors of the possible grounds on which they could have acquitted Leschi or found him guilty of a lesser charge—and thus spared his life? Was it impartiality that led the jury to conclude there was no reasonable doubt that the defendant had shot or assisted in the shooting of Colonel Moses when the only testimony placing Leschi at the scene was given by a devoted henchman of Governor Stevens—who had repeatedly vowed to have the Nisqually chief executed—and contradicted by a number of other witnesses and his own prior statements?

McFadden's opinion was on relatively solid ground in dismissing the belated submission of the Kautz map purportedly showing that Leschi and others who may have met the militia party on the prairie could not have reached the ambush site in time to attack the soldiers. The map was not conclusive evidence, nor did it clear Leschi of Rabbeson's charge that he had been on the prairie when the soldiers arrived and might have reappeared at the shooting site.

Much of McFadden's opinion was devoted to a laborious refutation of the appellant's claim that the site of his trial had been unconstitutionally shifted from Steilacoom to Olympia. Since Pierce County had been lawfully reassigned by the territorial legislature to the same judicial district as Thurston County, the plea was feckless and further burdened by the undemonstrable implication that Leschi could not obtain a fair trial in Olympia, the territorial capital. After carefully refuting the pleading over the change of venue, McFadden airily brushed aside the two substantive issues in Leschi's appeal—that the jury had ignored the preponderance of the evidence in reaching its verdict and that the trial judge had not charged the jury properly.

In his review of the evidence at the retrial, McFadden failed to note that none of the witnesses had identified Leschi as Moses's killer, the principal charge on which he was indicted. Nor did anyone testify that Leschi had masterminded the ambush or directed any of his warriors to harm the militia party. The entire case against Leschi came down to Rabbeson's testimony that Leschi had been at the prairie and shortly thereafter at the swamp, where he supposedly shot at Rabbeson from close range, missed, and then apparently ran off into the brush with two Indian companions instead of finishing off the lone militiaman. It was a story hard to credit on its face and one that none of Rabbeson's comrades supported, yet McFadden's opinion astonishingly asserted, "The testimony of Rabbeson . . . is clear and positive against the prisoner; he speaks with certainty of the fact of Leschi's presence . . . [and] he is fully sustained by the witness principally relied upon by the prisoner [Bradley], except that he did not see or recognize Leschi at the place where the shooting took place."

But Bradley had gone further. He testified emphatically that he had not seen Leschi at the ambush site, elsewhere in the swamp area, up on the prairie, or anywhere else that day. How, then, was Rabbeson "fully sustained" by Bradley's testimony, as McFadden's opinion stated? No one at the trial had fully sustained anything Rabbeson testified to. McFadden then fell back on the straw-man argument that jurors were always to be regarded as judges of the facts testified to at a trial "unless the evidence greatly preponderates against the verdict"—and he found no such preponderance. Not even enough evidence to raise a doubt in the jurors' minds, from which the defendant, of course, would have benefitted. The law's hallowed presumption of innocence in the absence of compelling evidence had been ruthlessly discarded.

McFadden's opinion was no more convincing in its dismissal of the claim that Judge Lander's instruction to the jury had been inadequate. The opinion never really engaged the appellant's argument that Lander should have apprised the jury that it could convict Leschi of second-degree murder despite the original indictment charging him with first-degree murder. And finally, McFadden balked at conceding Lander should have—as Chenoweth had done—cited the so-called rule of war that might have mitigated against convicting a legitimate combatant like Leschi as a murderer. Instead he wrote: "All the jury had to decide upon was the evidence given upon the trial. . . . We see nothing improper here. . . . We are, therefore, of the opinion that the judgment in this case should be affirmed."

Having exhausted their final remedy in the courts of law, Leschi's counselors apparently then urged their client to throw himself on the mercy of the justices before they reaffirmed the district court's sentence—or so Meeker's account suggests. For the first time, we read words directly attributed to Leschi. But there is reason to question both the date and the authenticity of the quoted remarks, which Meeker said were related to the Oregon Historical Society in January 1904 by Frank Shaw, Stevens's close aide, who apparently was on hand and transcribed them. Shaw said Leschi's words were uttered "concerning the sentence of death passed by the Court of Washington Territory in Olympia in 1857," but which court was he referring to—Lander's Second Judicial District Court or the territorial Supreme Court? Leschi's statement may have been given in March 1857, prior to his sentencing by Judge Lander at the retrial. Yet they are dated in Meeker's generally reliable chronology as December 18, right after Justice McFadden denied Leschi's appeal.

Leschi's reported remarks conveyed a sense of contrition but no real regret for what he had done, which he did not believe should cause him to be put to death. Mostly, there was resignation in his tone and a yearning to be understood by his tormentors. "I do not see that there is any use of saying anything," he began. "My attorney has said all that he could for me." Then he invoked the rule of war in his own behalf:

> I do not know anything about your laws. I have supposed that the killing of armed men in war time was not murder. If it was, then soldiers who killed Indians were guilty of murder, too.
>
> The Indians did not keep in order like the soldiers, and, therefore, could not fight in bodies like them, but had to resort to ambush and seek the cover of trees, logs and everything that could hide them from the bullets. This was their mode of fighting, and they knew no other way.
>
> Dr. Tolmie and [Frank Shaw] . . . warned me against allowing my anger to get the best of my good sense, as I could not gain anything by going to war against the United States, but would be beaten and humbled, and would have to hide like a wild beast in the end. I did not take this good advice, but nursed my anger until it became a furious passion.

At the end he gave voice to his profound grievance and proud
defiance:

> I went to war because I believed that the Indians had been
> wronged by the white men, and did everything in my power to beat
> the Boston soldier, but for lack of numbers, supplies and ammuni-
> tion I have failed. I deny that I had any part in killing Miles or
> Moses. I heard that a company of soldiers were coming out from
> Steilacoom, and determined to lay in ambush for it; but did not
> expect to catch anyone coming from the other way. I did not see
> Miles or Moses before or after they were dead, but was told by the
> Indians that they had been killed. As God sees me, this is the truth.

Leschi then made the sign of the cross, according to Shaw, and concluded in his own Salish dialect, "There is the Father, this is the Son, this
is the Holy Ghost—these are all one and the same. Amen."

Was Leschi capable of expressing himself in language of such sophis-
tication? Did his native tongue allow it? Certainly the vocabulary of the
Chinook jargon did not. Meeker's book says that Shaw, in his accompanying note to the historical society, indicated that he had rendered
Leschi's remarks "in substance." Several regional historians have supposed that Shaw was guilty of at least some, presumably respectful,
embellishment. For why, one may ask, would Leschi, facing the likelihood of hanging, have forsaken the spiritual heritage of his people and
genuflected to his white oppressors' faith?

The Indian spirits had not served him very well, Leschi might have
calculated; perhaps the whites had triumphed over his own race because
their gods were superior to his. But there was one other credible explanation for his apparent defection to the Christian deity.

About a month before the Supreme Court heard Leschi's appeal,
Father Louis Rossi, age forty, had arrived at Steilacoom to take charge of
the diocese there, centered around the little chapel on the grounds of the
army post, most of whose garrison was of Irish Catholic ancestry. In
Leschi, worn down by a year of close confinement, the priest seemed to
have found a pagan of quiet dignity whose soul was at imminent risk of
eternal damnation. Father Rossi may well have taught him the error of his
savage ways during a month of ministering, leading Leschi to invoke the
True Church's tripartite godhead at the close of his statement to the court
that held his life in its hands. Was this his ultimate submission to the

white man's power? Or was he just feigning having taken the cross in order to appear worthy of Christian mercy?

Either way, the court was unmoved. Leschi's execution was scheduled for January 22, 1858, between 10:00 a.m. and 2:00 p.m., at Steilacoom. From first to last, the adjudication of the Nisqually leader's case had exhibited all the forms of due process of law but none of the substance of justice.

I 2

All the Favors of the Law

Leschi HAD just one last hope to escape the hangman—a grant of executive clemency, either by the President of the United States or by the new governor of Washington Territory.

With little more than a month remaining before his scheduled execution, Leschi's friends knew it would be all but impossible geographically to send a coherent appeal to the White House by the speediest sea transport and allow James Buchanan time to consider it and reply before the fixed day of doom. The eastern portion of the nation was already crisscrossed with 25,000 miles of telegraph wire, but another ten years would pass before Western Union was established as a continental enterprise. Even then a detailed explanation by telegraph of Leschi's case and why he should be spared would have been prohibitively expensive. That left Governor Fayette McMullin, a lately transplanted Virginian, as Leschi's sole would-be savior, and at first he seemed surprisingly open to persuasion.

To the likely annoyance of the Stevens clique, who ruled Olympia even with their leader relocated in the East, McMullin traveled to Steilacoom to meet with Leschi, his lawyers, and supporters and, without the prosecutorial staff and other territorial officers present, to hear the Nisqually's story with fresh ears. William Tolmie provided the new governor with an extensive written statement about Leschi's character and dealings with white settlers before the Medicine Creek Treaty had been foisted on his tribe. In his letter Tolmie recounted Leschi's alarm that Stevens was bent on exiling all the Indians in his territory to some distant land of everlasting darkness, then added his own belief that "neither Leschi nor Quiemuth would have taken up arms unless virtually driven from their homes." On Christmas Day 1857, exactly three years after the Medicine Creek Treaty had been unveiled, more than 1,000 natives who had gathered on Squaxin Island to receive their annuities from the federal government placed their marks on a petition to the governor to spare Leschi. It was impressive testimony that hanging the Nisqually hero might only make a martyr of him and in no way help pacify the natives—quite the opposite, perhaps.

Even the faint suspicion that McMullin might be receptive to pleas to save Leschi's life galvanized most of the white community outside of Pierce County. Leschi's larger-than-life legend was wildly at odds with the reality of his and his tribe's frail condition. A spent force wracked by dejection, the caged Nisqually was nevertheless widely portrayed as a figure of charismatic appeal and power, still capable of rousing the natives to armed resistance against white migration. Among whites his very name inspired dread of torched houses and haystacks, stolen horses and butchered cattle, and lurid scenes of violent death.

A citizens' committee was hastily organized and gathered 700 signatures on a petition submitted to McMullin and the territorial legislature, urging the governor to deny the clemency appeal on the ground that Leschi had "counseled and advised, if he did not directly participate in, the several cowardly and cruel murders which were perpetrated on our unguarded and defenseless citizens"—a charge never brought against him in court. The petitioners declared that "an impartial upright intelligent jury" had found Leschi guilty of first-degree murder and therefore "no good" would come from his release; indeed, "justice demands his execution, however much his present condition may call for our sympathy." For good measure, the ill-tempered citizenry took a xenophobic swipe at William Tolmie for his "artful cunning and special pleading [to spare Leschi], worthy of the representatives of an unlawful, illegitimate foreign corporation. . . . He goes entirely beyond the bounds of truth in his statements . . . characterized by a stubborn and selfish disregard for the laws of the Territory."

Faced with such irascible opposition, McMullin would not risk his political standing so soon after assuming office, and so he denied Leschi clemency.

Hope fading now, his supporters paid a desperate visit to the Nisqually reservation. Lieutenant Kautz, from tribal connections through his Indian wife, Leschi's niece, had learned the identity of the man said to have been the actual shooter at the Moses ambush, a brave named Puo-

yontis. Joined by Tolmie and Leschi's attorney, Frank Clark, Kautz be-
seeched Puoyontis to come forward and admit his role in the ambush.
The retired Nisqually warrior admitted to his white visitors that he had
been at the site and fired at the party of militiamen, but he could not—or
would not—say for certain it was his bullet that had brought down
Moses. "He maintained that he was at war with the whites when he did
this," Kautz wrote in his diary, "and thought he was doing right. But he
would not surrender himself."

Even if he had, Puoyontis's selfless act would probably not have won
Leschi's release; he had been convicted as an accessory to the killing
since no one had claimed seeing him shoot Moses.

Now the scaffolding for the gallows was rising in a bowl-shaped hollow about a mile from Steilacoom and off the grounds of the army fort.
Commandant Casey, in response to a request from Pierce County's sheriff, George Williams, to provide twenty men to escort the prisoner from
the guardhouse to the execution site and oversee the proceedings, made
clear that he wanted nothing to do with Leschi's hanging, which he and
his whole garrison viewed as outright murder. He allowed as how he
would likely hand over the prisoner so that the sentence could be carried
out, but only if the transfer was requested of him by someone with
authority in the form of a legal warrant issued by the territorial Supreme
Court. Because Sheriff Williams and his deputy, Charles McDaniel, who
had been designated as hangman, were no more eager than Casey to see
the execution carried out, young Frank Clark was able to hatch a last-
minute effort to prevent Leschi from being delivered to the gallows
within the court-appointed hours.

On the eve or morning of execution day Clark had enlisted an Indian
to swear in an affidavit in front of U.S. Commissoner James Bachelder,
who also served as sutler (provisioner) to Fort Steilacoom, that Sheriff
Williams and his deputy had been selling liquor to local Indians—a serious enough offense to require the immediate arrest and detention of the
accused, pending a court hearing. Two army officers, one of them Gus
Kautz's brother, took the unresisting law officers into custody, thereby
preventing them from ushering Leschi to the gallows between 10:00 a.m.
and 2:00 p.m., as the courts had directed. Since Bachelder was in daily
contact with Casey and Kautz, the whole army post had to be aware of
Clark's maneuverings to forestall the execution.

Word of the conspiracy quickly reached members of the anti-Leschi
citizens' committee, many of whom had been planning to watch the

Indian be hanged, and a representative was sent at once to the Steilacoom jail to demand the death warrant the sheriff was holding on his person. Williams refused to turn it over, and when the irate committee member attempted to remove it forcibly, he was restrained. Two o'clock came and went, Leschi was still alive at the fort, and there was no authorization in place to carry out the hanging.

It was a transparent flouting of the law, no less blatant than Stevens's earlier shutdown of the judicial system in decreeing martial law. What were the conspirators thinking they could gain by their delaying game? Possibly a miraculous intervention from Washington, D.C., in the form of a presidential pardon? The reaction in Olympia was swift and predictably furious. Several hundred citizens gathered that same evening at the public school to protest "the high handed outrage perpetrated by the civilian authorities of Pierce County, the connivance of the military officers at Fort Steilacoom, and particularly the conduct of one James Bachelder." The citizens framed a resolution that took special aim at Casey and his officers for having disgraced their branch of service and their "most unusual and unreasonable sympathy for the Indian, who was shown to have engaged in the most fiendish massacre of helpless women and children on White River in the fall of 1855"—the same unsubstantiated accusation that was hurled against Leschi by those who had petitioned Governor McMullin to deny him clemency.

Casey was all innocence, claiming to be a stickler for proper procedure and that no one had presented him with a warrant to turn over the prisoner for escorting to the gallows. Even in the nearby town of Steilacoom, though, the normally Indian-tolerant residents were incensed by the abuse of the law to keep Leschi alive. A protest meeting hardly less aroused than the one at Olympia was held a few nights later at Steilacoom, and among its organizers was Ezra Meeker, whose refusal to vote for conviction had spared Leschi at his first trial. Meeker's name appeared first among the signers of the Steilacoom citizens' resolution denouncing Sheriff Williams as "a base hireling unworthy of the position he now occupies" and repeated the now hysterical outcry against Leschi for "murdering, in cold blood, our inoffensive and defenseless neighbors and their children." The document hysterically claimed that he would have, "had it been in his power, swept every civilized being from this fair land." At this point, the truth was irrelevant to the red-eyed citizenry. The rhetoric of hate had intensified to satisfy the level of frustrated vengeance.

Even so, Clark, Kautz, and Tolmie still hoped to persuade the white community that Leschi did not deserve to die. They wrote, paid for, and issued a four-page broadside they called *Truth Teller* that tried to justify their subterfuge in momentarily staying the execution. Leschi, Clark wrote in a signed article, had been "arrested by treachery for an offense of which he is not guilty . . . [and] convicted by the civil courts who have no jurisdiction in the case, for the offense was committed by other Indians in time of war." Trying to justify the ruse of detaining Sheriff Williams and his deputy, Clark insisted that the hanging of Leschi would have "plunged us almost immediately into an Indian war . . . one that would have arrayed the entire Indian force of the country against us." Perhaps, but the corollary was already evident: the deceptive delay of the execution had arrayed virtually the entire white population of the territory against Leschi. At the end of his apologia, Clark begged his fellow citizens to allow the President time to decide if Leschi should live or die—probably the only rational basis for the conspiratorial contrivance.

The intervention purchased time for Leschi. The territorial legislature, which was in session at the time, ordered the Washington Supreme Court to convene and again address the Leschi matter. The justices remanded the case to the Second District Court, where Judge Chenoweth, substituting for the still absent Judge Lander, rescheduled the execution for two weeks hence, February 19, 1858, still at Steilacoom, but directed the sheriff of Thurston County, not the now discredited Sheriff Williams of Pierce County, to carry out the hanging.

The extent to which the temperament of the territorial judiciary had been frayed by the delaying tactics of Leschi's camp may be inferred from the vehement language used by Judge Chenoweth, likely the least biased of the three Washington jurists who at one time or another heard Leschi's case, as the Nisqually chief appeared before the bench for the final time. Chenoweth flayed the hapless convict as if it were his fault he was still among the living: "You have had the benefit of all the favors of law that the most favored of our own race have in trials for murder. You have had much time to prepare for death unlike those of our own race with whose *murders* you have been charged" (emphasis added). Leschi had in fact been charged not with plural "murders" but with the criminal killing of *one man,* a soldier, who had orders to destroy any hostile natives his party encountered.

·   ·   ·

IN HIS FINAL days Leschi struck his closest friend at Fort Steilacoom, Gus Kautz, as all too human. Or perhaps the lieutenant, too, had been worn down by the death vigil and overreacted upon detecting the least drop of impurity in the shattered Leschi's character. In his harsh February 10 diary entry, Kautz wrote that he and Clark had gone to the guardhouse

> to receive a voluntary statement from Leschi, the sum and substance of which was to exculpate himself and implicate others. He misstated and prevaricated much. Knowing as much as I do about the war I have little difficulty in detecting the truth. He is coming down in my estimation very much. He is bringing his Indian nature to bear and while some petty jealousy leads him to expose some, he lets others more notorious go by.

The duration of his confinement and the emotional gyrations caused by all the legal proceedings must have taken their toll on Leschi. How could their outcome have failed to stir an understandable bitterness in him at death's door? Yet despite any erosion of his noble character as perceived by Kautz—who unwittingly disclosed his own latent racism by the diary reference to Leschi's "Indian nature"—the courageous army officer clung to the Nisqually's cause, noting, "Tolmie is going to assist us in getting out the next paper," a second issue of the *Truth Teller,* a last-ditch piece of pro-Leschi publicity. Kautz's diary entry the next day noted growing tension over the imminent hanging: "A great many Indians were here pleading for Leschi. Mr. Gosnell, the Indian agent, says that the Indians are very much excited and that he has apprehensions that trouble will follow the execution."

Evidence that Leschi maintained his composure for the most part as the last hours of his life slipped away was provided afterward by the man who probably attended him more closely than anyone else at the end, his jailer and executioner, Charles Grainger. A retired sailor, Grainger had been tapped by Thurston County officials to serve as Leschi's hangman because he knew a thing or two about ropes and knots. While acting as Leschi's part-time guard, Grainger would untie the prisoner's hands so he could feed himself, and on these occasions the two would converse, since Leschi's rudimentary English had apparently improved during daily contact with whites at the fort. Grainger remembered Leschi as saying that "people had lied about him and given false evidence," that Tony Rabbeson "had lied when he said he saw him in the swamp, and that he would meet him before his God and he would tell him there that he lied. He said he was miles away when Moses was killed. . . . If he was dying for his people, he was willing to die, that Christ had died for others."

It had snowed and rained throughout the prior week, but by late morning on February 19, 1858, the weather had turned fair and mild for winter. Silas Casey bid a regretful farewell to his stoic prisoner and handed him over to a party of twelve mounted deputy sheriffs from Thurston County for the short, doleful ride to the prairie hollow a little out of town. No women and few natives were among the 300 or so onlookers gathered before the scaffolding, according to the report in the *Pioneer and Democrat,* but Grainger later recalled a palpable tribal presence in the form of distant drums to accompany Leschi's passage to the spirit world.

The prisoner was assisted from his horse and led directly toward the platform, where he paused for a moment to contemplate the dangling rope. Then, the newspaper reported, he collected himself and ascended the jerry-built stairs "with a firm step, as if he desired to show the white men how fearlessly an Indian can meet his death." At the top he saw Grainger, who remembered that Leschi "was as cool as could be—just like he was going to dinner . . . and that is more than I can say for myself. In fact, Leschi seemed to be the coolest of all on the scaffold. . . . He thanked me for my kindness to him."

At first Leschi declined to make a final statement, but after his hands were tied behind him, he bowed his head "for some ten or fifteen minutes in fervent prayer"—a final indulgence that, if accurately reported, must have tried the patience of the breathless crowd. Then, in his native tongue and without making the sign of the cross, he said he was ready for the end and "bore malice toward none save one man . . . upon whom he evoked [*sic*] the vengeance of heaven." Whether he meant Rabbeson or the hateful governor who had unsheathed Rabbeson as his lethal weapon, we have been left no way of telling.

At 11:35 a.m., a black silk kerchief was tied over the prisoner's face. Hardly a moment later the scaffold drop gave way, "and Leschi, the brave in battle, was launched into eternity without having moved a muscle to indicate fear of death," the *Pioneer and Democrat* reported. "He made no disclosures whatever and proved 'as true as the needle to the pole' to his confederates." There was no outcry from the viewers, no display of anger or grief. Grainger's final reflection when Meeker interviewed him long afterward for his book was, "I felt I was hanging an innocent man—and believe it yet."

The white Indian agent at the Nisqually reservation drove up in a two-horse rig with a few of the dead man's tribesmen. They cut him down reverently and bore away his body for three days of above-ground repose in the heart of his reclaimed homeland. Then it was put in a coffin and buried near the reservation, away from prying white eyes and potential grave defilers.

ON THE FINAL day of May 1858, a few months after the last chief of the Nisquallies—the title would be buried with him—had been laid to his eternal rest, Isaac Stevens arose before the United States House of Representatives to defend his behavior toward the native people of Washington Territory and the war he had waged against them. He was obliged to speak out, Stevens asserted, because "it has often been charged against us that that war was brought on by outrages upon the rights of the Indians; that it was gotten up for the purpose of speculation; and that it was the treaties that caused the war."

The war had been fought, explained the new territorial delegate, to defend the white settlements; he would not concede that the settlers and the treaties designed to multiply their numbers were in themselves acts of aggression that drove the displaced natives to arms. "What account would an executive have had to render," Stevens asked, "who, when he heard the Indians were devastating the settlements, burning the houses, and massacring the women and children, had declined to protect those settlements on the ground that here and there a white man had outraged the Indians . . . ?" His gift for hyperbolic fabrication had not abated. Stevens's war was transformed from the inevitable result of his swindling treaties into a heroic response to a nonexistent tidal wave of apocalyptic slaughter engulfing the white pioneers.

Even if the treaties had incited the war, he continued, "was it the fault of the people of these territories?" No one, of course, had accused the settlers themselves of driving the Indians over the brink of forbearance and into battle. The natives had been willing to step back and share their homelands with the settlers before the governor began to press grossly inequitable treaty terms on the tribes and confined them to bleak, pint-sized reservations. "It was the act of your Government," said Stevens. "It was the act of your Congress. It was done under the orders of our President." He had only been honoring his orders, which were to protect at all costs the heroic settlers who "were carrying with them the arts and arms, the laws and institutions of their country, and there they planted empire and civilization." The arriving whites had been met by an indigenous people thoroughly hostile to them, Stevens said, claiming that only the imposition of his treaties had staved off far worse bloodshed. The conflict with the natives of his territory had been "a war entirely unprovoked . . . caused by no bad conduct of our people, but caused altogether by the feeling of antagonism between the races." It was simply human nature for the two races, revealing their basic characters, to hate and quarrel with each another—and for the more culturally advanced race to subdue the more backward one.

To bolster his argument to Congress, Stevens cited a report filed the year before by J. Ross Brown, a new Indian agent sent by the Interior Department to examine tribal conditions in Washington Territory and the extent of hostility between the races. Brown, like Stevens, failed to concede that the whites' seizure and occupation of Indian Country had stirred a profound grievance in the hearts of the native people. "I am satisfied that no public officer could have done better," Brown said of Stevens's efforts.

Well, if Stevens had not been the prime promoter of mutual rancor and strife on the tense frontier, who had? Brown had a ready answer:

Leschi, the celebrated Nisqually chief, was most determined in his hostility. Bold, adventurous, and eloquent, he possessed an unlimited sway over his people, and by the earnestness of his purpose and the persuasiveness of his arguments, carried all with him who heard him speak. He traveled by day and night, caring neither for hunger nor fatigue, visited the camps of the Yakimas and the Klickitats; addressed the councils in terms of eloquence such as they had never heard. He crossed the Columbia, penetrated to southern Oregon, appealed to all the disaffected there . . . to resist like braves so terrible a fate [as mass deportation to a land of eternal darkness]. The white men were but a handful now. They could all be killed at once, and then others would fear to come. But if there was no war, they would grow strong and many, and soon put all the Indians in their big ships to that terrible land . . . where torture and death awaited them.

No wonder Stevens had been singlemindedly devoted to hunting down and punishing so vile an evildoer. And no doubt J. Ross Brown had happened upon all this illuminating intelligence not by reliance on Stevens and his cronies but by a diligent and objective search for the truth among both the Indians and the whites before settling upon the Nisqually leader as the blameworthy malefactor-in-chief.

In fairness to Stevens and his rationalizations, he had indeed been hewing to a time-tested custom among his countrymen, dating back to their less-than-benign Puritan ancestors. Even a white officer as humanely inclined as Leschi's protector, Colonel George Wright, would eventually lose patience with the natives of eastern Washington who had the ill grace to keep fighting when resistance had become pointless. After both Stevens and Leschi had left the stage, Wright was still patrolling out of Fort Walla Walla, aiming new, highly accurate long rifles at any hostile movement by the natives in a determined drive to cleanse the region of violence for good. In the decisive battle, Wright's troops killed sixty Indians while suffering only a single, nonfatal casualty. As further draconian punishment, of the sort Stevens had long urged, Wright ordered 1,000 Indian horses butchered, ending the mobility of the plains tribes; destroyed the Yakimas' winter food supply; and directed their young chief, Qualchan, Leschi's cousin, to give himself up or all the Indian prisoners that the American soldiers had rounded up would be executed. Qualchan, probably hoping Wright would treat him with the same charity as he had accorded his now martyred cousin, rode into the army camp at nine o'clock that evening to satisfy the colonel's demand. He was hanged the next morning. Seventeen other warriors were given a military trial; all seventeen joined Qualchan at the end of a rope.

ISAAC STEVENS did such a good job representing his far-off constituents, extracting funds from Congress for internal improvements in Washington Territory and otherwise advancing the development of the region, that he was reelected in 1859 with 61 percent of the vote. When the Civil War began, retired Major Stevens heard a renewed bugle call to glory and sought to return to the army with a higher-ranking commission. Sponsored by the governors of Massachusetts, his home state, and Rhode Island, where his wife's family was highly regarded, he won a colonelcy in charge of a volunteer regiment and was eventually dispatched to take possession of the Sea Islands off South Carolina, where he overcame a case of yellow fever. His success won him promotion to brigadier general, in charge of the celebrated Seventy-ninth New York Highlanders in the Army of the Potomac. With Hazard, pulled out of Harvard to serve alongside his father as adjutant, Stevens's unit fought valiantly in the Virginia campaign, though his superiors were regularly outmaneuvered by the Confederate generals.

Ordered to cover a Union retreat toward Washington, D.C., Stevens's troops engaged forces under the command of Stonewall Jackson in the woods and cornfields around Chantilly on the main road to the capital, fifteen miles to the east. The Confederates rose up from cover and opened fire, driving Stevens's men back. He commanded them to hold fast, pivot about, and charge—a surprise reversal that forced the enemy to retreat. They regrouped in short order, though, and were soon putting down a murderous line of fire at the oncoming men in blue. Hazard was hit in the arm and hip and under his father's orders was helped from the field. Then, with the zeal that was his finest virtue but apt to turn him reckless, Stevens snatched up the regimental flag that had fallen with its color-bearer, dashed into the field of fire, and cried—or so it was reported—"Highlanders, my Highlanders, follow your general!"

They did, driving the rebels deeper into the woods. But a thunderstorm burst upon the hellish scene just then, all but obliterating the sound of gunfire and the extremity of the peril. A bullet hurtling through the midst of the chaos struck him in the temple, and Isaac Stevens was dead. The date was September 1, 1862; he was forty-four years old.

His biographer Kent Richards wrote of Stevens: "He died as he had lived, scorning opposition and tempting fate." He was posthumously promoted to major general. His widow, Meg, never remarried, returned to Washington Territory to see it become a state in 1889, and died in 1914 at the age of ninety-seven.

Stevens would have been proud beyond the telling of how Hazard conducted himself in the war after his father's death. Recovered from his wounds at Chantilly, he took part in many other major battles and was wounded again in the wilderness. But his heroism in the 1863 assault on Fort Huger in Virginia, leading to the capture of 9 officers, 130 noncommissioned men, 5 cannons, and 5 gunboats, earned him the Congressional Medal of Honor. His action at Petersburg in the final year of the war resulted in his elevation to brevetted brigadier general, making him at twenty-three the youngest general in the Union army. After the war he gravitated back toward Puget Sound, where his father's memory was honored by many in the white community. Among Hazard's other activities, he worked as an attorney for the Northern Pacific Railroad, operating over the route that his father and his party had surveyed in 1853, and as collector of internal revenue at Olympia, but he never became a pillar of the community.

In 1915, the year after his mother died, he was called to court, no doubt because his father had been the creator of the Medicine Creek Treaty (and perhaps because he himself as a twelve-year-old had been present at the signing), to testify on behalf of two Nisquallies charged with killing a deer out of season. "I don't think the whites," said Hazard Stevens, "now that the Indians are rapidly dwindling and unable to put up a fight, should back up on an agreement they made more than sixty years ago. It is a matter of right and wrong. The treaty is specific, giving the Indians the right to hunt and fish wherever they wish." He visited the Medicine Creek council site just before he died three years later but failed in his effort to have it named a national historic place.

Tony Rabbeson outlived Leschi by thirty-three years and one day. He had worked, among his other ventures, as a manufacturer and vendor of building supplies, operator of a coach service, and, when he died at sixty-six in 1891, as co-proprietor of the leading funeral home in Olympia. His obituary in the *Washington Standard* said of him: "Mr. Rabbeson earned considerable distinction in the Indian war of 1855–56, serving as Captain of a company of volunteers. He was a man of more than ordinary mental attainments, and was a genial neighbor, a kind husband, an indulgent father and a respected citizen."

A more forthright obituary appeared fourteen years later with the publication of Ezra Meeker's book, detailing Rabbeson's essential role in the conviction and hanging of Leschi. In so doing, Meeker wrote Leschi's obituary as well, calling him "a victim of judicial murder, if ever there was one . . . condemned through prejudice and perjury, hounded to his death" by an unsavory and cynical junta. Its ringleader, Isaac Ingalls Stevens, chosen by the President and Congress to rid Washington Territory of the natives' hold on the land, succeeded in no small measure by convincing the white community that the peace-loving chief of the Nisquallies was a bloodthirsty monster. The preponderance of the historical evidence is to the contrary, as the leading perpetrators of the charge very likely knew.

EPILOGUE

After Leschi

I. *Salmon and Survival*

S IX YEARS AFTER THE CIVIL WAR ended, Congress called off
the sham formality of treatymaking with tribal America. By then
most of the natives' soil had been commandeered for white settlement and economic use as the pacification process wound down to eradi-
cating what few pockets of Indian defiance remained in the Dakotas.

Meanwhile, the treaty-certified guardianship of the dispossessed
natives was, by and large, simply scandalous. Congress, saddled with
huge Civil War debts, was unwilling to spend enough to meet the government's commitments to the Indians. Promises of medical care, vocational
training, schools, farming equipment, and other supplies went unfulfilled. Salaries for U.S. Indian agents went unpaid or were insufficient to
attract qualified, conscientious men; too many who served in that capacity were corrupt, sadistic, or dysfunctional—sometimes all three.

In Washington Territory, as in many other western areas, the tribes
were placed on largely infertile land and expected to operate self-
sustaining farm cooperatives, even though they were rarely provided with
the required seed, fertilizer, plows, other tools and equipment, or with
instruction in crop-raising. Those who managed to put some reservation
acreage under cultivation had to live with the knowledge that their land
could at any moment be snatched from them by white settlers or that their
entire reservation could be moved elsewhere upon presidential order, as
the Medicine Creek Treaty and others like it allowed. Under such conditions, few tribesmen were motivated to farm. Nor could they obtain credit
to establish other kinds of businesses, such as sawmills to help harvest
trees on tribal land or to service thriving white loggers.

The Nisquallies had become dismayed war refugees, most of their villages taken from them and their sacred tribal burial grounds abandoned under the Medicine Creek Treaty. No leaders had emerged to succeed Leschi and Quiemuth. Many in the tribe were chronically sick, hungry, and destitute. Even in its more generous configuration as finally granted by Isaac Stevens, their reservation was composed of only a thin strip of rich bottomland near the river, patches of wooded terrain, and a prairie on the eastern side of the river covering several thousand acres of thin, sandy soil useful only for pasturing. Some chose not to remain within the narrowly confined reservation, seen as an internment camp without a fence, and drifted away. The men tried to survive by fishing and hunting, hiring out as loggers or herdsmen, or performing menial work for whites. Those left on the reservation, according to a report by its U.S. Indian agent, J. Ross Brown, filed just before Leschi's death, were "a very lazy, worthless set. . . . They say the government deprived them of their natural heritage, now let it support them."

A successor U.S. agent for the Bureau of Indian Affairs, R. H. Milroy, noted in his annual report for 1876 that only 10 percent of the reservation's 4,717 acres was good for crops and just 277 acres were under cultivation. On Nisqually property he counted 87 tribally owned horses, 33 head of cattle, and 225 sheep. No census figure was given for the human inhabitants, but the tribe's population likely did not exceed 200. While lamenting that the Nisquallies had been abused by whites acting "like Satan of old," Milroy saw no hope of salvation for the tribe in the "forced communism" of reservation life, denying residents the incentive to persevere, dooming them to wallow in poverty, and leaving the fifty or so children there unschooled and growing up "in the barbaric ignorance of their parents."

A new initiative in the federal government's sustained campaign to stamp out what little remained of Native America's sense of self-identity was launched in 1887. Titled the General Allotment Act and widely called the Dawes Act, the measure was sponsored by U.S. Senator Henry L. Dawes, a Massachusetts Republican who also declared that tribal "communism" was at the root of the natives' abysmal condition. In an unintentionally ironic explanation of the wide cultural chasm between the two races, Dawes instructed that the essential skill Indians needed to master was "selfishness, which is at the bottom of civilization."

The Dawes Act called for the breakup of reservations into personally—not tribally—held allotments of 160 acres given to each male household head, provided he agreed to farm the land and develop good work and thrift habits. Title to the allotments would be held in trust by the Department of the Interior for twenty-five years, at the end of which it would pass to the conscientious allottee, who would be rewarded with citizenship along with the obligation to pay state and local taxes previously unlevied against reservation dwellers.

While theoretically serving to encourage and reward such social desiderata as ambition, hard work, and self-sufficiency, the Dawes allotment plan had the corollary effect of diverting its participants' attention and energies away from the welfare and problems of the tribe as a whole. Selfishness was good, altruism bad; tribalism was un-American, and the old, pre-American ways were to be consigned to the ages. As carried out over the next half-century, the Dawes allotment program was a grievous failure if measured by its aspiration to turn the Indians into farmers. The land allotted to them was mostly arid or otherwise unsuited for crops, and few of the allottees had the financial resources or the proper training to succeed. Most natives who accepted a land allotment just lived on it the best they could manage and passed it on, in ever smaller pieces, to their heirs for whatever use they could make of it.

As the nineteenth century ran out, then, the condition of America's native people was poor and growing worse. The last gasp of armed Indian resistance was exhaled in 1890 at Wounded Knee Creek in South Dakota, where 200 natives were massacred by U.S. soldiers. A less-violent living death was in prospect for the tribal remnants being crowded out by the Industrial Age and its churning expansion into even the once remote corners of the Golden West. At the Nisqually reservation, the remainder of Leschi's tribe hovered close to bare subsistence.

THE IMMINENT participation of the United States in the First World War presented the citizens of Pierce County, especially those in its principal city, Tacoma, with an opportunity in 1917 to go to the aid of both their nation and their own pocketbooks. Much of the county's serene countryside east of Puget Sound, with its temperate climate, open farmland, deep forests, and crystal rivers—all within easy reach of railway and ocean-going transport—was standing unused by man. By white men, anyway. A perfect place, thought the good people of Pierce, for the federal government to construct a military base.

The Tacoma boosters found a receptive ear at the U.S. War Department, and before long the process was under way. The project was christened Camp Lewis (later changed to Fort Lewis) after Meriwether Lewis, co-leader of the early nineteenth-century expedition of discovery that opened the American West, and would eventually occupy nearly 90,000 acres, among the largest military bases in the U.S. One sticky problem arose, though, as Pierce County got to work condemning the land slated for the army's use under a long-term lease. The War Department wanted its new base to extend to the Nisqually River, Pierce County's western boundary; the prairie there would make an ideal artillery range. It so happened, though, that 3,500 of those acres, including the portion to be used for gunnery practice, constituted the eastern two-thirds of the Nisqually reservation, land that was supposedly sacrosanct by virtue of the amended Medicine Creek Treaty. The reservation acreage wanted for Camp Lewis was owned by twenty-five Nisqually allottees under the Dawes Act program. No matter. America was going to war, the army had to have its artillery range—apparently no other location would serve as well—and so the few dozen Indian families out there would just have to pack up and move somewhere else.

The Nisquallies, about to be victimized anew, were not happy. Their reservation was not a very large piece of real estate to begin with, and now they were being told they had to give up two-thirds of it. Pierce County proceeded to condemn the Nisqually land, and the War Department, after some haggling, agreed to pay its owners about $25 an acre, close to the going rate. Although the Medicine Creek Treaty gave the President unilateral power to move the reservations of the signatory tribes for any reason he thought necessary, the Nisqually reservation was not moved; it was just severely truncated. If the tribe had had the time, money, and knowledge to go to court and fight the taking, it might well have prevailed. But such opposition would surely have been resented in the surrounding white community; after all, American youth was being sent abroad to risk its life's blood trying to save the world for democracy, and the boys had to be trained somewhere for that mission.

After the First World War, the tribe asked for its land back from Fort Lewis. President Wilson's Secretary of War, Newton Baker, would not hear of it. The Nisquallies, he stated, had been paid fairly for their land and the artillery range was essential for training, so it was found "neither advisable nor necessary from any point of view that [the land] be returned to the Indians." And so for the better part of a century the percussive thud of exploding cannon shells has been heard in the neighborhood, the Nisquallies and their surrounding ecosystem be damned.

· · ·

AMONG THE rarely hailed aspects of the New Deal's sweeping reforms to save the nation from economic ruin was a program to rescue its native people. The 1934 Indian Reorganization Act attempted, with some success, to help participating tribes conserve and develop their land resources without interference by avaricious outsiders; to form businesses and acquire credit at normal rates; to institute home rule by drawing up tribal constitutions as a framework for self-government for a people long pushed around as unwanted wards by distant bureaucrats; and to allow Indians to practice their ancient customs and religious beliefs openly.

Of the 258 officially recognized tribes at the time, 177 agreed to reorganize themselves within the new federal oversight guidelines and assume direction, for the most part, of their own affairs. When the Nisquallies took up the question in late 1934, they had only forty adults registered with the Bureau of Indian Affairs (BIA), and just over half bothered to participate, voting nineteen to two for the plan. They were now so shadowy a remnant—and their nearest neighbors' ranks had likewise thinned—that a 1940 book-length study of their shared folkways by anthropologist Marian Smith of Columbia University concluded that "the Puyallup-Nisqually culture is gone."

As late as the 1960s neither running water nor electricity was available in the ramshackle dwellings at the bleak Nisqually reservation. For drinking, cooking, and cleaning water, "you had to drag an eight-gallon milk can to the nearest creek and fill it," recalled Lewis Squally, born in 1936. There were no community facilities to speak of. The only tribal gathering places were a tiny store on the reservation and the back room at a little Methodist church in the next-door village of Yelm. "Conditions were devastating," according to Georgeanna Kautz, whose husband was a mixed-blood descendant of U.S. Army officer (and ardent Leschi sympathizer) August Kautz of the Fort Steilacoom garrison. Kautz put the number of Nisqually families on the reservation in the 1950s and '60s at no more than two dozen, and while "many people here worked hard just to survive—fishing, hunting, berry-gathering, whatever it took—sometimes we starved." If tribal members fell ill, in an era when tuberculosis and spina bifida were common among them, "you had to drag yourself to an Indian hospital," since white facilities did not welcome natives as patients. Nisqually children who managed to attend Yelm public schools had to suffer constant racist taunts. A 1963 BIA survey on the sorry state of the tribes in the south Puget Sound region concluded that the worst of the social pathologies besetting the native population was a numbing idleness, stemming largely from low skill levels that reflected a sky-high school truancy rate, poor health habits, low self-esteem, and the related fear of competing—and being scorned—in the white world. An escapist alcoholic haze prevailed, further deepening dysfunction in one or more members of nearly every Nisqually household.

Caught in a vicious cycle of poverty and powerlessness and brimming alternately with rage and despair, a group of younger Nisquallies, Puyallups, and their tribal neighbors took note of the social protest movement by American blacks and their egalitarian allies beginning in the early 1960s. They saw in it a model for launching their own demand for civil rights and economic betterment. The catalyst for this effort was the suddenly escalating need for the tribes of the state of Washington to defend their claim on the one resource that had long sustained them in body and communal spirit—the salmon. The incomparable species is surely one of the earth's most satisfying gifts to *Homo sapiens,* at the top of the food chain. Its flesh is remarkable for its color, flavor, texture, and nutritional value; its life cycle, a parable of valor and athletic prowess. The Indians, who derived nourishment from every part of the once-abundant animal, paid reverence to it in a feast of thanksgiving each spring when the first Chinook or king salmon, largest of the species (averaging two and a half feet long), swam up the Nisqually.

Salmon were not only a staple of the Nisquallies' diet and culture but also a commodity they sold in quantity to white stores and markets. Thus salmon were a prime source of badly needed income, especially during the seasons in which white citizens were not permitted to fish under Washington State's wildlife regulations even though the treaty tribes were allowed to do so "in all their usual and accustomed places." When tribal fishermen persisted in claiming their off-reservation and off-season treaty rights during the Depression years of economic struggle, Washington State wardens began to crack down by fining or arresting them and confiscating their boats and nets. Resentment among the Nisquallies was fueled by their conviction that, aside from the meager 1,280 acres of reservation land the tribe was left with, it had won no real compensation under the Medicine Creek Treaty except the supposedly unimpeded right to fish and hunt as they always had.

As the salmon supply continued to drop in inverse ratio to the post–

World War II surge in the Northwest's human population, state game wardens stepped up their drive to limit the tribes' off-reservation access to the species. The salmon's fiercest enemies, however, were neither natural marine predators nor the native fishermen but the whites who came upon the Northwest paradise and assaulted it. They cut the timber, planted the fields and doused them with chemical fertilizer, built homes, factories, and shopping malls in sprawling profusion and roads to link them all, and disgorged torrents of waste. A no-less-lethal peril to the salmon emerged from the New Deal's paroxysm of dam-building in order to bring cheap hydroelectric power and flood control to one of the nation's wettest regions. In the Northwest, 400 dams were erected within a few decades, including a few small ones on the upper Nisqually River, built by municipal utility companies, which slowed the flow of the waterway and hindered the passage of its salmon. The Indians harvested somewhere between 5 and 10 percent of Washington's catch, but because the tribes were allowed to ignore fish and game laws that applied to non-Indians, they served as ideal scapegoats for the alarming drop-off in the salmon supply.

To protect the salmon, Washington State officials had begun undertaking conservation measures in the late 1940s. Native fishermen were increasingly badgered to cut down on their catches, even within their reservations. The tribes resisted the pressure as a blatant violation of their treaty rights and further objected because similar requests for restraint were not made of white sport and commercial fishermen, housing developers, and industrial polluters. Tensions grew along with restraining orders as state officials insisted that the Medicine Creek Treaty, in granting the signatory tribes the right to fish and hunt "in common with all citizens of the territory," required the Indians to bend to the needs of the population as a whole.

Washington courts held that the Indians' treaty rights to fish free of state regulation had been awarded only as a temporary expedient while tribal people were learning how to fend for themselves without the crutch of permanent federal paternalism—and a century was long enough for the natives to have adjusted. In 1963 Washington State's Supreme Court ruled that Indian treaty rights did not impair the policing power of the state, which was free to subject tribal members, like all other citizens, to "reasonable and necessary" regulations protecting salmon and to other forms of conservation. Soon the Nisqually River below the reservation was closed to all fishermen who did not abide by state rules about the duration of the fishing season, per-person catch quotas, and methods of angling. The river quickly turned into a combat zone.

For a decade, a group of militant younger Nisquallies, largely without the approval—and usually in defiance—of their tribal council and elders, was joined by neighboring and more distant tribesmen and some non-Indian allies in direct confrontations with state game wardens and law enforcement officers over treaty fishing rights. Patterned after bus and lunch counter sit-ins by blacks protesting segregated facilities, the Puget Sound rebels' efforts became known as "fish-ins" and won wide media coverage and considerable sympathy nationwide.

The state government launched day-and-night surveillance of the Nisqually, Puyallup, and other rivers by coordinated teams of patrol cars, high-powered speedboats, and helicopters, linked by radio and walkie-talkies and equipped with searchlights, in a warlike hunt for off-reservation Indian anglers. When found, alleged violators, who protested that they were acting within the law, were not treated tenderly. Shoves, fists, billy clubs, tear gas, and boat-ramming were regularly employed against the Indian resisters. Those arrested paid for their principles with fines, confiscated fishing equipment, and jail time.

To help dramatize their effort, tribal protesters attracted outside celebrities to join the fish-ins, most of them symbolically. Film idol Marlon Brando, though, then at the peak of his fame, participated actively in a well-publicized event in March 1964, on both the Nisqually and Puyallup rivers. After paddling a twenty-foot canoe a few hundred yards, Brando landed a pair of steelhead salmon as hundreds looked on, including a team of state Department of Game officers. They gathered him up when he landed, confiscated his catch, and ushered him unresisting to a waiting vehicle for a ride to police headquarters. There he was booked on a charge of game-fishing without a license, gave his home address as 2900 Mulholland Drive, Hollywood, and paid a nominal fine. The next day, in a trenchcoat and scarf, brown suede jacket, tight pants, and moccasins, Brando spoke at a protest rally in Olympia, telling a crowd of 2,000, lured by his glamour, "We made treaties as a young, weak nation when the Iroquois Confederation could have wiped us out. When we got stronger, we broke them. . . . The government has been trying to divide and conquer the Indians. Their rights must be protected."

By the late 1960s, the battleground shifted to the courts. Tribal protesters enlisted legal strategists from federal departments and agencies, including the new Office of Equal Opportunity, as well as from public-action groups like the American Friends Service Committee and the Native American Rights Fund. Their pooled talents permitted a sustained legal campaign well enough funded to hire expert witnesses to debunk the state's claim that it was Indian overfishing that had been killing off the salmon.

The climactic case in this effort, *U.S. v. Washington,* brought by the federal government in behalf of twenty-one tribes' treaty rights to fish as they pleased, came to trial in the U.S. District Court in Tacoma in September 1973. The judge assigned to the case seemed unlikely to lend a sympathetic ear to the tribes' argument. George H. Boldt, appointed by the Eisenhower administration, was regarded as a hard-shell, law-and-order jurist who interpreted issues within their narrowest context. He had no special acquaintance or experience dealing with Indian law—and he happened to be a sport fisherman. But Judge Boldt was also said to be fair-minded, and it was apparent during the month-long trial that he was letting the tribes present their case in all its dimensions. His court heard 50 witnesses, received 350 exhibits, and wound up with a transcript of proceedings that ran 4,600 pages. In February 1974, Boldt delivered a 203-page opinion that not only supported the Indians' position but elevated them to a level of recognition and respect that they had not enjoyed since Isaac Stevens set foot in Washington Territory.

The Boldt Decision, as the ruling came to be known, asserted that no act of Congress or any court decision had annulled the Stevens treaties. The state could impose fishing regulations, Boldt wrote, but they had to be reasonable and necessary for preserving fisheries, minimally intrusive, and nondiscriminatory toward the Indians. This last condition meant, he said, that the tribes were entitled to a fair share of the catch not needed for spawning. And a fair share of the salmon harvest, whether taken on or off reservations, the judge ruled, meant 50 percent—his interpretation of the Indians' right to take fish "in common" with the rest of the citizenry.

Nearly as cheering to the natives, Boldt held that the state of Washington was not the only sovereign entity that could regulate fishing by the treaty tribes; the tribes themselves could police fishing by their own members with fully legal enforcement power. The state and the tribes were directed to cooperate in overseeing Washington's fisheries, sharing data and framing regulations in a coordinated manner. State officials responded with years of obstructionist tactics until Judge Boldt finally lost patience with their noncompliance and placed all of Washington State's fisheries under federal court control. On July 2, 1979, the U.S.

Supreme Court upheld Boldt's rulings. The state of Washington had lost its diehard fight against the Treaty of Medicine Creek.

EVEN WITH its epic victory in the Great Fish War, the survival of the little Nisqually tribe remained in doubt. Salmon alone could not save another similarly endangered species. By the 1970s, hardly a hundred Nisqually tribe members lived on or close to the reservation.

Their numbers slowly grew after the Boldt Decision began to revive a tribal frame of mind. Families trickled back home from the diaspora, heartened by the opening of a federally funded $700,000 tribal headquarters in 1977. Yet true recovery from generations of desperately hard times was stymied by a struggle for power and status among the tribe's families, waged with an intensity inverse to the size of the reservation and the number of its dwellers. In a place where everyone was related to someone else not far away, emotions were always close to the surface, and infighting for supremacy erupted with regularity. Among the tribes of the south Sound, the Nisquallies were notorious for the instability of their government and the passion of their civil discord. Sometimes fists flew at general council meetings in the tribal gymnasium. The Nisquallies could equally be "a generous, friendly, open people," observed former New Englander Matthew Porter, a white outsider who put in a stint for several years as tribal educational director. But they were stricken, as so many other native people had been since the whites came to their land, by the plague of alcoholism. "It affected almost every family on the reservation," Porter recounted. Dysfunctional parents begat succeeding generations of likewise afflicted children in a seemingly unbreakable vicious cycle. The ravaging effects of addiction were compounded after Latin American drug lords targeted Indian reservations as both choice customer territory and, because of their relative remoteness, ideal bases for the processing and distribution of their lethal products.

A particularly insidious menace among the Nisquallies was methamphetamine, the ingredients of which were purchasable over the counter and could be cooked up on home stoves for domestic use or ready sale or sharing in a place as intimate as their reservation. The brain damage from meth, used as a lifestyle anodyne, was often immediate and permanent. By the last two decades of the twentieth century, getting arrested for using, carrying, selling, or antisocial acts as a result of taking drugs became almost a rite of passage among the Nisqually youth. One consequence was a rate of joblessness among tribe members in the 1990s that reached as high as 70 percent, according to BIA data. Even among tribal members who found work, 57 percent earned at or below the poverty line.

Why, then, did any Nisqually want to stay in the tribe and remain on a reservation, where life was so chronically stark and materially unrewarding? Part of the most often ventured explanation—perhaps most of it—was the strong, residual spiritual nature of the native people even in places like south Puget Sound, where encroaching modernity had all but overwhelmed what little remained of the Nisquallies' tribal identity. "People here say they sometimes see their ancestors walking down the path," reported one nontribal employee sensitive and respectful enough not to dismiss the phenomenon as group hallucination.

However humble, the tiny Nisqually reservation was not like other places. It was as much a comfort as a curse for those who chose to remain, returned there, or were incapable of leaving. It remains a community where life shuts down on the day of a funeral and everyone gathers at the gymnasium to pay respects to the departed, however modest a member of the tribe. It is a place where elder Jack McCloud still laments the disappearance of the cedars and charges timber giant Weyerhauser with destroying "a part of the one great sacredness. . . . Trees produce oxygen; companies produce poison." His cousin Jim McCloud, onetime sundancer and the closest present-day Nisqually to a traditional shaman, sums up why the tribe holds fast to its roots: "We're not going anyplace [else] because we need each other—we're just trying to take care of each other. . . . I admire how much we've been through—and we're still here."

II. *For Whom the Eagle Cries*

BY THE DAWN of the twenty-first century, Leschi's reputation—to the extent it was known at all in the white world, even within his native region—remained tarnished. Ezra Meeker's book in his defense had been issued nearly 100 years earlier, but it was regarded more as a collector's item than a creditable account of sordid events in Washington's territorial era. Clinton A. Snowden, in his six-volume *History of Washington,* which began to appear in 1909, had given the back of his hand to Meeker's heroic portrait:

Some have supposed, from all that has been said and written about [Leschi], that he was a great chief—the real organizer and leader of the uprising. But he did not hold even a second place among the leaders of that enterprise. He was not a great Indian in any sense. He was not a warrior of consequence. He was not an organizer or a manager. He was simply a glib-tongued orator, and like most other agitators, very competent to get those who listened to him into trouble, but wholly incompetent to get them out of it.

By midcentury, Leschi's reputation had not been rehabilitated. In an article about his execution in the March 1949 issue of the respected *Oregon Historical Quarterly,* Martin Schmitt wrote: "Leschi was definitely not 'a good Indian.' He did not like the whites. He waged incessant and bloody war against them when it became apparent they were driving him from the best part of the country." The last chief of the Nisquallies, moreover, remained listed in the judicial records of the state as a convicted murderer. Even at the Nisqually reservation, there was little overt recognition of the officially defiled Leschi as a benevolent spiritual presence. "The feeling here," one veteran tribal official recollected, "was 'Let's not talk about him.'"

One tribal member, though, Cecilia Svinth Carpenter, emphatically disagreed. Born of a Nisqually mother and a white father, a Lutheran minister of Danish ancestry, Carpenter was raised on a farm about a dozen miles northeast of the Nisqually reservation. She married at eighteen, devoted herself to raising a family, and did not complete her high school studies until she was thirty-eight. After earning bachelor's and master's degrees from nearby Pacific Lutheran College—her thesis was about the Medicine Creek Treaty—she taught social studies and language arts in the Tacoma public schools. Though she lived off-reservation, the tall, formidable schoolmarm never lost touch with her tribal roots. On discovering that the Indian role in Washington's past was omitted in the history textbooks given to her, she supplemented them with her own written accounts. Carpenter's professional attainments won her designation as Nisqually tribal historian, and in 1986 she began to transform the tribe's oral tradition into the written word by producing the first of her eight books—*Leschi: Last Chief of the Nisquallies,* published through her own imprint, Tahoma Research. What her writings may have lacked in depth and style they made up for in earnestness and authenticity. Carpenter nursed the hope that someday she could help get Leschi's name cleared from the state legal annals as a convicted killer and scrub away that stain on the tribe's honor.

The idea, though, remained a dream until the beginning of the twenty-first century, when a Nisqually tribe member from the next generation stepped forward to take up Leschi's cause as no one else had before. It helped that she was traceably related to Leschi himself.

Cynthia Iyall, born in 1961 and raised on her family's fifty-acre farm in Tumwater, ten or so miles west of the Nisqually reservation, had $^{13}\!/_{32}$ Indian blood. Her mother was of German and Irish ancestry; her father was part Cowlitz—a tribe based a little south of the Nisqually homeland—and descended from Leschi's half-sister, Margaret, who married into the Iyall family (the name means "gracious" in the Cowlitz language). Cynthia's great-grandfather Frank Iyall, a logger by trade and a champion of Indian causes, had lobbied in Washington, D.C., for, among other forms of recognition, the 1924 Citizenship Act for all native people. Two of her great-uncles, Paul and Dewey Leschi, were Quiemuth's grandsons and carried the Leschi name to honor and perpetuate it.

As a farmgirl, Cynthia heard a good deal of the native Salish dialect spoken, learned Indian songs and place-names, and explored the still-unspoiled vistas on Yelm Plain and the Nisqually watershed hills, where Leschi once roamed. She was, in short, a modern Indian maiden, but like Cecilia Carpenter, who would later become her mentor, she soon ventured into the wider white world. Attending Tumwater High School, Cynthia bloomed into a smart, highly attractive young woman with blue eyes, a strong, melodious voice, and a glow of cheery confidence. She married a white man and lived for several years on the Nisqually reservation until her husband's job as a police officer drew them away to the Tacoma suburb of Federal Way. There she worked seven years for Weyerhauser as an executive assistant in corporate services while raising a son. Then for six years she successfully ran a store that sold hockey equipment—her son, Richard, loved to skate—until her marriage fell apart. A tribal friend told her that the Nisquallies were looking for an economic development officer; it seemed the right moment to reconnect with her tribal roots. She won the job and, with her son, settled in a house a mile below the reservation.

The early 1990s were not a good time for starting over in Nisqually-land, and especially not for bringing up a son. The place was beset by joblessness, drugs, alcoholism, diabetes, truancy, and a tragic epidemic of suicides among the tribe's young men by hanging and drug overdosing. Iyall tried to arouse a spirit of enterprise at tribal headquarters. Among other projects, she rescued a HUD grant about to expire and got a long-delayed convenience store, the Rezmart, up and running across the highway from the tribal center. Iyall was sunny, energetic, and popular, especially with younger tribal members, while respectful of her elders, some of whom nevertheless sniped at her as more white than Indian, more Cowlitz than Nisqually, and an outsider because she had not grown up on the reservation. In 1997, harboring the hope of one day leading the tribe despite not belonging to any of the families that had long exercised oligarchic domination over its governing apparatus, Iyall ran for and won an at-large seat on the seven-member tribal council. After her three-year term, she was discouraged by the infighting and stepped away to concentrate on her development job.

During this time, Iyall grew close to two tribal elders, Cecilia Carpenter, the fount of wisdom on the Nisqually past, and her bachelor great-uncle, Sherman Leschi, the last of Quiemuth's line to bear his illustrious brother's name. On her Sunday morning visits with Sherman, it became apparent to Cynthia that he was haunted by Leschi's tragic story. "It came up in every conversation," she recalled. Other elders unrelated to the martyred chief, like Cecilia Carpenter, were similarly obsessed, Iyall discovered. "So many generations of Nisqually people had lived with this," she said. "For the older people it was hard even to talk about—you could see the pain in their faces and feel their anger when the subject arose." On one of Cynthia's Sunday morning visits with Sherman in June 2001, he was brooding, as if sensing his time left on earth was nearing an end. Finally he said to her, "I have something I want you to do." She looked hard into his imploring eyes as he added, "I want you to clear Leschi's name."

It was a daunting assignment. Iyall was only a junior tribal officer—persuading non-Indian Washington State to exonerate the all-but-forgotten hero of the little Nisqually tribe seemed about as easy a job as moving Mount Rainier. Still, she told Sherman that she would try. He died some months later, and soon thereafter Cynthia was walking along a trail through the reservation when suddenly an owl landed on a branch just above her head as she passed underneath. Of a spiritual nature, she took the bird for Sherman's reincarnation, or at least an urgent reminder of her pledge to him.

·   ·   ·

IN 2002, TO MARK the sesquicentennial of the creation of Washington Territory, the Washington State Historical Society (WSHS), which owned and ran the imposing new State History Museum in run-down Tacoma, had begun preparing a series of exhibitions, traveling shows, and websites to be rolled out over several years. The program was to conclude with "The Treaty Trail," an exhibit retelling how Isaac Stevens had enticed native tribes into surrendering their homelands to the U.S. government.

Among those on the WSHS curatorial staff assigned to the sesquicentennial project was Melissa Parr, an enthusiastic up-and-comer who steeped herself in the history of the period, in particular Stevens's encounter with the Nisquallies and his victimization of Leschi. It was a troubling story to Parr, whose father was of mixed Cherokee, Chickasaw, and English ancestry. She grew convinced that Leschi's tragic story was worth telling the public about in full and that the pending 150th anniversary of the Medicine Creek Treaty might provide the ideal occasion for the state of Washington to apologize officially for what had been done to the Nisqually chief.

A friend on the museum staff told Parr she ought to get in touch with Cecilia Carpenter, then seventy-eight and about to publish her latest book, *The Nisqually, My People,* the most comprehensive study yet about the tribe. Carpenter, aware that Cynthia Iyall shared her hope of winning posthumous redemption for Leschi, urged Parr to get hold of the younger Nisqually official (and, importantly, a Leschi relative). Iyall saw that Parr's institutional affiliation might be of great value in a cooperative effort to open up the Leschi matter to public awareness.

The three women formed the nucleus of a spontaneous Committee to Exonerate Leschi, a brainy sisterhood to whose ranks they soon recruited several other professional women of partly Indian ancestry, with Iyall serving as the committee chair. Parr asked her boss, WSHS director David Nicandri, if she could devote a portion of her work time and the historical society's resources to documenting the Leschi story, both for retelling through the museum's multimedia outlets and for advancing the campaign on which Iyall's committee had now embarked. Nicandri, an authority on the Northwest Indian tribes, told her that propagating knowledge of the Leschi injustice might prove the most instructive and beneficial facet of the museum's entire sesquicentennial celebration. Parr was invited to cast as wide a net as possible in gathering documentation on the subject, much of which had been buried in the tightly secured WSHS and Washington State archival vaults. The handwritten documents that emerged would require long hours to decipher and transcribe. Smart, nervy, and driven, Parr became, through her web of connections, the principal non-Nisqually in the emergent drive to reclaim Leschi from infamy. At its core, though, it remained a Nisqually initiative, and it was Iyall who functioned as the engine for the project even if Parr was the one whose foot was often on the pedal.

However flagrant the abuses Leschi had suffered at the hands of the territorial courts, the committee soon learned it would be hard to win a formal reversal of his conviction. Most problematic, the territorial courts that had tried Leschi were creations of Congress and under federal jurisdiction, so the Washington State courts might be loath to intercede.

To help the Leschi advocacy group better understand what it was up against, one of its members, WSHS graphic designer and writer Sharon Hultman, asked her lawyer husband, Carl, a former public defender in the Seattle area courts and a veteran member of the Pierce County prosecutor's office, to sift through the legal documents that Parr and the historical society's staff were assembling. Hultman could find no conclusive evidence that Leschi had been judicially railroaded. The forms of due process, he pointed out, seemed to have been honored: Leschi had had the benefit of lawyers, translators, a liberal instruction to the jury about the law of war at his first trial, enough time to find defense witnesses and build a case for his retrial, and recourse to the appeals process. The Nisqually chief, moreover, had offered no alibi, so far as anyone knew, and, indeed, admitted in a post-trial statement that his party of warriors had been camped at Connell's Prairie at the time Colonel Moses was ambushed.

Appreciative of the difficulties ahead, Cynthia Iyall appeared before the Nisqually tribal council at the end of September 2002 to report on her volunteer committee's efforts. The council was supportive of her group but worried that if it took its case to court, whether state or federal, and was turned down for any reason, Leschi would, in effect, have been reconvicted and the Nisqually tribal honor freshly insulted. Besides, Iyall was a relatively new and young presence within the tribal power structure and excited a degree of resentment for her initiative in a matter of such importance. "There were definitely some around here who wanted her to fail," recalled one veteran senior tribal official. "The older women especially were jealous of her."

Iyall persisted. In February 2003 she won the tribal council's official endorsement of her efforts in the form of a resolution, crafted to support both the tribe's and her committee's claim of legal standing to bring a formal plea for exoneration before the courts. The tribe, and Leschi's descendants in particular, said the council resolution, "have lived with the incorrect history of this event since 1857" and asked for the legal record to be cleansed and an official apology.

To gain these aims, what Iyall's group needed most was a legal strategist, preferably one with political clout. Melissa Parr and the Hultmans found just the person while holding an evening skull session on the Leschi project at a downtown Tacoma tavern. John Ladenburg, for fourteen years the highly successful Pierce County prosecutor, passed their table and paused to greet Carl Hultman, one of his former deputies. Ladenburg, in the middle of his first term as county executive and the ranking Democratic pol in Tacoma, was intrigued when told what the seated group was up to. His family had settled in the region in the 1880s, he had known a lot of Indians since childhood, and he was close to the Tacoma-based Puyallup tribe, whom he had helped win financial independence by facilitating the multimillion-dollar settlement of their lawsuit over long-violated rights to the tidelands beside their reservation on Puget Sound. Ladenburg offered to be of any help he could to the Leschi exoneration committee.

The group took him up on his offer at a meeting in his office in April 2003. As Ladenburg recalled the session, the committee seemed to be floundering over a realistic game plan. The least acceptable form of their objective was a gubernatorial pardon for Leschi from Democratic Governor Gary Locke, which might provide solace by recognizing the injustice done him but would not formally remove the stigma of the murder conviction. What Iyall's group wanted was an unequivocal apology from the state legislature, the people's branch of the government, and—of greatest importance to Cecilia Carpenter—a legally binding reversal of Leschi's conviction by either the federal or state courts on the grounds that, as a legitimate warrior defending his people, he should never have been charged with homicide.

But even if the legislature, not due to reconvene until January 2004, proved responsive to the Nisqually appeal, that would not expunge Leschi's murder conviction from Washington's judicial records—only the courts could do that. And Ladenburg had to point out the likely insuperable legal obstacles confronting the committee, which Carl Hultman had already detected. Particularly hampering a modern-day challenge to

Leschi's conviction was the lack of a verbatim transcript—or anything close to it—of the legal proceedings on which to build an appeal. Ladenburg broached an alternative planted in his mind by a reenactment he had recently seen on television of the Scopes "monkey trial" on the teaching of evolution. What if, instead of a formal court proceeding to revisit the Leschi conviction, some sort of quasi-judicial tribunal was conducted to review the circumstances of the case and whatever documentary evidence was now available and then to pass judgment on the fairness of the outcome? Perhaps the Washington State Supreme Court, or at least some of its members, could be persuaded to join such a panel outside their regular judicial duties, even as the high court's justices sometimes sat in on moot court proceedings at the University of Washington's School of Law. Such an exercise would not, of course, be legally binding, but might have a sufficiently moral and symbolic aura about it to bring a substantial measure of relief to the Nisqually people and thereby do honor to Leschi's memory.

"But what if they convict him again?" Cecilia Carpenter fretted upon hearing the idea. She contended that a staged reconsideration of the case ought to have a guaranteed "friendly" outcome—otherwise, why should the exoneration committee even consider sacrificing the opportunity to win a formal, legally valid reversal of Leschi's conviction, however problematic such an appeal might be?

The historical court idea was just food for thought, Ladenburg said, but he urged the committee, no matter what form of relief it might pursue, to do so at the state level. "He told us not to spin our wheels by taking the case to Washington, D.C.," Parr remembered. Congress was far away and had a lot more consequential matters to deal with than the grievance of a small, distant Indian tribe. And filing a petition with the federal courts, a process that could last years and cost a lot of money, seemed equally unpromising. Washington State's branches of government were far more likely to be responsive—and susceptible to pressure from the Native American community and its allies. "This is our case—we need to make it right," Ladenburg said to the committee, pointing out that most of the events Leschi's case dealt with and the Indian war itself had occurred right there in Pierce County, a few miles from where they were sitting.

THE LONGER John Ladenburg pondered the challenge facing the Leschi exoneration group, the more certain he became that the tribe's best hope for obtaining relief lay in the person of the chief justice of the Washington State Supreme Court, Gerry Alexander.

Alexander was known to be a keen student of history. He had majored in the subject at college and eventually served as chairman of the State Capital Museum's board of trustees. More to the point, Gerry (pronounced with a hard G, as in "good") Alexander, after thirty years on the bench, nine of them on Washington's highest court, was widely regarded by the state's legal community as a model jurist, principled yet undogmatic, dignified but not in the least stuffy, patient until abused by dilatory or devious advocates, respectful of precedent but not so worshipful of it as to spurn commonsense solutions equitable to all parties. "The test I apply," he confided to intimates, "is whether or not I can explain a ruling of mine to my barber."

A classic case of hometown-boy-makes-good without ever having wandered far afield, Alexander graduated from Olympia High School, which stood in the shadow of the state capitol, one of the handsomest in the nation and directly across the way from the Temple of Justice, as the majestic marble palace housing the Washington State Supreme Court was officially known. After earning his bachelor's and law school degrees from the academically superior University of Washington in Seattle, he joined a prominent law firm back in Olympia, where politics was the leading industry. Alexander's father was a Republican Party stalwart, but Gerry was less a political partisan than a legal craftsman who, after nine years in private practice, entered the judicial arena as a trial judge, won respect for his diligence, and advanced to the appellate level.

At the peak of his career now, Alexander was admired quite simply as a very decent man. His appearance and carriage—the white hair, the wire-framed glasses, the welcoming warmth, the caring inquiry that went beyond politeness—suggested the benign bearing of a man of the cloth, the kindly village pastor laboring in the fields of the Lord. Most co-workers agreed with his colleague on the state's high court, Justice Susan J. Owens, that the chief justice "has a genuine respect for people and treats everyone the same way—he's gracious to all and talks down to no one." On becoming chief justice, he made it a point of pride to be accessible to the public in a manner that probably few other high-ranking jurists in the nation were willing to risk. Unscheduled visitors could walk into his office, exchange a hearty handshake with the chief if he was not closeted, and perhaps receive the answer to a casual question or two. Alexander even listed his home number in the telephone book and selectively replied to e-mails from the public, provided the senders did not seek legal advice or inquire about a matter that was before his court (or likely to be).

John Ladenburg had never argued a case in front of Alexander during his prosecutorial career but had crossed paths and shared professional occasions with him enough times to pick up the phone and place an exploratory courtesy call to the chief justice. Alexander knew all about *Leschi v. Washington Territory,* the first death-penalty appeal reported in the state's judicial annals—and a notorious ruling it was, to the chief justice's way of thinking, as he had revealed in several public comments. But almost reflexively he told Ladenburg that the Nisquallies would likely be disappointed if they hoped the Washington Supreme Court would, or had the power to, rewrite history. Ancient history, at that.

According to the congressional enactment creating the state of Washington in 1889, cases like Leschi's that had been finally adjudicated by the territorial Supreme Court could not be reopened by Washington's new state Supreme Court. And even if that door had not been statutorily closed, the absence of a transcript of the Leschi retrial in and of itself made it all but impossible for a modern court to reconsider the outcome. And if a sentimental exception were made for a Leschi appeal, Alexander's court would be inviting an endless queue of petitioners to come forward, howling injustice over long-forgotten cases. Finally, the chief justice, a gentleman of the utmost propriety, let Ladenburg know he thought it would be unseemly for the present-day Supreme Court to denounce its judicial predecessors as bigots or blockheads, even if they had been.

At some point in their exchange, either Ladenburg or Alexander (both politely claim authorship) broached the idea of creating some sort of special tribunal, without legally binding force, to review the Leschi conviction. Both men were aware that, besides the Scopes trial, reenactments of such famous courtroom dramas as the Salem witchcraft, Sacco-Vanzetti, Lindbergh, and Rosenberg trials were occasionally staged for theatrical or educational purposes. Such an expedient would spare Alexander's court from formally having to confirm Leschi's conviction, since—to the chief justice's way of thinking—it could hardly do otherwise yet maintain its judicial credibility. The details, like how to avoid turning the event into a show trial and reducing the judges to actors bereft of true deliberative power, would take some figuring out, but both men thought the idea had merit. Alexander said he might even be willing to preside over such a staged proceeding. A less confident judge, eager to preserve his reputation as an immaculately disinterested arbiter, might have said it was not his job to lend comfort to the tribe.

By mid-September, thanks to the state historical society's labors, the exoneration group had assembled impressive documentary evidence. Cynthia Iyall announced that her group would soon ask the state legislature to issue an apology to Leschi's people. While waiting for the lawmakers to reconvene in the new year, Iyall e-mailed Alexander in early December, asking if he would meet with the exoneration committee to explore the idea of a "friendly trial." She added with insouciant directness that such an event, "exonerating Leschi on the record [and] correcting an almost 150-year-old wrong, is the right thing to do in 2004."

The imperative tone to her message, compounded by its call for an on-the-record proceeding—not merely a symbolic event—and Iyall's frank expectation that its ruling would exonerate Leschi, was so presumptuous that Alexander might easily have taken offense had it come from a more guileful correspondent. Instead, the chief justice replied to Iyall that "I was thinking of something like a re-enactment trial" to deal with the Leschi matter. No such tribunal could "have the force of law," the chief justice emphasized, but it could "be important symbolically." His reservations made known in advance, the chief justice agreed to meet with Iyall's committee.

To insulate himself and his court from possible charges of improper private communication with potential litigants, Alexander and Associate Justice Susan Owens, a former longtime tribal court judge, traveled to Ladenburg's office in Tacoma the week before Christmas to meet with the exoneration group. Alexander's notes on the meeting, recorded afterward, said, "They [the tribe] would . . . like members of the Supreme Court to participate in a historical court that would evaluate Leschi's trial and conviction and pronounce its findings regarding the fairness of the proceeding and the correctness of the determination." Iyall had a somewhat different memory. At that point, she believed, her group still favored asking the Supreme Court itself, not any special "historical court," to pass judgment on Leschi's conviction.

To lend his high office in an irregular fashion to a reexamination of the Leschi case, the chief justice also had to cover himself politically. Justiceships on the Washington Supreme Court were elective offices, and he could not afford to be cavalier about his perquisites. The judiciary did not initiate legal actions, even informal ones like a "historical court" (whatever that might turn out to be); rather, it responded to applications for a judgment from disputants. It was the executive and legislative branches that were constitutionally charged with framing policy initiatives and expressing the public will. Accordingly, Alexander's understandably self-protective notes stated, "It was generally agreed that . . . resolutions from the Legislature and the Governor should precede the deliberations of the historical court."

Nisqually tribal lawyer Bill Tobin, on hand for the meeting, saw it as a positive sign that Alexander had taken the trouble to show up, "though he seemed leery of what he might be asked to do . . . It was not at all clear by the end of the meeting where we were headed." Committee chair Iyall, awestruck at first by Alexander, who seemed to her "a strong, opinionated person," came away feeling that "once we connected with him, there was a sense things were going to happen—he seemed sincere and genuine about wanting to correct an injustice and was sympathetic to the tribe's pain." But first the chief justice needed to hear the views of the state legislature. With the lawmakers' 2004 session right around the corner, Iyall decided to enter the political fray directly now.

MARILYN RASMUSSEN'S farmhouse in rural Eatonville stood just a few miles from Leschi's birth village and close to the site of the territorial militia's 1856 Mashel River massacre of thirty or more Nisquallies. Rasmussen's district in the Washington State Senate extended from Mount Rainier, the 14,000-foot dormant volcano that loomed like a snow-shrouded sentinel over her family's beef and hay farm, to Puget Sound, encompassing all of Pierce County and crossing into eastern Thurston County, home of the Nisqually reservation.

Rasmussen, who had held her Senate seat for eleven years, knew all about Leschi. She had learned the history of her district and even kept a framed copy of a Leschi portrait, said to have been drawn from memory soon after his death, hanging near the top of the memorabilia on her soaring kitchen wall. "I was a big Leschi fan," she reminisced. But none of that was known to Cynthia Iyall when she came to Rasmussen's office at the state capitol. "She scared me to death at first—she seemed very firm and tough," Iyall recalled. "But after I finally spit out what we were after, she warmed right up."

The senator and her staff massaged the language of the proposed resolution, drafted by Nisqually tribal lawyers Bill Tobin and Thor Hoyte, to express the Senate's sorrow over the injustice done to Leschi and to ask the State Supreme Court to exonerate him. Then Rasmussen, a Democrat, went to the office of veteran Republican Senator Robert McCaslin, Judiciary Committee chairman and gatekeeper for all legal issues to come before the upper chamber. McCaslin scanned the Leschi resolution and handed it back, saying the agenda for the new legislative session had already been set and there was no time to consider such a marginal matter. "Besides," Rasmussen remembered his telling her, "your resolution will never pass."

But attitudes toward Native Americans had changed. Tribal grievances could no longer be brushed aside in Washington State as they had been before the Boldt Decision and especially since the arrival of big-time Indian gaming in the 1990s. Twenty tribally owned casinos were operating in Washington by the beginning of 2004, contributing substantially to the native people's liberation from abject economic dependency and bringing to nearby white communities employment opportunities. The tribes could also now afford to contribute to the political parties and back candidates friendly to their concerns. So Rasmussen pressed her case with the off-putting McCaslin. "This is something we have to do for these people," she told the Republican bigwig. "Give me just fifteen minutes for a hearing on our resolution," she implored. He offered five, then relented and told her to take her draft resolution to the Judiciary Committee's veteran senior counsel, Aldo Melchiori, to make it palatable to lawmakers who knew little about Leschi.

The crafty Melchiori did his homework and saw that phrasing the resolution to satisfy the tribe would raise problems. The available evidence would not allow the Senate to make a flat-out declaration of Leschi's innocence of the Moses killing. Nor was it clear why an apology for Leschi's mistreatment should come in the form of a joint resolution by the state legislature. It was the judicial branch that had fouled up Leschi's case by allowing it to be brought in the first place—now let the courts, at the legislature's behest, deal with reversing the conviction. Melchiori drew up the proposed resolution, including as much of the tribal lawyers' language as he dared but not venturing to spell out any specific mechanism or rationale by which the Supreme Court might justify scrapping the Leschi conviction.

His draft had two main points. First, Leschi, who had been "a victim of discrimination . . . because he was a non-Caucasian," had left Washington State a legacy "as a courageous leader whose sacrifice for his people is worthy of honor and respect." The second element in the resolution was a dicier matter, calling on the state's Supreme Court to "use its inherent power of providing justice to vacate the conviction of Chief Leschi and depublish the record in his case." Senator Rasmussen had little trouble rounding up twenty co-sponsors, and in early February 2004, the Judiciary Committee passed the resolution on the first of its two required readings. "I was aware it was going to give the Justices a problem—that it would get interesting real fast because of the separation-of-powers issue," said Melchiori. "But I was kind of having fun."

Gerry Alexander was not. While he welcomed an expression of support from the legislature for statewide recognition of the injustice done to Leschi, Alexander certainly did not like being told by another branch of government what his court should or should not do about the matter. A few days after the resolution had cleared its first hurdle, the chief justice, his ire edging him toward indiscretion, was overheard by a state employee at the capitol cafeteria railing to a luncheon partner, "I don't know how or why the court should review a decision by the Territorial Supreme Court—next someone will be asking us to vacate the conviction of Al Capone." The eavesdropper sent a letter to the daily *Olympian,* reporting the incident with disapproval but identifying the speaker only as a member of the Supreme Court. After seeing in print what he had intended as a private wisecrack, "I wanted to bite my tongue off," Alexander remembered.

The chief justice's growing distress was not relieved by the Senate Judiciary Committee hearing on the resolution, which ran closer to two hours than the five minutes that the panel's chairman had first offered. The packed hearing chamber, riveted by the grim history lesson that unfolded, heard the exoneration group's key ally, John Ladenburg, testify as chief executive of Pierce County that "we all need to have a hand in righting this wrong and recognizing that Leschi was not a murderer. And on behalf of Pierce County I apologize to the Nisqually tribe and the descendants of Chief Leschi for what happened to him in our county."

Invited by the media after the hearing to comment on the resolution being shaped by the Senate, Alexander gave a carefully balanced response that masked his annoyance. "We will look at it," he said, if the legislature passed the resolution, "but we won't do anything that would be unlawful. You just can't reach back 150 years or any length of time and wave away a conviction"—which, of course, was precisely what Leschi's tribe had in mind. And for the first time, Alexander publicly put forward the idea of a "historical court," without legally binding authority, to review the Leschi conviction, and said that members of his high court might be willing to participate in such an exercise. But Cynthia Iyall, with a strong pro-Leschi resolution progressing through the legislature, pressured the court to do more. She told the media that her tribe wanted a full-dress, on-the-record exoneration and that the current sesquicentennial of the Medicine Creek Treaty "is really the best time for this to happen. . . . People would be able to accept it now."

Alexander's unhappiness with the wording of the Leschi resolution forced Melchiori to blunt its pointed language. His second version respectfully asked the Supreme Court to examine the "unfortunate circumstances of this case, determine whether it had jurisdiction to hear a petition for relief . . . and, *if so,* to vacate the [Leschi] conviction and depublish the record in his case" (emphasis added). The "if so" condition seemed to give the justices all the wiggle room they needed if the court wanted to evade entanglement in an emotionally seductive but judicially parlous challenge. The new version quickly passed the Judiciary Committee, which sent it on to the Rules Committee to await call-up for a full Senate vote. But there the resolution stayed. The problem was that while the revised wording no longer presumed to tell the Supreme Court that it was empowered to deal with the Leschi matter, it nonetheless prescribed how the justices' deliberations on the matter should turn out.

Its author tried to soften the language further, but Iyall and her Nisqually contingent objected. "The tribe's expectations had been raised, and they didn't want to relent," Melchiori recounted. And though the second version of the resolution had already unanimously passed the state House of Representatives, Rasmussen and her co-sponsors lacked the votes to force it out of the Rules Committee so long as its wording seemed offensive to the Supreme Court.

As the legislative clock wound down in early March, sentiment persisted to do something for the tribe, so the Secretary of the Senate, Milton H. Doumit Jr., intervened by crafting a third version of the resolution. While preserving the earlier language that lionized Leschi as "a great and noble" figure, the new text said the Senate "joins with those who hope the Nisqually tribe is successful in its efforts to right a gross injustice through a vacation of his conviction by the Washington Supreme Court." This less hortative wording got the resolution out of committee and onto the Senate floor, where it passed unanimously. But the clock ran out on the legislative term before the Senate wording could reach the conference committee and the two houses' differing versions could be made to conform. Technically, then, the joint resolution failed to pass, although the media played the story as if it had succeeded—as it no doubt would have, had the calendar allowed. Iyall was sufficiently emboldened by the clear, if not quite complete, victory to tell the Tacoma-based *News Tribune* that the tribe now planned to petition the Supreme Court to review the case. She made no reference to a special "historical court" to deal with the matter.

Still more heat was applied to Alexander a few days later, reflecting the new political clout of the state's Indian population. A letter from the majority and minority leaders of both houses of the legislature, obviously meant to compensate for the lawmakers' failure to clear the joint resolution before the end of the session, was directed to the chief justice and called the Leschi conviction "a black stain upon the history of our state." The letter ended, as the second Senate version of the resolution had, by asking the Supreme Court to review the matter to determine whether it could exercise jurisdiction over it—and if so, to exonerate Leschi.

In a polite but stiff reply to the legislature's kingpins—a copy was directed to Iyall and her committee—Alexander pointed out that his court could not take up the Leschi matter simply because the legislature had asked it to: "Our court, like all other courts, may only act when a petition or other pleading is filed directly in the court" requesting it to intervene. "To date no one has filed a formal petition . . . relative to the trial and conviction of Chief Leschi." Then he alerted any such potential petitioner to "be prepared to address several issues, in addition to the jurisdiction issue," including the legal standing of a person seeking relief in a criminal proceeding for another person, especially a dead one. In short, the chief justice was advising Leschi's people, who were apparently ignoring his earlier straight talk to them, that if they supposed the Supreme Court would roll over and ignore the rigorous rules of jurisprudence just because the legislature had taken their side, the tribe had better think again.

LATE IN MARCH, the chief justice received an e-mail from Cynthia Iyall, citing the legislature's resolution and asking to meet with Alexander "to discuss the possibility of the Supreme Court examining the circumstances" of Leschi's case. Iyall's apparently ingenuous request for a second meeting with the chief justice suggested she might not have understood that would-be petitioners to the Supreme Court could not ask its members for advice on how to win favorable treatment for their appeal. Or perhaps Iyall believed—or was trying to imply—that Leschi's was a special case and so no ethical issue was raised by her group's seeking the court's guidance.

The chief justice replied to Iyall that he would have to discuss the subject with the other members of his court before he could agree to meet with her group, and then assigned his legal intern, James E. Brown, to look into the jurisdictional aspects of the Leschi matter and report back to him as soon as possible.

Brown's memo asserted that because the 1889 act of Congress creating Washington as a state had limited its new Supreme Court's jurisdiction over old cases to those still pending before the territorial high court, and since the Leschi case had been finally adjudicated thirty-one years earlier, his conviction seemed beyond the reach of the present-day state courts. Brown's memo also dashed cold water on any Nisqually claim of legal standing by arguing that under long-established constitutional standards—he cited none—the tribe would be required to show "an actual injury," defined as "invasion of a legally protected interest that is . . . concrete and particularized . . . not conjectural or hypothetical. A mere ideological grievance is not enough. . . . There must be a justiciable controversy." And the tribe's pleading, if based on its collective wounded pride, would be just too abstract and theoretical to qualify.

Alexander circulated Brown's findings among the other justices, who shared the chief's view that the Supreme Court ought not to be lured into an official review of the Leschi conviction, nor should they go on record with findings that implied their territorial predecessors had botched the case. Among his colleagues, only Justice Owens was sympathetic with the chief justice's inclination to grant some form of judicial—or at least quasi-legal—relief to the Nisqallies. The other seven members of the court had no objection, however, if Justices Alexander and Owens wished to participate in an unofficial hearing, provided that such a proceeding did not intrude on the Supreme Court's regular business and was held outside the hallowed Temple of Justice, lest confusion be sown in the public's mind over the legal status of the event.

Accordingly, Alexander wrote Iyall that he and Justice Owens would be glad to meet with her group in his chambers. But he cautioned that the justices were "bound by the canons of judicial ethics and cannot receive ex parte communications about factual or legal matters that are or may come before the court." The fact Alexander had not closed the door to them gave Iyall and her team reason to hope there might yet be some middle ground between a highly problematic formal Supreme Court hearing and a merely symbolic proceeding. But at the late April meeting in Alexander's chambers, the Nisquallies' hope was soon shattered.

The tribe had every right to bring an exoneration plea to his court, the chief justice told his visitors, "but I saw we weren't going to get in the door if we filed a regular petition," recalled Bill Tobin, the only lawyer among the Leschi delegation. They were kindly advised that they did not have a live case, that the issues of jurisdiction, legal standing, and moot-ness were towering, and that—though it was not spelled out in so many words—the court did not want to be put in the unsympathetic position of having to turn down a fatally flawed petition with a ruling that would only redouble the tribe's grief. Alexander then reintroduced the idea of a historical court as a means to advance the tribal healing process.

The tribe's choice was clear now: either file a formal petition in the teeth of an almost certain rebuff by the Supreme Court or settle for a staged judicial proceeding with the trappings of authenticity and the like-lihood—but no guarantee—of a friendly outcome. It took Iyall and her allies two and a half months to decide.

True, they might have managed, at considerable expense, to craft an ingenious appeal and argue it in open court, thereby attracting wide media attention to the injustice suffered by Leschi. But if they lost—and the odds were, Bill Tobin made clear to them, that they would lose—would the noble attempt be sufficient consolation to the Nisqually peo-ple? It was not an easy question. "You had to respect the tribe's wishes," Iyall recounted. "A lot of families felt the pain, and some were willing to go out and take their chances in a real courtroom." But one of Iyall's inner circle of advisors, attorney Tina Kuckkahn, of Native American ancestry and in charge of the Longhouse, the Indian cultural center at Evergreen State College in Olympia, offered the exoneration group a philosophical precept that resonated with them: the applied principles and procedures of the law did not, sad to say, necessarily result in justice, however effectively they might promote a stable, orderly society. Thus, if Alexander and his fellow justices felt bound by legal strictures to deny Leschi his chance to be exonerated by a new court in a new age, then per-haps a so-called historical court with enough resemblance to the real thing might place at least a quasi-legal imprimatur on the state legisla-ture's resolutions honoring Leschi's memory. Such an outcome might serve to publicize the enormity of the injustice done to Leschi. Yes, the historical court would be, at best, half a loaf, but wouldn't that be preferable, Kuckkahn counseled, to none?

Iyall thought so. But tribal historian Cecilia Carpenter held firm, favoring the risk of a formal appeal and fearing that even a historical court might conclude that it could not justifiably—under white man's law—quash Leschi's conviction five or six generations after the fact. In the end, though, Carpenter agreed to stand aside if the tribal consensus favored a compromise. Out of concern for Carpenter's anxiety, Iyall tried one last time to bargain with the chief justice to make sure the tribe would get its half loaf. On July 17, 2004, she e-mailed Alexander:

> It has taken me a while to get back to you, due to half our tribe wanting to pursue a historical court and the other half (an important half) wanting to pursue the official petition.
>
> I am making an executive decision and would like to pursue the historical court if we are not too late. Is it possible for you to reply and let me know as many details as possible?
>
> Cecilia Carpenter really wants to pursue the petition route. However, she will go with those of us who want the historical court, if she could get some kind of guaranteed outcome.
>
> Can you write back, explaining what you think this would look like for us and explain how you think the outcome would be? I truly appreciate your assistance.

In response, Alexander agreed to a hearing that would examine Leschi's trials and appeal as well as what was known about the events surrounding them. He envisioned an appellate court format with no jurors and the decision left to a seven-judge panel consisting of perhaps several Supreme Court justices, three tribal judges, and a top officer from the state bar association. The State History Museum in Tacoma, he thought, would provide a proper site for what Alexander intended to be an essentially educational, not judicial, event. And once more, to cover his robed derrière, the chief justice stressed that the court, "of course, would not have legal standing and any findings and conclusions it made would not disturb, in a legal sense, the decisions of the courts in the Washington Territory in the Leschi case." He was offering the tribe a gesture, not deliverance. As to Iyall's last-ditch request for the promise of an outcome favorable to the tribe, Alexander told her, for a take-it-or-leave-it final time, that any judge participating in even an unofficial court "with a pre-conceived notion of the outcome . . . would impeach the credibility of any decision the body reached."

The tribe, in other words, either had to trust the chief justice's evident goodwill or go to war against him, as it had against Isaac Stevens many moons ago. Gerry Alexander seemed the more trustworthy of the two.

To oppose the Nisqually petition and speak for the original territorial prosecution team, Alexander turned to its present-day counterpart, Pierce County prosecutor Jerry Horne, who assigned two veteran litigators from his office to stand up for Stevens and the territorial courts. One of them was Carl Hultman, who had helped the exoneration committee plot its course almost from the start. Hultman was too devoted a professional to consider faking his way through the hearing; he and his well-qualified co-counsel, the disinterested and accomplished Mary Robnett, a former law clerk to Alexander and a ten-year deputy prosecutor, could be counted on to put up enough resistance to provide the historical court with a semblance of impartiality. The other ground rules Alexander put in place, though, tipped his hand. Only the tribe's side would be invited to put on witnesses, most of them well-credentialed historians familiar with Indian culture and all of them preapproved by the chief justice. No cross-examination of the witnesses was to be permitted, in part because the State Museum had placed a four-hour time limit on the afternoon hearing, blaming it on a previously scheduled social event. Such restrictions underscored the reality: this was to be a performance, really a series of mini-lectures, not an adversarial proceeding that might rain fresh grief on Leschi's people.

To fill out his panel of judges, Alexander hunted for jurists likely to share his and Justice Owens's sensitivity to the social considerations of the case. It took some doing. No other Supreme Court justice besides Alexander and Owens had any interest in serving on the historical court. A U.S. District Court judge whom the chief justice approached said he felt it was "inappropriate" for him to take part. And the president of the Washington State Bar Association begged off due to a prior engagement. Alexander wound up with a group of solid but slightly less eminent members of the state's juridical hierarchy: two court of appeals judges, two county judges, and the Lummi tribal court judge from northern Puget Sound. One of those chosen, Judge Daniel J. Berschauer of the Thurston County Superior Court, was fascinated by the historical court idea. "I never heard of such a thing," he recounted. But he wondered on what basis the special tribunal could exonerate Leschi without doing what appellate courts rarely do: look behind the facts as determined by the jury and conclude that it could not have reasonably reached the verdict it did. If the historical court were to apply the normal rules of judicial review, "we'd probably need to let the decision stand," Berschauer remembered fearing, "and that could have been very difficult for the tribe." He and other participating judges said afterward, though, that in enlisting them Alexander had in no way hinted how he wanted the decision to turn out.

Bill Tobin's pretrial legal memorandum to the historical court judges on behalf of the Nisquallies argued that at the time Colonel Moses was shot to death at Connell's Prairie, (1) a state of war undeniably existed between the natives and the whites' government; (2) Leschi, who was appointed a chieftain by white officials, occupied a prominent position among the Indian belligerents; and (3) the Nisqually people enjoyed sovereign status as testified to by the Medicine Creek Treaty that Governor Stevens had negotiated with them. Thus, Leschi was a legitimate combatant who, under the rules of warfare, was entitled to kill enemy soldiers without later being susceptible to the charge of murder by civil authorities.

In the weeks preceding the event, the exoneration committee's de facto publicist, Melissa Parr, succeeded in attracting considerable media interest. National as well as regional TV, radio, and press coverage dealt with the Nisqually initiative; *The New York Times* spread the story over the top of its first national news page under the headline "Chief's Retrial, 146 Years in the Making" and accompanied it with a three-column picture of the photogenic Cynthia Iyall standing close to Leschi's gravestone. Not everyone who wrote about the impending historical court was enthusiastic. Thomas Shapley, a columnist and editorial board member of the *Seattle Post-Intelligencer,* reflected thus about Leschi's hanging:

> If shame remains from this act—part and parcel of a Western-style ethnic cleansing—it lies not on Chief Leschi or his tribe or descendants. The stain is not on him but on his killers, and the inhumane ethic too often used to "settle" the West. . . . There's no bill we can pass, no court decision we can render and no mock trial we can hold that can truly right this wrong. Perhaps, then, we should continue to wear this stain as a reminder, should we be tempted to do wrong again.

The newspaper's editorial page, however, praised Alexander for "finding a way to properly pursue justice in one of the state's most infamous cases of injustice."

AND SO, at one o'clock on Friday, December 10, 2004, Gerry Alexander donned the robes of his high office in a makeshift dressing room on the basement level of the State History Museum. The self-styled Washington Historical Court of Inquiry and Justice, a creation of his own making, was about to gather in the auditorium a few steps away. The tribunal that he had convened was to perform an autopsy on some sorry history, and thus its purpose was more educational than judicial—but wasn't teaching the public historic truths what museums were meant to do?

After meeting briefly for the first (and only) time with the other six judges, Alexander led them into the museum auditorium and saw that all of its 230 seats were filled. An overflow of 125 or so more spectators gathered on the second-floor mezzanine, where a closed-circuit TV screen had been installed. The glare of floodlights brought into the auditorium for the cameras of TVW, Washington's public television network, added to the theatricality of the moment. "We entered the room with some trepidation—I think we all felt some pressure," recalled Judge Berschauer. Attending tribal members had donned items of native dress for the occasion. Seated at the front of the auditorium was Cynthia Iyall, whose blood pressure had been spiking for the past year from worry over the course she and her allies had pursued. Nearby sat the tribe's eighty-year-old historian, Cecilia Carpenter. The night before, a Puyallup friend had presented her with a blue vest she had embroidered "for protection against evil spirits." Carpenter, a woman of both the Indian and white worlds, wore the vest over a red-figured blouse to comfort her throughout the proceeding, which she had half dreaded because the outcome remained in doubt.

What followed was a serious, dignified, but hardly gripping exposition of the Leschi affair. The two prosecuting attorneys put up more than a token argument against vacating the murder conviction. In her opening statement, Mary Robnett claimed that Leschi had not been judicially lynched; on the contrary, he had had the benefit of competent attorneys, interpreters, and the appeals process; and all court officers had done their jobs "well and professionally." Of the six expert witnesses testifying in Leschi's favor, University of Colorado law professor and Indian historian

Charles Wilkinson was the most pointed, stressing "the glaring and serious defect" in the Medicine Creek Treaty that denied Leschi's tribe a habitable reservation and noting that prior to resorting to armed rebellion, Leschi had "tried to negotiate for a change in the treaty but made no progress." A pair of military lawyers from the Judge Advocate General's office stationed at Fort Lewis testified that U.S. Army officials at the time had clearly viewed Leschi as "a lawful combatant" and then a prisoner of war, not a criminal terrorist. The final expert witness, Isaac Stevens's biographer Kent Richards, tried to put the best face possible on the governor's postwar pursuit of Leschi. He contended that Stevens believed the execution of the Nisqually chief "would bring closure to the war," notwithstanding that the U.S. Army from top to bottom believed precisely the opposite.

The sole soaring moment in the long proceeding came at the end. The Leschi team's attorney, Bill Tobin, turned over the petitioners' summation to John Ladenburg, who opened by telling the judges that the case before them was "more than just the facts presented. This case is about the future, not the past. This case is about humanity, not history. This case is a rare opportunity for the people of Washington, both Indian and non-Indian, to come together to heal old wounds and create a road towards understanding and respect." Rejecting the argument in summation by Carl Hultman, his former colleague, Ladenburg reminded the judges they were not an appellate court but one imbued with a historical perspective: "You have a right to examine all of the history, all of the things we have found out. . . . It's more than about the simple record."

But that record was damnable enough, he asserted, and perceptible to any objective modern examiner. The entire case against Leschi, Ladenburg said, was built on the highly questionable testimony of just one witness. That witness also served as foreman of the indicting grand jury—"the absurdness of it is shocking even if it didn't result in a man's death." Nobody, furthermore, had testified they saw Leschi fire the shot that killed Moses—and even if he had been there, "mere presence at the scene cannot be used to convict." At the end, Ladenburg shifted his rhetoric into high gear:

It is said that after Leschi died, a solitary bald eagle would often be seen circling Leschi's original home. And as it circled, that eagle would scream out a single cry and then disappear into the tall fir. It might be that that eagle represented the land itself, searching for

Leschi. Maybe the eagle represented the family of Leschi, searching for their lost kin. Perhaps the eagle was Leschi himself, cruelly separated from his land and family.

Today another solitary eagle circles that sacred land, and it too has a lonely cry. But this cry is not for Leschi but for us, the living. . . . This cry demands to know when we will have the courage to stand up as one people in Washington and admit the wrong of the past. Like the eagle from above, we can see the landscape of our heritage now in sharp focus. We can see the injustice done to Leschi and the Nisquallies. We can see the pain caused by the multiple trials, the lingering appeals, the obscene pressure to hang this man . . . whose crime was refusing to give up his land and possessions. This man whose crime was loving his family and his people so much that he could not see them cast away as a forgotten race . . .

The eagle demands that we right the wrong of so many years ago. The eagle now cries for simple justice. We cannot bring Leschi back to life. We cannot restore him to his land. We can, we must, restore him to his name. . . . We do this not for Leschi's descendants alone. We do this not for the Nisqually tribe or the tribes of the Northwest alone. The eagle cries for us—all of us.

The judges retired for about twenty minutes to reach a decision. There was some discussion about the totality of the evidence, but they all saw the difficulty of applying what Judge Berschauer called "even hybrid appellate rules." The clear avenue open to them stirred no dissent as they focused on whether Leschi had been a legitimate combatant or a perpetrator of terrorist atrocities—a distinction blurred by modern warfare in tumultuous settings. "All of us were aware of what was going on in Iraq and Afghanistan," one of the judges recalled.

The chief justice spoke for the court, delivering its brief, unanimous opinion. The historical tribunal, Alexander said, was not "bound by contemporary rules of appellate procedure" and, accordingly, exercised its right to examine all surviving records and consider all the intelligence it received from the witnesses who had come before them that afternoon. Nevertheless, the court was restricting its findings to only one issue and concluded that

on October 31, 1854 [he meant 1855], a state of war existed between the federal territory of Washington and several Indian tribes, including the Nisqually Indian tribe; and that A. B. Moses was a combatant in that war as a member of the territorial militia; that his death occurred in this war; and that, therefore, Chief Leschi should not, as a matter of law, have been tried for the crime of murder. Therefore, because that is the case, this historical court would exonerate Chief Leschi from . . .

The burst of cheers and applause drowned out Alexander's last few words.

It was an oddly jejune ruling. There was no ringing denunciation of the prejudicial conduct of Leschi's trials and appeal, as the tribe and the exoneration committee would have liked. Despite the chief justice's disclaimer that his historical court was not restricted by the usual rules and practices of real appellate courts in weighing claims of judicial error, the seven volunteer judges did not venture to find fault with any of the abundant censurable aspects of how their territorial forebears had dealt with the case except for the one glaring procedural matter—the murder indictment itself—that made the rest of the Nisqually chief's abhorrent treatment secondary and, apparently, not worth even mentioning. The ruling was based on the narrowest possible ground, in keeping with the common practice of appellate courts.

Yet even as a purposely confined, noninflammatory finding, the historical court's ruling seemed haphazard. The oral opinion stated that "as a matter of law," Leschi should not have been put on trial for murder—but exactly what law was that? The so-called law of war or rule of war, protecting legal combatants? Where was that written? If no statutory basis existed for it, then where was the case law? A true historical court, had it the time, funds, and inclination, might have cited whatever on-point legal literature existed, like the writings of Hugo Grotius, the seventeenth-century Dutch scholar who was still the principal authority on the "law of war."

The abrupt ending of the historical court raised another question. If the time limitations imposed on the event forced the judges to issue an on-the-spot, offhand, and unsourced ruling, why didn't they subsequently issue a detailed written opinion that explored the gravely suspect elements in the legal proceedings against Leschi, which, when taken *in toto,* amounted to a massive miscarriage of justice? If the historical court project had been intended as more than an earnest gesture of commiseration, a carefully documented opinion would have been far more instructive to posterity than a few spoken words of soft rebuke for egregious judicial misconduct. Composing such an opinion would no doubt have required considerable time and effort, but there was no need to rush it; after all, the injustice had been left to fester for generations.

The chief justice, a reflective man, said afterward that he wished such a comprehensive opinion had been drawn up to justify the undertaking and help present a clearer measure of the pain inflicted on the natives during the white settlement of the American Northwest. In fairness, though—and to spare the members of the historical court from the gibe that no good deed goes unpunished—it should be noted that the project was a labor of conscience for all involved. For the participating judges to have exhumed the Leschi case and produced an exhaustive legal and historical analysis would surely have taken them away from their pressing official duties. In voting even symbolically to exonerate Leschi by the least damning of the remedies available to them, Alexander and his fellow judges contributed more than their fair share to the cause of justice. In lending his prominence and honorable reputation to a display of empathy for hurting neighbors, the chief justice probably exceeded the mandate of his office. As David Hastings, a supervisory staff member at the Washington State Archives and a seasoned observer of the political scene at the state capital, remarked afterward about Alexander's involvement, "It was a pretty brave thing to do."

Within the Nisqually community the reaction to the historical court decision was largely favorable. As elder Reuben Wells Sr., a member of one of the tribe's most influential families, put it simply: "It was enough for us—in fact, a great relief." The court and its ruling may have been only symbolic, but in the natives' culture symbols possessed potency. Joe Cushman, veteran Nisqually tribal planner, thought the court's ruling had been "emotionally overwhelming" for the reservation and notably enhanced Cynthia Iyall's stature within the tribe. Cecilia Carpenter, while relieved that the historical court had not reimposed Leschi's conviction, was not exactly dancing a jig. "They did say that Leschi shouldn't have been tried," Carpenter reflected, "but it doesn't change the legal record. This was really a way for white people, for the state of Washington, to say, 'We're sorry'—and I accept it. It's the best we can do." Melissa Parr, who after Iyall was the prime catalyst of the exoneration effort, perhaps best evaluated its outcome: "It's easy to criticize or second-guess the process—maybe it wasn't perfect, maybe more could have been done. But I'd say we did pretty damn good—people will be thinking and writing about Leschi and social justice because of what we did. I was honored to be part of it."

In 2006, despite a costly advertising campaign against him by the building industry and hard-right conservatives, Gerry Alexander—with the overwhelming support of the state bar—won a third six-year term on the Washington State Supreme Court with 54 percent of the vote. When he stepped down as chief justice at the end of 2009, he had served longer in that position than anyone before him in Washington State history.

III. *Red Wind Rising*

TWO WEEKS AFTER the historical court had "exonerated" Chief Leschi from the crime of murder—and almost 150 years to the day since the tribes of south Puget Sound had gathered at Medicine Creek to hear what fate the American government had in store for them—an event occurred that marked the beginning of a dramatic reversal in the collective fortunes of Leschi's struggling descendants.

In the running public debate over civil rights, no issue had been more controversial during the closing decades of the twentieth century than whether a nation that had long and systematically degraded its blacks now owed them not only a fair shake but something more—labeled "affirmative action"—as a compensatory mechanism to broaden and quicken their educational and economic opportunities. Native Americans were hardly less needy than African Americans, but they were far fewer and less organized, and so they impinged lightly, when at all, on the national consciousness—and conscience. What could be done to help the Indians, white America comforted itself by asking rhetorically, other than leaving the sad souls in peace to drink themselves into early graves on their barren reservations?

That was when the idea began to dawn on a few small, desperate, and widely separated tribes that legalized gaming might be expanded into Indian Country as a possible economic lifeline. Since only a couple of states permitted legalized casinos, the licensing of big-time betting establishments on reservation land would amount to a promising program of affirmative action at no cost to federal or state governments. But arguments against the idea were formidable. Betting on games of chance was not a revenue source that sound social policy encouraged; gambling tended to siphon money from those who could least afford to lose it while too often enticing those who were least equipped to resist its addicting excitement. Indian people, moreover, were a spiritual and communal folk who ought not to be corrupted by such a tawdry practice as a way out of

their economic plight. Tribal members, it was further contended, had neither the acumen nor the ambition to operate big, complex undertakings
like casinos. They would be easily gulled and muscled in on by the high-
powered, Vegas-based gaming industry and organized crime.

There were, however, compelling counterarguments to these claims.
Far from being morally repugnant to the Indian cultural tradition, gambling had long been a pleasurable recreational activity among tribal people. And while entrepreneurial drive and the accumulation of wealth by
individuals were historically foreign to the native psyche, running a
casino would be a cooperative venture for the mutual benefit of every
member of the owning tribe, its profits used to fund enhanced social services and communal facilities. Gaming operations could also generate
jobs for tribal members willing and able to learn the trade. And if their
potential white casino customers were foolhardy enough to gamble away
more than they could afford, it would hardly be the fault of the Indians.
Besides, weren't the tribes entitled to some payback from the progeny of
those who had taken away their land long ago?

After a decade of debate and legal wrangling, President Reagan
signed the Indian Gaming Regulatory Act of 1988, granting federal
license to three categories of gambling on tribal land, from bingo halls
and card parlors to so-called Class III high-stakes, Vegas-type casinos
with lucrative slot machines. The new enterprises were to be jointly reg-
ulated by a National Indian Gaming Commission, the host states, and the
tribes themselves. Gaming earnings were subject to the federal income
tax but not to state income levies (because reservations were federal land
and exempt from many state regulations). Participating states were
granted some regulatory powers, such as determining the number of slot
machines each tribe was entitled to install, but the tribes themselves were
given the principal job of policing their gaming operations. Each had to
sign a revenue allocation plan with its state, disclosing how the tribe
intended to spend its casino profits for the well-being of all and prevent
larcenous members from ripping them off.

The Nisquallies waded into legalized gaming by stages. They began
modestly in 1992 with a metal-roofed, 3,000-square-foot bingo hall
offering modest $300 pots as the top prize—nothing fancy and geared to
a largely local clientele, given the reservation's rural setting fifteen miles
southeast of Olympia and ten driving miles off I-5, Washington's main
interstate highway. The bingo hall did reasonably well for a few years
until the novelty wore off, and by mid-1996 it was shut down. Elsewhere

in Indian Country, though, the gaming business was beginning to boom. With a singlemindedness rare among its historically discordant membership and a loan from the Bank of America, the Nisquallies converted the old bingo hall in 1997 into a 9,000-square-foot structure intended to resemble an old-style Indian longhouse. Its new, noisier, and more exciting diversions like rocket bingo, keno, and 300 high-tech slot machines with bells and whistles soon began to draw a great many new customers from a wider area.

To add an authentic cultural grace note to the casino, the tribe turned to its historian, Cecilia Carpenter, for an appealing name. She was drawn to the tribe's legendary spirit of the wind, Laliad, one of several supernatural essences the Creator had sent to nourish the rebirth of the woebegone Nisquallies after a terrible prehistoric flood. It was Laliad who brought them the gentle rains, spread sunshine over their glorious lands, and helped the blue camases bloom on the prairie and the cedars grow to the sky. Carpenter proposed naming the tribe's big communal project Red Wind, adding the adjective to suggest this wind was protector of the native people.

Red Wind grew steadily. Soon several big companies in the gaming industry were making overtures to partner with the Nisquallies or run the casino for them for a hefty rake-off. The tribe chose instead to run the casino itself, hiring outside managers and staff but retaining supervisory power through the tribal council and a newly created Nisqually Gaming Commission. After five years, Red Wind's annual gross reached $10 million. According to the revenue allocation plan the tribe had signed as part of its compact with the state of Washington, 10 percent of net profits were held in reserve and the remainder went to the tribe, with 41 percent allocated for social services and economic development, 20 percent for government activities, 15 percent for the long-term capital account to pay off loans and other debts, 10 percent for per capita cash distributions to every enrolled member of the tribe, 2 percent to help local governments meet higher costs caused by the casino's customer traffic, and 2 percent to local charities. High operating costs, though, and a conservative business plan calling for accelerated retirement of the bank loan to build Red Wind did not leave much profit to come across the Yelm Highway, at the southwest corner of the Nisqually reservation, where the casino stood. Tribal elders griped that so far the business had not much improved their lot.

What Red Wind needed was scale, more of everything—space, bodies, action, sound, food, drama—to make it big-time. There were few in the tribe opposed to a major expansion, in part because the existing small casino had not turned its members into addicted gamblers. Nisqually planning director Joe Cushman helped arrange a $30 million loan from Bank of America—the new plant would cost $40 million by the time the 85,000-square-foot brown monolith and its adjoining 928-stall parking garage were completed—and construction began in late 2003. Tribal council chairman Dorian Sanchez, a former state employee with extensive experience in the personnel area, pushed hard to get the new Red Wind up and running within a year. When it opened just before Christmas 2004, the Nisqually casino boasted the electric ambiance of over-the-top Vegas decadence. Operating from 9:00 a.m. to 5:00 a.m. Monday through Wednesday and around the clock the rest of the week, the cavernous hall featured 675 slot machines (the number would soon grow to nearly 1,000), several dozen card, dice, and roulette tables, and 3 restaurants. The customers flocked; the place was the most exciting recreational facility for miles.

Two staffing problems appeared within the first year or two of the new Red Wind's operations. The casino's size, while exponentially expanded, was still modest by the humongous scale of Caesar's Palace and the Bellagio in Vegas or Foxwoods, the immensely successful tribal enterprise in Connecticut, so Red Wind salaries were scaled accordingly. Its location as well did not make it alluring for experienced gaming personnel; as a result, it took several years to find a competent and knowledgeable manager in Quinton Boshoff, a South African with thirty years in the business. The other personnel difficulty stemmed from the unfulfilled hope that the casino would become a big, instant employer of work-needy Nisquallies. The culture gap was simply too wide. Tribal members did not much care for indoor labor, grubbing for tips, or hewing to a work ethic that demanded strict punctuality, repetitive tasking, sedentary labor, and steady attendance—you could not just take off for a day to fish or tend to Auntie when she got ill. A high school diploma or a G.E.D. was a requisite for almost all casino jobs, and detectable drug use was a cause for swift termination. Thus, of the 625 employees on the Red Wind payroll when the casino hit its stride after a few years, no more than 70 were Indian, and only 40 or so of them Nisqually. But the tribe's Gaming Commission agency, a separate on-site contingent tasked with policing the operation, employed 30 people by 2008 with a $2 million payroll independent of the casino's.

Problems aside, Red Wind was swiftly, hugely successful. Daily attendance, which ran at about 1,400 before the new building opened, more than tripled by 2008. Tourist buses arrived at all hours, and not just on weekends. Even at midmorning on a typical weekday, two-thirds of the slot machines were busy (the gaming tables did most of their business at night). It may not have been a stylish, big-bucks crowd, but the customers were constant, manageable, and appreciative of the opportunity to splurge at a glitzy, well-maintained diversion in a peaceful rural setting. By the end of 2008, Red Wind was grossing $90 million a year, and in 2009, a recession year, the casino take grew another 6 percent. "This is a very good business," manager Boshoff noted in his low-key manner—so much so that the tribe paid off its bank loan in full within just a few years, allowing a considerable saving in annual interest charges.

The new Red Wind's financial impact on the tribe was stunning. Its 2009 profits came to $35 million, or more than $52,000 for each of the tribe's 670 enrollees, the highest membership in living memory. Actually, only $10,500 (taxable) went directly into the pocket (or, for minors, a trust account) of each Nisqually. The rest was ticketed, in keeping with the tribe's state-approved revenue allocation plan, mostly for enhanced government, social, and health services, managing natural resources (including two fish hatcheries), and funding new business opportunities. The tribal coffers that year were also the beneficiary of $10 million in federal and other grants and subsidies, more than $4 million in profit from its Rezmart convenience store (virtually all of it from state cigarette taxes that Washington allowed the tribe to retain), $2 million from licenses and permits, a $1 million surplus from the operation of its well-run tribal jail (housing mostly non-Nisqually prisoners), and $1 million in yield from stocks, bonds, and bank accounts. The tribe's assets reached $126.3 million by the end of 2008. About 100 enrolled Nisquallies, roughly one-fourth of its adult population, worked for the tribe as it reached toward self-sufficiency.

THE DRAMATIC improvement in Nisqually finances was accompanied by a notable change in its demographics. By the first decade of the twenty-first century, 60 percent of the tribe was under the age of thirty-five, and one-third was eighteen or younger. There were few left who knew the old language or wore tribal dress except on rare ceremonial occasions.

Foremost among the younger tribal adults newly exercising a leadership role was Cynthia Iyall. Her initiative in mounting the campaign that won quasi-official exoneration for Leschi late in 2004 had helped restore honor to the Nisqually name and stamped Iyall as an emergent political figure. While still resented by some of the tribe's older women as too white-looking and too much an outsider to be taken for a true Nisqually, Iyall was gaining in popularity as a role model among the younger women, while a group of younger men had begun to gravitate around her because of her unlikely aquatic exploits.

The sharp decline in the salmon population had driven the younger and hardier among the Nisqually fishermen to learn to scuba dive in quest of geoducks (pronounced "goo-ee-ducks"), the giant clams that thronged the shallows of Puget Sound and fetched five dollars a pound for export to the Asian gourmet food market. Harvesting geoducks took real stamina and training; the equipment was heavy, finding the burrowing creatures required persistence and endurance, and resurfacing too fast could cause you to black out or worse. Cynthia Iyall, not a large woman, decided to give it a try, mostly for the money, not the sporting challenge, and succeeded—a lone female among her all-male fellow divers. Partnering with her brother Tom, she operated a boat of her own with a three-member crew, among the smallest in the Nisqually geoduck fleet, which she named *The Feisty* and took out in season, mostly over weekends. *The Feisty* won its owner both profits and a following of fraternal admirers.

Her geoduck venture prompted Iyall to dream up an entrepreneurial concept she called Nisqually Aquatic Technologies (NAT). The tribe would operate or help fund a company to train scuba divers and then seek contracts to put them to work on underwater projects when they weren't going after geoducks and other shellfish—jobs like cleaning out the insides of municipal water tanks, scraping ship hulls, removing creosote from dock piers, and eliminating other contaminants fouling the Sound, or any other submerged task that came along. After repeated rebuffs from the tribal council, Iyall rallied enough younger divers to her cause and was finally granted seed money to get NAT going. But the infant enterprise ran into trouble. The payroll and start-up expenses were high—full diving gear, for example, cost $6,000 per outfit—and it would take time to attract customers to its novel service. Soon the underfinanced business was suspended, and the tribe had to write off the loan—NAT was a worthy idea but would take time and money to develop. Iyall, though, had won the enthusiastic backing of forty to fifty certified tribal divers who, with their families, constituted a sizable voting bloc in so small an electorate.

On the face of it, tribal council chairman Dorian Sanchez should have had little to fear from challengers for his job. He had managed to get the new Red Wind opened on schedule, and it was proving a bonanza. But Sanchez was charged by critics with neglecting his duties and frequently being away, either out of town or, more often, lured across the highway to Red Wind, the tribe's glittery new funhouse, where he was said to march about issuing commands as if he were the casino's proprietor, even though he was not licensed to work in the gaming industry. Since Sanchez was the tribe's chief executive and the tribe owned Red Wind, it was not easy to deflect him when he played the big shot. Resentment grew over his use of an expense account and spreading around tickets to the tribe's season skybox at Seattle Mariners baseball games in order to win friends and political supporters. When he treated himself and a girl-friend to an all-expenses-paid (nearly $5,000) junket to Detroit to attend the 2006 Super Bowl featuring the home-state Seattle Seahawks, he earned the wrath of many at the reservation and brought the tribe a formal censure by the National Indian Gaming Commission for his intrusion into Red Wind's operations. The door was open to a challenger when Sanchez's three-year term as council chairman expired in 2006.

"The tribe was on the cusp of making it or failing," recalled Cynthia Iyall, who from her desk and duties in the Nisqually headquarters building had her finger on the pulse of its governmental activities. "It had endured decades of hard times, and we needed someone there to do things—not keep going off" and neglecting leadership duties. Hopeful since her return to the tribe a dozen years earlier of one day winning the Nisqually council chair, Iyall was ready to go after the job again after an unsuccessful run against Sanchez in 2003. In recognition of her leading the Leschi exoneration drive, the State Historical Society had presented her its 2005 Peace and Friendship Award for advancing public under-standing of cultural diversity. She wrote a series of opinion-page articles for *The Olympian,* the local daily, that graphically explained Nisqually culture. And her efforts establishing the NAT venture, though bogged down by underfunding and inept management, had won her a sizable bloc of loyalists. She promised, if elected, to lead the tribe into the mod-ern world without losing touch with its cultural heritage. "The idea was let's move into the new universe," Iyall said. "These old guys have had their time, and they've kept our people down." She won the election handily.

In a classic display of Nisqually political dementia, Sanchez refused to accept his defeat, charging that the election was improperly conducted. It took several months of wrangling and repeated hearings in the tribal court before a general council meeting of the entire tribe confirmed the election results. A sea change had come to the Nisqually people.

IYALL'S CHIEF obstacle was the makeup of the tribal council, stacked four to three against her. The vice chair, secretary, and two at-large council members came from the old-guard families used to running things. Initially, Iyall was unaggressive, letting her opponents have their full say and hoping to find common ground on important issues so that at least one member of the opposition camp would join hers. Viewed as smart, honest, and hardworking by her staff—especially by the tribe's legal corps, which dealt with her on a daily basis—she brought a disciplined approach to the trying job. She had to remind herself to keep cool and to remain respectful even in the face of harassment. "She was too tentative, too deferential at first," recalled Thor Hoyte, lead tribal attorney, with expertise in public planning. "You can't be nice and conciliatory all the time." By her second year on the job, Iyall had toughened up and took solace from tribal wise man Jim McCloud, who counseled her about the virulence of her antagonists, "Just remember—it's not your fault that they're angry."

Although Red Wind was proving a financial blessing, Iyall recognized that the tribe could not rely on gaming alone to attain economic security and social progress. The goose laying the golden eggs could throw a fit or drop dead at any time. Suppose, for example, the state decided, as a revenue-raising measure, to legalize casinos on nontribal land and tax their profits? Iyall's basic approach, what she called a "strategic investment" policy, was premised on leveraging casino profits to fund new moneymaking opportunities while resisting pressure, particularly from tribal elders, to parcel the gambling profits into ever larger per capita distributions.

The linchpin of her new, entrepreneurial program, for which she won tribal council backing, was the purchase of forty acres of prime commercial real estate at a major intersection on Interstate 5, six miles northwest of Nisqually tribal headquarters, in Olympia's booming suburb of Lacey. The tract, directly adjacent to a supersized shopping plaza already in the planning stage, cost $26 million, a hefty speculative outlay made possible by the tribe's quick retirement of its loan to put up its casino. The tribe would seek a partner to build and operate a major component of the new shopping complex on Washington's main north-south traffic artery, projected to become the largest retail hub in the state. Smaller land purchases soon followed, one of them involving payment of $2.5 million and land swaps with an electric power company and Fort Lewis for 470 acres close to the reservation to construct houses for sale or lease, with Nisquallies given first choice.

Another part of Iyall's entrepreneurial policy called for expansion of existing tribal businesses besides the casino. Among these was the Nisquallies' state-of-the-art correctional facility with eighty beds, at times filled to capacity with prisoners drawn largely from—and held under profitable contracts with—surrounding tribes and municipalities that either had no jail or did not want to expand their lockup. Recognized for running one of the best Indian-owned jails in the nation, with decent food, ample recreational facilities, and TV surveillance of virtually every square inch of the facility, the tribe planned to expand the lucrative operation to 250 or more beds. Another candidate for upgrading was the Rez-mart, a glorified tobacco shop also selling junk food, which might be turned into a small supermarket offering healthful, fresh produce. Meanwhile, NAT, the tribe's underwater diving business, off to a rocky start after Iyall had come up with the inventive concept, was restructured and brought directly under the tribe's ownership. Now with a lean core staff and only half a dozen fulltime divers on its payroll but a far larger pool of certified tribal divers available on an as-needed basis, the service company was in much better operating shape and its business picked up. Among new NAT customers were the state, Pierce County, the U.S. Army Corps of Engineers, other tribes, private companies, and boat owners. By early 2009, Nisqually Aquatic Technologies was close to breaking even, and the national news section of that year's August 25 edition of *The New York Times* ran a long article, with a large color photo, on NAT divers who, as part of the Obama administration's economic stimulus package, were removing submerged fishing nets lost or discarded decades earlier but still killing fish, birds, and other animals in Puget Sound.

Using Red Wind's profits to expand or at least sustain the tribe's flow of earnings had been Iyall's top priority, but putting its new-found wealth to good communal use was no less a challenge to the council chairwoman. Her emphasis, in light of the youth-skewed demographics of the tribe, was on educational programs and recreational facilities aimed at combating the old stranglehold of drug addiction.

Under Iyall's regime, the two main additions to the tribe's physical plant were a $2 million learning center, equipped with fifteen computers and attached to a multimedia library featuring works on Indian culture, and an $8 million, 34,000-square-foot youth and community center, which opened early in 2010. The learning center provided a well-lighted, no-pressure, drug-free haven for tribal youngsters, a home away from home and parental scrutiny. Truancy and drug addiction were on the decline, and soon about 30 school-age dropouts and 50 adults in the tribe were pursuing G.E.D.'s to qualify for better jobs or advanced schooling—encouraging numbers in a community with fewer than 700 members. Forty or so other Nisquallies were pursuing college degrees fulltime or parttime, many with financial assistance from the tribe. A vocational training program was also available for members who wanted to work at Red Wind or in tribal government. The new twenty-four-acre youth/community center, also serving as an emergency shelter, included a basketball court and grandstand with an elevated running track, a well-equipped fitness center, a cultural resources center (with a room devoted to woodcarving, a cherished tribal craft), a computer lab, teaching and meeting rooms, an electronic game room, and a large, modern kitchen. Adjacent athletic fields and an outdoor swimming pool were projected. To address other neglected tribal needs, Iyall also set in motion an $11 million project, to be paid for largely by federal funding, calling for construction of a new Nisqually administrative building and a major overhaul of the overcrowded old tribal headquarters to provide expanded space for health, counseling, and environmental protection services. The new administrative complex was scheduled to open in mid-2011.

Even as it pushed ahead on other fronts, the tribe under Iyall's leadership stepped up its efforts to save what was left of the Nisqually environment, in particular its river basin, and to reclaim parts lost to the inroads of modern developers. A prominent example of this conservationist impulse was the reclamation of a 420-acre farm on the Nisqually estuary that originally had been created from marshlands and estuarine shallows by dikes damming it off from the Sound. In 2006 Nisqually workers took down the old dikes and began flooding the farm, deeded to the tribe by its non-Indian owner at his death, and returning cropland to salt marsh, ideal spawning ground for Chinook salmon, which had all but disappeared thirty years earlier. Tribal members also planted 40,000 trees and shrubs to rebuild the marsh and surrounding forest into a habitat not only for juvenile salmon but for birds and other wildlife as well. Upstream, tribal volunteers were busy clearing the waterway and riparian areas of debris. As a result of such efforts, the tribe was the only one chosen by environmental officials to help create Mashel State Park, midway up the Nisqually River, due to become one of the largest state parks in Washington. Because the area, which includes the site of the 1856 massacre of tribal noncombatants, is of sacred memory to Nisquallies, a section of the future park is to be used as a retreat and for ceremonial occasions.

FOR ALL THE SUCCESS she enjoyed during her first term as leader of the "Nisqually nation," as she proudly referred to it in her 2008 State of the Tribe report, Cynthia Iyall encountered two serious challenges from the tribe's senior generation that might have caused her downfall.

One came from old-guard families whose resentment was fanned by Iyall's drive and popularity. Its angriest voice belonged to the tribal council secretary, a shrill obstructionist who led a rogue effort to purge the Nisqually membership roll of seventy to eighty newer, younger enrollees, largely partial to Iyall's progressive policies—and thus return control of the tribal government to the old-guard clique. At one point the tribal secretary and her allies seized control of a council meeting when Iyall and one other councilman were called away on other tribal business, and the conspirators voted to shut down the tribal courts—in violation of the Nisqually constitution—and fired the legal staff, plunging the Nisqually government into chaos. Iyall, directly challenged, was forced to call a general assembly of the whole tribe several times. As a result, the runamuck insurgents were finally all voted off the council and fined, greatly strengthening Iyall's hand.

She faced a different kind of threat from the tribe's most charismatic elder, Billy Frank Jr., spearhead of the 1960s "fish-in" uprising against state authorities and son of Willie Frank, the last full-blooded Nisqually when he died in 1983 at the age of 102. After attacking the old tribal leadership for collaborating with oppressive state wardens and conducting tribal affairs in secret, Frank shied away from seeking the council chairmanship as he had announced and tried to convert Frank's Landing, his family's fifteen-acre enclave a few miles downriver from the reservation, into a separate, rival mini-tribe. He got Congress to designate it an independent Indian community—the only one in the state of Washington. There Frank's sister Maiselle and her family operated a lucrative tobacco store, which took business away from the Nisqually tribe's Rezmart, and an Indian school almost entirely funded with federal dollars. Politically astute, Frank soon became the most powerful native leader in the state through his thirty-year tenure as entrenched director of the Northwest Indian Fisheries Commission, an intertribal agency set up after the Boldt Decision to ensure Indian participation in state efforts to save the endangered salmon and push environmental protection programs.

When, in 2007, federal and state law officers raided the Frank's Landing tobacco shop run by Billy's relatives, who later pleaded guilty to evading more than $9 million in cigarette taxes owed to Washington State, Frank became infuriated with the Nisqually tribe for blowing the whistle on his family. As payback, he talked Washington's governor, Christine Gregoire, into allowing the disgraced Frank's Landing community to rent out its shut-down smoke shop to the Squaxin Island tribe, defying the Nisquallies' claim that under a compact with the state, they had exclusive cigarette sales rights to that sector of Indian Country. Chairwoman Iyall and the tribal council promptly filed suit against Gregoire in an effort to prevent the embittered Frank from similarly leasing out his private community to another tribe to operate a casino there, posing a fatal threat to the profits of nearby Red Wind, the Nisquallies' cash cow. In reporting the clash between the Landing and the Nisquallies, the Tacoma *News Tribune* quoted Frank, by then nearly eighty, as saying of his native tribe, "Everything they touch turns to crap," wholly ignoring the great success of Red Wind and how the tribe under Iyall was building on it.

Some among the older generation of women at the reservation, most of them loyal to Billy Frank and drawn to him by the star power of his alpha-male persona, continued to resist Iyall's emergence as tribal leader. Few of her detractors were more outspoken than Frank's old colleague from the fish-in days, Georgeanna Kautz, Nisqually tribal representative on Frank's Fish Commission, who remarked in the spring of 2008, "We have to work together here, and Cynthia doesn't have the leadership skills to bring the tribe together—the families are fighting ugly, and she's letting it happen. I wish I weren't in this tribe now."

The tribal consensus, however, was far more generous. "Things have never been better for the tribe," said its octogenarian historian, Cecilia Carpenter. Of Iyall's skills in helping bring about the improvement, one tribal department head praised her vigor and professionalism, and chief Nisqually financial officer Eletta Tiam added, "She's respectful of everyone"—not the case, in Tiam's view, with Iyall's predecessor. A veteran administrative officer enthused about Iyall: "I've watched her blossom and grow. Some people just have that spark—she has a gift. This is what we've been waiting for. The old seat-of-the-pants crisis management approach to governing doesn't work here anymore. She's putting the tribe back to where it should be." Most upbeat of all was planning director Joe Cushman, whose family settled in Washington before statehood and who came to work for the Nisquallies in the 1970s. "I think the tribe is going to do incredible things over the next twenty years," he said.

The Nisquallies remain one of the smallest of the twenty-seven tribes in the state of Washington. And because the Nisqually constitution requires one-quarter Indian blood and a proven tribal ancestor to qualify for membership—and because so many enrollees keep marrying outside the race—the tribe's extinction in the not-distant future looms as a real possibility unless, among the other dramatic changes they are undergoing, the Nisquallies revise the rules governing who can belong. "This is definitely at the back of our minds," said Iyall, who has set up a tribal committee to study the possibility of reducing the requirement for new Nisqually enrollees to 12½ percent Indian blood.

Cynthia Iyall may yet get the chance to bring about a change in this regard as well as in many others she has inaugurated. On Saturday, May 2, 2009, Iyall was reelected as the Nisqually leader by a vote of 176 to 121 over a woman from a prominent old tribal family and a long-time employee at the Indian Fish Commission, Billy Frank's bailiwick. Iyall's efforts will help determine whether the diminutive Nisqually tribe will perish or endure as a sovereign entity after generations of trial and torment—and may perhaps even prosper anew as a subculture with its spiritual values largely intact amidst an immense, churning society that has spared it little love.

ACKNOWLEDGMENTS

As RECOUNTED in the Preface, I would not have undertaken this project if an alert staff member at the Washington State Supreme Court Library had not called my attention to the 2004 reconsideration, undertaken by a panel of state judges, of the injustices dealt to Leschi and his people a century and a half earlier. That law librarian was Dawn Kendrick Gibb, to whom I owe this first word of thanks. The building where she works, known as the Temple of Justice, was presided over during the years of my research by Washington State's then chief justice, Gerry L. Alexander, who welcomed me to his chambers and very graciously allowed me access to his file on the Leschi exoneration matter and the special Historical Court of Inquiry and Justice he devised for dealing with the thorny issue. I am greatly appreciative as well of the efforts to track down historical documents for my use by Roger Easton, a dedicated volunteer researcher at the Washington State Archives in Olympia, along with guidance from Dave Hastings, state records archivist. Of valuable assistance in the early stages of my quest was Melissa Parr, then a member of the curatorial staff at the Washington State Historical Society and History Museum, who also served as a key participant on the Committee to Exonerate Chief Leschi and urged me to "think tribal" as I tried to grasp Native American social and spiritual values.

For educating me about the history, culture, and activities of the Nisqually Indian Tribe and its ways of coping with—and lately beginning to overcome—its long intractable problems, I owe special thanks to four people, starting with Cynthia Iyall, chairwoman of the Nisqually Tribal Council since 2006, who trusted me to tell her people's story fairly and with understanding. Nisqually tribal historian Cecilia S. Carpenter was extraordinarily generous in sharing her memories, insights, and materials from her vast collection of documents. Thor Hoyte, Nisqually tribal attorney, was heroically patient in coping with my unending requests for information, and his insights, along with those offered by former Nisqually tribal lawyer (now of counsel) Bill Tobin, proved indispensable to my appreciation of life and poltical complexities at the reservation. Chief tribal financial officer Eletta Tiam was also helpful.

Others of valuable assistance to my research effort were Drew Crooks, Puget Sound regional historian, who also scrutinized the manuscript and made a number of helpful suggestions; Kelly Kunsch, research librarian at the Seattle University School of Law; Gary F. Reese of Steilacoom, a specialist in early Northwest history; Rob Carson, staff reporter for the Tacoma *News Tribune;* and John Ladenburg, former county executive of Pierce County and prominent ally in the effort to restore Leschi's name to honor. Thanks, too, to Connie Perry, Mr. Ladenburg's assistant, and Cindy Jennings, Justice Alexander's assistant, for cheerfully complying with my requests for help.

Finally, I am—more than ever—grateful to my wife, Phyllis, for sharing my literary adventures and the profound learning experience that this book, along with my earlier ones, has provided; she also reviewed the manuscript at all stages and offered many constructive suggestions throughout. To Jonathan Segal at Alfred A. Knopf, I am greatly indebted for his continuing encouragement of my work and his painstaking scrutiny of this text. And to Joy Harris, my literary representative, my thanks for shepherding me through this journey.

INTERVIEWS

The following people were kind enough to meet with me and enrich my knowledge of the subjects dealt with in the text: Gerry L. Alexander, Jennifer Ammons, Robert Anderson, Daniel Berschauer, Quinton Boshoff, Cecilia S. Carpenter, Rob Carson, Tom Chambers, Ronald Cox, Drew Crooks, Joe Cushman, Patrick Delahunty, Brion Douglas, Billy Frank Jr., Kathy George, Alexandra Harmon, Dave Hastings, Thor A. Hoyte, Carl Hultman, Sharon Hultman, Cynthia Iyall, Judith Joseph, Georgeanna Kautz, Kyle Kautz, Tina Kuckkahn, Kelly Kunsch, John W. Ladenburg, Barbara A. Madsen, Jack McCloud, Jim McCloud, Aldo Melchiori, David Nicandri, Susan J. Owens, Melissa Parr, Matthew Porter, Marilyn Rasmussen, Kent D. Richards, Steve Robinson, Mary Robnett, Stephanie Scott, Lewis Squally, Shanna Stevenson, Eletta Tiam, Bill Tobin, David Troutt, Reuben Wells, Charles F. Wilkinson, and David Zeeck.

CREDITS AND PERMISSIONS

The maps of Washington Territory and the Puget Sound region affected by the Medicine Creek Treaty were created for this book by Darin Jensen, staff cartographer and lecturer in the Department of Geography at the University of California–Berkeley.

The poem "Listen" by Jack Iyall, great-uncle of Cynthia Iyall, is included here as an epigraph through the kind permission of Terece Iyall-Williams.

Illustrations are reproduced through the courtesy and with the permission of the following:

Washington State Archives: Both pictures of Isaac Stevens, B. F. Shaw, Charles Mason, Michael Simmons, Ezra Meeker, first capitol building of Washington Territory, Nisqually woven basket, Edward Lander, Francis Chenoweth, and Fayette McMullin.

Washington State Historical Society: Drawings of Leschi and Quiemuth, painting of Mount Rainier, and photos of Antonio Rabbeson, William Tolmie, George Gibbs, John Wool, and Frank Clark.

Tahoma Research: Photo of August Kautz.

Nisqually Indian Tribe: Photos of Cynthia Iyall, Nisqually Tribal Youth and Community Center, and Red Wind Casino.

Gerry Alexander photo by Gayle Rieber; Cecilia Carpenter photo by Olan Mills.

SELECTED BIBLIOGRAPHY

American Friends Service Committee. *Uncommon Controversy: Fishing Rights of the Muckleshoot, Puyallup, and Nisqually Indians.* University of Washington Press, 1970.

Asher, Brad. *Beyond the Reservations: Indians, Settlers, and the Law in Washington Territory, 1853–1889.* University of Oklahoma Press, 1999.

Bancroft, Hubert Howe. *History of Washington, Idaho, and Montana, 1845–1889.* The History Co., 1890.

Beardsley, Arthur. "The Bench and Bar of Washington: The First Fifty Years, 1845–1900." Unpublished ms., ca. 1940. University of Washington School of Law, Gallagher Library, Special Collections.

Beckham, Stephen D., "George Gibbs, 1815–1873: Historian and Ethnologist." Ph.D. dissertation, Department of History, University of California at Los Angeles, 1970.

Binns, Archie. *Northwest Gateway: The Story of the Port of Seattle,* Doubleday, Doran, 1941.

Bond, James E. *The Rights of Riot: Internal Conflict and the Law of War.* Princeton University Press, 1974.

Boyd, Robert. *The Coming of the Spirit of Pestilence.* University of Washington Press, 1999.

Cahn, Edgar S., ed. *Our Brother's Keeper: The Indian in White America.* New Community, 1969.

Canby, William C., Jr. *American Indian Law in a Nutshell.* Thomson-West, 2004.

Carey, Charles H. *A General History of Oregon Prior to 1861.* Metropolitan, 1935.

Carpenter, Cecilia S. *Fort Nisqually: A Documented History of Indian and British Interaction.* Tahoma Research, 1986.

———. *Leschi: Last Chief of the Nisquallies.* Tahoma Research, 1986.

———. *The Nisqually, My People.* Tahoma Research, 2002.

———. *Stolen Lands: The Story of the Dispossessed Nisquallies.* Tahoma Research, 2007.

———. *Tears of Internment: The Indian History of Fox Island and the Puget Sound Indian War.* Tahoma Research, 1996.

———. *Where the Waters Begin: The Traditional Nisqually Indian History of Mount Rainier.* Northwest Interpretive Association, 1994.

Clark, Ella E. *Indian Legends of the Pacific Northwest.* University of California Press, 1953.

Costo, Rupert, and Jeanette Henry. *Indian Treaties: Two Centuries of Dishonor.* Indian Historian Press, 1977.

Crooks, Drew W. *Past Reflections: Essays on the Hudson's Bay Company in the Southern Puget Sound Region.* Fort Nisqually Foundation, 2001.

Darian-Smith, Eve. *New Capitalists: Law, Politics, and Identity Surrounding Casino Gaming on Native American Land.* Wadsworth-Thomson Learning, 2004.

Deloria, Vine, Jr. *Custer Died for Your Sins: An Indian Manifesto.* Rev. ed. University of Oklahoma Press, 1988.

Deloria, Vine, Jr., and Clifford M. Lytle. *American Indians, American Justice.* University of Texas Press, 1983.

Eastman, Charles A. (Ohiyesa). *Indian Heroes and Great Chieftains.* University of Nebraska Press, 1991 (orig. pub. 1918).

Eckrom, J. A. *Remembered Drums: A History of the Puget Sound Indian War.* Pioneer Press Books, 1989.

Emmons, Della Gould. *Leschi of the Nisquallies.* T. S. Dennison & Co., 1965.

Ficken, Robert E. *Washington Territory.* Washington State University Press, 2002.

Ficken, Robert E., and Charles P. LeWarne. *Washington: A Centennial History.* University of Washington Press, 1989.

Gibbs, George. *Indian Tribes of Washington Territory.* Ye Galleon Press, 1978 (orig. pub. 1855).

Grotius, Hugo. *The Rights of War and Peace.* Book III. Ed. Richard Tuck. Liberty Fund, 2005.

Haeberlin, Hermann Karl, and Erma Gunther. *The Indians of Puget Sound.* University of Washington Press, 1930.

Hansbury, Matthew J. "The Three Trials of the Nisqually Chief Leschi." Master's thesis, Department of History, Washington State University, 2006.

Harmon, Alexandra. *Indians in the Making: Ethnic Relations and Indian Identities Around Puget Sound.* University of California Press, 1998.

Hunt, Herbert. *Tacoma: Its History and Its Builders.* S. J. Clarke Publishing Co., 1916.

Hunt, Herbert, and Floyd C. Kaylor. *Washington West of the Cascades,* vol. 1. S. J. Clarke Publishing Co., 1917.

Jackson, Helen Hunt. *A Century of Dishonor: A Sketch of the United States Government's Dealings with Some of the Indian Tribes.* Dover, 2003 (orig. pub. 1881).

Johnson, David Alan. *Founding the Far West: California, Oregon and Nevada, 1840–1890.* University of California Press, 1992.

Kappler, Charles J., ed. *Indian Affairs: Laws and Treaties,* vol. 2. U.S. Government Printing Office, 1904.

Koning, Hans. *The Conquest of America: How the Indian Nations Lost Their Continent.* Monthly Review Press, 1993.

Meany, Edward S. *History of the State of Washington.* Macmillan, 1943.

Meeker, Ezra. *Pioneer Reminiscences of Puget Sound: The Tragedy of Leschi.* Lowman and Hanford, 1905.

Morgan, Murray. *Puget's Sound: A Narrative of Early Tacoma and the Southern Sound.* University of Washington Press, 1979.

Page, Jake. *In the Hands of the Great Spirit: The 20,000-Year History of the American Indians.* Free Press, 2003.

Prucha, Francis Paul. *American Indian Policy in the Formative Years.* Harvard University Press, 1962.

———. *American Indian Treaties: The History of a Political Anomaly.* University of California Press, 1994.

Richards, Kent D. *Isaac I. Stevens: Young Man in a Hurry.* Brigham Young University Press, 1979.

Rosen, Lawrence, ed. *American Indians and the Law.* Transaction Books, 1976.

Ruby, Robert H., and John A. Brown. *A Guide to the Indian Tribes of the Pacific Northwest.* University of Oklahoma Press, 1986.

Smith, Marian W. *The Puyallup-Nisqually.* Columbia University Press, 1940.

Snowden, Clinton A. *History of Washington: The Rise and Progress of an American State.* Century History, 1911.

Splawn, A. J. *Ka-Mi-Akin: Last Hero of the Yakimas.* Kessinger Publishing, n.d. (orig. pub. 1917).

Stevens, Hazard. *The Life of Isaac Ingalls Stevens.* 2 vols. Kessinger Publishing, n.d. (orig. pub. 1901).

Swan, James G. *The Northwest Coast: Three Years of Residence in Washington Territory.* University of Washington Press, 1992 (orig. pub. 1857).

Territory of Washington. *Laws of the Territory of Washington.* Edward Furste, 1857.

Tolmie, William F. *The Journals of William Fraser Tolmie—Physician and Fur Trader.* Mitchell Press, 1963.

Underhill, Ruth. *Indians of the Pacific Northwest.* U.S. Department of the Interior, 1945.

Washburn, Wilcomb E. *The Indian and the White Man.* Anchor Books, 1964.

Wilkinson, Charles. *Blood Struggle: The Rise of Modern Indian Nations.* Norton, 2005.

———. *Messages from Frank's Landing: A Story of Salmon, Treaties, and the Indian Way.* University of Washington Press, 2000.

ARCHIVAL MATERIALS

The Washington State Archives in Olympia holds the most comprehensive collection of documents pertinent to the subjects dealt with here. Although the original documents in this collection are limited to the Territorial Volunteer Papers, which include some 2,000 pages of Isaac Stevens's correspondence as self-designated commander-in-chief of the territorial militia during the Puget Sound Indian War as well as his journal as superintendent of Indian affairs for the territory, Washington Archives also holds in microfilm copy or facsimile the following: Isaac Ingalls Stevens Papers, 1831–1862, at the University of Washington, pertaining to his military career, his leadership of the Northern Pacific Railway Survey, his terms as Washington territorial delegate to Congress, and his service as general of the Seventy-ninth Regiment Volunteers in the Civil War; Isaac Stevens Collection, Bienecke Library, Yale University, concerning aspects of his military career and service as territorial governor; letters and reports filed by Washington's territorial governors to the U.S. Department of State, two reels, covering 1853–1872, held by the Federal Archives and Record Service, Department of State Territorial Papers; Isaac Stevens Papers, Washington State Library, Olympia, including his outgoing letters and a history of his term as governor; Stevens Family Papers, Washington State Historical Society, Tacoma, covering various aspects of his career dating from the Mexican War; and the Isaac I. Stevens and Family Papers, 1832–1939, Western Washington State Historical Society, Spokane, consisting of family correspondence. Also dealing with aspects of events and individuals discussed here are collections of William F. Tolmie's papers at the University of Washington and the British Columbia Provincial Archive in Victoria, B.C.; "Recollections of Edward Huggins" in the University of Washington's special collections; papers of B. F. Shaw held by the Oregon Historical Society, Portland, and the documents on Indian affairs gathered by Gary F. Reese and held in the Northwest Room at Tacoma Public Library, including an edition of August Kautz's diaries. Two useful online files of articles and documents dealing with personalities and events discussed in this book have been created by the Washington State History Museum—"The Treaty Trail: U.S. Treaty Councils in the Northwest," at www.washingtonhistoryonline

.org/treatytrail, and "Leschi: Justice in Our Time," at www.washingtonhistoryonline
.org/treatytrail.

COURT CASES

Ex Parte Quirin, 317 U.S. 1 (1942).

Montoya v. U.S. 180 U.S. 261 (1901).

Puyallup Tribe v. Wash. Dept of Game, 391 U.S. 382 (1968); *Wash. Dept. of Game v.
Puyallup Tribe,* 414 U.S. 44 (1973) and 433 U.S. 165 (1977).

Sohappy v. Smith, 302 F. Supp. 899 (D.Or., 1969).

State v. Alexis, Wash. S. Ct. no. 13084 (1915); *State v. Alexis,* Whatcom Cty. Super. Ct,
no. 1720, August 17, 1915.

State v. McCoy, 63 Wash. 2d 421, 387 P. 2d 942 (1963).

State v. Tulee, 7 Wash. 2d 124, 109 P 2d 280 (1940); *Tulee v. Washington,* 315 U.S. 681
(1942).

Territory of Washington v. Leshi [*sic*] 1, F. Cas. 113–122, 2d Jud. Dist., Terr. Wash., 1857;
Leschi v. Washington Territory, 1 Wash. Terr. 13–30, 1857, Wash. State Archives,
Supreme Court Opinions.

United States v. Washington, 384 F. Supp. 312 (WD. Wash., 1974)

Worcester v. Georgia, 31 U.S. (6 Pet.) 515 (1832).

NOTES ON SOURCES

For full citation of books mentioned below, see the Selected Bibliography. In some cases, quoted or paraphrased material is sourced in the text itself and not duplicated here.

ABBREVIATIONS USED IN CITATIONS BELOW

DRNRUT Documents Related to the Negotiation of Ratified and Unratified
            Treaties with Various Indian Tribes, 1801–69, National Archives
    WSA Washington State Archives, Olympia
  WSHS Washington State Historical Society, Tacoma
   WSIA Records of the Washington Superintendency of Indian Affairs,
            1853–74, National Archives, Record Group 75

Mention of the *News Tribune* refers to the daily newspaper published in Tacoma, Washington.

1. *"I Know What I Am About"*

The two best sources on Isaac Stevens's life are the biographies by his son Hazard and historian Kent Richards. The former, not surprisingly, is an apologia for a checkered life; the latter is a well-written and balanced, though overly admiring, portrait that fails to mention Ezra Meeker's criticisms. Stevens was a profuse letter writer, and inquirers into his career will find much grist in the correspondence and other archival materials listed above. See also Sherburn F. Cook Jr., "The Little Napoleon: The Short and Turbulent Career of Isaac Stevens," *Columbia,* vol. 14, no. 4 (Winter 2000 -1): 17–20.

2. *Paradise for Free*

Morgan's *Puget's Sound* is a readable popular history of the region prior to its becoming U.S. territory. See also Asher, *Beyond the Reservations;* Bancroft, *History of Washington, Idaho, and Montana;* Boyd, *The Coming of the Spirit of Pestilence;* Carey, *A General History of Oregon Prior to 1861;* Carpenter, *Fort Nisqually;* Ficken, *Washington Territory;* Ficken and Warne, *Washington: A Centennial History;* Hunt, *Washington West of the Cascades;* Meany, *History of the State of Washington;* Snowden, *A History of Washington;* and Tolmie, *The Journals of William Fraser Tolmie.* This author dealt with the clash between Britain and the United States over the possession of the Oregon Territory in a chapter of his book *Seizing Destiny* (Knopf, 2007). See also John M. McClelland Jr., "Almost Columbia, Triumphantly Washington," *Columbia,* vol. 2, no. 2 (Summer 1988).

3. *The Northwest Express*

Chapters 16–20 of vol. 1 of Hazard Stevens's biography offer a colorful account of his father's adventures leading the Northern Railroad Survey party. The affecting plea by an Assiniboine elder is described in Stevens on pp. 343–44. See also Beckham, *George Gibbs;* Richards, *Isaac I. Stevens,* chapters 6–7; Robert Johansen, "Reporting a Pacific Railroad Survey," quoting Stevens's letters to Stephen Douglas, *Pacific Northwest Quarterly,* no. 47 (Oct. 1956); D. W. Meing, "Isaac Stevens: Practical Geographer of the Early Northwest," *Geographical Review,* vol. 45 (Oct. 1955); and Prucha, *American Indian Policy.* On Stevens's aggressive stance against the rights of the Hudson's Bay Company in Washington Territory, see William Tolmie's letter to Stevens, Dec. 27, 1853, Stevens corr., WSA, and Yale University collection.

4. *A Credit to His Race*

For an overview of American Indian history and issues, see Page, *In the Hands of the Great Spirit;* Washburn, *The Indian and the White Man;* Cahn, ed., *Our Brother's Keeper: The Indian in White America;* and the writings of Vine Deloria Jr., but there is a vast literature of worthy works on the subject. Perhaps the most informed and artfully crafted book on the Native Americans in the Northwest is Harmon's *Indians in the Making;* see also Underhill, *Indians of the Pacific Northwest;* Gibbs, *Indian Tribes of Washington Territory;* Ruby and Brown, *A Guide to the Indian Tribes of the Pacific Northwest;* Clark, *Indian Legends of the Pacific Northwest,* and Haeberlin and Gunther, *The Indians of Puget Sound.* On the Nisquallies and Leschi, the leading works are Smith, *The Puyallup-Nisqually,* and Carpenter, *The Nisqually: My People* and *Leschi: Last Chief of the Nisquallies.* As a Native American, Carpenter has performed a valuable service for her tribe by producing a body of works (see Selected Bibliography) that bridge the gap between the Nisqually oral tradition and written scholarship. For a view of Leschi by his third and youngest wife, Mary, see text of interview with her by Ezra Meeker ca. 1915, Meeker Papers, WSHS, box 16. For a contemporary view of Leschi by a well-positioned white settler, see Tolmie's letter to Washington Territory Gov. Fayette McMullin, Jan. 12, 1858, quoted by Meeker, *Pioneer Reminiscences,* pp. 447–49, also in William Tolmie Papers, University of Washington Library, accession no. 4577–1, box 2, folder 3. On federal officials' instructions regarding treaties with the Indians, see George Manypenny's letter to Stevens, May 9, 1853, and Charles Mix to Stevens, Aug. 30, 1854, both roll 7, WSIA National Archives; letter to Stevens from Secretary of State William L. Marcy, June 3, 1853, Yale University collection, Hudson's Bay Company folder, copy in WSA. For Stevens's initially more liberal view, see his letter to Manypenny, Dec. 26, 1853, cited in U.S. Court of Claims, *Duwamish et al. v. United States,* University of Washington microfilm collection, A7374, 725–28. On treatymaking efforts in Oregon Territory prior to Stevens's arrival in Olympia, see Charles F. Coan, "The First Stage of the Federal Indian Policy in the Northwest," *Oregon Historical Quarterly,* vol. 22 (March 1921).

5. *Christmas at Medicine Creek*

On treatymaking with Indians generally, see Jackson, *A Century of Dishonor,* and Prucha, *American Indian Treaties.* The two earlier books that report on the Medicine Creek

Treaty are vol. 1 of Hazard Stevens's biography of his father, chapter 25, pp. 448–80, covering as well other treaties with the Indians that Stevens imposed, and Meeker's *Pioneer Reminiscences,* chapters 30–34, pp. 229–75, providing a far more critical view of the treaties and notable for its interviews with tribal witnesses to the event. The most extensive periodical treatment of the subject is the special Fall 2005 issue of *Oregon Historical Quarterly,* vol. 106, no. 3, titled "The Isaac I. Stevens and Joel Palmer Treaties, 1855–2005" and edited by Stevens biographer Kent Richards. The most valuable material in this issue, other than Richards's introductory essay, is the article "Medicine Creek to Fox Island: Cadastral Scans and Contested Domains" by SuAnn M. Reddick and Cary C. Collins, pp. 374–97, which extensively reviews archival documents and speculates on what really may have transpired at the Medicine Creek treaty council. The only substantive memoir by a direct participant at the council is Benjamin Franklin Shaw's "Medicine Creek Treaty," a speech delivered on Oct. 20, 1903, and published in *Proceedings of the Oregon Historical Society,* 1906, appendix C, pp. 24–32. Shaw argues in his remarks that the entire Indian treaty process was a cynical charade, imposed on the natives who accepted it because they were powerless to do otherwise. See also Shaw's letter titled "Did Leschi Sign the Medicine Creek Treaty?" *Seattle Post-Intelligencer,* Jan. 31, 1904. Principal official documents surviving include: Commission to Hold Treaties with the Tribes of Washington Territory and the Blackfoot Country, council proceedings, Dec. 7, 1854–March 3, 1855, see Records of Washington Superintendency of Indian Affairs (WSIA), 1853–1874, roll 26, M5, National Archives; Treaty of Medicine Creek, Dec. 26, 1854, 10 Stat. 1132 (ratified by U.S. Senate Mar. 2, 1855); *Ratified Indian Treaties, 1722–1869,* microfilm of possible original draft of Treaty of Medicine Creek, frames 66–83, roll 11, M668, National Archives; and minutes of Medicine Creek council, box 26, WSIA, and DRNRUT, reel 5, Washington State Library. Notable among the letters dealing with the Medicine Creek council are: Stevens to Michael T. Simmons, March 22, 1854, WSIA, roll 1, National Archives; Stevens to Manypenny, acknowledging "disputed points" after the treaty was initially read to the tribes, Dec. 30, 1854, roll 5, DRNRUT; Stevens to Manypenny, May 11, 1855, roll 1, WSIA; and George Gibbs to Stevens, Dec. 29, 1854, WSIA, roll 23; Dec. 31, 1854, and Jan. 6, 1855, DRNRUT, both on roll 5, WSA and National Archives. See also Maria Pascualy and Cecilia S. Carpenter, *Remembering Medicine Creek* (Firewood Press, 2005). A worthwhile study of the treaty and its aftermath undertaken a generation after the events but while some participants still survived is "The Indian Side of the Puget Sound Indian War," a paper delivered by James Wickersham on Oct. 9, 1893, Wickersham Collection, MSS TS-120, box 1, folder 3, WSHS, as well as Elwood Evans, "Wickersham Roasted," *Tacoma Ledger,* Oct. 17–18, 1893.

6. *Blood in the Autumn Air*

Hazard Stevens offers moving examples of Indian objections to his father's treaties west of the Cascades on pp. 462–80, drawing on minutes of council meetings in WSIA records cited in notes to Chapter 5, but fails to convey Chief Seattle's affecting speech of resignation at the Point Elliott council (for which see American Friends Service Committee, *Uncommon Controversy,* pp. xxx–xxxi, and Eckrom, *Remembered Drums,* p. 17, among many other reports of his remarks). On council sessions east of the Cascades, where Stevens encountered serious resistance, see Clifford E. Tratzer, "The Legacy of the Walla Walla Council, 1855," *Oregon Historical Quarterly,* vol. 106, no. 3 (Fall 2005). His biog-

raphers put Stevens's treaty activities in a favorable light, his son unabashedly at pp. 448–
49 and Richards at p. 206, but the latter is critical of Stevens on p. 207 for inviting white
settlement onto tribal lands before treaties were ratified. Gibbs is similarly critical in his
Jan. 1857 letter (see Swan, *The Northwest Coast,* p. 428), and in general gainsaying
Stevens for unseemly haste in his treaty dealings and the insufficiency of the reservations
assigned the treaty tribes. Chapter 3 of Harmon's *Indians in the Making* is a sophisticated
account of how the treaty tribes had been swindled and came to recognize as much. On
Leschi's prewar efforts to rouse tribal opposition to the treaties, see Splawn's life of
Kamiakin, p. 40; Swan's *The Northwest Coast,* p. 426 quoting Gibbs's letter; and Snowden's treatment of the Indian war in his history of Washington. On the McAllister family's dealings with Leschi, see "Early Reminscences of a Nisqually Pioneer" by Sarah
McAllister Hartman, 1893, Northwest Room collection, Tacoma Public Library. James
McAllister's Oct. 16, 1855, letter to Acting Governor Mason on Leschi's suspicious
activity, in the WSHS and WSA collections, is quoted by Carpenter in *Fort Nisqually,*
p. 175 (see footnote 10 for chapter 20). Mason's proclamation of Indian peril and call for
four additional militia companies, Oct. 22, 1855, WSHS and WSA collections, was tantamount to a declaration of war. On the escalation of tensions between settlers and Indians, see E. T. Gunn, "Governor Stevens' War," *Puget Sound Courier,* Oct. 19, 1855.

7. *The Territory in Dread*

J. A. Eckrom's *Remembered Drums* is a lively popular account of the Indian war at Puget
Sound. Meeker's *Tragedy of Leschi* deals with the early stages of the war and the White
River massacre in chapters 36–37. For John King's memories of the atrocity, see pp. 292–
300. See also Wade Vaughan, "Puget Sound Indian Invasion," 1978, in the Tacoma Public Library's Northwest Room collection. The Indian ambush of Tidd's express party at
Connell's Prairie resulting in two militiamen's deaths and Leschi's eventual prosecution
for murder was recounted by Rabbeson and Tidd in the *Pioneer and Democrat,* Nov. 9,
1855, WSA and WSHS; for more detailed discussion, see Chapters 10 and 11 in this
book.

8. *An Impressive Performance*

On Leschi's bold landing at Fox Island to pursue peace negotiations and later visit to the
McLeod farm for the same purpose, see Meeker, pp. 330–37, and Eckrom, pp. 114–16.
On the Seattle raid, see Binns, *Northwest Gateway,* chapter 8; Charles M. Gates, ed.,
"Seattle's First Taste of Battle, 1856," *Pacific Northwest Quarterly,* vol. 47 (Jan. 1956);
Meeker, pp. 348–52; and Splawn, pp. 56–57. On Leschi's link, if any, to the raid, see
Report on Proceedings of a military commission convened at Seattle, May 15, 1856, to
investigate the January raid there, WSA. For an early round of their epistolary duel, see
Stevens to Gen. John Wool, Dec. 28, 1855, and Wool to Stevens, Feb. 12, 1856. Most of
their correspondence, along with Stevens's pointed exchanges with Lieut. Col. Silas
Casey and Col. George Wright, are in Yale Library's William W. Miller Collection.
Stevens's speech to the Washington Territory legislature promising to exterminate every
last hostile Indian was reported in the *Pioneer and Democrat* on Jan. 25, 1856. On Eliza-
beth Stevens and Charles Mason, see her letter to her sister, Mary Howard, Feb. 1, 1856,
in "Leschi: Justice in Our Time" file on WSHS website. On Leschi's military reversals,

see Meeker, pp. 352–64; Eckrom, starting with Patkamin's attack on Leschi's remote camp, pp. 119–37; and "Leschi and Patkamin" by Elwood Evans, Stevens Collection, Beinecke Library, Yale University. Gary Fuller Reese edited a useful file of documents titled "Leschi, the Officers and the Citizens," available since 1986 in the Tacoma Library's Northwest Room collection. On the atrocity perpetrated by Maxon in April 1856, see Eckrom, pp. 145–48; Meeker, pp. 367–69; and a pamphlet by local historian Abbi Wonacott, *Where the Mashel Meets the Nisqually: The Mashel Massacre of 1856,* Bellus Uccallo Publishing, Eatonville, Wash.

9. *The Wages of Zealotry*

Two detailed accounts of Stevens's misadventure into martial law appeared in the *Pacific Northwest Quarterly:* Samuel F. Cohn's "Martial Law in Washington Territory," vol. 27, July 1936 issue, and Roy Lokken's "The Martial Law Controversy in Washington Territory, 1856," vol. 43, April 1952 issue. Official court and executive department documents on the martial law crisis may be found in WSA under Territorial Supreme Court case files; see Cause #2. For Gibbs's leading role in opposing Stevens's despotic conduct, see *Pacific Northwest Letters of George Gibbs,* edited by Vernon Carstensen and published by the Oregon Historical Society, 1954, as well as documents composed mostly by Pierce County lawyers with Gibbs as likely lead writer, including proceedings of May 7, 1856, meetings of bar members of the Third Judicial District to protest the arrest of Judge Lander and his clerk and of a mass meeting of citizens in Steilacoom on the same date and an accusatory screed titled "A Brief Notice of Recent Outrages Committed by Isaac I. Stevens" by Whig lawyers, sent to Pierce administration officials in Washington, D.C., and the national press, WSA. Meeker covers this episode in detail on pp. 382–402, including the text of Secretary of State Marcy's Sept. 12, 1856, letter to Stevens advising him of President Pierce's disapproval of his conduct, p. 401. On Stevens's call for ongoing combat against hostile Indians and insistence on apprehending and punishing Leschi even after the war west of the Cascades was over, see his letters to BIA director Manypenny, May 5, 25, and 31, 1856, roll 2, WSIA; Aug. 28, 1856, letter on Fox Island council; council minutes, Puyallup Indian Tribal Archives, Tacoma; and on the continuing need to try Leschi and other Indian war leaders, Oct. 22, 1856. Further disclosures of Stevens's vehement frame of mind are contained in his letters to Secretary of War Jefferson Davis, March 9 and Aug. 1, 1856; crowing about the massacre at Grande Ronde as a great victory, WSHS, and his letter to the *Pioneer and Democrat* on the alleged Indian betrayal of whites who trusted them most, Feb. 27, 1857, WSA. Stevens foe George Gibbs concurs with him on the importance of pacifying Indians, in a letter to James Swan, July 31, 1856, quoted in Swan, *The Northwest Coast,* p. 390. The gap between Stevens's thinking and the army's is well illustrated by the governor's exchange with Col. Wright in the summer of 1856, Stevens to Wright, June 18 (and Oct. 4) on the danger he believed posed by Leschi et al., and Wright to Stevens, July 23. On this schism, see also Gen. Wool's letter to J. S. Cummingham at the Department of War on the hostility of whites and governors of the Washington and Oregon territories toward Indians, April 4, 1856, and the letter from Wool's aide to Casey advising of the general's accord with not surrendering Leschi for trial, Nov. 19, 1856, WSA. Meeker's chapter 55, "The Unrelenting Foe," pp. 409–14, further samples the argumentative letters between Stevens and top regional army officers Wright and Casey. Carpenter discusses the Fox Island council providing new reservations for the Nisquallies and Puyallups in *Tears of Internment,* pp. 57–60 and 83–90.

10–12. *Judgment Day—and Night;*
With Malice Aforethought; All the Favors of the Law

On the hunt for and apprehension and trials of Leschi, see Meeker, pp. 409–46, especially chapter 55, "The Unremitting Foe," and his account (pp. 415–23) of the first trial, in which he served as a member of the jury. On Leschi's frame of mind after he laid down his arms but remained a fugitive from Stevens's wrath, see *Pioneer and Democrat* article of Oct. 17, 1856, on the meeting between Tolmie and Leschi at Fort Nisqually and Tolmie's account of it in the Feb. 25, 1858, *Truth Teller*, in WSA, as well as Col. Wright's July 17, 1857, letter to Leschi defense lawyer Frank Clark, WSHS collection of Wright papers. For a comprehensive review of Leschi's judicial treatment, see Kelly Kunsch, "The Trials of Leschi: Nisqually Chief," *Seattle Journal of Social Justice*, vol. 5, no. 1 (Fall–Winter 2006). Contemporary assessment of the Leschi case and related documents may be found in Elwood Evans's "The Trial of Leschi" at Yale's Bienecke Library. The principal authority on the exemption of lawful combatants from the charge of murder for killing a foe in wartime is Grotius, *The Rights of War and Peace*, vol. 3, pp. 274–79. On the efforts by Leschi's friends and admirers to spare his life, see Martin Schmitt, "The Execution of Chief Leschi and the *Truth Teller*," *Oregon Historical Quarterly*, vol. 50, no. 1 (March 1949); Alexander Olson, "Our Leschi: The Making of a Martyr," *Pacific Northwest Quarterly*, vol. 95, no. 1 (Winter 2003–4): 26–36; Col. Wright's letter to Leschi's lead defense attorney Frank Clark in *Pioneer and Democrat*, July 19, 1857, and Gary F. Reese, ed., *Nothing Worthy of Note Transpired Today: The Northwest Journals of August V. Kautz*, 1858, 1978 (see entries for Dec. 29, 1857–Feb. 19, 1858). A biographical sketch of Leschi's lawyer Frank Clark ran in *Steilacoom Historical Museum Quarterly*, vol. 15, no. 4 (Winter 1987). On Leschi's taking the cross near the end of his life, see Victor W. Wortley, "Perceptions and Misperceptions: A European Cleric's View of the American Indian," about Father Louis Rossi, *Pacific Northwest Quarterly*, vol. 72 (Oct. 1981). On the murder of Quiemuth, see Drew Crooks, "Quiemuth: Remembering the Nisqually Leader . . . ," *Occurences*, published by Fort Nisqually Living History Museum, vol. 26, nos. 1 and 2 (Winter/Spring 2008); James Goudy, "An Account of the Capture and Killing of Quiemuth," Bienecke Library, Yale University, and the account by James Longmire, who took Quiemuth into voluntary custody, in *Tacoma Sunday Ledger*, Aug. 21, 1892, and *Told by the Pioneers*, Washington Pioneer Project, 1937–38. Stevens wrote to Manypenny on the surrender and murder of Quiemuth, Nov. 21, 1856, and on the outcome and alleged fairness of the Leschi trial, April 3, 1857, WSA collections. For Stevens's apologia to Congress for his conduct as governor of Washington Territory, see proceedings in U.S. House of Representatives on May 31, 1858. Contemporary newspaper accounts include *Pioneer and Democrat*, short article on Leschi's whereabouts, Oct. 17, 1856; "Leschi, Quiemuth, etc.," Nov. 28, 1856; "Trial and Conviction of Leschi," March 20, 1857; and articles on citizens' condemnation of the plan to prevent Leschi's execution, Jan. 29 and Feb. 12, 1858, WSA, and *The Oregonian*, "Capture of Leschi, the War Chief," and article on Winyea trial, Nov. 22, 1856, and "Quiemuth, Nisqually Chief, Killed at Olympia, Nov. 29, 1856. The two issues of the *Truth Teller*, Feb. 3 and 25, 1858, are available in the Washington State Archives; see also Tolmie's letter on Leschi's character to Governor Fayette McMullin, Jan. 12, 1858, quoted by Meeker, *Pioneer Reminiscences*, pp. 447–49, and in William Tolmie Papers, University of Washington Library, accession no. 4577–1, box 2, folder 3. Collected court documents relating to the Leschi trials and appeal are in Washington State Archives' Territorial Supreme Court case files, Cause #3; many were transcribed in 2003 for use by the ad hoc Committee to Exonerate

Leschi, see Epilogue below, section II, "For Whom the Eagle Cries." Meeker deals with the efforts, in the courts and extralegally, to spare Leschi's life and describes his execution on pp. 450–54.

Epilogue
I. *Salmon and Survival*

On the condition of the Nisqually reservation, see annual report for 1876 by U.S. Indian Agernt R. H. Milroy to Bureau of Indian Affairs, National Archives. The best sources on the subject of salmon-fishing and its importance to the Northwest Indian tribes are the Boldt Decision, *United States v. Washington,* 384 F. Supp. 312 (WD. Wash., 1974), and the American Friends Service Committee book *Uncommon Controversy.* See also "25 Years After the Boldt Decision: The Fish Tale That Changed History," *Seattle Times,* Feb. 7, 1999, and "Tribal Triumph," *News Tribune,* Feb. 15, 2004. On the "fish-ins," see "Brando Steals Lead in Mutiny on the River" and related articles, *News Tribune,* March 2, 1964. For a sense of Nisqually life and status at the end of the twentieth century, see Lorrine Thompson's "What It Means to Be Nisqually: Preserving Their Tradition" in *The Olympian,* Nov. 25, 1999.

II. *For Whom the Eagle Cries*

On the Washington State Historical Court of Inquiry and Justice, see *Los Angeles Times,* "A Matter of Justice and Honor," Dec. 28, 2004, describing Iyall's leadership of the exoneration effort; *News Tribune:* "Effort Underway to Clear Chief Leschi's Name," Sept. 16, 2003; "Chief Leschi 'appeal' gets legislative support," March 7, 2004; "Second Chance at Justice," Dec. 9, 2004; "Justice 146 Years Later," Dec. 11, 2004; "What the Leschi Verdict Tells Us About Us" (editorial), Dec. 14, 2004; *New York Times:* "Chief's Retrial, 146 Years in the Making," Dec. 5, 2004, and "Indian Chief Hanged in 1858 Is Cleared," Dec. 12, 2004; *The Olympian:* "Senate Hears Case to Clear Chief's Name, Rewrite History," Feb. 19, 2004; "Legislators Right Historical Wrong," March 5, 2004; "Leschi's Descendants Deserve to Have His Name Cleared," op-ed column by Cynthia Iyall, March 5, 2004; "Chief Leschi Exonerated for History Books," Dec. 11, 2004; *Seattle Post-Intelligencer:* "Leschi Wasn't a Murderer, Tribe Says," Sept. 15, 2003; "Exonerate Chief Leschi, Say Tribe, Lawmakers," Feb. 19, 2004; "Some Wrongs Are Beyond Righting" and "Historical Revision Rights a Wrong," columns by Thomas Shapley, Sept. 26 and Dec. 19, 2004; "Hero or Murderer? Trial Aims to Clear Name of Chief Leschi," Dec. 4, 2004; "Historical Court Clears Chief Leschi's Name," Dec. 11, 2004; "Leschi Exonerated: Historical Wrong Righted" (editorial), Dec. 14, 2004; *Seattle Times:* "Seeking Justice for the Chief," Dec. 5, 2004, and "Historic Nisqually Chief Exonerated," Dec. 11, 2004; *Seattle Weekly:* "Wrongheaded Murder," Dec. 8–14, and "Ending an Indian War," Dec. 15–21, 2004. Other sources: Memoranda and correspondence dealing with the special Washington Historical Court of Justice convened on Dec. 10, 2004, were obtained from Washington Supreme Court Justice Gerry Alexander, who presided over the tribunal and retains the documents in his chambers; responsible researchers seeking access to these documents should apply directly to Justice Alexander. Upon his mandatory retirement at the end of 2011, his file on the Leschi exoneration is likely to be domiciled at Washington State Archives, Olympia. Other documents consulted: Nisqually

Indian Tribe, Council Resolution No. 5, Feb. 14, 2003; State of Washington, Senate Joint Memorial 8054, first reading, Feb. 11, and Senate Resolution 8727, March 4, 2004; House of Representatives Resolution 4708, March 4, 2004: letter from the majority and minority leaders of both houses of the Washington State Legislature to Chief Justice Alexander, March 9, and Alexander's reply, March 15, 2004; and James E. Brown's memorandum on Leschi exoneration issues for Chief Justice Alexander, April 5, 2004. For the writings and judicial philosophy of Justice Alexander, see: "Abe Lincoln and the Pacific Northwest," *Columbia,* no. 3 (Winter 2002–3); "The Courts of the Washington Territory: 1853–1859," *Washington State Bar News,* Nov. 2003; "Technology, Values, and the Justice System," *Washington Law Review,* vol. 79, no. 1 (2004); "The Fox and the Shellfish," *UWLaw,* vol. 53 (Spring 2005); and his concurring opinion in *Andersen v. King County,* 158 Wash. 2d 1, 138 P. 3d 963 (2006). A videotape of the proceedings of the Historical Court of Inquiry and Justice can be purchased from Washington public TV station TVW. A transcript of the tape was made by the author and copies contributed to Washington State Archives and the State Law Library. For an evaluation of the historical court's proceedings, see Kelly Kunsch, "The Trials of Leschi," *Seattle Journal of Social Justice,* vol. 5, no. 1 (Fall/Winter 2006), which also contains the fullest legal bibliography of the Leschi case.

III. *Red Wind Rising*

On Red Wind Casino: The Nisqually Tribe's gaming revenue allocation plan is on file with the National Indian Gaming Commission and the Washington State Gambling Commission. For a description of the casino's activities, visit its website: www.redwind casino.com. For data and information on tribal casinos in the United States, consult the National Indian Gaming Commission, Washington, D.C., and www.nigc.gov. On other Nisqually commercial activity, see "Nisqually Indian Tribe to Purchase 9.6 Acres of Prime Commercial Property along I-5 in Thurston County," tribal press release, April 1, 2008, and "Moving Off the Reservation: Indian Tribes Look Far Afield for Places to Invest Casino Wealth," *New York Times,* Sept. 29, 2007.

On Cynthia Iyall's advance to tribal chair, see her op-ed columns in *The Olympian,* May 14, July 30, Oct. 8, Dec. 17, 2004, and March 11, May 20, July 29, and Oct. 7, 2005. On efforts against Chairwoman Iyall by tribal council dissidents, see decision in *Nisqually Indian Tribe v. Carmen Kalama et al.,* case nos. CR-08–06–016 through 018, Nisqually Tribal Court. On the clash between the Nisquallies and Billy Frank Jr. and the Frank's Landing Community, see letter from Nisqually tribal chairman Dorian Sanchez to Cindi Yates, Washington Dept. of Revenue, protesting sale of cigarettes without tax stamps at the Landing's smoke shop and claiming violations of Nisqually cigarette compact with state, July 19, 2005, Nisqually tribal files. Also, "Nisquallies Sue State Over Cigarette-Sales Area," *Seattle Times,* Feb. 8, 2008; *Nisqually Indian Tribe v. Christine Gregoire, Governor of the State of Washington,* U.S. Dist. Court, WD. Wash., Case 3:08-cv-05069-RBL, litigation ongoing; "The Swoop on Frank's Landing," *Works in Progress,* Thurston Co. Rainbow Coalition, June 2007; "$9.2 Million Sentence in Frank's Landing Smoke Shop Case," *News Tribune,* March 10, 2009, and especially "Indian Country Infighting: Tiny Community Battles the Nisquallies to Maintain Its Independence," by Rob Carson, *News Tribune,* April 27, 2008, an example of press coverage often skewed toward enhancing Frank's stature as Native American leader. Frank's attack on the policies of the Nisqually Tribal Council, charging secrecy, malfeasance, and selling out to state officials while announcing his intention to seek the tribal chairmanship, was stated in a Dec. 27, 1976, letter to tribal members, files of Tahoma Research; see also *William Frank et al. v. Rogers C. B. Morton,* Civil Action 1134–73 filed Feb. 19, 1974, U.S. Dist. Court, District of Columbia, and *Herman John, Jr. et al. v. Zelma Kalama McCloud et al.,* complaint no. 76–1635 filed in U.S. Dist. Court, WD. Wash., July 8, 1976. For examples of Frank's activities, see *News Tribune* files on "fish-ins," 1963–65; "Nisqually Indian Leader Fights to Bring Back the Salmon," Dec. 22, 1982; "Billy Frank Jr. Fishes Political Waters Now," Feb. 15, 1984; "Nisqually Leader Billy Frank Honored by Common Cause," May 4, 1985; profile of Frank, *Seattle Times,* Feb. 7, 1999; "Northwest Tribal Perspectives on the Endangered Species Act," Frank's testimony before U.S. Senate Subcommittee on Fisheries, Wildlife and Water of the Committee on Envirnment and Public Works, Sept. 21, 2005, and "Being Frank" columns in Northwest Indian Fisheries Commission *News.* On Frank's political pull in obtaining federal recognition for Frank's Landing Indian community, see additions and deletions section of PL 100–153 (HR 2937), 100th U.S. Congress, first session, Nov. 5, 1987, and of PL 103–435 (HR 4709), 103rd Congress, second session, Nov. 2, 1994. Regarding heavy federal funding of Frank family's Wahelut School (it reached $20,000 per pupil for 2006–8), see Bureau of Indian Education records.

For examples of the Nisqually effort to improve the habitat, see "Salt Water Returns to Nisqually Field," *News Tribune,* Nov. 1, 2006, and "Tribal Fund Will Preserve Nisqually River Watershed Habitat," Washington Department of Ecology press release, July 31, 2006. On the percentage of Indian blood required for tribal membership, see "Blood Won't Always Tell" by Rob Carson, *News Tribune,* Feb. 17, 2002. On Indian-white relations, see "Walking a Mile: A First Step Toward Mutual Understanding" by John Doble and Andrew L. Yarrow with Amber N. Ott and Jonathan Rochkind, a report by Public Agenda, 2007.

INDEX

Page numbers in italics refer to maps.

A NOTE ABOUT THE AUTHOR

RICHARD KLUGER, a native of Paterson, New Jersey, graduated from Princeton University and worked as a journalist and book-publishing executive before turning to writing books. His works include *Simple Justice,* the classic account of the U.S. Supreme Court's landmark decision *Brown v. Board of Education*, ending racial segregation in the nation's public schools, and *The Paper: The Life and Death of the* New York Herald Tribune, both finalists for the National Book Award. His critical history of the tobacco industry, *Ashes to Ashes,* won the Pulitzer Prize for general nonfiction in 1997. *Seizing Destiny: The Relentless Expansion of American Territory* was published in 2006. He is also the author of six novels, including *Members of the Tribe* and *The Sheriff of Nottingham*, and two others written with his wife, Phyllis. They live in northern California.

A NOTE ON THE TYPE

The text of this book was set in a typeface called Times New Roman, designed by Stanley Morison (1889–1967) for *The Times* (London) and first introduced by that newspaper in 1932.

Among typographers and designers of the twentieth century, Stanley Morison was a strong forming influence—as a typographical advisor to the Monotype Corporation, as a director of two distinguished publishing houses, and as a writer of sensibility, erudition, and keen practical sense.

Composed by North Market Street Graphics,
Lancaster, Pennsylvania
Printed and bound by Berryville Graphics,
Berryville, Virginia
Designed by Virginia Tan